The Publications of James Edward Oglethorpe

The Publications of
James Edward Oglethorpe

Edited by Rodney M. Baine

Foreword by Phinizy Spalding

The University of Georgia Press *Athens and London*

© 1994 by the University of Georgia Press
Athens, Georgia 30602
All rights reserved

Designed by Sandra Strother Hudson
Set in 10 on 13 Janson Text by Tseng Information Systems, Inc.

Library of Congress Cataloging in Publication Data

Oglethorpe, James Edward, 1696–1785.
The publications of James Edward Oglethorpe / edited by
Rodney M. Baine ; foreword by Phinizy Spalding.
p. cm.
Includes bibliographical references and index.
ISBN 0-8203-1546-X (alk. paper)
1. Georgia—History—Colonial period, ca. 1600–1775—Sources.
2. South Carolina—History—Colonial period, ca. 1600–1775—Sources.
I. Baine, Rodney M. II. Title.
F289.03625 1994
975.8'02—dc20 92-38271

British Library Cataloging in Publication Data available

Reissue published in 2021

Most University Press titles are available
from popular e-book vendors.

Printed digitally

ISBN 9780820361086 (Hardcover)
ISBN 9780820361079 (Paperback)
ISBN 9780820361062 (Ebook)

For my grandsons
Leonard Brenner
John Anderson Baine
Oscar Baine

Contents

Foreword to the Reissue	ix
Foreword by Phinizy Spalding	xv
Preface	xxix
Quisquis amissam (1714)	3
A Duel Explained (1722)	5
The Sailors Advocate (1728)	7
A Preliminary Report on the Fleet Prison (1729)	44
A Report from the Committee appointed to Enquire into the State of the Goals of this Kingdom: Relating to the Fleet Prison (1729)	48
A Report from the Committee appointed to Enquire into the State of the Goals of this Kingdom: Relating to the Marshalsea Prison; and farther Relating to the Fleet Prison (1729)	83
A Preliminary Report on the King's Bench Prison (1730)	119
An Addendum to the Fleet Prison Report (1730)	122
A Report from the Committee appointed to Enquire into the State of the Goals of this Kingdom. Relating to the King's Bench Prison (1730)	125
An Appeal for the Georgia Colony (1732)	159
Select Tracts Relating to Colonies (1732)	167
A New and Accurate Account of the Provinces of South-Carolina and Georgia (1732)	200
A Description of the Indians in Georgia (1733)	241
An Account of Carolina and Georgia (1739)	245

An Account of the Negroe Insurrection in South Carolina (1740)	252
A Thanksgiving for Victory (1742)	256
The King's Bench Prison Revisited (1752)	259
The Naked Truth (1755)	270
Some Account of the Cherokees (1762)	296
Shipping Problems in South Carolina (1762)	298
Three Letters on Corsica (1768)	302
The Adams Letters (1773–1774)	311
The Faber Letters (1778)	321
Three Letters Supporting Lord North (1782)	328
Appendix 1: Spurious Attributions	335
Appendix 2: Probable Attributions	337
A Refutation of Calumnies (1742)	338
Praise for John Howard (1777)	342
Notes	345
Index	387

Foreword to the Reissue

James Edward Oglethorpe directed the group of founders of the thirteenth British colony in North America in 1733. He would return to England for the final time ten years later and live another half century as a minor political figure and friend to such famous men as James Boswell and Samuel Johnson. Oglethorpe has been described as a liberal and an idealist, a man responsible for the only colony that was to be prohibitionist, abolitionist, and egalitarian. But he, like all historic figures, is much more complicated than a simple listing of traits reveals.

This new foreword to *The Publications of James Edward Oglethorpe* comes more than a quarter century after the original publication. There has been a dearth of writing on the Georgia founder since the glut of scholarship in the late 1980s and early 1990s coinciding with the 1983 semiquincentennial of Georgia. With the exception of Thomas D. Wilson's *The Oglethorpe Plan: Enlightenment Design in Savannah and Beyond* (2012), which focuses mostly on Georgia's colonial capital but also discusses Oglethorpe in depth, and a handful of articles in the *Georgia Historical Quarterly* on specific aspects of Oglethorpe's life and legacy, this volume, republished in a more accessible and e-book format, will hopefully lead to a renewed interest in the unique (and final) British colony and its enigmatic founder.

Edited by Rodney M. Baine, longtime University of Georgia professor, the present volume is the only collection of Oglethorpe's published writings, with the exception of a few widely available Georgia propagandic pamphlets. *The Publications of James Edward Oglethorpe* was most likely a preview of Baine's planned (but never realized) *The Papers and Speeches of James*

Edward Oglethorpe, almost three thousand pages of which are in his Hargrett Rare Books and Manuscript Library archival collection at the University of Georgia. Containing more than twenty complete works from Oglethorpe's verified print record, ranging in time from Oglethorpe's early life as a young man (1714) to just three years before his death (1782), this volume offers a chronological snapshot of the Georgia founder's philosophies, influences, and leanings. Baine even tempts the reader that other treasures of anonymous or lost articles or letters penned by Oglethorpe await discovery. (In fact, in the current age of digitization of archival material and periodicals, time might be ripe for a new historical investigation!)

So how does the current reader, with a twenty-first-century lens, assess an eighteenth-century nobleman? Is it ever possible to evaluate a historic figure without either forgiving based on contemporariness or convicting based on modernity? As Phinizy Spalding, imminent Oglethorpe scholar and longtime historian at the University of Georgia, wrote at the beginning of his original foreword, "The best introduction to Oglethorpe is in his own words." But before a person's own words can be evaluated, one must understand the life and world of the character.

The last of ten children born to Lady Eleanor Wall and Sir Theophilus Oglethorpe, James was christened on December 22, 1696. He attended Eton and then entered Corpus Christi College, Oxford, in 1714. James temporarily left Corpus Christi to serve under Prince Eugene of Savoy in Austria against the Turks. In 1722, Oglethorpe was elected to Parliament from the same district previously represented by his father and two older brothers. There, he would begin to develop his own principles outside the influence of his politically active family. He would serve in the House of Commons until 1754.

In 1728, Oglethorpe lost his friend Robert Castell to smallpox contracted while Castell was jailed in London's Fleet Prison for unpaid debts. A year after Castell's death, Oglethorpe formed a Parliamentary committee to investigate debtor prisons in England and recommend reforms. The spotlight encouraged less corruption between the prison system and the judiciary, and overall conditions improved. The improvements, in turn, gained Oglethorpe national fame, and he used his newfound platform to garner support for the

Foreword

establishment of a colony in British North America to offer financial and social equality for those who could achieve neither in England.

In 1732, George II granted a charter for the colony of Georgia, partially inspired by Oglethorpe's idealistic plan but also to create a buffer between Spanish Florida and the rest of colonial Great Britain. On February 12, 1733, Oglethorpe led the settlers to Yamacraw Bluff, the future site of the colony's capital city of Savannah. He had explored the area with Yamacraw chief Tomochichi, the local Native American leader with whom Oglethorpe would form a lifelong relationship. The most exactingly planned of new colonial cities, Savannah was to embody Oglethorpe's egalitarian vision with its predetermined plot sizes, identical homes, and individuals working their own land. The charter guaranteed religious freedom for all non-Catholics ("papists" were excluded to guard against Spanish interference), and Oglethorpe would even fight for the acceptance of Jewish settlers in Georgia. Slavery was banned, though the colonial government would soon legislate that runaway slaves from other colonies be returned to their owners if found in Georgia.

Military threats from the Spanish began to take up more and more of Oglethorpe's time. He earned military fame during the War of Jenkins' Ear with his victory at the Battle of Bloody Marsh in July 1742 proving fatal to Spanish plans to capture Georgia, and George II promoted Oglethorpe to the rank of brigadier general. The next year, Oglethorpe would attempt one last time to expand British influence into Florida by attacking St. Augustine. The unsuccessful invasion led a disgruntled soldier to accuse Oglethorpe of misconduct, and Oglethorpe was summoned back to London to answer the court-martial. In 1744, he was cleared of all charges.

Now permanently back in England, Oglethorpe married Lady Elizabeth Wright, baroness and heir to a considerable annuity. Being the youngest child, Oglethorpe would need the financial security of his wife to live out his life as a retired general and member of the gentry. He and Lady Elizabeth would spend much time in London, where they became active among the intelligentsia.

In 1745, Oglethorpe again served England militarily by attempting to put down an invasion by the supporters of Charles Edward Stuart, the "Younger Pretender." His campaign strategy led to another court-martial, but he was again acquitted. There was concern that Oglethorpe intentionally slowed his arrival due to influence from his Jacobite sisters, known supporters of Bonnie Prince Charles. Oglethorpe was later asked to return to British North America to fight his former colonists, but he refused, favoring Edmund Burke's push for conciliation between Britain and its colony. In 1785, Oglethorpe met John Adams, America's first ambassador to Britain, in London. That same year, six months shy of his eighty-ninth birthday, Oglethorpe died after a brief illness. Lady Elizabeth died two years later.

With an understanding of the life and experiences of the man, how should the reader evaluate Oglethorpe based on his published words? Ideally, a figure's own writings shed light on the person's character and motivations. To simply read selected writings, however, even with historical background, does not allow us the permission to evaluate solely with the lens of our own time and experiences. Baine offered context but, of course, made decisions on what writings to include and what to leave out. The Sisyphean task of the historian is to remove as much bias as possible and evaluate the character through the lens of objectivity. Of course, no historical figure can be completely represented. No minds may be read for motives. No time travelers can bring a people into the present and quiz them on their reaction to circumstances or occurrences.

In his waning years, Oglethorpe himself would inflate his earlier liberality. He would recall that his abolitionist vision for Georgia stemmed from an acceptance of the equality of all men. He would forget that laws were passed in the colony to ensure the return of runaway slaves to South Carolina. He would forget that enslaved Africans were used to clear the site of Savannah. He had briefly served as a governor of the slave-trading Royal African Company but also was instrumental in the emancipation of Job ben Solomon, a prince who had been kidnapped into slavery. Oglethorpe wrote sympathetically of the Native Americans (though in a paternalistic and patronizing way) but unsympathetically of the Stono Slave Rebellion. He wrote of great respect for his friend Yamacraw chief Tomochichi but equated English Jews with traitors who placed love of money above love of country. Oglethorpe would offer religious freedom in Georgia to Jews and Lutherans but not Catholics—even though his mother was raised Catholic and his sisters practiced Catholicism in France.

Foreword

But maybe it is a human trait to remember with more optimism than reality. Based on the political tone of the writings here as they move chronologically, Oglethorpe *did* appear to become more progressive in his later years. His progressiveness was, of course, built on the foundation of his family's political activity and his own penal reformation and liberal colonial intentions. In letters to the editor, he supported the protection of the Commons to guarantee that the regular man would be able to have the financial stability to ensure the success of his family, even blaming the rich and their capitalistic motives for the eventual extinction of the shared space.

Since this collection was originally published a quarter century ago, readers of history have become much less likely to lionize historical figures while ignoring the more complicated parts of their life, behavior, or legacy. As students of history know, all people are real, three-dimensional characters living in a time and place, responding to events around them as best as they can. History does not change, of course, but our understanding of it can evolve as more voices are able to join the discussion. This is not an erasing of history but rather a widening of historical remembrance and study. James Edward Oglethorpe, based on the writings included here, is worthy of continued assessment, and this reprinted volume will, hopefully, bring more voices into the conversation.

ELI ARNOLD

Foreword

Phinizy Spalding

How does one who has worked and, in a sense, lived with James Edward Oglethorpe for more than thirty years, do a foreword to such an ambitious, scholarly, and useful volume as this? Where is the proper starting place; where should it end? In fact, should there be a foreword at all? After mulling over these and allied problems I concluded the obvious: Oglethorpe speaks for himself today just as he did two centuries and more ago. So the best introduction to Oglethorpe is in his own words.

Still, there is a need for some kind of interpretation, particularly as the tricentennial of Oglethorpe's birth looms and as the world faces only its second millennium since the birth of Christ. Not that Oglethorpe and Jesus had much in common, even though the former's enemies or friends on two continents probably thought a comparison not completely inappropriate.

Other points indicating that a foreword might be useful relate to Oglethorpe's personality and the way he handled himself. He was controversial, outspoken, driven; he always carried a message with him. Oglethorpe was certain of his own rectitude; he did not brook fools lightly. In most respects he was fearlessly outspoken, but Oglethorpe was certainly no martyr, unless his sacrifices for Georgia be put in that context. He was opinionated, obstinate, and probably not very easy to get along with, particularly as a young man. "Things" pretty much had to go his way, and it is part of the determined nature of Oglethorpe that they generally did. Except, once again, in Georgia—his province and, in a sense, his major disappointment. So in spite of my own inclinations, and in spite of the presence of Oglethorpe's own words, a foreword of some sort seems at least marginally desirable. As we used to say half-mockingly in graduate school on the subject of one another's research topics, "It needs to be done!"

From his youth this unusual man James Oglethorpe showed the signs of independence that never left him throughout his long life. It is possibly quite true that "Jamie," as some of his family called him, was badly spoiled. As the last of a long series of children born to Eleanor Wall and Theophilus Oglethorpe, he was adored by his parents and by his siblings, particularly his sisters who lived to see their youngest brother reach maturity and prominence. An irony of this strong bond of affection — a bond powerfully returned by their brother — is that James's three married sisters wed French husbands. And Oglethorpe detested France. Although he carefully distinguished between the French themselves — "a gay and agreeable people" — and French policy, he had contempt for those he termed "Frenchified" or for the "Bourbonite Pensioner." These "leeches" on society were, though, English, a development Oglethorpe viewed as uniquely deplorable. So he consistently denounced French influence in English society, even blaming it for the deterioration of relations between England and her American colonies. In his opinion, French bribes in an unreformed, cynical Parliament were behind the passage of the disastrous Stamp Act of 1765, and kept William Pitt, a leader for whom Oglethorpe had abiding admiration, out of power at crucial times. In addition, the influence of France's tactics exacerbated Whig-Tory strife in England, turned Scots and Irishmen against Britons, put "Churchman and Presbyterian" at odds, and even got "cyder and malt" counties on bad terms.

Oglethorpe must have been aware of the hyperbolic nature of some of his writings about France, and he was certainly conscious of the occasionally humorous picture his words created. The image conjured by his vivid word description of effete Frenchmen permeating English cities and countryside surely struck his readers as at least charmingly simplistic. The reality of "legions of friseurs and dancers amongst the women; and pimps, taylors, and cooks" agitating "the rich families," all of which presumably spread continental corruption, creates a delicious Fieldingesque scene. His fear of French influence in America, however, was never handled lightly; France was England's most dangerous foe and posed particular challenges to frontier outposts such as Oglethorpe's own Georgia. Such a palpable danger was no laughing matter. His published works, official reports, and correspondence are studded with schemes, most of them imaginary, outlining vicious French plots to undermine Georgia's — hence all of British America's — security. Oglethorpe was, if such a term be permissible, a kind of professional Francophobe, a trait appropriately reflected in his writings. His heirs were French, as implied earlier, an irony of which the old general was well aware.

Oglethorpe's incident with Arthur Onslow might today be ascribed to youthful indiscretion. He was, after all, a high-spirited lad in his midtwenties when this affair occurred. Even so, it is hard to view the young Oglethorpe in this unhappy role as more than a rather brutish fellow with an egotistical bent. This latter tendency ultimately formed another pattern in Oglethorpe's life. His personal vanity, observed at first hand by James Boswell as well as others, was legion. Rodney Baine has even caught Oglethorpe praising his own previously printed (but anonymous) work. There was, some might say, a touch of the academic reflected by such an exposé.

With maturity, the political rigidity, to which Oglethorpe fell heir from his mother and sisters, altered. James Oglethorpe evolved, particularly after assuming the seat in Parliament that his father and brothers had held before him, into an avowed independent. He became an intense and dedicated public servant whose interest in hard work and moderate reform within the framework of the existing system caught the attention even of the ruling political elite. This devotion to achievable aims and his determination to bring these goals to reality are best reflected in Oglethorpe's various reports on English jails and in his stirring writings on the sorry plight of imprisoned debtors.

Oglethorpe's obsession with such issues and his search for solutions to these sorts of social ills led logically to his advanced concept for the colony of Georgia. Although he was no utopian, Oglethorpe aimed at the improvement of English society, at least partly by the creation of a colony in British America where the forces that drove him might be documented through settlement, practice, and prosperity. Georgia was, then, his brainchild completely, as John Percival, the Earl of Egmont, readily confirmed. Oglethorpe looked upon his province in much the same way John Winthrop viewed Massachusetts Bay and William Penn saw Pennsylvania: as a sort of holy experiment where rational reforms, once safely in place and proven, might be transplanted to the mother country's own soil. Oglethorpe's Georgia was to be a sort of secular, rational, eighteenth-century Zion. It looked to him to be so good, so achievable, so commendable. His basic optimism on the beneficial role Georgia was to play in the national scheme of things is most cogently expressed in his published works contained in the body of the present volume.

Perhaps it would all have been possible, this earthly paradise where lawyers and black slavery and "spiritous liquors" were barred. But the person responsible for bringing the loose ends together—Oglethorpe himself—was incapable of the sort of intellectual resilience the New World demanded. His staunch independence in England, a stand most interested parties could accept at face value, also had a fixed side to it. "At home," the rigidity remarked upon by some could, given the circumstances, be an asset. "In the plantations," though, Oglethorpe's approach more often than not took on a doctrinaire tone that even his best advisers could do little to modify. In a kind of late-medieval society, aspects of which still existed in eighteenth-century England, men knew their places; they recognized their betters and followed their lead. This was particularly true in rural counties such as Surrey, where Oglethorpe's role as lord of the manor had more than simply ceremonial significance.

Once in the New World Oglethorpe found his position to be subtly altered. Recognized as *the* leader of the Georgia experiment, although lacking a specific title, he discovered to his chagrin that his position on a subject was no longer necessarily the definitive one. Even before the ship *Anne* sailed from Gravesend controversies had surfaced, and more appeared during the voyage to America. No few of the early settlers grumbled openly under his leadership; they were frankly worried about basic questions relating, for example, to female inheritance of land in Georgia. Slavery—to have it or not—was an immediate issue, just as the availability of rum or strong drink other than beer and wine. It would be stretching the situation unbearably to maintain the view often expressed by American historians that the Atlantic Ocean was the first liberating step for colonists as they left the Old World. Even so, Oglethorpe found himself, once in America, faced by a new environment in more than simply the physical sense. So did his settlers. The leader's resourcefulness and his ability to compromise were immediately tested, just as surely as was his body on this wild riverbank in this bizarre, challenging New World.

Some like to think of Oglethorpe's reforms, if thus they may be called, as harking back to the Middle Ages. But to view Oglethorpe's efforts in this direction poses the danger of interpreting his opposition as more politically and intellectually "liberated" than Oglethorpe. Nothing can be farther from the truth. Historians too often tend to view events as black or white, and to fit developments into presentist molds to suit their own approaches to contemporary situations. Fortunately there is no easy way to "fix" Oglethorpe in the eighteenth century, much less in the twentieth. To paraphrase Charles A. Beard, each person must search the record— in this case Oglethorpe's written corpus—and decide for himself. He was perceived by his contemporaries as intelligent, determined, and free from cant. To a typical twentieth-century eye such an interpretation may appear hopelessly naive. But Oglethorpe should, I think, be looked at within his own frame of reference, not ours, and his record upon examination is a good one.

Politically, Oglethorpe went far beyond the stand taken by his energetic and foolish mother and sisters. His position is probably best reflected by his early break with the Stuarts and the "fringeites" who agitated for the overthrow of the Hanoverians and a return to High Toryism. And yet he shared much in common with those dissatisfied by a system that produced a George I and, most particularly, a Robert Walpole. The Jacobites yearned for a more centralized—perhaps even despotic—church and monarchy, and for a time when such families as the Oglethorpes had been in favor. "Jamie" Oglethorpe could never quite shake the feeling that these simpler times had been somehow more honest and that civic virtue was more often rewarded then than during the rule of "the Father of Corruption," as he described Walpole, who "slept over the Helm of State." In his last years Oglethorpe even reminisced to James Boswell on the many virtues of late-Stuart England.

This inclination to reflect on the period before the Glorious Revolution in an objective yet faintly romantic fashion caused Oglethorpe to be viewed with suspicion throughout his career. In fact it helped bring him a courts-martial after he bungled an assignment during the fateful invasion of England by Prince Charles Edward in 1745–46. The Duke of Cumberland, George II's son, considered Oglethorpe a secret Stuart supporter. Cumberland saw to it that Oglethorpe never actively commanded English troops again, even though the charges against him were dismissed as groundless.

It is this curious admixture of concept and behavior that is part of the Oglethorpe enigma. In his writings he spoke for the downtrodden, for those with little or no voice in society. His sympathies lay with the farmers and agricultural workers, displaced by enclosures and demographic changes none then understood; for common sailors, whose grievances were legion but who had no constituency; for imprisoned debtors, whose position in eighteenth-century British society seemed hopeless. Oglethorpe also claimed to speak for a broad cross-section of the English middle class—for merchants, shopkeepers, landowners, and the like, who bore the brunt of the nation's war effort. Although he was born into a secure position in society, based on a solid relationship to the land and to the then-ruling house of Stuart, Oglethorpe disliked favoritism and the sort of special treatment given, for example, to influential prisoners who enjoyed wide freedoms and creature comforts not unlike some of the semipalatial minimum security prisons, complete with golf courses, that we hear of today. Oglethorpe was, in some respects, a creature of the society he critiqued, and yet this too says something about the powers of observation that permitted him to sense the failings in a system from which he himself sprang.

In this regard Oglethorpe was not unlike America's Thomas Jefferson. Was Oglethorpe, then, inconsistent? If so, Jefferson was as well. My reaction on this question is that Oglethorpe would have agreed wholeheartedly with his friend Samuel Johnson's definition that consistency was a characteristic most often found lodged comfortably in small, smug minds.

The Jefferson reference leads me to another observation. Both men were strongly pro–laissez faire in their approaches, although Oglethorpe's ideas in this regard precede Adam Smith's famous publication of 1776. Oglethorpe *knew* that it was the yeoman farmer who jelled English society and gave it the strength and resilience it possessed. The prosperity of the lower class was immediately mirrored in the influence and impact that the English upper class possessed. It was a kind of "trickle up" economic system as Oglethorpe viewed it and it worked for all concerned when not tampered with. This was particularly clear in the area of international trade and in English commerce generally. It was sound British mercantile practice that made Britain great.

Just as with Jefferson, Oglethorpe deplored changes in the simpler system, particularly the evolution of industrialism and the desertion of the countryside. He warned that such a serious movement meant lowering the status of the urban laborer to the subsistence level materially, and to the emotional and spiritual point of personal despair. His interest, just as Jefferson's, appears genuinely to have been for that elusive "common man," whom Oglethorpe consciously set out to help by reshaping certain fixtures of English society and by founding Georgia. Jefferson tried to achieve the same goal by simplifying and economizing government and by orienting it toward the elements he perceived to be the productive ones in American society. In Oglethorpe's "perfect" colony all would be ruled by an agrarian law he best articulated in *Select Tracts*. There would be no manufacturing in Georgia, hence no industrial class to be downtrodden. Georgians would raise "Silk, Wine, and Oil"; trade and commerce would come from these products. Georgia's productivity would benefit the mercantile system and the average citizen; her people would bask in the reflected glory of Oglethorpe's province. Thomas Jefferson could hardly have said it better.

Georgians most certainly disliked the liquor prohibition, particularly those nascent Indian traders who saw in rum an invaluable exchange commodity. No few of the natives resented it too, particularly those called by the eminent historical anthropologist Charles Hudson "the trading Indians." Their influence was founded in some part upon the trade in "kill devil" and their relations with the white man. To Oglethorpe, who tended to deal at times in oversimplifications, it was obvious that the English traders had debauched the natives by the use of rum, for "they are miserable sights" when under its baleful influence. Still he thought it "a vulgar Error" to assume that all natives were "addicted to this Vice." Many were strong of limb, admirable in their honesty and integrity, and excellent associates. Obviously, however, Oglethorpe was not above using the native Americans against Britain's enemies; but what other position could he realistically assume, located, as Oglethorpe and Georgia were, on a troubled international frontier where there was a larger concentration of indigenous peoples than in any other single area of North America?

In his writings Oglethorpe could be extremely graphic when he set out to be. His hard-hitting report on the Stono River uprising of 1739 is, in my opinion, the best surviving account of that incident. His views on the suppression of this rebellion are fairly shocking to the twentieth century, just as they were—intentionally—to the eighteenth century. He wrote plainly, eloquently, and with a double-barreled purpose: to speak out in no uncertain terms on slavery itself, and to outline vividly what terrifying dangers were inherent in a province where slavery was permitted. After all, the Stono Rebellion has been recently described in appropriately lurid terms as "the most violent slave uprising in the entire history of the mainland colonies before the coming of the nineteenth century," in Katz, Murrin, and Greenberg's *Colonial America: Essays in Politics and Social Development*, 4th ed. (New York: McGraw-Hill, 1993). Those who observed the rebellion and its effects, such as Oglethorpe, were profoundly moved by the experience. Slavery, once planted, tended, like kudzu, to dominate the area where it was permitted. The mind as well as the pocketbook of the slaveholder became hypnotized by the institution, but as the number of slaveholders increased—as was occurring rapidly in South Carolina— fear of insurrection ballooned. Life was hard, Oglethorpe wrote, on the Southern Frontier, but neither Carolina nor Georgia would act leniently when faced by slave revolt; such a weakness would simply play into the hands of England's enemies, especially Spain, who took a role in the Stono affair. Spain's part in the rebellion was actually wildly exaggerated by the Carolinians, who lived in fear of a joint native-slave insurrection backed by either France or Spain or—unspeakably—both. Time and effort, Oglethorpe seemed to say, might best be concentrated elsewhere. He did not have to exaggerate, though, when he wrote in a rather offhand way that no Stono slaves were tortured once caught but were "only put . . . to an easy death." Many were pardoned, he said, and cited this "Humanity" as playing a major role in putting down the rebellion. There is no reason whatever to suspect that Oglethorpe was being facetious in these remarks. A leniency of spirit, he went on, had sapped "the very Spirit of Revolt," but who knew what the dastardly Spaniard might do next? Or the slaves?

It is fairly well documented in his writings that Oglethorpe had a certain way with words. He does not compare to many of his contemporaries and friends, such as Johnson, Boswell, and Goldsmith, but then who does? Oglethorpe's writing style is not always what I might call "elevated," but only rarely if ever did he address a subject that called up elegance of style. Debtors, sailors, imperial trade, Gallic intrigues, slave uprisings, Carolina provincials satiric attacks upon his person, political jottings—none of these excited whichever of the muses encouraged finely honed phrases and thrilling syntax. But Oglethorpe could, at rare times, be earthy and altogether surprising. His story about the "Clap and Pox," which refers to an internal English political situation, is daring and focuses attention through its grim but humorous allusion. It reminds me of the rather wicked (and human) remark in one of his official letters to the government during the War of Jenkins's Ear, that although his troops lacked ammunition and proper support, at least they had the balls to meet an onslought as it should be met.

Oglethorpe could also coin a phrase. It is rather surprising that none of his best quotations has been picked up as a monograph title. On the settlement of Georgia, "the Asilum of the Unfortunate" would seem to hold all kinds of possibilities for an author with a strong message to impart. My own favorite phrase, though, is "By a *lucky Kind* of *Poverty*," which, continued to its logical ending, maintains that the British overseas plantations had been fortunate in never discovering the fabulous riches claimed by the Spanish. Spain's dependence upon American treasure held back the development of trade in her empire, held down the status of the common laborer and yeoman farmer, and fixed the mother country in a continuous search for what had really proven to be fool's gold and not the real thing. Without the gold and silver, England developed her trade, her farms, her middle-class merchants, her Indian traders, and her staple crops, all of which redounded to the benefit of the mother country. Spain's and France's empires shriveled by comparison. He had a point.

Oglethorpe could be perfectly blunt in discussing such a matter as economics. "Profit and Gain," as he viewed it, was "the meanest Motive" on which to found a colony. His calling out for "prudent Beneficence" was intended to touch uneasy consciences, possibly even his own. This simple phrase, in fact, might best describe Oglethorpe's public career as reflected in his writings. Oglethorpe, classical scholar, could write with tongue-in-cheek in his witty, if not very subtle, line on the subject of the government of South Carolina: "All Carolina is divided into three Parts." A sharp sense of humor, though, was never one of his defining features. This, taken with his inability to accept constructive criticism and his well-developed ego led him into problems at home and in America that could have been avoided. His judgment in making appointments was often faulty, and his abhorrence of the dull particulars of finance are well known and need no discussion here. In my estimation, however, the sympathetic prose he devoted to the plight of those imprisoned for debt more than makes up for deficiencies of personality and wit in other areas.

Oglethorpe's notion of prohibiting female inheritance of Georgia's land sprung from no misogynist's mind. Rather it reflected his concern that Georgia's frontier women, unaccustomed to the use of firearms and defensive military measures, might be easy prey for Britain's enemies. He also feared that unscrupulous elements of society would take advantage of widowed property owners and, in one fashion or another, end up with title to their land. The end result, he feared, might be concentration of land in but a few hands. Such intensive elements, with economic interests that ran beyond the production of silk and oils, would agitate for slavery and, given the tenor of the British House of Commons, might succeed in having this regulation, one of Trustee Georgia's only three laws, revoked. The agrarian economy would be undermined, the purified agrarian law (which was to dominate the province) would be but a faint memory. Trading interests and manufacturing elements would assume control of the colony. Again the similarities, especially in the theoretical field, between Oglethorpe and Jefferson are worth making.

It was not just the slaves who were recipients of Oglethorpe's pity and sympathy, but the native Georgians as well. From his first day in the colony Oglethorpe had felt a rapport with the Indians, and they with him. His triumphant return to England, with a delegation of natives in tow (could Oglethorpe have been thinking of Christopher Columbus or of Raleigh?) proved a brilliant public relations success. The London newspapers, who could sense a good story, covered almost every move the native "Americans" made. Interviews with the royal family and the Archbishop of

Canterbury would naturally be given full attention, but the natives could hardly draw a private breath without having it reported in the journals and magazines of the day. The most dramatic incident during the visit came with the death from smallpox of one of Tomochichi's warriors. Oglethorpe provided the native entourage with sufficient time for mourning at his own country house in Godalming, following the warrior's burial in the church yard of St. John the Evangelist.

Although he angled for peaceful relations for Georgia through his hospitality, and although he rather shamelessly kowtowed to the Yamacraws in order to give them status among larger tribes, it is clear that his affection for the native people was genuine. His romanticized picture of Tomochichi, the man of natural integrity and honesty, surely influenced later writers, such as Philip Freneau, who were in part responsible for the emergence in literature—and history too—of the myth of the natural man, the Noble Savage. There is no legitimate reason to doubt Oglethorpe's sincere affection for these people, an affection that extended to the Creeks, Cherokees, Chickasaws, Choctaws, and other tribes. His working relationship with Mary Musgrove, the invaluable "half-breed" who acted as Georgia's spokeswoman among her mother's Creek family, was always conducted on an equal basis. Nor should Oglethorpe's sorrow, openly expressed at the impressive funeral given Tomochichi in 1739, be questioned. These two men "got along" well and spoke easily and confidentially to one another. Oglethorpe's grief at his old ally's death was sincere. It may be worth noting that it was only after Oglethorpe left Georgia in 1743 that relations between the colony and the backcountry Creeks began to fall apart.

The admiration Oglethorpe had for native Americans he found in Georgia is nicely reflected in his writings. His descriptions in *New and Accurate Account* were verified by firsthand experience. He admired especially the absence of guile, and their charming use of metaphor and simile—traits Oglethorpe stressed in his own writings, but not always with the effect he intended. As a garrulous, opinionated Britisher, Oglethorpe enjoyed hearing his own voice on a subject, and was accustomed to the experience. It appears that he treasured his stays among the natives, particularly his important visit to the backcountry in 1739, when he succeeded in underscoring England's urgent desire for alliance and peace with the Creeks. How much better it must have seemed to him to smoke the peace pipe and drink the black drink with the Creeks than face down the raucous and déclassé Georgia malcontents or the arrogant, rude Carolinians.

Oglethorpe thought it was preferable, I suspect, to parlay with the natives than engage in the cat-and-mouse political game he sometimes found himself playing with William Stephens, secretary for the trustees in Georgia. In fact, as the years went by Stephens, through his capacity as secretary, assumed the role of competitor with Oglethorpe for the good will of the Georgia board. Although the two men remained roughly civil to one another, at least as far as the official record goes, there could only have been powerful tensions between them. Stephens was Oglethorpe's senior by a full generation, but the two had careers that overlapped in the Parliament of the 1720s. The men *must* have known one another, for England was a tight little island in those days, especially socially and politically, but there is no sign of recognition between the men in their correspondence, or in Stephens's exhaustive *Journal* and letters sent to London from Yamacraw Bluff.

One plank in the Georgia Trustees' platform for Georgia affected the natives directly and mirrors, in part, Oglethorpe's paternalism toward them as well as toward the English settlers. Before coming to America he had been advised by those who knew the situation—including several highly considered natives themselves—that it would be wise to prohibit the use of rum or strong liquors in the Indian trade. Those were the staples used by the Carolinians and Virginians to close a deal to the traders' benefit. The traders knew no shame, Oglethorpe heard, and often plied the natives with rum until the latter were drunk and unable to bargain rationally. Oglethorpe himself disliked strong liquor and extended the ban on hard drink, formalized by an act of the trustees in 1735, to include his colonists as well as "the Georgia Indians." His idealism was, then, to be spread all round; the colony as a rather mildly structured biblical state began to form. The huzzas from England echoed and re-echoed. He was to be the vessel by which achievable British reform of the 1720s and 1730s was to be realized.

Oglethorpe's image for Georgia was to see a colony of closely knit farmers, traders, and artisans living within reasonable proximity of one another. As a result of limiting the size of land grants to fifty acres for the average male landholder, he aimed to create a self-sufficient society where each property holder raised the necessities of life for himself. In times of crisis these close neighbors could gather quickly and effectively to fend off attackers—an impossibility in rural South Carolina owing to the huge landholdings, many of them uninhabited except for roving bands of natives. These virtual empires were held by important provincials as well as Briton for speculative purposes only and were detrimental to the security and defense of the colony. In Georgia, the modest white farmer would not have to compete with a plantation economy and a system of slave labor. Speculators, a major scourge of the Southern Frontier in Oglethorpe's eyes, would have to search elsewhere to satisfy their insatiable desire for money and power; Oglethorpe's colony would not be turned into just another Carolina.

His opposition to slavery and large land grants uncovered for Oglethorpe few admirers in America, and even fewer at home. Oglethorpe found that he was having particularly to defend the slave prohibition over and over again, even within the trustee ranks, and before the House of Commons. As his determination grew that Georgia would not bow to special interests, so did his opponents', who sent Thomas Stephens, son of William, as their agent in London. Pamphlets, booklets, and general rhetoric on the subject of Georgia and how it was to develop filled the air. Once again this avowedly "different" colony to the south of Carolina became a "hot" news item in the 1740s that could not be ignored.

As for his adamant stand on the question of slavery, it was pointed out with telling effect that Oglethorpe was listed in London's *Historical Register* for 1731–1732 as a deputy governor of the influential slave holding firm known as the Royal African Company. Oglethorpe, though, had not taken an active role in the affairs of this organization and found it reasonably easy to fend off attacks from that direction. But it also was bruited about that in spite of what his official position on large landholding might be, it was indisputable that Oglethorpe himself leased significant acreage in South Carolina where slave labor was utilized, or so wrote William Stephens. Still, Betty Wood's balanced and carefully considered assessment that Oglethorpe was sincere in his antislavery stance and was, in fact, far ahead of his time, should be looked upon as an accurate interpretation of this difficult man.

At the very least, the charge against Oglethorpe made by William Stephens did nothing to cement a friendship that apparently did not exist robustly in any case. Stephens's contention weakened Oglethorpe's position along the high road of moral rectitude and tended to lessen his authority in Georgia. Moreover, Stephens reported that Oglethorpe had tried to get South Carolina to establish a ferry from his property across the Savannah, a river "equal to the Rhine," he said. (His financial interest on one bank of this noble stream probably made him view the river in a more romantic light than he might otherwise have done.) Rhine or no Rhine, the South Carolina Assembly demurred; Oglethorpe's scheme came to nothing. The publication of these startling bits of news may have been the immediate cause of the friction between Stephens and Oglethorpe, and might well be viewed as retribution for a slight Oglethorpe directed toward Stephens's son, Thomas. William Stephens disliked subterfuge and deception, and his discovery that Oglethorpe was capable of speaking out of both sides of his ample mouth may have led the older man to develop an urge to puncture at least one segment of the "palladin of philanthropy" image that Oglethorpe nourished about his person.

One of the most valuable aspects in the present collection of Oglethorpe's published writings is that it reflects a sharp image of what English society was like during this period. And Oglethorpe, of course, is juxtaposed against this historical scrim. His writings underscore some of both the weaknesses and strengths of eighteenth-century England and, for this reason, have a virtue in themselves. But they do more than just that, obviously. They reflect one influential man's desire to improve society while being keenly aware, at the same time, that what England already had was the best the civilized world offered in the areas of politics, social virtue, and opportunity. And it was never Oglethorpe's notion to change the status quo radically.

Obviously, Oglethorpe did not work alone for these ends. Oglethorpe's England, and this phrase embraced virtually the entire century, groped for reform of a system that would not at the same time destroy its strengths and undeniable assets—that would not throw out the baby with the bath. At first his efforts, and England's, were sporadic and sluggish, but by the time the French Revolution came such attempts assumed a sense of understandable urgency for the reformers. Oglethorpe's active and most productive years preceded the "revolutionary generation," but he continued to embrace various efforts to make the system a more manageable one. Even as an octogenerian, when most such citizens of the land denounced change as they shakily lifted their Madeira glasses in London's public houses, Oglethorpe kept in mind a more equitable England by supporting William Pitt, by continuing to express sympathy for America and Americans, and through his involvement with prison reform. He also added his voice to the movements that aimed to topple slavery from its imperial pinnacle. Oglethorpe backed Georgia's move in the American Revolution, but he thought that the push for complete independence was premature. His denunciation of English administrative and political mismanagement continued until his dying day, although he was out of any spheres of influence and was seen by most contemporary politicians as an ancient carryover from an earlier age.

As is apparent in his writings, it is certain that Oglethorpe was no radical; the reforms he pushed were moderate and rational. He was, after all, a man of the Enlightenment—well read, outspoken, fair-minded, self-conscious, opinionated, a trifle stuffy perhaps, but on the whole not an unattractive figure. If he lacked the humor and wit of some of his sharper contemporaries, such as Fielding, Swift, Addison, Sheridan, or Goldsmith, at least he had a quickness and unmistakable style. He loved give-and-take, whether it be with young or old, and he was afraid of nothing. This slightly crotchety old gentleman in 1785 had the same feeling of relevancy to England that he had fifty years earlier.

At the very end of his life Oglethorpe had a courtesy visit from John Adams, first ambassador of the United States to the Court of St. James. Even Adams was struck by the vivacity, the youth, and the spirit that the founder of one of the original thirteen states personified. Their meeting was cordial, brief, noncommittal. Oglethorpe returned Adams's call, and not long after, the old Georgian was dead. If only the caller, instead of the staid, reserved New Englander, had been Thomas Jefferson! But historians must not deal in "if" history. They must be satisfied with the record as it is. And Oglethorpe's, I submit to the impartial reader, is a good one.

Preface

Oglethorpe's published writings are collected here for the first time. Hitherto only two of his tracts have been published together. In 1972, *Select Tracts Relating to Colonies* and *A New and Accurate Account of the Provinces of South-Carolina and Georgia* were included by Trevor R. Reese in *The Most Delightful Country of the Universe*. There, however, the first is unascribed and the second attributed to both Oglethorpe and Benjamin Martyn. It seems unjust that although collections of the writings of some colonizers, such as William Penn, have been available through the centuries, only now have the writings of James Edward Oglethorpe been brought together. Like Penn, he was a distinguished philanthropist. He was a pioneer in championing the rights of the British sailor and was the first reformer of the English prison system, anticipating the work of John Howard by almost half a century. Among the colonizers, moreover, he was apparently the first to envision the British empire as a British Commonwealth.

Reprinted here, with separate introductions and with notes both textual and explanatory, are all the tracts, important committee reports, and letters to the press so far identified as written or edited for publication and published either by Oglethorpe or, like the parliamentary reports, with his cooperation. His "Instruction which was published in pamphlet to settle Island of St. Johns" (Prince Edward Island) does not appear here, for contrary to the general's belief, it was apparently never printed.[1] During his parliamentary career Oglethorpe authored many reports that also do not appear here; but they were either never printed, or were at most, like the reports on the state of the British fisheries, represented in the *Journals of the House of Commons* not by any narrative, exposition, or argument by Oglethorpe, but by a page or two of testimony from witnesses. Though published separately, his 1749 parliamentary report designed to assist the Moravians in America was actually assembled by their leader Count Zinzendorf, his London agent, and his London solicitor. Excluded are Oglethorpe's *Some Account of the Design of the Trustees for establishing Colonys in America*, which was first published by the University of Georgia Press in 1990; and his speeches, letters, and papers, which I hope to incorporate in a separate volume.

Excluded also are a number of items that have been attributed to Oglethorpe at one time or another, but on slender and unreliable evidence. These spurious attributions I examine in Appendix 1. In Appendix 2, I include two pieces that Oglethorpe probably wrote.

The text is always that of the first edition. I have, however, incorporated all Oglethorpe's substantive changes. Thus in *A New and Accurate Account* I have incorporated Oglethorpe's own manuscript corrections and improvements; *The Sailors Advocate* I have reprinted from the corrected state; and in *The Naked Truth* I have incorporated the substantive changes that Oglethorpe made in the second edition. All such changes I have recorded in my notes. I have not modernized dates in Old Style, in which until 1752 the new year began on March 25. In separate introductions I have tried to date each publication, establish Oglethorpe's authorship, give its printing history, and place the piece in some historical perspective. In the notes I have tried to clarify Oglethorpe's allusions and identify the persons named.

In preparing this edition of Oglethorpe's writings, I have been assisted by the prompt and helpful responses of historians and librarians in the United Kingdom, Canada, and the United States. Their particular assistance I have attempted to acknowledge in appropriate notes. The valuable assistance of my colleagues Phinizy Spalding, of the History Department, and Jerome Mitchell, of the English Department, calls for special recognition. Professor Spalding has generously shared with me his copies of Oglethorpe materials among the Boswell Papers, at Yale, and has assisted me with this edition from its inception, suggesting numerous corrections and improvements. Professor Mitchell has for several years generously shared his office with me and has even scheduled his appointments so as to allow me quiet working time. I am also indebted to the English Department for defraying the expense of numerous microfilms and photocopies of Oglethorpe's writings; and for word processing there I am grateful to De Anna Palmer, Connie Perry, and Karen Myers.

For permission to reprint I am indebted to several libraries and a publisher: to the Rare Book and Manuscript Collection, Cornell University Library, for the first edition of *The Naked Truth*, and to the Peabody Institute Library of Baltimore, Maryland, for the additions and revisions in the second edition; to the Baker Library (Kress Collection), Harvard Business School for the first edition, corrected state, of *The Sailors Advocate;* to the Hargrett Rare Book and Manuscript Library of the University of Georgia for first editions of *Select Tracts Relating to Colonies* and *A New and Accurate Account*, including Oglethorpe's manuscript corrections in the latter; to the Newberry Library for the "Account of Carolina and Georgia" included in the 1739 edition of Thomas Salmon's *Modern History* published by Bettsworth and Hatch; and to the Beinecke Rare Book and Manuscript Library, Yale University and to the Edinburgh University Press for copies of the Faber letters.

The Publications of James Edward Oglethorpe

Quisquis amissam (1714)

"Quisquis amissam," Oglethorpe's first publication and only known poem, laments the death of Queen Anne and celebrates the coronation of King George I. It appeared in 1714 in *Pietas Universitatis Oxoniensis in Obitum Serenissimae Reginae Annae et Gratulatio in Augustissimi Regis Georgii Inaugurationem*, a volume to which most of the contributors were eminent Oxonians. Oglethorpe's Sapphic stanzas (a form developed by Horace) are not distinguished, but they are competent. Oglethorpe had had a good classical education at Eton, and at Corpus Christi he had studied with the renowned classical scholar Basil Kennet.[1] For some years Latin had provided the medium of his education; and Oglethorpe was apparently a good linguist. French came easy to him; and on his voyage to Georgia in 1736 with the Moravians, he learned some German. Earlier, in 1734, he and August Gottlieb Spangenberg had been forced to converse in Latin.[2] His facility in that language he apparently retained. On a visit to the general in 1783, James Boswell recorded that Oglethorpe "quoted several of the Latin poets."[3] But perhaps the most significant aspect of the poem is its declaration of allegiance to the Hanoverian king, for Oglethorpe's mother, brother, and sisters were all loyal to the Stuart Pretender.

"Quisquis amissam" was reprinted by Rudolf Kirk, in "A Latin Poem by James Edward Oglethorpe," *Georgia Historical Quarterly* 32 (1948): 29–31, with a prose translation by Dorothy Flint. My text follows the original, in *Pietas Universitatis Oxoniensis*. For the translation I am indebted to Robert R. Harris, of the Classics Department at the University of Georgia.[4]

Quisquis amissam lacrymis Parentem
Heu! pius frustrà repetis, molestum
Auferas planctum, atque, malè ominata
    Verba, querelas.
ANNA Se fleri vetat: *Illa* cœlos
Assidens Divis tenet, inde terras
Spectat, & curat Decus Imperîque
    Fata *Britanni.*
Mortuam stultè querimur, perenni
Fama *Quam* pennâ vehit, & superbos
Cui dedit nuper titulorum honores
    Flandria victa.
Musa virtutum memor arcet *Illam*
Luridis Orci tenebris: & alto
Laetus exemplo fit Imago viva
    GEORGIUS ANNÆ.
Ille, seu Martis studium fatiget,
Seu colat Pacem, nova sylva Laudum
Crescit, aut Lauro caput aut virenti
    Cinctus Olivâ.

    Jacobus Oglethorpe Eq. Aur. Fil. è C.C.C.
    Sup. Ord. Commens.

[All you who piously, yet in vain, alas! recall with tears your lost Mother, away with this tedious dirge, with these lamentations, ill-omened words.

Anna refuses to be bewailed: she herself, seated amongst the saints, holds the heavens whence she looks down upon earth and cares for the glory and the destiny of the British Empire.

Foolishly do we complain that she is dead when Glory bears her up on everlasting wing, and Flanders, conquered, has but recently conferred upon her the honor of proud titles.

The muse, mindful of her virtues, keeps her from the lurid darkness of Orcus, and George, rejoicing in her lofty example, is become the living image of Anna.

Whether he wears out the pursuit of Mars, or whether he cultivates Peace, a fresh forest of Praises springs up; for he is crowned, now with Laurel, now again with verdant Olive.

    James Oglethorpe, son of a gold-accoutered knight, of
    Corpus Christi College. Gentleman-commoner.]

A Duel Explained (1722)

Oglethorpe's account of his encounter with Captain Richard Onslow and Mr. Sharp was prompted by a news note that appeared in the *London Daily Journal* on March 27, 1722: "We are inform'd from Haslemere in Surry, that Mr. Oglethorpe drew his Sword there on Mr. Sharp (Secretary to the present Bishop of London) and wounded him in the Belly: Which Insult being resented by Capt. Onslow, Mr. Oglethorpe and he Drew, and in the Re-encounter both being slightly wounded, the Capt. disarmed Mr. Oglethorpe without pushing his Resentment so far as the Provocation deserved."

Captain Richard Onslow, a younger brother of Speaker Arthur Onslow, was in 1727 to be elected to Parliament as a supporter of the administration. Mr. Sharp was not the private secretary of John Robinson, Bishop of London; but the bishop doubtless required numerous secretaries or assistants for his manifold administrative and parliamentary responsibilities.[1]

My text reproduces Oglethorpe's response as published in the *London Daily Journal* for March 29, 1722.[2]

To the Author of the *Daily Journal*.

SIR,   London, March 29, 1722,

AN untarnish'd Reputation is dearer to every honest Man than Life, and printing Lies without the Author's Name, is like Stabbing in the Dark; News-Writers, in whose Power it is to blacken the most spotless Character, should have very good Authority before they publish Things prejudicial to any one's Reputation, since the Injury they do thereby is almost irreparable, Men being more willing to believe the Scandal, than the Recantation. I am lead into these Reflections by the falseness of the Article from Haslemere, publish'd in your Paper of Tuesday last, and must desire you, in Justice to me, to publish the following true Account of what happen'd there.

On Sunday the 25th, after Evening Service, Captain Onslow and Mr. Sharpe, meeting Mr. Burrell and Mr. Oglethorpe in the Market-Place at Haslemere, Mr. Oglethorpe tax'd Mr. Sharpe with some Stories that he had rais'd, Mr. Sharpe giving him a warm Answer, Mr. Oglethorpe corrected him for it; Captain Onslow stepping in between[,] Mr. Sharpe drew his Sword, on which Mr. Oglethorpe, Captain Onslow, and Mr. Burrell also drew. In the Scuffle Mr. Oglethorpe wounded Mr. Sharpe in the Belly, and Captain Onslow in the Thigh, Mr. Burrell beating down Mr. Oglethorpe's Thrusts, of which Captain Onslow taking advantage seiz'd on the Blade of Mr. Oglethorpe's Sword with his Left Hand, and said, your Life is in my Power, Mr. Oglethorpe answer'd, do your worst, and struggling, tore his Sword thro' the Captain's Hand which is very much disabled. The Mob being gathered, no more happen'd; Mr. Oglethorpe (who was not wounded) bound up Capt. Onslow's Wounds and sent for a Surgeon to him.

These are Facts; for the Truth of which I appeal to Captain Onslow himself, I am, SIR,
            JAMES OGLETHORPE.

The Sailors Advocate (1728)

Like most of Oglethorpe's subsequent publications, except for the parliamentary reports, *The Sailors Advocate* appeared anonymously. In his 1777 reprint Oglethorpe credited the pamphlet to "some of the most respectable Members in the Opposition" (p. v). They probably contributed mainly to the appendix; and doubtless they furnished ideas and suggestions for the central essay. But apparently Oglethorpe wrote that essay, edited the appendix, and later wrote the introduction. In his catalog of his own works Granville Sharp listed as No. 16 "Addition to the Preface of the Sailor's Advocate. (A Work of General Oglethorpe.)" Sharp's biographer, Prince Hoare, confirmed that the pamphlet was "written by his [Sharp's] veteran friend";[1] and in the second edition of the *Memoirs of Granville Sharp* he added, "In a copy sent to me by a friend, is the following marginal note, in Mr. Sharp's hand-writing: 'No part of this work was written by G.S., except the Letter to the Editor (Old General Oglethorpe), from p. x to p. xvii of the Introduction.'"[2] Sharp was certainly in a position to know. Not only did he contribute to the "eighth" edition, of 1777, but he was a close friend of the general during the last decade of his life and an executor and legatee of Mrs. Oglethorpe.

Among those who contributed to *The Sailors Advocate* must be listed John Drummond of Stirling, probably Captain Edward Vernon, and perhaps Giles Earle. John Drummond must have contributed appendix 3, for among the members of Parliament only he could be called a "Dutch Trader." In the debates on naval legislation he advocated two shillings a month additional pay and other benefits for volunteers.[3] Vernon may have collaborated with Oglethorpe on the central essay: the scenes where the writer appears aboard a press-smack and at the Admiralty Office come more plausibly from Captain Vernon than from Oglethorpe. An M.P. who was to serve on both of Oglethorpe's prison committees, Vernon protested to the Admiralty his dislike for the restraint and confinement that the system of impressment placed on seamen, and in advocating reform went to lengths not always tactful or practicable. Thus during the 1728 debate on the payment of seamen, he incurred public reprimand when, in

7

order to make copies, he removed a paper from the desk of the Speaker of the House while debate was ongoing.[4] Appendix 1, by someone "*bred in the Land-service,*" may have been contributed by Giles Earle. He had been deprived of his military commission for opposing the administration, had served 1718–20 as Groom of the Bedchamber to the Prince of Wales (George II) while Samuel Molyneux was his secretary, and was to be one of Oglethorpe's principal assistants on the prison committees.

In *The Sailors Advocate* Oglethorpe attacked the injustices that were suffered by the sailors of the Royal Navy, particularly their forcible recruitment by press-gangs.[5] The navies of France, Holland, and Sweden, Oglethorpe made clear, relied upon no such practice. But in spite of the Briton's fabled constitutional rights, the British Admiralty had, under the plea of alleged necessity, continually utilized this method of recruitment, citing legal precedents to sanction the practice.[6] Impressment had been lamented and attacked for centuries; and in 1696 a method of voluntary naval registration had been instituted, but it was awkwardly devised and ill-administered, and it proved useless.[7]

Another major injustice that Oglethorpe attacked in *The Sailors Advocate* was the amount of the sailor's pay and the method of payment. Since 1696 the rate had not increased. Moreover sailors were paid only infrequently; their pay was always several months late; and they were given not cash, but promissory tickets redeemable only at the London Pay Office or by a dockyard commissioner.[8] The sailors were usually forced to cash these tickets at a considerable discount. The families especially suffered from such a practice, for voyages sometimes lasted for more than a year; and when the sailors came home, they were often "turned over" — transferred to an outgoing vessel.

A number of proposals for reform had appeared toward the close of the previous century, when the act of 1696 was being considered,[9] and again in 1720, when naval legislation (eventually aborted) was pending, especially John Orlebar's *A Scheme Whereby His Majesty Would Never Want a Choice of Able Seamen.* A member of Parliament who had been Oglethorpe's contemporary at Eton and who was to serve on both of his prison committees, Orlebar advocated prompt payment of wages in cash at the end of a cruise, and concern for the sailors' families.[10] In or about 1727, other pamphlets proposed similar reforms.[11]

The immediate occasion of *The Sailors Advocate*, however, was the opening address of King George II to Parliament, on January 23, 1728. Possibly at the suggestion of his former secretary, Samuel Molyneux, who was now an M.P. and a Lord of the Admiralty, King George informed Parliament that he wished "to see the Foundation laid of so great and necessary a Work, as the Increase and Encouragement of our Seamen in general, that they may be invited, rather than compelled by Force and Violence, to enter into the Service of their Country."[12]

Hitherto dated only 1728, *The Sailors Advocate* appeared on or about February 13. On that day the *Daily Journal* advertised it as published "This Day," the first number of a new periodical. Thus *The Sailors Advocate* was printed only three weeks after George II recommended voluntary recruitment and apparently one day before a motion was made in Commons to bring in a bill "for encouraging Seamen, entering voluntarily into his Majesty's Service."[13] The second and last number appeared in April, while discussion was still deadlocked — merely a reprint of the anonymous *An Enquiry into the Causes of our Naval Miscarriages* (1707).[14]

Since the three weeks that elapsed between the king's speech and the publication of *The Sailors Advocate* would hardly have allowed Oglethorpe time to solicit contributions, prepare the central essay, gather the material for the appendixes, and have the pamphlet printed and advertised, he probably had some prior notice of the king's intentions, possibly through his friend John Percival, later Lord Egmont, a relative of Samuel Molyneux. Molyneux "formed schemes for the improvement of the navy," and may have authored "Some Considerations relating to the Seamen of the Kingdom," written about 1726–27 and discovered among the papers of Prime Minister Sir Robert Walpole.[15] The author there admitted pressing as "the *ratio ultima* to supply any sudden occasions and to fill up our ships complements when the volunteers shall not be numerous enough to do it."[16] But the thrust of this extensive report, with its numerous recommendations, was to promote enlistment by granting numerous special concessions and privileges to volunteers.

Through Percival, Molyneux himself, or Vernon, Oglethorpe apparently learned that the Admiralty and the Walpole administration intended to frame and force through Parliament a bill that would make some improvements in the recruitment of sailors, but would in effect recognize pressing as a legal means of manning the navy; and he must have anticipated that the committee of the House would be stacked in favor of the Admiralty. When the bill to encourage voluntary enlistment was ordered, on February 14, the small committee was indeed dominated by the Admiralty and the administration.

In naval history there has been some misinformation about the purpose and effect of *The Sailors Advocate*, even the allegation that it helped to defeat the intended improvements.[17] But several ameliorations were made in the legislation of 1728 because of the determined opposition to the Admiralty-drafted bill and doubtless, in part, because of *The Sailors Advocate*. These reforms were introduced into the bill by the opposition on the floor of the House. For example, on March 6 the House ordered that the committee "receive a Clause for preventing Seamen from being arrested for small Debts, during such Time as they do actually belong to any of his Majesty's Ships of War."[18] This provision became part of the new law.[19] A few days later, after the House discovered that the Admiralty had been misapplying funds specifically designated for sailors' pay and that it had consequently been forced to pay in promissory tickets, it ordered that the committee of the whole House "receive a Clause, for providing for the punctual Payment of what Moneys shall become due to the Seamen for short Allowance" and another "to provide, that all impressed Seamen, in his Majesty's Service, shall be discharged, and paid off, after a certain Time to be limited."[20] On April 15 it ordered a clause "for preventing Seamen being left in foreign Parts,"[21] a measure shortly enacted into law.[22] Perhaps because these measures unduly complicated the original bill, on May 2 the consideration of pay was separated from the original bill; and a small committee was appointed to bring in a bill providing for "the constant, regular, and punctual Payment of Seamens Wages."[23] Dominated by the legal administration and the Treasury, the new committee included Robert Jacomb, of the firm of Gibson, Jacob, and Jacomb, money leaders who specialized in discounting seamen's tickets. When on May 17 a motion was made as an instruction to the new committee "for preventing Persons from making unjust Advantages of the Necessities of Seamen in the Service of the Crown," it was voted down.[24] Reform was difficult when vested interests opposed. But in the opinion of Daniel A. Baugh, distinguished historian of the British navy, the bill that provided for proper pay was "the first statutory attempt to put the system of payment on a modern footing."[25] Oglethorpe's first pamphlet had at least played a part.

Of the 1728 edition, a quarto in half sheets, there are uncorrected and corrected states, represented respectively by the Goldsmith copy, in the Library of the University of London, and the Kress copy, in the Baker Library of Harvard University.[26] The pamphlet, as Oglethorpe stated, was hurriedly prepared and printed in order to sway public opinion and especially Parliament toward honoring the king's plea for better conditions for the seamen and the abolition of impressment. Oglethorpe apparently read proof late and hurriedly. Most of the copies that I have been able to examine represent the uncorrected state; and even in the corrected state glaring errors occur that remained uncorrected until 1777, like "morality" for "mortality," "Duth" for "Dutch," and "belive" for "believe."

In the "seventh" edition Oglethorpe added an introduction; and in the "eighth" he added a letter from his friend Granville Sharp. In strict bibliographical terminology there were evidently only three editions: those of 1728 and 1777 and the reprint, slightly abridged, in Abel Boyer's *Political State of Great Britain* for 1728 (35:245–65). Perhaps Oglethorpe counted as editions also his 1728 reprint of the anonymous *Enquiry* and its reprint in 1744 in *The Harleian Miscellany*.

The text and appendix I reprint from the corrected, Kress copy. Since the 1777 text is a page-for-page reprint of the 1728 edition, at least through appendix 2, and incorporates only one substantive change, I record the change in a note, but ignore the many modernizations in punctuation and spelling. The introduction I reprint from the "seventh" edition, of 1777.

THE
Sailors Advocate.

To be continued.

LONDON:

Printed for *H. Whitridge*, under the *Royal-Exchange*; and sold by *J. Roberts* in *Warwick-Lane*, and by the Book-sellers of *London* and *Westminster*, and the principal Towns in *Great-Britain*.

[Price Six Pence.]

Advertisement.

THOSE who please to favour the Author with their Correspondence, are desired to direct to the SAILORS ADVOCATE *at Mr.* Whitridge's *the corner of* Castle-Alley, *under the* Royal-Exchange, Cornhill.

INTRODUCTION BY THE EDITOR OF THE SEVENTH EDITION.

STATESMEN from the most antient times have had a kind of *itching* Palm: to quiet which, and to fill their purses, they continually filch from the people under the pretence of *loyalty* and *zeal* for the Service of the Crown, using *"the Tyrant's Plea,* — NECESSITY*."[27]

This *Thing* of Pressing is a good Milch Cow to the Admiralty. Protections, Passports, Exemptions, Accompts and Charges of Press Gangs without checque, &c. &c. are perquisites, which mount higher than those of the Chancellor, Chief Justices, and Judges put altogether.

The Revolution remedied the evil, but the Admiralty thought it too sweet a morsel to be parted with, and have continually been *nibbling* to get at it again; but the Courts of Law, and the People of England, being always aware of them, like *Cats* have watched the *mice*, and every now and then *have given a Gripe* to the Admiralty Court. Some of the Admiralty have been smartly punished for exceeding their powers, but still the *Mouse* had a mind to the *Cheese;* and in the Year 1727, Sir Charles Wager,[28] by the advice of *Jacome* and *Gibson* (two money Scrivenors and buyers of Sailors Tickets) strove to knaw a hole that he might once more get at the sweet morsel. But the Spirit of the Constitution was, at that time, so high in Parliament, that the Promoters of Admiralty Powers durst not publicly set their faces against *the Laws* and *Rights* of the Kingdom; and therefore, that they might steal a confession of their absurd method of kidknapping the Men and the Cash of the Kingdom under the name of PRESSING, they intended to deceive and surprize the King and Parliament by *"the fair flattering"* † *Pretence* of manning the Navy in an open and generous manner.

The King, in his speech of that year, nobly recommended to the House

---

*Milton.

†The *like Deceit* procured the wicked Act of 11 Hen. VII. c. 3. so justly condemned by the great Sir Edward Coke, whose description of it, is *equally* applicable to the *Admiralty Bill* above mentioned, — It — *"had a fair flattering preamble, pretending to avoid divers mischiefs,"* &c. —— But *"the Purview of that Act tended in the execution contrary ex diametro."* — 4 Inst. p. 40.[29]

of Commons to consider the method of manning the Navy by *Encouragement*, in order to prevent all complaints of Grievances: but the *Admiralty* drew up a Bill, which pointed at the very contrary! It was to *oppress* the Subject; — and this they thought to obtain by making an express distinction in the Bill between *Volunteers* and *pressed Men*, hoping that a Court of Law by seeing the Words *Pressed Men* mentioned in the Act, would from thence draw an inference that such a thing as *pressing* was recognized by Parliament to exist in law.

With this View a Bill was moved for, drawn by the Admiralty Clerks, brought in, Read twice, and committed; when the Design appeared so bare-faced that it raised a general opposition, and the Minister "*who had not seen Pharsalia,*"[30] and had not, therefore, lost all shame, blushed at the absurdity of his Admiralty-Friends.

Besides which, the Opposition of Sir Joseph Jekyll, Serjeant Pingelly, Mr. Lutwyche, Mr. Shippen, Mr. Arthur Onslow, then Speaker (as also some Persons even now alive) the Landed Gentlemen, Sir James Lowther, the Cities of London and Bristol, and the Out Ports, gathered such strength, that in spite of the Court they threw out the mention of *Pressed Men* in every part of the Bill. In the Debates it was discovered that the Admiralty had misapplied the money appropriated for paying Seamen, and had left a debt *upon the Head of Wages*, which, by obliging them to give Tickets instead of Cash, so much distressed the Seamen, that it was manifestly one of the causes which prevented them from inlisting into the Service.

Out of this Oppression the Ticket Buyers made their great perquisite. To remedy which, the Opposition pointed out that the Charge of the Navy was divided into Heads of Payment, one of which was *Wages;* they therefore gave £ 500,000 to clear that *Head of Wages*, and thereby *to prevent for ever* the pretence of not paying the *Wages* when they became due.

Wages are the motive upon which Freemen give their service: but if men are forced to serve without their own consent, they are *Slaves* and not Freemen. By this proceeding it plainly appeared to be *the sense of Parliament* that PRESSING is not only *illegal*, but that the true method of raising Men was to provide and pay them Sums equal to the Value of their Service.

During the agitation of this Question many Petitions came to Parliament setting forth the Grievances of *Pressing;* and the annexed Tract, THE SAILORS ADVOCATE, was then printed, having been composed by some of the most respectable Members in the Opposition, of whom we are happy to say some yet survive, and still maintain the same public Spirit.

This little Tract is now republished to keep up in the people of the present age the Knowledge and Spirit of their Predecessors. Many Years after the Correction of the abovementioned Bill, Sir Charles Wager, who could not leave off *nibbling*, served up once more the former Absurdities, like chewed meat in a French Ragout; for in the Year 1741 he brought in another Bill, under the Title indeed of "An Act for the *Encouragement and Increase of Seamen;*" but the "PURVIEW," as before, "*tended in the execution contrary ex diametro,*" viz. to authorize all the Absurdities of *Pressing.* The House, after many Debates, threw out every word that expressed any Idea of countenancing *Pressing;* and those Debates are wonderfully curious and of great Authority, on account of the very eminent characters at that time in the House who were engaged in the examination of this Question.

The present Editor has subjoined to this little preface the Titles and Preambles of the two Acts which were the occasion of the following Essay,[31] called THE SAILORS ADVOCATE, and also references to some other Statutes relating to this subject, in order to shew that the *Admiralty Court* hath no power of *Acting* within the Realm, and much less of selling *Protections,* (levying money without consent of Parliament) and of seizing the Persons of Men *without* a legal *process* in a Court of Record, according to the *common Law of England.*

As for the *Admiralty Court,* it is not (in its ordinary Process) a Court of *English Law,* but acts upon corrupt *Traditions* and Tyrannical Maxims growing out of the Lees of the Roman Tyranny, being a mere Farrago of Prerogative, which is so justly exposed by the excellent Fortescue.*

This Court however hath not, as yet, been *completely* consigned to the deserved fate of the Court of the Lord President of Wales, and of the Court and Council of the Lord President of the North, of the Star Chamber, Council Table, &c. &c. all which, upon full examination, were taken away as insufferable grievances.

The First Publication of THE SAILORS ADVOCATE was occasioned by the Debates on the Two following Acts of Parliament:

Anno primo Georgii II. Regis, c. 14.

An Act for Encouraging Seamen to enter into His Majesty's Service.

WHEREAS *nothing will more effectually contribute to the promoting and advancing the Naval Strength of this Kingdom, than the endeavouring by* DUE AND

---

*See his valuable Tract "*de laudibus Legum Angliæ.*"[32]

FITTING ENCOURAGEMENTS *to invite Mariners and Seamen to enter willingly into the Service of their Country, as often as Occasion shall require; and whereas His Majesty, out of His Princely Concern for the Increase and Encouragement of His Seamen, hath been most graciously pleased to recommend the same from the Throne, as a Consideration of* THE GREATEST IMPORTANCE; *be it therefore enacted,* &c. In the enacting part, however, the Admiralty Interest would have added a power *of pressing*, in full contradiction to the declared intentions of his Majesty in the preamble, which the Spirit of the House would not bear, but rejected the *Pressing* Clauses with Disdain, and left only what was innocent in the Bill, as the Act now remains. And if the same crafty Adm——lty Interest hath deceived any subsequent Parliaments, by procuring captious expressions to be inserted in any other Acts whereby the general Rights of the Kingdom may be affected by *innuendo*, the COMMON LAW will certainly rescue the Subject from any such snares; and JUDGES and JURIES will understand the Acts of Parliament in a Just and *legal* sense to redress the injured.

Anno primo Georgii II. Regis, c. ix.

An Act for granting an Aid to His Majesty of *Five hundred thousand Pounds*, towards discharging Wages due to Seamen, and for the *constant, regular, and punctual* Payment of Seamens Wages FOR THE FUTURE; &c.

MOST *Gracious Sovereign; Whereas several just and necessary Measures were, upon account of the late perplexed and disturbed Situation of Affairs in Europe, entered into and concerted between Your Majesty's late Royal Father, of Glorious Memory, and Your good Allies; and in order to preserve and restore the Peace of Europe, and to secure the Trade, Navigation, and other valuable Rights and Possessions of these Kingdoms, great Fleets were employed abroad in divers remote Parts, whereby a great Arrear or Debt has been contracted for the Service of the Navy, and particularly* ON THE HEAD OF SEAMENS WAGES; *and Your Majesty having now, by the Blessing of God on Your Care and Concern for the general Good, so far obtained a settlement of Affairs abroad, as that there is no present occasion for employing so great a number of Seamen in Your Majesty's Service; and the immediate payment of the said Arrears of Wages is judged adviseable, not only as it will save and prevent a further great Expence, but also as it will render* a regular, constant, *and* punctual payment of Seamens Wages *more practicable and easy* for the future; *which will be an Encouragement to able and experienced Seamen,* AT ALL TIMES HEREAFTER, *to enter themselves voluntarily into Your Majesty's Service, when occasions shall require the same; and Your Majesty's most loyal and dutiful Subjects, the Commons of Great Britain in Parliament assembled, having taken Your Majesty's most gracious Recommendation from the Throne into their most serious Consideration, have for these purposes freely and* UNANIMOUSLY *given and granted to Your Majesty the Sum of* Five hundred thousand Pounds, *to be raised in manner herein after mentioned,* &c. *And to the End, Intent, and Purpose, that as well all Arrears of Seamens Wages, as their growing Wages, may be* CONSTANTLY, REGULARLY, *and punctually paid, be it enacted by the Authority aforesaid, That not only as to such Monies as have been granted in this Session of Parliament for the Service of the Navy, but also as to such Supplies as shall be* HEREAFTER GRANTED IN PARLIAMENT FOR THOSE SERVICES, *such Parts or Proportions thereof as shall be* ON THE HEAD OF SEAMENS WAGES, *shall from time to time be issued and applied for those Services* constantly, regularly, *and* punctually, *in manner following,* &c.[33]

It is well worth while for a true honest hearted Englishman in the House of Commons to enquire, whether this solemn enacted Appropriation of public Money has been *"constantly"* applied according to the enacted purposes; if not, it may have occasioned the backwardness of Seamen to enlist: and it is to be hoped that no such obstacle could have been thrown in the way with design to furnish the stale pretence of Necessity, in order to obtain their *favourite morsel.*

[Granville Sharp's letter, added in the "eighth" edition, of 1777, is here omitted.]

Numb. I.

THE

Sailors Advocate.

To be continued.

The Welfare of THESE NATIONS undoubtedly depends upon their being powerful at Sea, for whilst they are Masters there, they are secure from Foreign invasions, and may carry the produce of their industry to all parts of the World: It is the *Royal Navy* and *Trade* of BRITAIN which makes it a powerful and envy'd State; Were either of these lost, we should be as despicable Slaves as some of our Neighbours; yet by oppressing those by whom our *Liberties* are preserved, and our *Riches* encreased, we take effectual methods to destroy both.[34] Our *Trade* and *Power* are so linked, that they must stand or fall together; suppose us once inferior in Force to any Nation which rivals us, and our Trade is gone: Suppose our Trade lost, and there's an end of our Force; for Money is the support of the Navy, and Trade the source of Riches. It is the Wealth acquired by means of our Trade, that makes us, at least, equal to our Neighbours, to whom we are inferior both as to the extent of our Dominions, and the fertility of our Soil.

The Interest of the *Funds*,[35] which makes us superior to the rest of Europe, is paid out of the Duties arising from *Trade*; and if those Duties should decrease, it is needless to mention the effects which it must have upon the *Funds*. *The advantage of Trade. The Funds depend upon it.*

By Trade Lands are made more valuable; by Trade the King's Revenues are paid; and to Trade it is owing, that this ISLAND, which with difficulty could, in the Time of RICHARD I. pay 100,000 marks,* now raises yearly above five millions of pounds Sterling. Every discouragement therefore given to Trade, prejudices the *King's Revenues*, the *landed Interest*, the *Funds*, and consequently the whole Nation. Yet not only Trade, but Liberty also is in danger of being subverted, by a custom which is supported under pretence of necessity.

This custom is the *pressing of Seamen*, a proceeding authorized by nothing but forced Constructions of laws, or Unwarrantable violence. The *Magna Charta* says, *that no freeman may be taken or imprisoned, or be disseized of his freehold or liberties, or his free customs, or be outlawed or exiled, or in any manner destroyed, but by the lawful judgment of his Peers, or by the law of the Land.*[37] This is confirm'd by the *Petition of right*;#[39] And† the Courts at Westminsterhall have, in the case of Pressing, explained this so strongly, that the killing an Officer or Sailor, in this manner striving to usurp the liberties of mankind, is by them only deemed Manslaughter. As it seems surprizing how so open an Evasion of the Laws should escape with impunity, it may not be amiss to give a short account of it. *Pressing prejudicial to Liberty, and contrary to Law.*

---

*For to raise 100,000 marks only, in the time of *Richard* I. was impos'd upon every Knight's fee twenty shillings, the fourth part of all Laymen's revenues, and the fourth part of all the revenues of the Clergy, with a tenth of their Goods. Daniel's Hist. p. 121.[36]

#16 C. 1.[38]   †5 El. 795. 48.[40]

The Kings of England formerly contracted with the Captains to furnish Bands of men for the Sea-service at a certain price: these Officers, when they could not get Men by other means, prevailed upon them by drinking, &c. as Land-Officers raise Recruits; and when this failed, they forced on board, under pretence of drunken broils, or their having received *Prest money,[41] such fellows as none thought fit to claim. But though at first this happened only to the worst of men, it was afterwards carry'd so far, that it became a *complaint* in Parliament. Some Officers were punished, and the *Admiralty* issued out orders not to press any *Freeholders*, imagining that under that name would be comprehended all such as were able to prosecute the *pressing Officers*, and that the rest would be forced to submit, because they could not bear the expence of a suit. Thus is *Pressing* carried on with impunity: and the man who is poor has no remedy. The *Admiralty*, it is said, upon these occasions defrays the charge of the Suit of the *Pressing officer*, and, if he is cast, pays the fine for him †. *The original of Pressing.*

This abuse which has crept in by degrees is at last come to such an height that it calls aloud for remedy; since it is not only an injury to the *Liberty* of the *Subject*, but tends to the destruction of the *Government* it self: It ruins *Trade* for the present, and by its consequences must destroy the *Royal Navy*, for whose support it is pretended to be design'd. It is a maxim generally allow'd, that Free nations make the best Soldiers; when Liberty leaves them, Courage soon follows; Oppression certainly debases the mind, and what can be a greater Oppression than forcing Men as prisoners on board a Man of war without necessaries, without allowing them time to order their affairs, or to take leave of their families. How can it be expected, that a Man should fight for the Liberty of others, whilst he himself feels the pangs of Slavery, or expose his Life to defend the property of a Nation, where his dearest pledges, his Wife and Children, are pining a way with want. *Destructive of Liberty, and of the Royal Navy it self, by abateing the Courage of the Sailors.*

Pressing and *hard Usage* not only abates the courage, but lessens the number of the *Sailors*. How easy it is for them to remove from one country to another, is self evident; nor need it be proved by the example of the DUTCH, whose Fleets are above half mann'd by Foreigners; and the wealth of Holland is founded on the *Pressing lessens the number of Sailors.*

---

* Prest is an old French Word, signifying ready, and this Money was given as earnest.
† See *Appendix*.

ill treatment of the Flemings by the Spaniards; for, to avoid Slavery, they chose rather to live free in Unwholesome marshes, than be oppress'd in the Fruitful plains of Flanders.

That the *Common sailor* is not insensible of hardships, is proved by the numbers who have left their native country, and now help to mann the *Russian Fleets* and *Spanish Privateers.* The *Ostend ships* were navigated by *British sailors*,[42] and all countries are benefitted by Englishmen, who have been banish'd by this unhappy practice. Besides, too many of them have turned Pirates, which has put the *Government* to great expences, to protect Trade against those whom we have thus made enemies to all mankind, *Forces them into Foreign service, and induces them to turn Pirates.*

But there is a third and much more terrible manner in which the *sailors* of England are lessened by *pressing;* for the dreadful *mortality* that has of late raged in our *Squadrons*,[43] and helped to disappoint the schemes laid for the peace of Europe, in some measure proceeded from the *miseries* which the men endured on board the *guard-ships;* where many hundreds being confined together without necessaries, occasioned such a stench as gave rise to many distempers, of which several died immediately; but in others of stronger constitutions the distemper lurked, till the heat of the climate into which they went, gave such a ferment to their blood, as brought out the distempers which they had contracted by this ill usage in England; and they soon became contagious. Besides which, the men not being permitted to go on shore to provide necessaries, can with difficulty keep themselves clean; and the want of change of cloathing is often it self the cause of infection; and this has been so manifest in the *West-Indies*, that two or three thousand men are said to have been lost on board that *Squadron;*[44] for when ships are once infected, the bringing fresh men into them is but encreasing the mortality. Tradesmen and others not used to the Sea, being prest on board Ships of war, are so far from being serviceable to the King, that they are a detriment in general to the intended expedition; but particularly because their eating salt provisions often corrupts the blood, and hurries them into such a sickness as spreads a contagion thro' a whole Fleet. This was the case of *Admiral Wager's* Squadron, fitted out in great haste two years ago for the *Baltick*,[45] as well as that in the *West Indies* since. *Causes mortality on board the Squadrons.*

It is not the Timber nor the Iron of the *Ships* of *War* which gives the *Dominion* of the *Seas;* but the *Sailors* who mann them, that are the strength of the NATION; it is their skill and courage on which the safety of the Ships themselves depend; and should they be destroyed by distempers occasioned by ill usage, want of care, &c. or be frighted into Foreign service; what then must become of the *Royal Navy*, is too evident. That this may be the case, is not impossible, since *Sailors* grow every day more and more scarce, which is manifested from the difficulty of manning the Squadrons, and from the Merchants being obliged to augment their wages. The more *Sailors* perish, and the more hardships they endure, the scarcer will they be, and the greater will be the difficulty of manning the *Navy*: and where this will end, is not fit for me to say; but *Sailors* cannot easily be made, nor can we keep the *Dominion* of the *Seas* without them.

When a *Squadron* is to be mann'd the *Merchants ships* are forced to lie idle in their ports, their men are taken away when ready to sail, their perishable cargoe spoil'd, whilst Foreigners supply the markets abroad; which is a damage to *Trade* more considerable than any but Merchants can be sensible of: Thus the Service of the *Navy*, is made a pretence for destroying the very means by which *Navigation* it self subsists. *Pressing very prejudicial to the Merchants*

THE ENGLISH, under a long succession of Monarchs, boast a native liberty, and are born with many privileges which no other kingdom enjoys; neither their bodies nor purses are at their Kings arbitrary disposal; no law is or ought to be past without their own consent. How comes it then, that so very useful a part of his Majesty's subjects as the *Sailors* are, should be prest into the Service, denied their liberty, and turned to slaves? For *Slavery* is nothing but *service* by *force*. The *prest person* is assaulted and seized on the King's high way, and hurried into a floating prison, without being allowed time to speak or write to his friends. The *Crew* forces him along, as Bailiffs do those who resist upon being arrested for debt, often insulting them, and knocking them down before they seize them: sometimes if the unhappy man has money to give, the Gang will let him go;* but if he has not, he is infallibly put on board the smack, which is a vessel fitted up like a prison, with iron grates and bolts. A poor fellow who perhaps hath six or seven children, and makes hard shifts to bring them up, by labouring in lighters, fishing-boats, or plying as a waterman, and is not willing to leave his family to go a long voyage, is the first who is thus laid hold of; while the single man, who is fittest for the Sea, can leave his place of abode, and hide himself till the *press Warrants* are called in, or else go into Foreign service, and often times *Hardships of the persons pressed.*

---

*See the App.

the father of a hopeful family is hurried into a King's ship or press-smack, and his children immediately left without subsistence to seek charity; thus many become *shoe-cleaners* and *vagabonds*, instead of being bred up *Sailors*. I my self saw a *waterman's wife*, with five clean children about her, crying at the *Admiralty office* for her husband then hurried aboard the *Baltick Fleet*; but it being the case of so many in the *Mediterranean* and *West India Squadrons*, it was in vain for her alone to expect relief. And it is very melancholy to consider what great numbers of *women and children* have been brought to beggary, and left destitute, especially of late, by the mortality that has reign'd in some of our *Squadrons*.

This so discourages the generality of our men, that they study to breed up their children to any Trade or manner of living, rather than they should go to Sea; so that none but the worst sort of men will, by this means, be left to serve in the *Royal Navy*, and to them the *floating Bulwarks of England* must be intrusted, if we continue this method to mann our *Fleet*. No wonder then if our breed of *Seamen* grow worse and worse, since *slavery* will make the calling itself contemptible.

The expences of manning the Fleet by *pressing* amounts to a very large sum: It is commonly reckoned, at a medium, to be fifty shillings or three pounds per head; though the charge of keeping the Ships till they are manned, must certainly make it more than double that sum; to say nothing of the hindrance to the service. But what is still worse, this method of *pressing* sets up numbers of little Tyrants in all our Sea-ports, and even so near the Royal court, as in the city of London; where you shall see droves of these lawless fellows, armed with great sticks, force such as they think proper into the service, and knock down any who will not submit to appear before their magistrate, who is sometimes a Lieutenant, but oftner an Officer of the lowest rank, in an Alehouse at Wapping, or St. Catherine's, a Midshipman, a Boatswain's mate, or some such like *Judge* of *Liberty and Property*. This mighty lawgiver, according to his will and pleasure, sends the innocent prisoner aboard a *press Smack*, to lie in bulk, or the hold of the vessel, till he is ordered on board a Man of war, unless discharged as useless by the aforesaid Marine minister, or the Regulating captain appointed to view them in London, if the man has time to appeal there; but in all the Out-ports, the poor captive has none to appeal to but the Officer who presses him, nor any hopes of liberty, unless an order from the Admiralty sets him free, which generally comes so late that the poor man is sailed, and his family left a charge to the Parish. Perhaps the reader may be better pleased with

The present manner and charge of pressing.

an account of this from a sufferer, in his own words, which I happened to hear on board a *Press-smack*, on the Thames. A poor fellow just turned into the hold, looking up to the iron Grates over him, passionately broke out in these terms; ****"I'm in a Dungeon! what have I done, to be dragged from my wife and children in this manner? why was I shut in here! I that am born to be free; are not I and the greatest Duke in England equally free born? if I have done nothing, who has power to confine me? where is the liberty of an English-man? or why is not my Lord Mayor here as well as I?"

When a man is taken out of a homeward bound vessel, if he has any small private adventure, such as Tea, Wine, Rum, &c. it is generally sacrificed to the *Gang* that searches the Ship; but it is too often the practice, first to take what the poor creatures have thus brought home, as the only fruits of their labour and hardships, and then acquaint some other *press-gang* in the River, who come aboard, and take away the very same men, and hurry them immediately out to Sea again, attended with all these distresses of mind and body.

From this barbarous treatment of our People, arises this observation, that in all Foreign ports where our Ships of war arrive, they have so many of these discontented wretches a-board, that, rather than live under such hardships, or venture to return home, many have chosen to swim a-shoar at all hazards, though they have often failed in the attempt, and afterwards been seen dead, floating on the water. What a reproach is this to our Nation? thus to force Seamen to take all opportunities to enter into Foreign service, and to work and fight for Nations, who don't pretend to *Liberty*, and whom we justly scorn for living under the oppressions of *Arbitrary Government*. *The desperate condition of prest men.*

Pressing is not an *oppression* to the *private Sailor* only, but high *injustice* to the *Officers* themselves; for even the *chief Officers*, who sign the warrants for *pressing*, are laid under great difficulties, since it makes them liable to a prosecution, for doing what is necessarily required by their Office: On the one hand, they are bound to obey orders; and on the other, it is criminal by the *Laws* of the *Land* to confine any man, without crimes first alledged against him upon oath; though those Laws have not, in this case, been executed for many Years, yet is their force not lessened: And is it not an exceeding great hardship, for a considerable Officer to be eternally liable to a prosecution, whenever he hath enemies of power and malice sufficient to take advantage of it. 'Tis vain to imagine *Pressing an hardship upon the Officers employed in it; makes them liable to prosecutions, &c.*

that custom can be any defence, since the Highest officer of the Law was, within these few years, punished for violating a Statute scarcely ever read or known,⁴⁶ and which had been look'd upon as so obsolete, that three successive Chancellors had publickly sold the Masters places, which plainly shewed, that they imagined that Law to be no longer in force; yet this was not allowed as any plea in his defence; but in answer to his pleading the practice of his predecessors, and their not being punished, nor even blamed for it, the reply was: *That a blot was no blot until it was hit; and that though murder had been frequently practised, yet that did not make murder lawful, and that the more frequently the crime was committed, the greater necessity was there for punishing it.*⁴⁷ Those Gentlemen therefore must needs be in an uneasy situation, who are liable to a *parliamentary* prosecution for doing their duty. But if this is the case of the *chief Officers* of the *Admiralty*, how much worse is that of the *Lieutenants*, though they are sometimes Gentlemen of the best families in England, yet are they forced to do the duty of Bailiffs on shoar, and Goalers on board; to sit smoking in spunging-houses, to be obliged to Scour the streets, to herd with ruffians, and, which is worse to a compassionate man, to be the *Instruments of oppression*, and to tear away unhappy men from their wives and families. It may be of dangerous consequences for *Officers* to be accustomed to obey *Orders* absolutely contrary to the *Laws* of the *Land*: If in obedience to the former they should kill any unhappy wretch, what a load must that man's blood be upon their consciences; besides which, they must stand tryal for it, and, by the *Law*, murder is death, and it is doubtful whether there can be a pardon where there is an appeal for blood. On the other side, if they should meet with resistance, and lose their lives, what an unfortunate end is it to be kill'd in a mob, or amongst drunkards in a midnight broil: And the man who, in his own defence, kills any of the *press-gang*, is acquitted by Law.

But notwithstanding all these disadvantages, which the Service, the Trade of the Nation, and Particular men labour under from the practice of *pressing*, one general answer serves, viz. that the *Navy* cannot be manned without it, and that if men will not list voluntarily, they must be pressed. Supposing this be true, and that it is not want of *Sailors*, but want of inclination to serve, that makes the scarcity of men; it will be highly necessary to remove the reasons of their unwillingness, to enter. If it proceeds from forcing men to stay an unlimited time in the *service*, and from keeping them all that time like prisoners; from their being paid their wages in such a manner, as often reduces it above two thirds in its value; from the treatment which they receive

Reasons given for pressing.

after they are come on board, they being frequently sent from one extream of climate to another, as from the *Baltick* to the *West Indies*, without any regard to the Health of the men, the time they have already *served*, or their *merit* in *service*; to say nothing of their treatment by some *Inferior Officers*, who are suffered to use them more like dogs than men. If these are the reasons from whence their unwillingness to serve arises, the causes being removed, the effects will cease: And that some of these are the causes, we hope, is already demonstrated; nor can it be expected that any men will go on board a Man of war, where they are treated with severity, whilst they can have larger pay on board a Merchant ship, from whose service they are discharged, and readily paid off, at the end of the voyage.

The Pay on board a Man of war, clear of all deductions, is but 22 *s.* 6 *d.* per month; but out of this most of them do not actually receive above one third part. For not being allowed time to provide themselves with necessaries at home, *viz.*[48] bedding, cloaths, &c. they are forced to take them up at extravagant prices, though they might provide themselves with them at much cheaper rates; but that they cannot do, since they must not go on shoar, lest they should desert. *Sailors receive not above one third of their pay.*

Whilst their pay is thus squandered at Sea; their poor wives and families on shoar must take up their food, and other necessaries, at the utmost extortion, and be likewise obliged to those who supply them at 50 *l.* per cent. discount, on so precarious a security as a *Sailors wages* on board a Man of war; for, if he dies, the purser is generally the principal creditor.[49] But supposing a man out-lives the voyage, and after being several times turned over from *West-India* to *Baltick* voyages, comes home, and a ticket given him for payment; the creditors who furnished his family with subsistence during his absence, fall upon him, perhaps arrest him, and force him to sell or deliver up his ticket at 20 or 30 per cent. loss; or at least not knowing when he shall receive his money, he disposes of his ticket at six or seven shillings in the pound discount to those persons, who employ people in all the Ports for this abominable purpose. Can it then be expected that the love of glory, and the prospect of wooden legs and Greenwich Hospital, should make poor men prefer the King's pay, which is seldom 10 *s.* per month clear, to 30 or 40 *s.* in the Merchant's service.

The grievances of pressing, already set forth, will probably be sufficient to convince every man that they ought to be remedied; but the difficulty is, how to bring it about, and yet to be able to mann the Navy. The fault is easily *The best remedies for pressing to learned from experience.*

found, but it requires the utmost skill to prescribe a remedy. No particular scheme or project is here laid down, but only the different methods that are used in other Countries to mann their ships, that from proceedings approved by experience, better remedies may be collected than from the crude notions of speculative men.

To begin with the VENETIANS, who were once masters of the Mediterranean, they, upon the loss of the Indian trade, when a way round the Cape of Goodhope to the East Indies was discovered by the Portugueze, found their number of *Sailors* diminish, and that voluntiers sufficient to mann their Navy did not list; upon which they fell into a method of forcing men aboard; and this, together with their making *Noble Venetians* commanders, without considering their qualifications, lost them their power at sea, and reduced their Fleets to the wretched condition which they are now in. *The Venetian method of manning their Navy.*

In FRANCE, tho' it is an arbitrary Government, there is no *pressing*, but all *Sailors, Watermen,* &c. upon the sea-coast are enroled (by an Officer, called the *Commissary of the Classes*)[50] from the age of 16 to 60; that they may be ready upon any occasion for the Kings service: So that when any Ships are to be fitted out, an order is put up at every parish church about 14 days before, by which the men are required to repair to the Commissary in every respective district appointed for that purpose. Out of the whole the Commissary chuses a certain number, to each of whom he gives a printed passport, in which is incerted their names and place of abode, and the Port to which they are to repair in a certain limited time; allowing *Conduct-money* to enable them to perform their journey, at the rate of one peny per mile. When they come to the place appointed, they make their appearance before the Commissary of the Navy, who distributes them on board their respective ships; the Clerk entring down their names. Their *wages* begins from the day on which they come a-board, and eight days before the Ship sails, they, and the whole Ship's company, including the Officers, receive two month's advance-pay, to buy them necessaries: and when a Ship returns into their own harbours, they are paid the rest that is due to them; and if the Ship is laid up, a Commissary of the Navy, of which there is one in every Port, tho' they are paid their *wages,* gives them *conduct-money,* and a passport, in order to return home. *The French method.*

No *sailor* that is entered in these *Classes* can be arrested for debt, and if any desire leave to go into the Merchants service, the Commissary seldom refuses them a certificate, if they are not required on duty; but then the Master of such Merchant-ship, when he returns from his voyage, is to be accountable for every such man. It is said, that there are above thirty thousand men thus enroled in France for the King's Ships, who may not be inlisted for Land service.

The DUTCH, in the greatest extremity, never yet had recourse to *pressing;* but their method for manning their Ships is, first, to beat up for voluntiers, as we do, and sometimes they offer a small bounty of about six or seven Guilders a man; but generally they give a month's pay in advance, and no bounty; allowing the men about three Guilders, that is, about five shillings English a week, whilst they stay on shoar; for which their Landlords, or other friends are security, that they may not desert before they go on board; and in order to make the Service begin more agreeable to them, the Ship is compleatly fitted for the Sea, with all her provisions and stores on board, by the Officers, Sailors, Labourers, &c. kept for that service in the places whence the Ships are fitted out; so that the whole Crew goes on board at once on the beat of a Drum, that gives notice when the Ship is ready to receive them. *The Dutch method.* [51]

But if several Ships are to be fitted out at the same time, and this encouragement is not sufficient to raise Men soon enough, they encrease their bounty, or advance two month's pay in hand; and if that don't succeed, they lay an embargo upon all Merchant-Ships; and as their men are never entered into pay, or subsisted during an embargo, they are forced to go into the STATES service for a maintenance; by which means, it was scarce ever known to last above a month, or six weeks; in which time the Men of war have been always well manned; and there has not been above two embargoes since the year 1672. in which year only, the STATES being hard prest with a heavy War, they were forced to lay an embargo, and to raise the *Seamens* wages to fifteen Guilders per month.

The readiness of *Sailors* to enter into the DUTCH SERVICE, does not proceed from their pay being better than ours, since it is seldom more than eleven Guilders a month, which is not so much as twenty shillings English, out of which there is a deduction for the Surgeon: But the reason of their willingness to enter is, their treatment from their *Officers*, and their being sure of a discharge at their return home: For when a Ship comes into Port, to end her voyage, their *Admiralty* immediately either visits the Ship, or sends a deputation on board to enquire into the manner of the *Sailors* being treated by the *Captains* and *Officers*, particularly in respect to the *victualling*, which the Captain undertakes, at the rate of eight or nine pence per day a man; and if it appears that they have been oppressed, or defrauded of their provisions, the Captain is at least mulcted of his pay, and often rendered incapable of serving the STATES; after this, in three or four days they are paid off, and though there is a necessity for sending the Ship out again immediately, the men are not compelled to serve against their inclinations; but very often, upon liking their Captain, &c. the whole Ship's company enter again. If any man hath received a wound, or is otherwise hurt in the STATES SERVICE, he is allowed a bounty in proportion to his misfortune, but no yearly pension is given. And instead of taking advantage of the necessities of the men, during the voyage, by the Purser's or Sutler's selling of what they may want, at exhorbitant prices, they are supplied with some Money by the Captain, or his Clerk, for necessaries when in Foreign countries; and the mens wives, or those with whom they leave a power of Attorney, receive at home one month's pay in every three or four months, after the Ship has been six or eight months from Holland.

In SWEDEN, there are generally enroled upon the establishment upwards of 8000 Seamen, the inferior Officers, as Mates, Boatswains, Gunners, &c. being included; they are divided along the Seacoast in several districts, where they have cottages and lands assigned them, for the support of them and their children. They are mustered by the Officers, and have very compleat and uniform cloathing given them every year, almost like the Water-men in the river of Thames: When their service is required, orders are sent to their respective parishes, to declare from the pulpit, that the King's service requires their appearance upon such a day, at a certain place, where proper Officers attend, who, at the King's charge, carry them to the Port where the Ships are, and there the inspector makes choice of those that are to serve, if they are not all wanted at that time, and distributes them to their respective Ships, and from that time their pay begins. They have several considerable privileges, and among others, that of not being arrested for any debt whatsoever. *The Swedish method.*

When the Ships are fitted, some days before they are ready to sail, all the Company, from the Captain to the Cabin-boy, receive two month's pay, and returning from a voyage, though continued in the service, they receive what remains due to them; and whenever they are going abroad, they are again paid two month's pay, in order to provide themselves necessaries, though the voyage is often very short.

Every respective district meets once a month, and sometimes oftner, at which meeting the nearest Officers muster them, and send the muster-roll to the High-admiral, that he may know if their number is always compleat; and at the same time they are exercised with Fire-arms.

In time of peace an order is published, giving leave to any of the King's Seamen to sail in the Merchants service, and they who have a mind to go, declare it to the superior Officer of each respective District, who gives them a licence: These Seamen, who shipping themselves in this manner on board Merchant Ships to gain experience, are generally first preferred in the King's service, and more esteemed by the Merchants than others, because they are liable to be severely punished, and turned out of the King's service upon any just complaint made against them by the Master of these Ships during their voyage, which makes them behave better than other Seamen.

Every Master who ships these Seamen, is obliged to appear with them before the chief Magistrate of the Town where they are enroled; their names, age, and places of abode, as well as a description of their Persons, are also registered, the Master being accountable for the appearance of these men at his return, or give a good account what is become of them; for which purpose he has a certificate given him of all the qualifications of the men entred by him, which he must produce at his return to port, or he cannot be cleared; and he is obliged to victual, and treat them well in the voyage.

If the King has at any time occasion for a greater number of Sailors than is enroled, they beat up for voluntiers, and each voluntier receives a month or two month's pay for bounty-money. The Seamen in their Navy are under a very good discipline and regulation; Divine worship is strictly kept up every day a-board all the King's Ships at Sea, and no swearing heard, or beating allowed by the Inferior officers a-board them; those are preferred and encouraged most that merit best, and not often, if ever, by favour without it; and when the Father of a Family is killed in the service, a certain Fund is alotted for the maintenance of their Wives and Children, until they can provide for themselves.

The hardships of pressing have, in some measure, been represented; as also the methods made use of in other Countries to raise men for the Sea-service without it; these Papers were intended to have been more compleat, but as the Parliament are now sitting, it was thought necessary to hurry these sheets to the Press; before there was an opportunity of getting such information as was requisite, for drawing up any thing compleat upon this subject. What is now done, is only to induce others to communicate their thoughts to the Publick, or, if they please, to send them to the Publisher of this Paper, they shall be faithfully inserted in the next, as they shall direct, the Author being ready to assist any that shall contribute toward the remedying this abuse; for if the Publick can be served, it is indifferent to him who are the Instruments.

N. B. The Appendix comes from different hands, and vouchers for all the Facts can be produced, if required.

APPENDIX.

NUMBER I.

A Letter from one who was bred in the Land-service, concerning a method for the more easy manning of the Navy.

SIR,
IT is a work of the greatest difficulty to form a practicable scheme, by which *pressing* may be prevented, and the *service* not prejudiced.

The great CECIL, Queen Elizabeth's favourite-Minister, used to say, that the remedies for abuses were to be sought out of the laws and customs of our ancestors; by that means they will be of a-piece with the constitution. Supposing we were to follow his advice on this occasion, we should look back to see how the former Kings of England manned their Navy. I find that, till Henry the 8th's time, the King retained Captains, with whom he covenanted by indenture to furnish him with a band, consisting of a certain fixed number of men, which the Captains were to raise and recruit at their own expence; and that this was the method of the Sea, as well as the Land-service, appears by what follows:

7 H. 7. *Be it therefore ordained by the authority of this present Parliament, that if any Captain be* retained, *or hereafter shall be to serve the King on the Sea, or beyond the Sea, in feat of War, which hath not his or their whole and perfect number of Men and Soldiers, according as he shall be* retained *with the King, or give not them their full wages, without shortning, as he shall receive of the King for them, except for Jackets, for them that receive* Land *wages, that is to say, 6 s. 8 d. for a yoeman, and 13 s. 4 d. for a gentleman, for a whole year, he shall, for such default, forfeit to the King all his goods and chattels, and their bodies to prison.*

And if any Soldier, being no Captain immediately retained *with the King, which hereafter shall be in wages and* retained, *or take any* prest *to serve the King upon the Seas, or upon the Land beyond the Sea, depart out of the King's service without licence of his Captain, that such departing be taken, deemed and adjudged felony.*

3 H. 8. *Provided always, That no Captain be charged by this act for lack of his number* retained, *as is abovesaid, whose Soldiers happen to die, or otherwise depart, not in the default of the Captain; so that the said Captain, if he be at* Land wages, *shew the departing, or lacking of the said Soldier unto the King's Lieutenant there, and to the Treasurer of the wars: Or, if the Captain be at the* Sea wages, *if he shew the departing, or lacking of the Soldier so lacking, to the Admiral of the Navy where he is retained, at the next meeting with the said Admiral.*[52]

Those who are employed in the Navy may, perhaps, in these Clauses find the desired remedy; supposing when a Ship is put into commission, that the Admiralty should agree with the Captain to mann her at a certain price, say 3 l. a head; I name that sum, because, by calculation, every prestman stands the Government in that sum at least. It is not to be presumed, that a Captain would refuse a Ship, rather than take upon him the trouble of manning her: For his own reputation he would take care to provide good men, since both his character and safety would depend upon their behaviour: Besides, he would not be the less careful of the Sailors, when it would be for his advantage to preserve them. This method could not be called a hardship upon the Captains, since, if they pleased to be a little industrious, they might be gainers, by getting men at a cheaper rate than what the Government would allow them. We have seen instances in every Squadron, that some Officers have had their Ships overmanned in a few days. In the Land-service, the Captains raise and recruit their Companies without levy-money, and are at great expence to procure tall proper men, yet do not they complain, but pride themselves in the beauty and compleatness of their Corps, because, by that means, they shew their zeal to the service. And doubtless, the Sea-Officers have as much zeal for his Majesty, and much better abilities of shewing it, since their profits are larger.

This would take away, at once, almost all the complaints of the Common Sailors, since, by making it the Captain's interest to preserve his men, you make him their protector. At Land, the Officer visits the sick, and is as careful of his Soldiers as if they were his children, for the loss of a man is the loss of as much money as a Recruit would cost; and perhaps the Sea-Captain's good nature would not be decreased by its being his interest to take care of his Men.

The Seamens great complaint of their being turned over, might probably be remedied by this method, since, if the Admiralty gave notice to a Captain, to have a compleat Crew, there would be no need of turning over from any Ship newly come in. It may be objected, that it would be an expence to the Government, to pay levy-money to every Ship put into commission; but that, I beli[e]ve, can have little force, since it is not to be supposed, that the Parliament would scruple a small additional expence to preserve the Sailors, who are the Sinews of England, which so chearfully hath come into much larger expences for rebuilding, so sumptuously, the publick Offices and Admiralty in London, the yards of Deptford, &c.

Another complaint of the Sailors is, the Discount of their Tickets, and the great Usury at which their families are obliged to take up necessaries. This might be remedied, by giving the Sailor a power to leave a letter of Attorney with his wife, to receive some part of his wages, as he went on in service: By this means, their Wives would become Press-masters, for whenever they wanted money, they would be for sending their husbands to sea.

These are my first thoughts on a subject, of which I am very far from being master, and I hope you will either amend or excuse the errors I have committed, since good nature will rather look at my intentions, than at my performance, and consider that I have neither had time to finish what I designed, nor access to such papers as were necessary for that purpose. I am,

Sir,
your very humble Servant.

NUMBER II.

An account of the usage of prest men a-board Guard-ships.[53]

THE last two summers, that we have been expecting a War, Guard-ships were kept at the Nore, to receive the prest men from London and the River of Thames, who were a-board in Yatchs and Smacks, in the manner as I shall instance: One of them was called the Royal-Transport, a Vessel of about forty tonns burthen; her hold was secured with strong iron bars, and gratings on the hatches and deck, with only a small place left open, guarded with centinels, who let down the Prest men, one at a time, through a narrow scuttle, or trap-door, so that no goal could be more wretched; and they were not suffered to stir out, or so much as to take breath, till they got to the Guard-ship; which, sometimes, were several days together crouded so close with men, that they could not lie down, nor scarce have room to sit on the bottom or side of the Vessel, which made them so hot, dirty and faint, that there were often several of them sick, and some expiring, before they got to the Nore: And what was still more discouraging, they found seldom less on board the Guard-ship, than six, seven, or eight hundred at a time in the same condition that they were in, without common conveniences, being all forced to lie between decks, confined as before, and to eat what they could get, having seldom victuals enough dressed, which occasioned distempers, that sometimes six, eight, and ten, died of a day; and some were drowned in attempting their escape, by swimming from the Guard-ship; many of whose bodies were seen floating upon the River, and one of them was drove into a Creek at Chelsey. The rest that survived were parcelled out, to be divided to each Ship that was ready to receive them, where they carried the sickness, that spread itself so as to infect our Squadrons, before they sailed on their expedition.

NUMBER III.

A Letter from a Dutch Trader.

SIR,

IN the year 1725. a Sloop in which I had some concern, returned with Passengers and Goods from Holland; the men knowing that there was pressing in the River, would run into Margate-Road; so that the Master was forced there, to hire old disabled men that were past being prest, who, with the help of two Custom-house Waiters put on board, with much difficulty got into the River. When they came to the Nore, they met a man of War's boat with a Lieutenant, who, coming on board with his Crew, would bring the Vessel to an Anchor, with all her sails out; the Master, in vain, urged the danger of it; but he commanded, as if on board a prize, bringing her under the Man of war's stern; afterwards, the Master desiring him to walk down into the cabin, the Lieutenant being there, grew merry, began to quarrel with the Passengers, and threatned to press them; but one of them, Mr. P—— being as sturdy as himself, he let him alone, and only prest two of the other Passengers, who were gentlemen, and one of them, soon after, a Commission-officer. This being done, he viewed the ship's company, and found it to consist of old and lame men, hired at Margate, which put him in a great fury, so that a Custom-house boat coming on board at the same time, he would have prest them; but his wrath being somewhat over, he resolved to return on board, with two gentlemen-passengers whom he had pressed; but he had lost all his crew, for they had got between decks, where, having drank all the liquor they could find, they hid themselves, hoping to escape, for they also served against their wills on board the Man of war. Upon this the Lieutenant, in great indignation, called out to the ship for help, or he should be run away withal, though there was not a man that stirred to get up the Anchor; upon which another boat came on board; and whilst the other Officer, being a Midshipman, was talking with the Master of the Vessel, his crew rummaging also between decks, got drunk; but at last they got them up upon the deck, and the master desiring the officer of the Man of war to take care that none of these men carried any thing out of the vessel. They replied, He might look to it himself, for their men were all honest; upon which he desired the Custom-house waiters to have an eye to them; which he did, and one of them found a man carrying a pound of Tea, and took it from him; the master complained to the Lieutenant, and he promised to punish the man, but immediately pressed the waiter who had discovered him, and after keeping the vessel five hours in great confusion and danger, left her, carrying away two gentlemen-passengers, and this waiter, to help mann a King's Ship, who narrowly escaped being drowned in one of the boats. This shews the abuse of pressing, and it was no great recommendation of our Country to the Foreigners, who were in the vessel, to see men used in this manner like slaves, where liberty is so much talked of.

P. S. There was linen, and many necessaries in the mens cabins, all lost, to the value of above fifty pounds; and in many vessels much more is plundered under pretence of pressing.

NUMBER IV.

An Instance of the hardships of *Pressing* in a Letter from one of the people called Quakers.[54]

IN the year 1718, as well as my memory will serve, (for I have no minutes of the case by me, altho' I was in some measure concerned in it) the Philip and Mary, burthen 300 tons, or thereabouts, Wm. Haslam Master, was coming from Norway laden with Mats, Deal and Timber, and sailing up the Swin near Harwich having a fresh gale at N.E. and a flood tyde a little above the Shoe-beacon was met by a Penace belonging to the *** Man of war that was then riding by the Buoy of the Mouse.[55] The said Penace having come along side of the Philip and Mary, there being a Lieutenant in her, and about 16 men; the men from the said ship flung the Penace a cope to make her fast, and the side mann'd by Philip and Mary's men, and an entering cope put into the hands of the said Lieutenant, and he helpt in with much respect, after whom the rest of the Crew entred, except a man or two, who staid in the Penace; soon after, the Crew got on board the said ship, she sailing at a very great rate; the Lieutenant gave command to let go the anchor, that they might not be carried past the *** Man of war; but the Mate of the Philip and Mary answered, and said, it was not proper to let go the anchor when the ship was under sail, and so fresh under way, for if the anchor took hold 'twas enough to part the cable, or tear the ship's bows out, however the said Coxton being forward enough to obey the Lieutenant's command, called the rest of the Crew forward to let go the anchor; he was answered by the Mate of the ship (whom I shall have occasion to mention hereafter) Were they madmen? what did they mean to ruin the ship? and so went to hinder them, upon which the Coxton ordered the Penace's crew to draw their cutlashes, which they did accordingly, and the men on board the Philip and Mary took up hand-spikes in their own defence, and a skuffle or fray arose, in which the Philip and Mary's men had the better on't. The Lieutenant struck one of the men belonging to the Philip and Mary over his head with his cane that had an ill effect; but the Lieutenant seeing that he had not force enough to impress these hand-spike-men, gave orders to the Penace's crew to go on board the man of War for more, which accordingly they did, and as they were stepping into the Penace, the Coxton said, D——n the dogs, we'll be revenged on them, and I doubt not would have done his endeavour to have accomplished it, had he not in the scuffle received a wound on his head, supposed by his own Cutlash, being prest by the hand-spike so that it proved fatal to him. The Lieutenant keeping as it were the possession of the Philip and Mary all the time the Penace was returning to the Man of war, which when got on board, nine of the men belonging to the Philip and Mary took their own boat, being apprehensive that if the Penace brought more forces, some of them would be in danger of losing their lives, so away they go, making for the Essex shore, the Penace following them, filled with armed men, but they got on shore before the Penace. The Man of war seeing that the Philip and Mary was got several miles above her, slipt her cable, and makes all the sail that she could to come up with her. And coming up with the said Merchant-ship, the said Captain fires a Gun with shot and all, and ran up so near that he called to them to let go their anchors, or else he threatned to fire a broadside into her and sink her. Now the Man of war and the Merchant-ship being along side one of another, the Captain of the former calls to his Lieutenant, to bring the master on board the Man of war; (what to do there, we shall hear anon,) the Lieutenant answered, that the master would not come; at which the Captain called to his Lieutenant, Skin the dog (meaning the master of the Philip and Mary) skin him alive: so that being terrified between Captain and Lieutenant, he consented to go, and had ne'er a boat to go in but his long-boat, and she upon deck; the Lieutenant commanding the said master and Mate to hoist out this heavy boat, which they did with much ado, after a great deal of labour and toil, and the master and mate rowed themselves and the Lieutenant on board the Man of war: the said master coming upon the quarter deck first, and being a peaceable quiet man, and one of the people called Quakers, the first salutation he met with from the Captain was, How dare you, you quaking dog, come before a Commission officer with your Hat on; then he ordered some of his men to pull off his Hat, who pulled his Wig off also, the Captain with his left hand, taking hold of the master's right ear, and with his right fist clinch'd, said; I know you won't strike, no more will I, but with his fist clinched, punched him till his eyes were almost out of his head. The Captain being quite tired with punching, after some respite, took hold of both the poor Master's ears, and said, he would shew him Tower-hill-play; so holding him fast with his hands by his ears, flung his head in his face so often, that the poor Master was used in a most barbarous manner, being beat and abused much worse than by an avowed enemy, though he had not been active in the least on board his own ship, save when the Lieutenant, as I hinted before, gave one of his men such a blow over his head with his cane, by which blow the poor man lingered about three weeks and died.

But after he had given the blow, he was about drawing his sword, which the master seeing, prevented it by going behind him, and holding back the Lieutenant's arms, saying, He was afraid there was like to be mischief enough without his drawing his sword. The said Captain after he had shewed the master Tower-hill-play, took him by one of his ears, pulled his head down to the gunnel, and swore he'd cut his ears off, called to the

Carpenter to bring him mallet and chissel, which the Carpenter did, and the said Captain bid the Carpenter strike; to which the said Carpenter answered and said, Noble Captain, I've obey'd your commands in bringing the mallet and chissel, but I dare not cut a man's ears off: so the poor master escaped with his ears. The said Captain not being satisfied with the barbarity exercised over the Master, calls for his Mate, viz. John White, and when he appeared, fell upon him with his cane, beat him over his head and arms till the ferrel flew off, and the cane shievered in pieces, till the poor man lay senseless in the scuppers. The Captain had a Monkey on board, who seeing the Captain in a passion, fell also upon the poor mate, and bit and knawed 30 or 40 holes about his head and neck; the Captain standing over laughing all the time. This did not suffice, but the Mate was put into the billbows, when he had recovered his senses, for some days; then put on board the *** Man of war, which was Guard-ship of the Buoy of the Nore, stapled down upon his breech a top of the forecastle, and the commanding Officer would not suffer so much as a tarpauling, nor any thing to be cast over him, to keep the weather off him day or night, and thus this poor man was confined for about 10 days, I was informed that they would not suffer him to rise out of this posture to ease nature, but he did it as he sat, till he was almost dead. Now I shall leave the poor Mate, and return to the Master, who coming to London after he had reported his Ship at the Custom-house, and going down to his Ship, was arrested by a *** Writ, and hurried to the Marshalsea-prison without bayl, the mate being sent for, and two of the said Master's apprentices, who were taken by the Penace's crew,[56] were put into the said prison, and laid there 6 or 8 months, at last were bailed with much to do, and no Indictment being preferred against them, the recognizance was discharged; after which the Captain was ordered to Carolina, and upon his return was prosecuted by the Mate for an assault and battery, the Jury brought in their verdict for the Prosecutor 100*l.* and costs, which the Captain thought was hard, and desired a re-hearing, which was granted him, he first paying the prosecutors costs, which was about 71 *l.* It was heard a second time, and I well remember upon the Jury bringing in their verdict for the prosecutor 100*l.* damages and costs, the Judge said, "Gentlemen of the Jury, I think you have brought in a just verdict." After which, the Master of the Ship brought his action against the said Captain, and recovered 100*l.* damages and costs of suit; but being so long in prison, his Ship lying by the walls all the time, it was a means of his and his Family's ruin; as also the poor Mate's, who has been disordered ever since, and falling into fits, by the cruelty he met with, which he could never recover.

N. B. We have left out the names and some aggravating circumstances, that we shall be ready to insert at length, if any persons think themselves aggrieved by this relation.

A Letter to the Author of the Seaman's Advocate.

SIR

I HAve read over your account of the *Sailors Hardships*,[57] of which, tho' you have inserted many, yet are there more than probably any one person can be acquainted with; as it is of the last consequence to GREAT BRITAIN to encourage our *Navigation*, if the following thoughts may be of any use in promoting so good a design, my views will be answered; and I shall readily become your Correspondent as far as capable.

The intention of this *Letter* is, to propose some method by which our sea-faring-men may meet with encouragements to render the *Service* both agreeable and beneficial, and at the same time induce them to make this way of life (so useful to the *common welfare*) their own *choice*; which they have always endeavoured to fly from, when most wanted for the defence of their *Country*[.]

There has been a particular care taken to have a greater number of *fine Ships* in this than any other Nation; but the building new, and repairing the old, is now become a vast expence to the *Publick*, and so far from being a service to us, that it is rather an useless load, if we are not always able to mann them out sooner than our neighbours, when they may rival us with a Fleet, which may be built or procured before we expect it; for *Ships* are easier got *ready* than *seamen* raised; but were it possible *Sailors* could be made with the same ease a *Man of war* is built, and were they also as mere Machines, yet even then we ought to be careful of their preservation, which is too plain we have not hitherto been.

As you have produced examples from the French, Dutch and Swedes, who *mann* their *Fleets* without the barbarous custom of *pressing;* no doubt but the English, if they will give themselves the trouble, may fall upon methods adapted to the genius of the nation, which may prove as advantageous and easy to us, as those in use amongst our neighbours, are to their respective States.

This seems to be a proper juncture to endeavour at so good a work, since his Majesty has been pleased to recommend it in his most gracious Speech to both Houses of Parliament.

If you think fit, you may add this Letter to what you are about, it may perhaps bring to light other thoughts of more weight from such as have the same good design, of being *Advocates* for the *Seamen,* and *Trade* of GREAT BRITAIN.

The uncertainty of the *Sailors-pay* in ships of War is a very great grievance, because it destroys their credit, and starves their families in their absence; for when the *Common Seamen* want money in any of the ports where our ships of War resort, there are always about them numbers of *Ticket-buyers,* pettyfoggers, and others who live upon their ruin, by getting *Wills, Tickets,* and *powers* of *Attorney,* &c. from them, on very slight considerations: and too often when poor ignorant fellows are in liquor, they fall into the hands of different sharpers, who draw them in to sign more than one will or power; and these vermin are often known to make forged ones after the *Sailors* are dead; by which means their poor Families are left starving, and their Creditors defrauded: for, where money is received for *Wages* due in the *Navy* by a false power of attorney or will, the person to whom it is justly due, and produces the lawful one, is totally defeated, and loses his debt; which is a disadvantage peculiar to the *sailor* only; for if the same happens at the Bank of ENGLAND or to any other body or private man, the true power remains in full force, and must be satisfied; and when those are detected, who by *forgery,*[58] have defrauded the *Sailors,* their punishment is at most the Pillory, a short imprisonment and generally a small fine, which the poor *Sailor,* or *Creditor,* tho' he is at the charge of the prosecution, is not benefitted by: all these fines in London going to the *Sheriffs,* and in other places to the *Crown.*

To forge a *power,* whereby money is received from the BANK, EXCHEQUER, &c. is death, and can it be thought a less crime to defraud the *poor Sailors,* who dearly earn their *wages!* To prevent this the *Seamen's power* may be registered aboard the ship of war by the Captain's Clerk, or some officer appointed for that purpose, and a duplicate sent to the Navy or Pay-office, attested by the Captain, First Lieutenant, and Master; or where either of the last two Officers are wanting, the two next to the Captain, may sign instead of them: This would make our *Seamen's powers* authentick, and in great measure prevent *Forgery* and *Extortion,* or the *Sailors* giving more than one power, and running too much in debt.

When such a power is produced, though the Sailor is prickt Run,[59] yet his pay due, ought to be paid his Attorney; and such a punishment as shall be directed by Law for desertion be deemed sufficient. Two months pay in six may be advanced, endorsed on it every six months, till the Sailor is discharged, and the ship paid off; which ought to be where she is fitted out, or notice there given of the place where she is to be paid. This would be a great means of supporting the *Sailors* credit, given to their Families in their absence; for by this means the Creditor will be at as little trouble as possible in receiving his debt, which will make them give credit on better terms than they yet have done; And our ships being the best victualled of any in the world, the Seamen can never need above 3 or 4 shillings per month, to supply them with what little necessaries they may want aboard, more than the ship's allowance.

Every six Months after the Ship has been at sea, a *Ticket* for all the time over and above the two months advance, may be given to every *Sailor*, who has not left any power behind him: And Ships should never be above two years, or rather eighteen months unpaid, during which time a strict charge should be given to all Captains, to send home regular muster-rolls every month.

Were it practicable for the *Seamens* powers of attorney and tickets, after they have been six months due, to be circulated by a Banker, or proper office appointed for that purpose; it would very much contribute to the encouragement of the *Seamen*, and the Pay-office in London might take them up, in order to pass them to account.

Good usage, and as much liberty as is consistent with the nature of the Service, and a discharge at the end of every voyage, as soon as the Ships are got home in safety, would undoubtedly in our *Navy*, not only save a vast *expence* to the *Publick*, but procure *Seamen* on all occasions, and give them a new spirit; and instead of our *Ships of war* being terrible to, and avoided by our *sailors*, no doubt but they will chuse the *King's Service* preferably to the *Merchant's*, as soon as they can experience this just treatment.

These *Indulgences*,[60] together with the above method for subsisting their Families, preventing *frauds* in their powers of Attorney, and by that means raising them credit, without passing through the hands of *Extortioners*, would be more advantageous and agreeable to the Sailors, than even the raising of their wages on the foot they now are; which cannot be done without prejudice to the *Merchant*, (who must advance in proportion) and a considerable expence to the *Government*. Not but that in time of a hot *War*, when a great many ships are to be fitted out, it may be necessary to add four or five shillings a month to their wages, and therefore a discretionary power may be lodged in the Lords of the *Admiralty*.

HIS MAJESTY's NAVY being now very large, will alone require more *sailors* to mann them, than are in the three Kingdoms at any one time; and if but two-thirds, and the Tenders and Transports that they usually have depending on them, are ordered for service; they will employ forty four thousand men. And the *Merchants Service* hath not been carried on with less, these many years past, than twenty six thousand always employ'd, and fourteen thousand, or there-abouts, will be at home, or constantly fitting out; which makes forty thousand; so that when but two-thirds parts of the *Navy* are employed, we must have eighty four thousand men in the KING's and MERCHANTS Service: and, by all that I have learnt, we have not had above fifty thousand, for several years past, in the three Kingdoms, allowing for Fisher-men, Water-men, Bargemen, Lighter-men, &c. who must be always at home; and if they could be brought to go to Sea, there would be very few of them better than able-bodied Land-men, who, as well as Marines, may be of great use, and at any time can be detached from the Land-forces which we keep on foot; or rather might be a separate body formed for *Sea-service,* which has been found of great use in the *Navy,* and, if kept in our Ports, may be always improving, and contribute very much towards manning out any Squadron at a short warning. By this computation, unless such a body of *Marines* be established to encrease the *Sea-men,* at least thirty four thousand employed in our Navigation must be *Land-men,* if but two-third parts of our *Navy* are fitted out: Land-men sufficient may no doubt be encouraged to go volunteers, and the Officers may procure abler Men, who would provide themselves in a better manner, and much sooner make *Sea-men* than those who have been *prest* into the *Service,* and kept there by force, the consequence of which you have justly shewn.

For some time past it has been allowed, that if any *Ship of war* sets out half mann'd with *Seamen,* they are tolerably fit for Service; and with good usage and encouragement, Land-men may, in a short space of time, be made very serviceable at Sea, and almost as good in an engagement as Sea-men; but these must be such as are mixed with their own consent among them; for when they are forced on board, and drove about by the inferior Officers (as is too much practis'd in some ships) it makes them learn little of Sea-affairs, as they act without spirit; Examples may be found, of *King's-ships* being commanded by very good Officers, who have behaved in engagements with less reputation than usual, when they have met an enemy at first putting to sea, after they have been newly mann'd with *press'd men;* amongst whom they seldom, if ever, have one-half able *Sailors;* and even such must necessarily prove worse than volunteers.

As I have not the advantage of knowing fully the expence of the *Navy* and *Admiralty-Offices,* and all other charges which depend on the manning our *Ships of war* by *Pressing*, 'tis impossible for me to make any Proposal which is not subject to error. For which reason I have only wrote this to encourage others who are more capable, to demonstrate whether that charge is not greater than advancing two month's pay and subsistence (till the Ships are ready) with Conduct-money, or, on occasion, some small Bounty to encourage VOLUNTIERS, as our Neighbours have practis'd to mann their ships? Or whether a certain Sum established by Parliament for enroling a body of Men, under proper Regulations to be always near at hand, whenever the Publick-service requires them, will not be more effectual than the methods we have some time followed? I submit to better Judges.

If my leisure allows me opportunity of being farther informed, I shall give you my Thoughts very freely. In the interim I am,

Sir, Yours, &c.[61]

FINIS.

A Preliminary Report on the Fleet Prison (1729)

As chairman of the committee of the House of Commons appointed, on February 25, 1729, to inquire into the state of the English prisons, Oglethorpe prepared and delivered three major reports: those concerning the Fleet, the Marshalsea, and the King's Bench. He delivered also three brief preliminary and supplementary reports, of which this is the first.

What occasioned this preliminary report was the attempt of Thomas Bambridge, the warden of the Fleet, to prevent his prisoners from giving information to the investigating committee and his mistreatment of Sir William Rich, fourth Baronet Rich of Sunning, Berkshire, whose grandfather Sir William Rich had been a member of the House during the years 1698–1705. Imprisoned for debt, the fourth baronet, on January 25, 1729, had stabbed the warden while Bambridge and his minions were, Sir William alleged, assaulting him. Rich was then closely confined and shackled. His treatment was described by Sir Edmund Knatchbull, a member of Oglethorpe's committee:

> We went to the Fleet and was there by eight in the morning, and first visited the several apartments, many of which were so nauseous that we were forced to hold our noses; there were many poor people in sort of dungeons without light or fire and some in chains and others 30 or 40 in a room packed so close that it was likely in hot weather to breed a distemper; the poor wretches were overjoyed when we came in and with a general God bless us we were saluted. We then proceeded to examine Mr Bambridge, the warden . . . ; being asked how many were in irons, he said one for stabbing his man viz. Sir William Rich, and one for an escape; so the committee proceeded to examine Sir William Rich, having ordered his irons to be knocked off during his examination (they weighed 15 lb.), which proved a very cruel usage of him.

On the following day "they found Sir William Rich's irons had again been put on after the committee went away yesterday and he loaded with treble the weight and so close that his hands and arms were swelled greatly and he had been in torture all night, and this was done, as they apprehended, by the warden for the discovery he had made of his usage the day before to the committee and to intimidate the other prisoners from any complaint; and Maj. Selwyn declared he was there and overheard him intimidating and threatening others if they made complaints...."[1]

My text is taken from *The Journals of the House of Commons* (London, n.d.), 21:243, 247.

Veneris, 28° *die Februarii,*
Anno 2° Georgii 2di Regis, 1728.

. . . .

Mr. *Oglethorpe,* from the Committee, appointed to enquire into the State of the Gaols of this Kingdom, acquainted the House, that the Committee had entered upon their Enquiry into the State of the *Fleet* Prison; and had directed him to report to the House, how highly the Warden of the said Prison had misbehaved himself upon that Occasion: And he read the Report in his Place, and afterwards delivered it in at the Clerk's Table; where the same was read, and is as follows; *viz.*

That, upon the Receipt of a Letter this Morning, being the 28th Day of *February,* 1728, from Sir *Wm. Rich,* Baronet, complaining of severe Treatment from Mr. *Bambridge,* Warden of the Fleet, since his Examination before the Committee, the Committee thereupon examined the said Sir *Wm. Rich,* and found,

That, as soon as the Committee adjourned Yesterday, he, the said Sir *William,* had his Legs loaded with Irons, and Handcuffs put on, by an Agent of the Warden's, much straiter than those, that were on before his Examination; so that his Wrists were much swoln, and he was in Torture all Night;

Mr. *Bambridge* being called in, and examined, what induced him to change Sir *Wm. Rich's* Handcuffs, and put on straiter, by which he was in great Pain and Torture all Night;

The said *Bambridge* answered, that one of the Handcuffs was broke Yesterday; and that he had no other Reason for changing them.

That, upon the Inspection of the Committee Yesterday, it appeared, that the Handcuffs, which Sir *Wm. Rich* had on, before he was brought to the Committee, were sound and good, and, after they were weighed, were returned unbroken to Mr. *Bambridge,* or his Agents.

That it further appears to this Committee, that the changing the Handcuffs of Sir *William Rich,* and the ill Treatment he has met with from the Warden, and his Agents, was the Consequence of Sir *William Rich's* having given Evidence to this Committee, and was in order to intimidate others from giving further Evidence to this Committee.

Resolved, nemine contradicente, That *Thomas Bambridge,* Esquire, Warden of his Majesty's Prison of the *Fleet,* having misused, in a very cruel and barbarous Manner, Sir *William Rich,* now a Prisoner in his Custody, for having given Evidence before a Committee of this House, is guilty of a high Indignity to this House, a Contempt of the Authority, and a Breach of the Privilege, thereof.

Ordered, nemine contradicente, That the said *Thomas Bambridge* be, for his said Offence, taken into the Custody of the Serjeant at Arms attending this House.

A Report from the Committee appointed to Enquire into the State of the Goals of this Kingdom: Relating to the Fleet Prison (1729)

On March 20, 1728/9, Oglethorpe delivered his report to the House of Commons concerning the Fleet Prison; and on that same day the Speaker of the House ordered that it be printed.

Although Oglethorpe had the assistance of Luke Kenn, one of the parliamentary secretaries, to help him keep notes of the depositions and transcribe his final reports, Oglethorpe almost certainly authored his prison reports himself. Doubtless he entertained and implemented numerous suggestions from other members of his committees, but the members were so numerous and heterogeneous that it must have been the chairman who obtained and implemented a consensus.

It is difficult for us to visualize the state of the prisoners in the jails of eighteenth-century London. They were detained in overcrowded buildings administered by wardens who ran their prisons as capitalistic enterprises. There the surroundings and treatment depended upon the prisoners' purses: if they could raise the adequate money, they could take apartments or rooms "within the rules," that is, outside the walls of the prison but within its legal precincts. If their means were moderate, they could rent furnished or unfurnished rooms on the master's side. If they were paupers, they shared a room or ward on the common side, lying on the floor if they were unable to afford beds and subject to starvation and prison fever. Since the warden frequently cared nothing about repairing the prison or keeping it healthy, diseases were rife. Moreover starvation prevailed in many prisons, since wardens often misappropriated the charity monies given for feeding the poorest prisoners; and some wardens even prohibited the display of the traditional begging-box at the prison gate.

Many of these wardens were given a free hand by the courts whose duty it was to regulate and supervise their conduct.

In their annual petitions to Parliament the imprisoned debtors appealed for relief, but their petitions were usually laid upon the table or were referred to committees that gave most of their attention to petitions from creditors whose debtors had escaped. Even if a bill for debtor relief were presented to the House, it was generally voted down, or was not returned from the House of Lords. Oglethorpe himself had in 1724 served on the last such committee.[1]

On February 6, 1729, a committee was appointed in the House of Lords to consider the imprisonment of debtors; and a week later an analogous committee, of eight members, was named in the House of Commons. Though not a member of the original committee, Oglethorpe became one after the bill had its second reading, on March 12.[2] But far more important to Oglethorpe than an occasional and generally abortive bill to relieve imprisoned debtors were the broader concerns of prison conditions and management. After he learned that his friend Robert Castell, architect and author of *The Villas of the Ancients Illustrated* (1729), had died in the Fleet not because of obdurate creditors, but greedy and implacable jailors, Oglethorpe apparently began a private investigation of the plight of imprisoned debtors.[3] Their situation under the present penal system, he became convinced, was intolerable. Fortified with such emotional appeals as Castell's death and Sir William Rich's shackling, on February 25, 1729, Oglethorpe moved for the investigation of the English prisons; and a committee of ninety-six members was named "to enquire into the State of the Gaols of this Kingdom."[4] Oglethorpe was named chairman. They turned their attention, first, to the Fleet.

The Fleet Prison was located along the Fleet River near present Farringdon Street, London. Not originally designed as a prison, it was first built not long after the Norman Conquest, certainly by 1170–71. It was rebuilt in the reign of Edward III, again after it had been destroyed in the Peasants Revolt of 1381, and still again after the Great Fire of 1666. Used during the reigns of Henry VIII and his successors, until 1641, to receive prisoners sentenced by the Court of the Star Chamber, it subsequently became primarily a debtors prison. It was a freehold, part of the manor of Leveland, and was operated by the warden for his own profit; and though it was legally controlled by the Court of Common Pleas, the keeper rarely suffered legal intrusions or investigations. In 1691, in his *Cry of the Oppressed*, addressed to Parliament, which was then investigating conditions under Warden Richard Manlove, Moses Pitt cited his refusing to deliver bodies of dead prisoners to their families until debts were paid and his forcing prisoners to sleep side by side with dead bodies.[5] During 1698–99 Henry Pocklington chaired a select committee to investigate the Fleet, but it accomplished nothing. Sometimes Sir Peter King, Chief Justice of the Common Pleas, intervened on behalf of the prisoners; but his successor, Sir Robert Eyre, in 1725, seemed firmly in the interest of law and order — that is, the keeper. The keeper was now Thomas Bambridge.[6]

For three weeks Oglethorpe conducted a vigorous investigation of the Fleet, meeting with his committee daily and often twice daily — before and after the sitting of the House.[7] During this time the committee frequently visited the prison itself, certainly on March 4, 5, and 8, and evidently March 10,[8] but usually met either in the Speaker's Chamber or a convenient tavern. In his report on the Fleet, Oglethorpe showed clearly the "disastrous results of converting the keeping of a prison into a private profit-making concern."[9] The defects that he found in the Fleet were varied and serious: the warden's failing to keep adequate records, charging excessive and illegal fees, using the attached sponging-houses to extort even higher fees than those permitted in the prison itself, taking "fees" for permitting prisoners to live outside the prison and thus enabling them to escape, and refusing to release eligible prisoners unless he was bribed. Moreover the common side of the prison was both overcrowded and "noisom," for there ninety-three prisoners were huddled together in three small wards, locked in overnight in shockingly unsanitary conditions; and even on the master's side the sick were not separated from the well. Most shocking of all, the last wardens, Huggins and Bambridge, had introduced into the Fleet practices of torture; and the instruments were prominently displayed in Hogarth's group portrait of the committee.

When the House of Commons heard Oglethorpe's report on the Fleet, it adopted, *nemine contradicente*, the resolutions of the committee to disable Bambridge from acting as warden; to prosecute Huggins, Bambridge, and their underlings for their crimes against prisoners; and to better regulate the Fleet. Oglethorpe was thereupon named chairman of the committees of four to disable Bambridge and to better regulate the prison. The bill to disable Bambridge received priority. On April 3 Oglethorpe presented it to the House, and on May 13 a revised version was adopted, quickly approved by the House of Lords.[10] On May 13 Oglethorpe also read his bill "for the better regulating the Prison of the *Fleet*, and for more effectual preventing, and punishing, arbitrary and illegal Practices of the Warden of the said Prison." Although it was resolved that the bill should be read a second time, it died, perhaps dropped after opposition from members of the judiciary. Doubtless Oglethorpe realized his weakness in the knowledge of the law, for on April 27 he had entered Gray's Inn, where his uncle Sutton Oglethorpe had read law.[11] His purpose was obviously not to prepare himself to practice law, but with the assistance of a Master to become better familiar with the laws that regulated the prison system.

The three major reports are here reproduced from their first published versions rather than from *The Journals of the House of Commons*, where they were later printed from transcriptions of the original journals.[12] For the first publication, an official report ordered by the House, the printer probably took few liberties with Oglethorpe's text; but in the *Journals* the editors normalized paragraphing, punctuation, capitalization, and sometimes spelling.

A REPORT FROM THE COMMITTEE APPOINTED TO ENQUIRE

Into the State of the GOALS of

this Kingdom:

Relating to the FLEET *Prison.*

WITH THE

Resolutions and Orders of the House of Commons thereupon.

[Printer's ornament]

LONDON:

Printed for *Robert Knaplock, Jacob Tonson, John Pemberton,* and *Richard Williamson.* MDCCXXIX.

Jovis 20 *die Martii*, 1728.

By Vertue of an Order of the House of Commons, this Day made, I do appoint *Robert Knaplock, Jacob Tonson, John Pemberton*, and *Richard Williamson*, to Print this *Report*, and the *Proceedings* of the said House thereupon: And that no other Person presume to Print the same.

Ar. Onslow, Speaker.

A REPORT FROM THE COMMITTEE

Appointed to enquire into the State of the GOALS *of this Kingdom.*

Jovis 20 *die Martii,* 1728.

MR. *Oglethorpe,* from the Committee appointed to enquire into the State of the Goals of this Kingdom, made a Report of some Progress which the Committee had made in their Enquiry into the State of the *Fleet* Prison, with the Resolutions of the Committee thereupon; and he read the Report in his Place, and afterwards delivered the same (with Two Appendixes) in at the Table, where the Report was read, and is as follows, *viz.*

The COMMITTEE *having, in pursuance of the Order of this House (of the Twenty Fifth Day of* February, 1728) *to enquire into the State of the Goals of this Kingdom, Adjourned to the* Fleet, *and at several Times examined into the State of that Prison, have made some Progress therein, which they have thought fit to lay before the House.*

THE Committee find That the *Fleet* Prison is an ancient Prison, and formerly used for the Reception of the Prisoners committed by the Council-Table, then called the *Court of the Star-Chamber,* which exercised unlimited Authority, and inflicted heavier Punishments than by any Law were warranted.[13]

And as that assumed Authority was found to be an intolerable Burden to the Subject, and the Means to introduce an Arbitrary Power and Government, all Jurisdiction, Power, and Authority belonging unto or exercised in the same Court, or by any the Judges, Officers, or Ministers thereof, were clearly and absolutely dissolved, taken away, and determined, by an Act made in the Sixteenth Year of the Reign of King *Charles* the First.[14]

And thereby the Committee apprehend all Pretences of the Warden of the *Fleet* to take Fees from Archbishops, Bishops, Temporal Peers, Baronets, and others of lower Degree, or to put them in Irons, or exact Fees for not doing so, were determined, and abolished.

That after the said Act took place, the *Fleet* Prison became a Prison for Debtors, and for Contempts of the Courts of *Chancery, Exchequer,* and *Common-Pleas* only, and fell under the same Regulations as other Goals of this Kingdom.

That by an Act of the 22d and 23d of King *Charles* the Second, the future Government of all Prisons was vested in the Lords Chief Justices, the Chief Baron, or any Two of them, for the Time being; and the Justices of the Peace in *London, Middlesex,* and *Surrey;* and the Judges for the several Circuits; and the Justices of the Peace, for the Time being, in their several Precincts:[15] And pursuant thereunto, several Orders and Regulations have been made, the last of which is hereunto annexed (in the Appendix marked Letter *A*) which the present Warden of the *Fleet* hath not regarded or complied with, but hath exercised an Unwarrantable and Arbitrary Power, not only in extorting exorbitant Fees, but in oppressing Prisoners for Debt by loading them with Irons, worse than if the *Star-Chamber* was still subsisting, and contrary to the great Charter,[16] the Foundation of the Liberty of the Subject, and in defiance and contempt thereof, as well as of other good Laws of this Kingdom.

It appears by a Patent of the Third Year of Queen *Elizabeth,* recited in Letters Patents bearing Date the Nineteenth of King *Charles* the Second, That the *Fleet* Prison was an ancient Prison, called *Prisona de le Fleet,* alias, *The Queen's Goal of the Fleet;* and that certain Constitutions were then established by Agreement between *Richard Tyrrell,*[17] Warden, and the Prisoners of the *Fleet,* and a Table of Fees annexed, in which the Fees to be paid by an Archbishop, Duke, Marquis, Earl, or other Lord Spiritual or Temporal, are particularly mentioned, and the Fine ascertained which they are to pay for the Liberty of the House and Irons; and that these Constitutions and Orders were confirmed by the said Letters Patent of King *Charles* the Second: Which Letters Patent grant the Office of Warden of the *Fleet,* and of the Keeper of the Old Palace at *Westminster,* the Shops in *Westminster-Hall,* certain Tenements adjoining to the *Fleet,* and other Rents and Profits belonging to the Warden, to Sir *Jeremy Whichcot* and his Heirs for ever. And the said Sir *Jeremy* rebuilt the said Prison at his own Expence, as a Consideration for the Grant thereof.[18] But the said Prison, and the Custody of the Prisoners, being a Freehold, and falling by Descent or Purchase into the Hands of Persons incapable of executing the Office of Warden, was the Occasion of great Abuses, and frequent Complaints to Parliament, till at length the Patent was set aside.[19]

And a Patent for Life was granted to *Baldwyn Leighton* Esq; in consideration of his great Pains and Expences in Suing the former Patentees to a

Forfeiture;[20] and he soon dying, *John Huggins* Esq; by giving 5000*l.* to the late Lord *Clarendon*, did, by his Interest,[21] obtain a Grant of the said Office for his own and his Son's Life.

That during the time the said *Huggins* possessed the said Office of Warden of the *Fleet*, *Thomas Periom*,[22] a Prisoner in that Prison, charged with 40000 *l.* Debt, (the greatest Part thereof to the Crown) escaped, having the Liberty of the Rules by Permission of the said *Huggins*, for which Escape *Huggins* pretends he hath obtained a *Quietus*; and since that time *Joseph Vains*, charged with 10000 *l.* Debt to the Crown, having like Liberty of the Rules, also escaped.[23]

That *Thomas Dumay* made several Voyages to *France*, whilst a Prisoner in the *Fleet*, and in Custody of the said *Huggins*, and there bought Wines, some of which were delivered to the said *Huggins*, and *Dumay* drew several Bills whilst in *France* to the value of 320*l.* on *Richard Bishop* one of the Tipstaffs of the said Prison,[24] who paid 300*l.* and the said *Huggins* paid the rest. That by the punctual Payment of the said Bills *Dumay* acquired a Credit in *France*, and drew for a further Sum, and then returned to *England*, and when the Bills came for Payment the said *Richard Bishop* refused to accept them, and the Merchants upon *Dumay*'s Return endeavouring to get the Money of him, who was the Drawer of the Bills, found him a Prisoner in the Rules, and had no Remedy.

The said *John Huggins* owned to the Committee, that so many Prisoners had escaped during the time he was Warden, that it was impossible to enumerate them, he having kept no List of the Persons so escaped.

He also owned to the Committee that in his Time *Oliver Reed* made his Escape when there was a great Funeral, and whilst the Doors were open he went off; that afterwards being retaken he the said *Huggins* sent him to a Spunging-house, kept by *Richard Corbett*, one of the Tipstaffs belonging to the said Prison, where he was locked up, Ironed and Stapled down by his Order, tho' not condemned by any Court of Justice.[25]

That it appeared to the Committee, That in the Year 1725, one Mr. *Arne* an Upholder was carried into a Stable which stood where the Strong Room on the Master's Side now is, and was there confined (being a Place of Cold Restraint) till he died, and that he was in good State of Health before he was confined to that Room.[26]

That the said *John Huggins* growing in Years, and willing to retire from Business, and his Son not caring to take upon him so troublesome an Office, he hath for several Years been engaged in continual Negotiations about the Disposal of the said Office, and in *August* last concluded a final

Treaty with *Thomas Bambridge* and *Dougal Cuthbert* Esqrs; and for 5000*l*. to be paid unto him, obliged himself to surrender the said Patent for his and his Son's Life, and procure a new Patent for the said *Bambridge* and *Cuthbert*, which the said *Huggins* did accordingly obtain, and *Cuthbert* paid in Money, or gave good Security to pay 2500*l*. for one Moiety of the said Office of Warden, and *Bambridge* gave Land and other Security, which the said *Huggins* was then content with, for 2500*l*. being for the other Moiety of the said Office.[27]

That upon Inspection and Examination on the Common Side of the Prison, in the three Wards, called the Upper Chappel, the Lower Chappel, and *Julius Caesar*'s, Ninety three Persons were Confined, who are obliged to lye on the Floor, if they cannot Furnish themselves with Bedding, or Pay 1 *s. per* Week to such Prisoner as is so provided.

That the *Lyons* Den and Womens Ward, which contain about Eighteen Persons, are very Noisom, and in very ill Repair.

That there are several Rooms in the Chappel Stairs, for each of which 5*l*. a Year is now paid, but did formerly belong to the Common Side, and for which nothing was paid, until charged by Mr. *Huggins* at 3*l*. a Year each. And on this Floor, there are several Persons who are uncertain what Chamber-Rent they shall be obliged to pay, and are at the Mercy of the Warden.

That in some Rooms Persons who are Sick of different Distempers are obliged to lye together, or on the Floor; One in particular had the Small-Pox, and two Women were ordered to lye with her, and they pay 2*s.* 10*d. per* Week each for such Lodging.

That in all the Rooms (except very few) the Furniture is provided by the Prisoners, and those which are furnished by the Warden are extreamly bad.

That there was a Regulation by the Judges in *Trinity* Term 1727,[28] by which the Warden ought to furnish all the Rooms, and in such Case the Prisoners to pay 2*s.* 6*d. per* Week for each Room so furnished; but now there are several Rooms, in each of which there are two, three and four Beds, and in each Bed two, and sometimes three Persons, who pay 2*s.* 10*d.* each *per* Week, for such Lodging.

That the Walls which secure the Prison are 25 Foot high, with Pallisadoes on the Top, and in good Repair, and no seeming possibility for any Prisoner to Escape.

That at the End of the Place called the *Bare*, a Watch-House was built about a Year since, wherein are kept several Muskets and Bayonets, as are likewise several others in a Room fronting *Fleet-Ditch*, whereas formerly only Pikes and Halberts were kept in that part of the Prison which is called the *Lodge*.

That several Men called *Watchmen*, and under the Pay of Mr. *Bambridge*, belong to the Prison; one of which *Bambridge* ordered to fire upon Captain *Mackpheadris*,[29] upon the Dispute which happened between them, but the Watchman fearing the Consequence, refused to obey him.

That the Windows of the Prison are in very bad Repair, to the great prejudice of the Health of the Prisoners, tho' by a late Order of the Judges they ought to have been kept in good Repair by the Warden.

That there are three Houses adjoining and belonging to the Prison, which are kept as Spunging-Houses by Tenants to Mr. *Bambridge*, as Warden, in one of which, kept by *Corbett*,[30] 26 Prisoners are confined.

That many of these Prisoners pay 2*s*. a Day for the Use of a Room in this House, and for Firing 1 *s*. and the other Prisoners 1 *s*. a Night for a Bed, but, notwithstanding such Payments, they are obliged to lye two or more in the same Bed. The Sums paid by these Twenty Six Prisoners, (Two at 2*s*. *per* Day, and Twenty Four at 1*s*. for the Use of the Lodgings only, being in the whole 1*l*. 8*s*.) amount Yearly to 511*l*. besides the Money paid for Firing at 1 *s*. a Day by such as have any, and 1 *s*. a Day for their Board.

Some of these Prisoners not being able to pay the 1 *s*. a Day for Eating, procured Necessaries to dress their own Meat, but *Corbett*, the Tipstaff, would not suffer them so to do, and they are under the Necessity of being supplied by their Friends, or starve.

That Lieutenant *Jenkin Leyson* (now a Prisoner with *Corbett*) paid the following Fees upon his being taken into Custody, for one Action, *viz*.[31]

	l.	*s*.	*d*.
To the Judge's Clerk	1	2	8
To the Phillizer[32]	0	4	0
To the Warden of the *Fleet*	2	6	8
To *Corbett* the Tipstaff	0	10	6
To Ditto, for being taken into Custody	1	10	0
To the Turnkeys	0	2	6
Total	5	16	4

It also appeared upon the Examination of several other Prisoners, that they paid the like Fees for every single Caption. And,

That every Prisoner removed by *Habeas Corpus* from one Place to another, pays to the Tipstaff 4s. 2d. every one brought out the Country by *Habeas Corpus*, and committed in Court for want of Bail, pays 13s. 4d. and every Prisoner carried to *Westminster-Hall* by *Habeas Corpus*, in Order to be Charged in Execution, pays 10s.

That every Prisoner pays at his Entrance into the House of the Tipstaff 6s. towards a Bowl of Punch.

That *Thomas Hogg* who had been about three Years a Prisoner in the *Fleet* Prison, and was then discharged by Order of Court, about eight Months after such Discharge, passing by the Door of that Prison, stopped to give Charity to the Prisoners at the Grate, and being seen by *James Barnes* (one of the said *Bambridge*'s Agents and Accomplices) the said *Barnes* seized and forced him into *Corbett*'s Spunging-House, where he hath been detained ever since (now upwards of Nine Months) without any Cause or Legal Authority whatsoever.[33]

That *Corbett* being examined touching the Discharge of his Prisoners, own'd he never made any regular Entry, and that all the Original Discharges of Prisoners committed to his Custody since Mr. *Guybon*'s Time were not received by him from the Warden,[34] but left with the Turnkey, from whom he only receiv'd verbal Directions.

The Committee could not get from Mr. *Bambridge*, or his Officers, any List of such Prisoners as have the Liberty of the Rules and Precincts of the *Fleet* Prison; but the Committee obtained, by another Hand, a List of Three Hundred and Eighty Two Persons, with an Account of what each Person hath paid to the Warden for such Liberty, and the annual Gifts every *Christmas*, amounting to near 2828*l*. 17s. 4d. and it appeared to the Committee that the Prisoners for the greatest Debts have not sign'd the Book. That the Gratuity to the Warden for the Liberty of the Rules, is exacted in proportion to the Greatness of the Debt; and if all paid, that Account would be Three times the before-mentioned Sum. These Sums so paid appear to be very extraordinary Exactions from the Prisoners, and are the more unreasonable because all Prisoners who have the Liberty of the Rules enter into Bonds in very great Penalties, with sufficient Sureties, for not escaping, the least of which Penalties are always double the Sums they stand committed for.

Mr. *Cotton*, Clerk of the Papers, upon his Examination concerning the Money taken by him for Day-Rules granted to Prisoners, confessed that every Prisoner who has the Liberty to go abroad in Term-Time pays 5s. 6d. for each Day, and for the first and last Days of the Term 6s. which he said is divided in the following Manner, *viz.*

	s.	d.
To the four Judges 3*d.* each	1	0
To the Secondary	1	8
To the Warden	1	0
To the Clerk of the Papers	1	10
	5	6
More to the Clerk of the Papers the first and last Day of the Term	0	6
Total	6	0

And that in about two Years Time one Gentleman paid 30*l.* for obtaining Day-Rules.

That an Act having passed in the Sixth Year of the late King, for the Relief of Insolvent Debtors, Mr. *Fytche* did thereupon declare in the Name of the said Mr. *Huggins* (who had directed him so to do) that unless every Prisoner within the Rules would give him two Guineas they should not be listed, in order to be discharged in pursuance of that Act,[35] for that he the said *Huggins* would refuse to swear them his Prisoners, as that Act required, and would not suffer his Deputy to do it; but a List was delivered of about Twenty Prisoners then in the Rules, who were discharged; having given two Guineas each to *Huggins*, for inserting them in the List, and for swearing them to be his Prisoners; and three hundred Prisoners were carried up to *Guild-hall* in order to their Discharge, but some were refused to be listed, and lost the Benefit of the Act, because they had not Money enough to pay for being put into the List.

That Mr. *Huggins* being examined touching an Instrument signed by him in *November* 1724, appointing *Richard Corbett* one of the Five Tipstaffs of or belonging to the *Fleet* Prison, acknowledged that he had no Power by Vertue of any Patent from the Crown to Constitute such Tipstaff, but that when he came to his Office he found that such an Officer had been so constituted, and he took that for a Precedent to do the same.

That there are five Commitment-Books, wherein the Names of all Prisoners committed to the *Fleet* Prison are or ought to be entered. The Commencement of the Date of the first Book is the twenty sixth of *March* 1708, and the last the sixth of *May* 1728, to this Time.[36]

There is one Book wherein the Names are inserted of those Prisoners who are removed to the *Fleet* by *Habeas Corpus*, beginning in *Michaelmas-*Term 1727, to this Time.

There is one Declaration-Book, wherein the Names of those Creditors are inserted who declare against their Debtors, beginning the 23d of *January* 1728, to this Time.

There is one Lodge-Book, wherein the Prisoners Names are entred when they come into the Prison, beginning *November* 1728.

There is one Security Bond-Book without Date.

That he the said Mr. *Huggins*, on *Saturday*, *Sunday*, and *Monday*, the First, Second, and Third of *March* 1728, (since the Committee was appointed) did exonerate or discharge out of the Commitment-Books One Hundred and Nineteen Persons, for several Sums, amounting to about 17099*l*. 6*s*. 7*d*.

He owned that he has in his Custody Fifty Two Discharges more, which ought to have been long since discharged, and amount to very great Sums of Money.

That by the Dates in the List which Mr. *Huggins* delivered to the Committee of One Hundred and Nineteen Persons so discharged, and the Fifty Two to be discharged, it appeared that many of them ought to have been discharged in the Years 1718, 1719, 1720, and so on to this Time.

That there are two Escape-Warrants, one of which the Judge grants, the other the Warden; that which the Judge grants, carries the Prisoner to *Newgate*, there to remain during Life, unless the Debt be paid; and that which the Warden grants is on some Information, or Pretence, that the Prisoner is out of the Rules, and so remands him to the Prison.

One ill Use which is made of keeping the Prisoners so long on the Commitment-Book, is, That the Warden may at his Pleasure Issue his Escape-Warrant against any such Person continued on the Commitment-Book, and carry him to the Spunging-House, or to the Prison, and there detain him until he squeezes from him all the Money that can possibly be got.

Another ill Use, and Inconveniency is, That Persons who have been Seven Years or more out of the Rules, or out of the Prison, (their Names remaining in the Commitment-Book) return, after having contracted new Debts, and so become Prisoners again fraudulently, to obtain the Benefit of the usual Acts for Relief of Insolvent Debtors.

That the Date of the *Habeas-Corpus* Book being but in *Michaelmas*-Term 1727, the Date of the Declaration-Book the 23d of *January* 1728, and the Date of the Lodge-Book *November* in 1728, the Committee conceive from such late Dates that there must be a Concealment of former Books of that kind, or that they are destroyed; either of which must tend to the great

Prejudice of the Prisoners and the Creditors, and to the suppressing the Truth in this Enquiry.

That since the said *Thomas Bambridge* has acted as Warden, the Books belonging to the Office of the Warden have been very negligently kept, and the Discharges not duly entred, to the great Prejudice of many of His Majesty's Subjects; and he hath not regularly taken Charge of the Prisoners committed to his Care by his Patent; and hath not, as he himself confesseth, ever had any Authentick List of the Prisoners in the Rules delivered him, so he cannot have executed the Trust of keeping his Prisoners in safe Custody, when he did not know who or where they were.

The Committee find that the said *Thomas Bambridge*, who for some Years acted as Deputy-Warden of the *Fleet*, and is now actually Warden of that Prison, hath himself been aiding and assisting in an Escape; That He caused a private Door to be made through the Walls of the Prison out of the Yard where the Dogs are, the Key of which Door was kept by himself, and he with his own Hands opened the Door and let out *Boyce*, the Smugler,[37] charged at the King's Suit with upwards of 30000*l*. and was afterwards seen at *Islington*, and hath been several times let out of the Prison by *Bambridge*.

That *William Kilberry* was allowed by *Bambridge* to go out of the Prison and the Rules thereof, though charged at the Suit of the Crown with the Sum of 5820*l*.[38]

That *William Booth*, charged with 5820*l*. at the Suit of the Crown, though committed close Prisoner, was also suffered to go out of the Prison and the Rules thereof.[39]

That *William Talure*, committed by the Court of *Common-Pleas* for 740*l*. upon mesne Process, and charged with Forgery, hath been suffered to go out of the *Fleet* Prison to *Wem* in the County of *Salop*, where the Committee are informed he still remains.[40]

That the said *James Barnes* (tho' a Prisoner in the *Fleet* Prison upon Execution) hath been permitted during this Enquiry to come from thence to *Westminster* to the said *Bambridge*, when in Custody of the Messenger to the Serjeant at Arms attending this House.[41]

The Committee find that the said *Bambridge* hath by himself and his Agents often refused to admit Prisoners into the Prison, though committed by due course of Law, and in order to extort Money from them, hath often, contrary to an Act of the Twenty Second and Twenty Third of King *Charles* the Second,[42] without their free and voluntary Consent, caused them to be carried away from the Prison Gate unto a publick Victualling or Drinking House, commonly called a Spunging-House, belonging to him the said *Bambridge* as Warden, and rented of him by *Corbett* his Tipstaff, and hath there kept them at Exorbitant Charges, and forced them to call for more Liquor than they were inclined to, and to spend more than they were able to afford, to the defrauding of their Creditors, and the distressing of their Families, whose Substance they are compelled there to consume; and for the more effectual making them stretch their poor Remains of Credit, and to squeeze out of them the Charity of their Friends, each Prisoner is better or worse treated according to his Expences, some being allowed a handsome Room and Bed to themselves, some stowed in Garrets, three in one Bed, and some put in Irons.

That these Houses were further used by the said *Bambridge* as a Terror for extorting Money from the Prisoners, who on Security given have the Liberty of the Rules; of which Mr. *Robert Castell* was an unhappy Instance, a Man born to a competent Estate, but being unfortunately plunged in Debt, was thrown into Prison; he was first sent (according to Custom) to *Corbett*'s, from whence he by Presents to *Bambridge* redeemed himself, and, giving Security, obtained the Liberty of the Rules; notwithstanding which he had frequently Presents, as they are called, exacted from him by *Bambridge*, and was menaced, on refusal, to be sent back to *Corbett*'s again.

The said *Bambridge* having thus unlawfully extorted large Sums of Money from him in a very short time, *Castell* grew weary of being made such a wretched Property, and resolving not to injure farther his Family or his Creditors for the sake of so small a Liberty, he refused to submit to further Exactions, upon which the said *Bambridge* ordered him to be recommitted to *Corbett*'s, where the Small-Pox then raged, though *Castell* acquainted him with his not having had that Distemper, and that he dreaded it so much, That the putting him into a House where it was would occasion his Death, which, if it happened before he could settle his Affairs, would be a great Prejudice to his Creditors, and would expose his Family to Destruction; and therefore he earnestly desired that he might either be sent to another House, or even into the Goal itself, as a Favour. The melancholy Case of this poor Gentleman moved the very Agents of the said *Bambridge* to Compassion, so that they also used their utmost Endeavours to disswade him from sending this unhappy Prisoner to that Infected House: But *Bambridge* forced him thither, where he (as he feared he should) caught the Small-Pox, and in a few Days dyed thereof, justly charging the said *Bambridge* with his Death; and unhappily leaving all his Affairs in the greatest Confusion, and a numerous Family of small Children in the utmost Distress.

It appeared to the Committee, That the Letting-out of the *Fleet* Tenements to *Victuallers* for the Reception of Prisoners hath been but of late practised, and that the first of them Lett for this Purpose was to *Mary Whitwood*, who still continues Tenant of the same, and that her Rent has from 32*l. per Ann.* been encreased to 60 *l.* and a certain Number of Prisoners stipulated to be made a Prey of to enable her to pay so great a Rent; and that she, to procure the Benefit of having such a Number of Prisoners sent to her House, hath, over and above the encreased Rent, been obliged to make a Present to the said *Bambridge* of Forty Guineas, as also of a Toy, (as 'tis called) being the Model of a *Chinese* Ship made of Amber set in Silver, for which Fourscore Broad-Pieces had been offered her.[43]

This is the first Method of extorting Money from the unhappy Prisoners; and when they can no longer bear the Misery and Expence of a Spunging-House, before they can obtain the Privilege of being admitted into the Prison they are obliged to comply with such exorbitant Fees as the said *Bambridge* thinks fit to demand, which if they do not, they are sure, under various Pretences, of being turned down to the Common-Side, if not put in Irons and Dungeons; and this has been done to those who were willing and offered to pay the Fees established by the Regulation made by the Judges of the *Common-Pleas* in *Trin. Term* 1727, which ought to have been hung up in some publick Place in the Prison, to which the Prisoners might have free Access, but was secreted by the said *James Barnes*, pursuant to the Orders of the said *Bambridge;* which Table of Fees seems to be unreasonable, because it obliges Men who are committed for not being able to pay their Debts, to pay such Sums of Money as their Curcumstances render them altogether unable to comply with.

And this Table of Fees was fraudulently obtained by the said *Bambridge*, for it appeared to the Committee, That upon Complaint of the Prisoners of the *Fleet* to the Court of *Common-Pleas*, the Order made by Lord Chief Justice *Herbert*,[44] establishing the Fees of that Goal, was ordered to be read, which Order was founded upon Institutions made in the Year 1651, in which was a Table of Fees, two *Items* whereof being taken away, the rest remained as follows;

	l.	*s.*	*d.*
To the Warden, for the Liberty of his House and Irons	1	6	8
For the Dismission Fee	0	7	4
To the Clerk, for making the Obligation	0	2	4
For Entring the Name and Cause	0	0	4
To the Chamberlain	0	1	0
To the Goaler	0	1	0
To the Porter	0	1	0
To a Gallon of Wine	0	2	8
And a Fee added by Order of Court to the Chaplain	0	2	0
Total	2	4	4

And the said *Bambridge* read the said Order, and instead of reading the particular *Items*, he read only the said Sum Total of 2*l*. 4*s*. 4*d*. and thereby he induced the Judges to believe that the said Sum was the Fee due to the Warden, and accordingly they ordered that 2*l*. 4*s*. 4*d*. to be paid as due to the Warden for a Commitment-Fee, and ordered the other Fees due to the Chamberlain, Goaler, and others, to be paid, over and above the said 2*l*. 4*s*. 4*d*. and the same have been ever since taken, besides the 7*s*. 4*d*. to the Warden upon the Prisoner's Discharge, notwithstanding they are all included in the 2*l*. 4*s*. 4*d*.

The said Judges of the *Common-Pleas* seeming to be of Opinion that every Action to which a Prisoner was rendred in Discharge of his Bail was a seperate Commitment, and that there was a seperate Commitment-Fee due upon each Action; the said *Bambridge* has thereupon received Six or Seven times 2*l*. 4*s*. 4*d*. of a single Person, as his bare Commitment-Fees, whereby the Prisoner has paid Six times for the Liberty of the House and Irons, Six Dismission-Fees, for Six Obligations (tho' none given) Six Fees to the Chamberlain, Porter, Goaler, *&c.* and Six Gallons of Wine; and the Prisoner pays the Chamberlain, Goaler, *&c.* for his Discharge besides.

The said *Bambridge* likewise takes a Fee of 3*l*. 6*s*. 8*d*. from every Prisoner committed by the *Exchequer* or *Chancery*, whereas there is no such Fee due, nor any Distinction in the Table of Fees between the Commitment of one Court or another.

And for a more particular Account of the Fees, Chamber-Rent, and Dues to the Chaplain, the Committee refer to the annexed *Appendix* marked with the Letter (*B.*)

And notwithstanding the Payment of such large Fees, in order to extort further Sums from the unfortunate Prisoners, the said *Bambridge* unjustly pretends he has *a Right as Warden* to exercise an unlimited Power of changing Prisoners from Room to Room; of turning them into the Common Side, tho' they have paid the Master's Side Fee; and inflicting Arbitrary Punishments by locking them down in unwholsome Dungeons, and loading them with torturing Irons; some Instances of which follow: *viz.*

Jacob Mendez Solas, a *Portuguese*,[45] was, as far as it appeard to the Committee, one of the first Prisoners for Debt that ever was loaded with Irons in the *Fleet;* The said *Bambridge* one Day called him into the Gate-house of the Prison, called the *Lodge*, where he caused him to be seized, fettered, and carried to *Corbett*'s, the Spunging-House, and there kept for upwards of a Week, and when brought back into the Prison, *Bambridge* caused him to be turned into the Dungeon, called the *Strong Room of the Master's Side.*

This Place is a Vault like those in which the Dead are Interr'd, and wherein the Bodies of Persons dying in the said Prison are usually deposited, till the Coroner's Inquest hath passed upon them; it has no Chimney nor Fire-place, nor any Light but what comes over the Door, or through a Hole of about Eight Inches square. It is neither Paved nor Boarded; and the rough Bricks appear both on the Sides and Top, being neither Wainscotted nor Plaistered: What adds to the Dampness and Stench of the Place is, its being built over the Common-Shore, and adjoining to the Sink and Dunghil where all the Nastiness of the Prison is cast. In this miserable Place the poor Wretch was kept by the said *Bambridge*, Manacled and Shackled for near Two Months. At length, on receiving Five Guineas from Mr. *Kemp*, a Friend of *Solas*'s, *Bambridge* released the Prisoner from his cruel Confinement. But tho' his Chains were taken off, his Terror still remained, and the unhappy Man was prevailed upon by that Terror, not only to labour *gratis* for the said *Bambridge*, but to swear also at random all that he hath required of him: And the Committee themselves saw an Instance of the deep Impression his Sufferings had made upon him; for on his surmising, from something said, that *Bambridge* was to return again, as Warden of the *Fleet*, he fainted, and the Blood started out of his Mouth and Nose.

Captain *John Mackpheadris*, who was bred a Merchant, is another melancholy Instance of the cruel Use the said *Bambridge* hath made of his assumed Authority. *Mackpheadris* was a considerable Trader, and in a very flourishing Condition until the Year 1720, when being bound for large Sums to the Crown, for a Person afterwards ruined by the Misfortunes of that Year, he was undone. In *June* 1727 he was Prisoner in the *Fleet*, and altho' he had before paid his Commitment-Fee, the like Fee was extorted from him a Second time; and he having furnished a Room, *Bambridge* demanded an extravagant Price for it, which he refused to pay; and urged, That it was unlawful for the Warden to demand extravagant Rents, and offered to pay what was legally due: Notwithstanding which, the said *Bambridge*, assisted by the said *James Barnes* and other Accomplices, broke open his Room, and took away several things of great Value, amongst others, the King's Extent in Aid of the Prisoner (which was to have been returned in a few Days, in order to procure the Debt to the Crown, and the Prisoner's Enlargement) which *Bambridge* still detains. Not content with this, *Bambridge* locked the Prisoner out of his Room, and forced him to lye in the open Yard, called the *Bare*. He sat quietly under his Wrongs, and getting some poor Materials, built a little Hut to protect himself, as well as he could, from the Injuries of the Weather. The said *Bambridge* seeing his Unconcernedness, said, *Damn him! he is easy. I will put him into the Strong Room before To-morrow*; and ordered *Barnes* to pull down his little Hut, which was done accordingly. The poor Prisoner being in an ill State of Health, and the Night rainy, was put to great Distress. Some time after this he was (about Eleven a Clock at Night) assaulted by *Bambridge*, with several other Persons his Accomplices, in a violent manner; and *Bambridge*, tho' the Prisoner was unarmed, attacked him with his Sword, but by good Fortune was prevented from killing him; and several other Prisoners coming out upon the Noise, they carried *Mackpheadris* for Safety into another Gentleman's Room, soon after which *Bambridge* coming with one *Savage*, and several others, broke open the Door, and *Bambridge* strove with his Sword to kill the Prisoner; but he again got away, and hid himself in another Room. Next Morning the said *Bambridge* entred the Prison with a Detachment of Soldiers, and ordered the Prisoner to be dragged to the Lodge, and Ironed with great Irons; on which he desiring to know for what Cause, and by what Authority he was to be so cruelly used; *Bambridge* replyed, *It was by his own Authority, and Damn him, he would do it, and have his Life*. The Prisoner desired he might be carried before a Magistrate, that he might know his Crime before he was punished; but *Bambridge* refused, and put Irons upon his Legs which were too little, so that in forcing them on[,] his Legs were like to have been broken; and the Torture was impossible to be endured. Upon which the Prisoner complaining of the grievous

Pain and Streightness of the Irons, *Bambridge* answered, *That he did it on purpose to torture him:* On which the Prisoner replying, *That by the Law of* England *no Man ought to be tortured;* Bambridge declared, *That he would do it first, and answer for it afterwards;* and caused him to be dragged away to the Dungeon, where he lay without a Bed, loaded with Irons so close rivetted that they kept him in continual Torture, and mortified his Legs. After long Application his Irons were changed, and a Surgeon directed to dress his Legs, but his Lameness is not nor ever can be cured. He was kept in this miserable Condition for Three Weeks, by which his Sight is greatly prejudiced, and in danger of being lost.

The Prisoner, upon this Usage, petitioned the *Judges*, and after several Meetings, and a full Hearing, the *Judges* reprimanded Mr. *Huggins* and *Bambridge*, and declared *That a Goaler could not answer the Ironing of a Man before he was found guilty of a Crime;* but it being out of Term, they could not give the Prisoner any Relief or Satisfaction.

Notwithstanding this Opinion of the Judges, the said *Bambridge* continued to keep the Prisoner in Irons till he had paid him Six Guineas; and to prevent the Prisoner's recovering Damages for the cruel Treatment of him, *Bambridge* Indicted him and his principal Witnesses at the *Old Baily*, before they knew any thing of the Matter; and to support that Indictment, he had recourse to Subornation, and turned Two of his Servants out of Places which they had bought, because they would not swear falsly that the Prisoner had struck the said *Bambridge*, which words he had inserted in Affidavits ready prepared for Signing, and which they knew to be false. As soon as they were apprized of it, they applyed to the Lord-Mayor, who ordered the Grand-Jury down to the *Fleet*, where they found that *Bambridge* was the Aggressor. But the Bill against the Prisoners being already found, the Second Enquiry was too late.

The Prisoners being no longer able to bear the Charges of Prosecution, which had already cost 100*l*. and being softned by Promises and terrified by Threats, submitted to plead Guilty, on a solemn Assurance and Agreement made with *Bambridge* before Witnesses, of having but One Shilling Fine laid upon them; but so soon as they had pleaded Guilty, *Bambridge* took Advantage of it, and has continued Harrassing them and their Securities ever since.

The Desire of Gain urged the said *Bambridge* to the preceding Instances of Cruelty; but a more Diabolical Passion, that of *Malice*, animated him to oppress Captain *David Sinclair* in the following manner.

At the latter end of *June* or beginning of *July* last, the said *Bambridge* declared to the said *James Barnes*, one of the Agents of his Cruelties, *That he would have* Sinclair'*s Blood;* and he took the Opportunity of the first Festival Day, which was on the first of *August* following, when he thought Captain *Sinclair* might, by celebrating the Memory of the late King, be warmed with Liquor so far as to give him some Excuse for the Cruelties which he intended to inflict upon him. But in some Measure he was disappointed, for Captain *Sinclair* was perfectly sober, when the said *Bambridge* rushed into his Room with a dark Lanthorn in his Hand, assisted by his Accomplices *James Barnes* and *William Pindar*, and supported by his usual Guard, armed with Muskets and Bayonets, and without any Provocation given, run his Lanthorn into Captain *Sinclair*'s Face, seized him by the Collar, and told him he must come along with him: Captain *Sinclair*, tho' surprized, asked for what and by what Authority he so treated him? Upon which *Barnes* and the rest seized Captain *Sinclair*, who still desiring to know by what Authority they so abused him? *Bambridge* grosly insulted him, and struck him with his Cane on the Head and Shoulders, whilst he was held fast by *Pindar* and *Barnes*. Such base and scandalous Usage of this Gentleman, who had in the late Wars always signalized himself with the greatest Courage, Gallantry and Honour in the Service of his Country upon many the most brave and desperate Occasions, must be most shocking and intollerable; yet Captain *Sinclair* bore it with Patience, refusing only to go out of his Room unless he was forced; whereupon the said *Bambridge* threatned to run his Cane down his Throat, and ordered his Guard to stab him with their Bayonets, or drag him down to the said Dungeon called the Strong Room, the latter of which they did, and *Bambridge* kept him confined in that damp and loathsome Place, till he had lost the Use of his Limbs and Memory, neither of which has he perfectly recovered to this Day.[46] Many aggravating Cruelties were used to make his Confinement more terrible; and when *Bambridge* found he was in danger of immediate Death, he removed him, for fear of his dying in Duress, and caused him to be carried in a dying Condition from that Dungeon to a Room where there was no Bed or Furniture; and so unmercifully prevented his Friends having any Access to him, that he was four Days without the least Sustenance.

It appeared to the Committee by the Evidence of a Surgeon and others, who were Prisoners in the House, that when Captain *Sinclair* was forced into that loathsome Dungeon he was in perfect Health.

Captain *Sinclair* applyed for Remedy at Law against the said Cruelties of *Bambridge*, and had procured a *Heabeas Corpus* for his Witnesses to be brought before the Sessions of *Oyer* and *Terminer*, when the said *Bam-*

bridge by colour of his assumed Authority as Warden, took the said Writs of *Habeas Corpus* from the Officer whose Duty it was to make a Return of them, and commanded him to keep out of the way, whilst he himself went to the *Old Baily*, and immediately indicted Capt. *Sinclair* and such of his Witnesses as he knew he could not deter by Threats or prevail with by Promises to go from the Truth.

Captain *Sinclair* had Temper enough to bear patiently almost unsupportable Injuries, and to reserve himself for a proper Occasion, when Justice should be done him by the Laws of the Realm.

But the said *Bambridge* has forced others by Wrongs and Injuries beyond human bearing, to endeavour the avenging Injuries and Oppressions which they could no longer endure.

And it appeared to the Committee, that the said *Bambridge*, in order to avoid the Punishment due to these Crimes, hath committed greater, and hath not only denied Admittance to the Sollicitors, who might procure Justice to the injured Prisoners, and in open Defiance to the Law, disobeyed the King's Writs, but hath also seduced some by indulging them in Riot, and terrifyed others with fear of Duress, to swear to and subscribe such false Affidavits as he thought fit to prepare for them, on several Occasions; in all which Wrongs and Oppressions *John Everett* also acted as one of the said *Bambridge*'s wicked Accomplices.[47]

That the said *Bambridge* being asked by the Committee, *By what Authority he pretended to put Prisoners into Dungeons and Irons?* Answered, *That he did it by his own Authority, as Warden*, to preserve the Quiet and Safety of the Custody of the Prison.

But it appeared to the Committee by the Examinations of many Witnesses, that, before the time when *Gybbon* and the said *Bambridge* acted as Deputy-Wardens under Mr. *Huggins*, the Quiet and Safety of the Custody were very well preserved without any use of Irons or Dungeons.

That the two Dungeons, called the Strong Room on the Master Side, and the Strong Room on the Common Side, were both built within these few Years; and that the old Method of punishing drunken and disorderly Persons was putting them in the Stocks; and the Punishment of those who had escaped, or attempted to escape, was putting them upon a Tub at the Gate of the Prison, by way of publick Shame, or securing them, without Irons, in their proper Rooms for some Days.

And that the said Dungeons were built in defyance of and contrary to the Declaration of The Lord *King*,[48] when Lord Chief Justice of the *Common-Pleas*; who, upon an Application made to him on behalf of the Prisoners of the *Fleet*, when Mr. *Huggins* and —— *Gybbon* urged,⁴⁹ that there was danger of Prisoners escaping, DECLARED *that they might raise their Walls higher, but that there should be no Prison within a Prison.*

That upon the strictest Enquiry, the Committee could not find that any Prisoners in the *Fleet* for Debt had been put in Irons, before the said Mr. *Huggins* had the Office of Warden.

That it is not the only Design of the said *Thomas Bambridge* to extort Money from his Prisoners, if they survive his inhuman Treatment, but he seems to have a further View, in case it causes Death, of possessing himself of their Effects. One remarkable Proof of which the Committee think proper here to insert, *viz.*

Mr. *John Holder*,⁵⁰ a *Spanish* Merchant, was a Prisoner in the *Fleet*, and had a Room which he fitted up with his own Furniture, and had with him all his Books, Accounts and Writings, and other Effects, to the value of about 30000*l.* which he declared by Affidavit, upon the following Occasion.

The said *Thomas Bambridge* by force turned the said Mr. *Holder* over to the Common Side, and took possession of his Room in which all his Effects were.

Mr. *Holder* remonstrated strongly against this Usage, and *Bambridge* refusing to restore him to his Room or Possession of his Effects, he made a proper Affidavit in order to apply to the Judges for Relief, and declared that he feared his Effects might be Embezelled whilst he was thus unjustly forced from them, and that he feared *Bambridge*'s cruel Treatment of him would be the Cause of his Death: The Miseries of the Common Side, which he dreaded, had such an Effect upon him, (being a Man of an advanced Age, and accustomed to live in Ease and Plenty,) that it threw him into such a fit of Sickness as made his Life despaired of, and in his Illness he often Declared, *That the Villain* Bambridge *would be the Occasion of his Death.* Which proved true, for *Bambridge* finding Mr. *Holder* like to die in the Duress which he had put him into, (for his own sake, to avoid the Punishment inflicted by Law upon Goalers who so inhumanly destroy their Prisoners) permitted him to be carried back to his Room, where in a few Days he died of the said Sickness, contracted by the said forcible Removal of him to the Common Side by *Bambridge*, as aforesaid.

Mr. *Holder* by his last Will appointed Major *Wilson* and Mr. *John Pigott* Trustees for his Son,⁵¹ a Youth of about 13 Years of Age, who had accompanied him in the time of his Confinement.

This Young Gentleman after his Father's Death locked up his Effects in several Trunks and Boxes, and delivered the Keys thereof to Mr. *Pigott* as his Trustee, who locked up the Room and took the Key with him; But the said *Thomas Bambridge* caused the said Room to be broke open by *Thomas King*, another of his Accomplices, and caused the said Effects to be seized, after that he, *Bambridge*, had forced Mr. *Pigott* out of the Prison (though a Prisoner in Execution) and locked down Major *Wilson* (the other Trustee) in the Dungeon, to prevent their taking any Inventory in behalf of the Heir at Law, then an Orphan.

These evil Practices of letting out Prisoners, extorting Exorbitant Fees, suffering Escapes, and exercising all sorts of Inhumanity for Gain, may in a great measure be imputed to the Venality of the Warden's Office; for the Warden who buys the Privilege of punishing others, does consequently sell his Forbearance at high Rates, and repair his own Charge and Loss at the wretched Expence of the Ease and Quiet of the miserable Objects in his Custody.

Upon the whole Matter, the Committee came to the following Resolutions, *viz.*

Resolved, That it appears to this Committee, That *Thomas Bambridge*, the Acting Warden of the Prison of the *Fleet*, hath wilfully permitted several Debtors to the Crown in great Sums of Money, as well as Debtors to divers of His Majesty's Subjects, to Escape; hath been guilty of the most Notorious Breaches of his Trust, great Extortions, and the highest Crimes and Misdemeanors in the Execution of his said Office; and hath Arbitrarily and Unlawfully loaded with Irons, put into Dungeons, and destroyed Prisoners for Debt under his Charge, treating them in the most Barbarous and Cruel Manner, in high Violation and Contempt of the Laws of this Kingdom.

Resolved, That it appears to this Committee, That *John Huggins* Esq; late Warden of the Prison of the *Fleet*, did, during the time of his Wardenship, wilfully permit many considerable Debtors in his Custody to Escape, and was notoriously guilty of great Breaches of his Trust, Extortions, Cruelties, and other high Crimes and Misdemeanors in the Execution of his said Office, to the great Oppression and Ruin of many of the Subjects of this Kingdom.

APPENDIX (A.)

Serjeants-Inn Hall, Trinity Term, 1727.

The TABLE of FEES *Ordered by the Judges to be paid by the Prisoners of the* Fleet, *to the Warden and his Agents, and to be hung up in the Hall of the said Prison.*

WHEREAS several Matters in Controversy between the Prisoners and the Warden of the *Fleet* were heard by the Right Honourable Sir *Robert Eyre* Knight, Lord Chief Justice of His Majesty's Court of *Common-Pleas* at *Westminster*, the Honourable *Robert Price* Esq; Sir *Francis Page* Knight, and *Alexander Denton* Esq; Justices of the said Court, at *Serjeants-Inn* Hall in *Chancery-Lane*, on *Monday* the 24th Day of *April*, on *Wednesday* the 26th Day of the same Month of *April*, on *Monday* the 1st Day of *May* following, and on *Friday* the 5th Day of the same Month of *May*, in *Easter* Term, in the 13th Year of the Reign of our Sovereign Lord King *George, Annoq; Domini* 1727: Upon which Hearing the Lord Chief Justice of the said Court came to the following Resolutions, *viz.*

	l.	s.	d.
That there is due and ought to be paid to the Warden of the *Fleet*, for every Commitment-Fee (exclusive of Commons) from all Persons of the Degree of an Esquire, Gentleman, or Gentlewoman, or any other Person under those Degrees, who shall enter on the Master's Side of the said Prison, 2*l.* 4*s.* 4*d.*	2	4	4
And that there ought to be paid to the Warden for every such Person, for the Use of the Minister of the said Prison, 2*s.*	0	2	0
That there is due, and ought to be paid to the Warden of the *Fleet*, for a Commitment-Fee for every Prisoner in Wards, or Common-Side, not taking Part of the Poors Box, 1*l.* 6*s.* 4*d.*	1	6	4
And every such Person ought to pay the Warden for the Use of the Minister of the said Prison 1*s.*	0	1	0

And every Prisoner taking part of the Poors Box ought to pay to the Warden 7*s.* 4*d.* and no more,

for his Commitment-Fee, and nothing for the Minister.   0   7   4
That there is due, and ought to be paid to the
Warden of the *Fleet*, for every Render in each Cause
2*l.* 4*s.* 4*d.* and nothing to the Minister.   2   4   4
That there is due, and ought to be paid to
the Chamberlain as his Fee for every Prisoner's
Entrance into the House 1*s.* and no more.   0   1   0
That there is due, and ought to be paid to
the Warden for every Prisoner's Discharge, either
by Creditor or Supersedeas, as a Fee for his
Dismission out of Prison, without any Regard
to the Number of Causes wherewith he stands
charged, 7*s.* 6*d.* and no more.   0   7   6
That there is due, and ought to be paid to
the Clerk of the Papers, for every Discharge of
every Action, 2*s.* 6*d.*   0   2   6
And for the Copy of every Cause, not
exceeding Three, 1*s.*   0   1   0
And for every Cause exceeding three Causes,
4*d.* (besides the 1*s.* a piece, for each of the said
first three Causes.)   0   0   4
That there is due, and ought to be paid to the
Clerk of the Papers, for his Certificate of the
Prisoner's Discharge delivered to the Prisoner
himself, without any Regard to the Number of
Causes he stood charged with, 2*s.* 6*d.* and for his
Certificate to the Warden for such Discharge 2*s.* 6*d.*   0   5   0
That there is due, and ought to be paid to the
Clerk of the Enquiries on the Discharge of a
Prisoner by the Creditors, and not by Supersedeas,
2*s.* 6*d.*   0   2   6
That there is due, and ought to be paid to the
Turnkey (who is now both Porter and Goaler) for the
Prisoner's Entrance into the House, 2*s.* and for
such Prisoner's Discharge to the Turnkey (being
Porter and Goaler) 2*s.* 6*d.*   0   4   6
That there is due, and ought to be paid to
the Turnkey, for every Declaration delivered to
him for a Prisoner, 1*s.*   0   1   0

That there is no Fee due to the Warden upon
his accepting Security, on the Prisoner's having
the Benefit of Day-Rules.

That there is no Fee due to the Warden for
Lodging and Chamber-Rent, where the Prisoner
has not actual Possession of the Chamber; but there
is due to the Warden for every Prisoner or
Prisoners, his or their Lodging or Chamber-Rent
2s. 6d. per Week, such Lodging or Chamber being
Furnished. 0 2 6

That there is due to the Minister that
Officiates and performs Divine Service within the
said Prison, for the Time being, from every Prisoner
within the Walls of the said Prison, or without the
Walls, or within the Rules, Four Pence per Week, to
be paid to the Warden for the Use of such Minister;
and that no such Minister or any other Clergyman,
being a Prisoner within the Walls or Rules of the
Fleet, do presume to Marry any Person without
Licence, within the Prison or Rules of the *Fleet*;
and that the Warden and his Officers do use
their utmost Vigilance to prevent all such Marriages.

That there is no fresh Commitment-Fee due to
the Warden upon the Prisoner's bringing himself
back to the *Fleet* by *Habeas Corpus*, (when the
Warden himself had removed him thence by *Habeas
Corpus*) and that there is no Fee, Gratuity or
Reward due to the Warden for his returning a
Habeas Corpus; but there is a Fee of 5s. 4d. due
to the Clerk of the Papers for the Allowance of
every Writ of *Habeas Corpus*, and 4s. for the
Return of the first Cause, and 2s. for every other
Cause, and no more. 0 11 4

That when a Prisoner dies in the *Fleet*, the Warden shall detain the Body
no longer than till the Coroner's Inquest be finished, which shall be done
with all reasonable Speed; and immediately afterwards the Body shall be
delivered to the Prisoner's Friends or Relations, if they desire it, without
Fee or Reward.

That this is the Duty of the Warden, and belongs to him, to keep the

Prison-House and Windows in necessary and good Repair, and to keep the Bog-House and Dunghil as clean and free from Stench and Noisomness as possible.

That a Table of Gifts and Bequests made for the Benefit of the Prisoners in the *Fleet*, expressing the particular Purposes for which the same were given, be prepared by the Warden, and hung up in the Hall of the said Prison.

That the Ward-Gates be opened at five of the Clock in the Summer, and seven of the Clock in the Winter, and do stand constantly open in the Day-time, according to the Order made the 17th *Feb.* 1727.

And whereas this Court, upon further Consideration of the Premisses, this present *Trinity* Term in the 13th Year of the Reign of our Sovereign Lord King *George*, is of Opinion that the said Resolutions are just, It is hereby Ordered that the same be observed by the Warden and Prisoners, and all other Persons therein concerned.

Robt. Eyre.
Robt. Price.
F. Page.
Alexr. Denton.

A LIST *of Bequests* &c. *which the Warden of the* Fleet *has set up in the* Common Hall *in the said* Fleet-Prison, *the* 20th June 1727, *which he allows of.*

	l.	*s.*	*d.*
Received from the Court of *Common-Pleas* 3*l.* each Term.	12	0	0
From the Court of *Exchequer*, 6*s.* 8*d.* every Term.	1	6	0
The Gift of *Edward Thatcher*, 40*s. per Annum*, the King's Tax allowed out.	1	16	0
The Gift of Mr. *Parker*, 30*s. per Annum* payable from Merchant-Taylors Company, King's Tax allowed out of it.	1	7	0
The Gift of *John Grubham* Esq; 3*l.* Allowed out of it 10*s.* for a Sea Breach in a Fence of Land in *Somersetshire*, called the Close.	2	10	0
The Gift of Mr. *John Kendrick* 30*s.* payable from the Drapers Company.	1	10	0

Received from the running Boxmen, *Christmas*, *Easter* and *Whitsontide*.	3	12	6
Received from the Honourable Master of the *Rolls*.	2	0	0
The Gift of Mr. *Dawson*, which has not been paid these several Years, to be given by the Church-Wardens of *Estrel* Pleas.	0	9	0
The Gift of Mr. *Carter*, which has not been paid, as appears from the Church-Wardens of *Underhurst*.	0	17	0
Received from the Leather-Sellers Company.	0	18	0
Received every *Christmas* 33 Penny Loaves, parted at the Dividing Table.			

APPENDIX (B.)

AN ACCOUNT *of the Profits arising Yearly to the Warden of the* Fleet, *by Rents payable for Lodgings, and other Rents, Perquisites and Profits which appear to be made therefrom.*

	l.	*s.*	*d.*
In the first Gallery, Ten Prisoners at 2s. 10d. *per* Week each.	1	8	4
In the Second Gallery, Eleven Prisoners at 2s. 10d. *per* Week each.	1	11	2
More in the same Gallery, *viz.* one at 3s. 6d. two at 10s. and three at 5s. 4d. each, which comes to	1	19	6
In the third Gallery, Nineteen at 2s. 10d. two at 3s. 9d. four at 5s. 4d. and two at 5s. 8d. each, which comes to	4	14	0
In the fourth Gallery, Thirty at 2s. 10d. each, which comes to	4	5	0
In the Garden Rooms, Twelve at 2s. 10d. each.	1	14	0
Total *per* Week	15	12	0

Which for Fifty two Weeks, or one Year, comes to	811	4	0
To which add			
The Cellar, lett *per Annum* at	80	0	0
The Coffee Room, lett *per Annum* at	14	0	0
The several Rooms in the Chappel Stairs, lett *per Annum* at	79	0	0
The Thirteen Houses fronting *Fleet-Ditch* between the two Walls and the Prison, Ten of which are lett at 310*l.* there is also three unlett at 90*l. per Annum*, and comes together to 400*l.*	400	0	0
Rent paid Annually by the Sherrifs of *London*, to the Keeper of the Palaces of Westminster,	8	0	0
Ditto to the Warden of the *Fleet*,	10	0	0
The Commitment-Fees, at 2*l.* 4*s.* 4*d.* each Commitment, being computed by Mr. *Bygrave* and Mr. *Cotton*, the former and present Clerk of the Papers, to be at least *Communibus Annis* three hundred and twenty in Number, amount to *per Annum* 646*l.* 18*s.* 8*d.* and the Dismission Fees at 7*s.* 6*d.* each Prisoner amount to *per Annum* 120*l.* and make in the whole *per Annum*,	766	18	8

Besides the vast Number of Extortions over and above these Fees, particularly from *Walter Newbury*, 11*l.* 4*s. John Dudley*, 16*l.* 12*s. Benjamin Wakeling*, 5*l.* 5*s. Peter Jordain* 6*l.* 10*s. Thomas Goulder* 8*l.* 19*s.* 6*d. Alexander Sydall*, 6*l.* 10*s. Alexander Leickey*, 3*l.* 6*s.* 8*d. Jeremiah Miles*, 4*l.* 14*s.* 6*d. James Bayley*, 13*l.* 8*s.* 8*d.* and several others.

By Liberty of Rules and New-Years Gifts, from the best Accounts that are given, or can be learnt, *per Annum* upwards of	1500	0	0
Shops in *Westminster Hall* Lett at 117*l.* and when all are Lett,	150	0	0

The Chaplain's Fees for Entrance of Three Hundred and Twenty Prisoners at 2*s.* each, amount to 32*l. per* Annum, besides 4*d. per* Week from at least One Thousand Prisoners in the Prison and the Liberty of the Rules, amounting to 865*l*. 16*s*. *per Annum*, and together make 897*l*. 16*s*. But Dr. *Franks*, Dean of *Bedford*, being the Officiating Chaplain, has been allowed but 40 Guineas a Year, and 40 Guineas a Year more when there was a Real Chaplain, which together make 80 Guineas *per Annum*; so Deducting the said 80 Guineas from the said 897*l*. 16*s*. there will remain a Clear Profit to the Warden *per Annum*,   813 6 0

Total *per Annum*   4632 18 8

Besides the Appointment of the following Officers.

The Clerk of the Papers gave for his Place 1500*l*.
The Clerk of the Inquiries Place worth 150*l*. *per Annum*.
The Turnkey's Place 50*l*. *per Annum*.
The Chamberlain's Place 40*l*. *per Annum*.
The Tipstaff to the Court of *Chancery* gave for his Place 328 Guineas.
The Tipstaff of the *Rolls* gave 150 Guineas.
The Tipstaff of the *Exchequer*, 150 Guineas.
The Tipstaff of the *Common-Pleas*, 210 Guineas.
The other Tipstaff there 200 Guineas.

THE Resolutions of the Committee being severally read a Second time, were, upon the Question severally put thereupon, agreed unto by the House, and are as follow, *viz*.

Resolved, Nemine Contradicente, That *Thomas Bambridge*, the Acting Warden of the Prison of the *Fleet*, hath wilfully permitted several Debtors to the Crown in great Sums of Money, as well as Debtors to divers of His Majesty's Subjects, to Escape; hath been guilty of the most notorious Breaches of his Trust, great Extortions, and the highest Crimes and Misdemeanors in the Execution of his said Office: and hath Arbitrarily and Unlawfully loaded with Irons, put into Dungeons and Destroyed Prisoners for Debt, under his Charge, treating them in the most Barbarous and Cruel Manner, in high Violation and Contempt of the Laws of this Kingdom.

Resolved, Nemine Contradicente, That *John Huggins* Esq; late Warden of the Prison of the *Fleet*, did, during the time of his Wardenship, wilfully permit many considerable Debtors, in his Custody, to Escape; and was notoriously guilty of great breaches of his Trust, Extortions, Cruelties, and other high Crimes and Misdemeanours in the Execution of his said Office, to the great Oppression and Ruin of many of the Subjects of this Kingdom.

Resolved, That it appears to this House That *James Barnes* was an Agent of and an Accomplice with the said *Thomas Bambridge* in the Commission of his said Crimes.

Resolved, That it appears to this House That *William Pindar* was an Agent of and an Accomplice with the said *Thomas Bambridge* in the Commission of his said Crimes.

Resolved, That it appears to this House That *John Everett* was an Agent of and an Accomplice with the said *Thomas Bambridge* in the Commission of his said Crimes.

Resolved, That it appears to this House That *Thomas King* was an Agent of and an Accomplice with the said *Thomas Bambridge* in the Commission of his said Crimes.

Mr. *Oglethorpe* acquainted the House, That he was directed by the Committee to Move That an humble Address be presented to His Majesty, That He will be graciously pleased to direct His Attorney-General forthwith to Prosecute, in the most Effectual Manner, the said *Thomas Bambridge*, for his said Crimes.

And He Moved the House accordingly.

Resolved, Nemine Contradicente, That an humble Address be presented to His Majesty That He will be graciously pleased to direct His Attorney-General forthwith to Prosecute, in the most Effectual Manner, the said *Thomas Bambridge*, for his said Crimes.

Mr. *Oglethorpe* also acquainted the House, That he was directed by the Committee to Move That an humble Address be presented to His Majesty, That He will be graciously pleased to direct his Attorney-General forthwith to Prosecute, in the most Effectual Manner, the said *John Huggins*, for his said Crimes.

And He Moved the House accordingly.

Resolved, Nemine Contradicente, That an humble Address be presented to His Majesty That He will be graciously pleased to direct His Attorney-General forthwith to Prosecute, in the most Effectual Manner, the said *John Huggins*, for his said Crimes.

Resolved, That an humble Address be presented to His Majesty That He will be graciously pleased to direct His Attorney-General forthwith to

Prosecute, in the most Effectual Manner, the said *James Barnes, William Pindar, John Everett,* and *Thomas King,* for their said Crimes.[52]

Ordered, That the said Addresses be presented to His Majesty by such Members of this House as are of His Majesty's most Honourable Privy-Council.

Ordered, That the said *Thomas Bambridge* be committed close Prisoner to His Majesty's Goal of *Newgate,* and that Mr. *Speaker* do Issue his Warrants accordingly.

Ordered, That the said *John Huggins* Esq; be committed close Prisoner to His Majesty's Goal of *Newgate,* and that Mr. *Speaker* do Issue his Warrants accordingly.

Ordered, That the said *James Barnes* be committed close Prisoner to His Majesty's Goal of *Newgate,* and that Mr. *Speaker* do Issue his Warrants accordingly.

Ordered, That the said *William Pindar* be committed close Prisoner to His Majesty's Goal of *Newgate,* and that Mr. *Speaker* do Issue his Warrants accordingly.

Ordered, That the said *John Everett* be committed close Prisoner to His Majesty's Goal of *Newgate,* and that Mr. *Speaker* do Issue his Warrants accordingly.

Ordered, That the said *Thomas King* be committed close Prisoner to His Majesty's Goal of *Newgate,* and that Mr. *Speaker* do Issue his Warrants accordingly.

Mr. *Oglethorpe* also acquainted the House, That he was directed by the Committee to Move That Leave be given to bring in a Bill to Disable the said *Thomas Bambridge* to Hold or Execute the Office of Warden of the Prison of the *Fleet,* or to Have or Exercise any Authority relating thereto.

And he Moved the House accordingly.

Ordered, Nemine Contradicente, That Leave be given to bring in a Bill to Disable the said *Thomas Bambridge* to Hold or Execute the Office of Warden of the Prison of the *Fleet,* or to Have or Exercise any Authority relating thereto; and that Mr. *Oglethorpe,* Mr. *Earle,* the Lord *Percivall,* and Mr. *Hughes* do prepare and bring in the same.

Mr. *Oglethorpe* also acquainted the House, That he was directed by the Committee to Move, That Leave be given to bring in a Bill for better Regulating the Prison of the *Fleet,* and for more effectual preventing and punishing Arbitrary and Illegal Practices of the Warden of the said Prison.

And he Moved the House accordingly.

Ordered, Nemine Contradicente, That Leave be given to bring in a Bill for better Regulating the Prison of the *Fleet*, and for more effectual preventing and punishing Arbitrary and Illegal Practices of the Warden of the said Prison; and that Mr. *Oglethorpe,* Mr. *Cornwall,* Mr. *Glanville,* and Mr. *Hughes* do prepare and bring in the same.

Ordered, That the Report from the Committee appointed to enquire into the State of the Goals of this Kingdom (this Day made to the House, in relation to the State of the *Fleet* Prison) with the Appendixes, and the Proceedings of the House thereupon, be Printed; and that Mr. *Speaker* do appoint the Printing thereof, and that no Person, but such as he shall appoint, do Presume to Print the same.

FINIS.

A Report from the Committee appointed to Enquire into the State of the Goals of this Kingdom: Relating to the Marshalsea Prison; and farther Relating to the Fleet Prison (1729)

n May 14, 1729, Oglethorpe delivered to the House his report on the state of the Marshalsea. On that same day, the Speaker arranged for its printing.

With the addition of eleven more members, named on March 24, 1729, Oglethorpe had conducted his second prison investigation—that of the Marshalsea. The Marshalsea Prison was in Southwark, fairly close to the London Bridge. Mentioned as early as 1332, it had been attacked by Wat Tyler's rebels in 1381. It became, under Henry VIII, Mary, and Elizabeth, second only to the Tower of London in importance, but thereafter became gradually a debtors prison. The prison had for some time developed a bad reputation. In 1718 it had been described in an anonymous poem entitled *Hell in Epitome*. Petitions read in the House of Commons on May 23, 1715, alleged "That a great Number of miserable Debtors have been starved to Death in the said Prison," and on December 19, 1722, characterized it as "the worst Prison in the Nation; where there is no Allowance but Water; by which Hardship many poor Souls die."[1] On December 12, 1724, five hundred debtors petitioned "That they are so numerous, and so closely confined, that they may occasion an epidemical Distemper to the whole Nation, in case of a hot Summer, they having no Allowance but Water; and many of their fellow Sufferers daily die, for want of a necessary Support."[2]

Members of the augmented committee made their first visit to the

Marshalsea on March 25. "Finding there, among many other miserable Objects, upwards of 30 Persons in immediate Danger of perishing with Sickness and Extremity of Want, they were so moved with Compassion to those unhappy Wretches, that they thought fit, to make a Bountiful Contribution out of their own Pockets, toward their Support; and to give Orders that they should be provided with an Apothecary, Nurses, Food, and all other Necessaries, till further Relief can be obtained."[3] The committee was back at the prison on May 8 and probably made visits before and after this date, but conducted its usual business in the Speaker's Chamber or in a convenient tavern.

On May 14 Oglethorpe presented his report to the House. At the Marshalsea he had encountered not only the same abuses that had prevailed at the Fleet, but conditions that were even worse. Debtors there were daily dying of prison fever and hunger, starving because charity monies had been misappropriated by the warden. They were also being tortured by instruments characteristic of the Spanish Inquisition: sheers, thumb screws, an iron collar, and an iron skull cap. These were soon engraved and reproduced in *The Representation of the several Fetters, Irons and Ingines that were taken from the Marshalsea Prison*, a single sheet folio included in *The Arbitrary Punishments and Cruel Tortures Engraved from the Originals laid before the House of Commons* (London, 1729). Perhaps even worse, some prisoners were confined, as long as a week, with bodies of the dead.

In his report on the Marshalsea, Oglethorpe was highly critical of the Court of Record of the King's Palace of Westminster, which had control over the prison.[4] He indicted that court, first, for permitting debtors to be incarcerated for debts of sometimes no more than a shilling, in spite of a recent act of Parliament against frivolous and vexatious arrests. Next, he rebuked the court for accepting gifts from the prison officials whose appointments they approved and for selling the offices of the court. "As the present Inquiry is not into the Nature and Practice of this Court, (the Abuses of which well deserve a particular Inquiry)," Oglethorpe remarked impertinently, "The Committee do not enlarge upon the ill consequences of such corrupt Sales, but. . . ."

The report closed with the recommendation that the wardens John Darby and William Acton should be prosecuted for their crimes. It was adopted *nemine contradicente;* and Acton was subsequently tried for the murders of Thomas Bliss, Captain John Bromfield, Robert Newton, and James Thompson, but was found innocent in each trial. He was accused also of the murder of William Crane, but the grand jury did not bring charges.[5]

But even while the main committee was investigating the Marshalsea and small subcommittees were working on bills to disable Bambridge from ever again holding office at the Fleet and to improve conditions there, the committee continued its investigation of the Fleet; and its report on the Marshalsea embodied a considerable supplemental report on the Fleet, a good deal of it concerning Sir William Rich.

My text is the separate report of 1729.

A REPORT FROM THE COMMITTEE APPOINTED TO ENQUIRE

Into the State of the GOALS of
this Kingdom:

Relating to the MARSHALSEA *Prison; And farther Relating to the* FLEET *Prison.*

WITH THE

Resolution of the HOUSE *of* COMMONS *thereupon.*

[Printer's ornament]

LONDON:
Printed for *Robert Knaplock, Jacob Tonson, John Pemberton,*
and *Richard Williamson.* MDCCXXIX.

Mercurii 14 *die Maii,* 1729.

BY Vertue of an Order of the HOUSE of COMMONS, this Day made, I do appoint *Robert Knaplock, Jacob Tonson, John Pemberton,* and *Richard Williamson,* to Print this *Report;* And that no other Person presume to Print the same.

AR. ONSLOW, Speaker.

A
REPORT
FROM THE
COMMITTEE

Appointed to enquire into the State of the GOALS *of this Kingdom.*

Mercurii 14 *die Maii,* 1729.

MR. *Oglethorpe,* from the Committee appointed to enquire into the State of the Goals of this Kingdom, made a Report of some Progress which the Committee had made in their Enquiry into the State of the Prison of the *Court of Marshalsea,* and of the *King's Palace Court of Westminster;* AND ALSO of a further Progress which the Committee had made in their Enquiry into the State of the *Fleet Prison;* with the Resolutions of the Committee thereupon; and he read the Report in his Place, and afterwards delivered the same (with the Appendixes) in at the Table, where the Report was read, and is as follows, *viz.*

The COMMITTEE *having, in pursuance of the Order of this House (of the Twenty Fifth Day of* February, 1728) *to enquire into the State of the Goals of this Kingdom, Adjourned to Prison of the Court of the* Marshalsea *and of the* King's Palace Court *of* Westminster, *and at several Times examined into the State of that Prison, have made some Progress therein, which they have thought fit to lay before the House.*

IT appeared to the Committee, That the Prison of the *Marshalsea* doth belong to the Court of the *Marshalsea* of the King's Household and to the Court of Record of the King's Palace of *Westminster:* And that the Person who hath the Care of the Prison and Custody of the *Marshalsea,* is styled Deputy Marshal of the *Marshalsea* of the King's Household and Keeper of the Prison of the same Court, and of the Prison of the Court of Record of the King's Palace of *Westminster,* and is appointed by the Knight Marshal for the time being.

That Sir *Philip Meadows,*[6] then Knight Marshal of the King's Household, did by Deed Poll, given under his Hand and Seal the 25th of *November* 1720, constitute *John Darby* Gent. Deputy Marshal of the *Marshalsea* of the

King's Household, and Keeper of the Prisons aforesaid, during the term of his natural Life.

And the said Knight Marshal by Articles of Agreement indented bearing even Date with the said last mentioned Deed Poll, declares the Conditions under which the said *John Darby* is to enjoy the said Offices, and among others, that if the said *John Darby*, without the Knight Marshal's Consent in Writing, shall at any Time let to Farm the said Offices, or any of the Fees, Profits, Advantages, or Benefits thereof, the said Grant shall cease, determine, and be void.

That *John Darby*, contrary to the said Conditions, hath let the Profits of the said Offices without Consent of the said Knight Marshal, and by Indenture of Lease bearing Date the 21st Day of *March* 1727, did grant and to Farm let to *William Acton* Butcher the *Marshalsea-Prison* for 140*l.* per Annum,[7] and by the same Lease did let the Benefit of the Lodging of the Prisoners, and other Advantages, for the further Yearly Rent of 260*l.* to be paid to him clear of all Taxes, for the Term of Seven Years.

That to make the Profits of the Prison arise to answer the said exorbitant Rents, no kind of Artifice or Oppression hath been unpractised.

It appears upon the Examination of many Witnesses, that on the Entry of Prisoners into the said Prison, Money has been extorted from them for obtaining the Liberty of going to the Masters Side, tho' the said *Darby* himself acknowledged he had no Right to any Fees till the Prisoner was discharged; and in order to create a greater Profit by vending Liquors and Food, the Servants of the Keeper have obstructed the bringing in necessary Liquors and Provisions, contrary to the express Words of the Act of Parliament of the Twenty-Second and Twenty-Third Year of King *Charles* II.[8] And have often, under the pretence of searching for Liquors, treated very rudely and indecently Women who came to Relieve and Support their Husbands labouring under the Hardships and Necessities of the Goal: And they raise the Price of Liquors, and other Necessaries, insomuch that the necessitous Prisoner is obliged to pay Three-pence *per* Quart for worse Beer than he can buy out of the Prison for Two-pence Half-penny; and they have also encouraged a Practice among the Prisoners, of forcing those newly Committed to pay Garnish, and of levying Fines upon each other under frivolous Pretences, the Money arising from which is to be spent at the Tap-House, so that he who is most active in exacting it is favoured as the greatest Friend to the House. This method of levying Garnish-Money and Fines is so publickly allowed, that there are Tables hung up in each Room of the stated Garnish Fees, some of which amount to 7*s.* 6*d.* some to more; and if the unhappy Wretch (which is the general Case) hath not Money to pay them, the Prisoners strip him in a Riotous manner, which in their Cant Phrase they call, *Letting the black Dog walk.*[9]

This shews the Inconveniency of the Keepers having the Advantage of the Tap-House, since to advance the Rent thereof, and to consume the Liquors there vended, they not only encourage Riot and Drunkenness, but also prevent the Needy Prisoner from being supplyed by his Friends with the meer Necessaries of Life, in order to encrease an exorbitant Gain to their Tenants.

And these Extortions, tho' small in the Particulars, are very heavy upon the unhappy Prisoners, many of whom are so poor as to be committed for a Debt of One Shilling only; for by the Usage of the said Court of Record, Processes are issued for the smallest Sums; and tho' the Cause of Action is but One Penny, a Process is issued, the Process is returned, and the Proceedings are carry'd on, till such time as the Costs amount to above 40*s*. and thereupon the Debtor is thrown into Prison, and by adding the Costs to the Debt the late Act of Parliament against frivolous and vexatious Arrests is eluded;[10] nor is it probable, that he can be from thence Released, for if he was incapable before to pay the Cause of Action, he must be much more so, when the Costs are added thereto; and if his Creditor then relents, he is detained for the Goaler's Fees and Costs of Suit, infinitely greater than the Original Debt.

It appeared to the Committee that there was no List of Fees publickly hung up in any part of the Prison, tho' required by Law; as to which the said *John Darby* being Examined, he acknowledged that no such List of late had been hung up, but he delivered to the Committee a Paper which he informed them was a Schedule of Fees established by the Judges of the Court of the King's Palace of *Westminster* the 17th of *December* 1675, hereunto annexed in the first Appendix marked with the Letter (*A.*) which Fees seem very exorbitant, in regard there are different Fees paid by the same Prisoner to the same Officer, and the whole amounts to more than is proportionable to the Smallness of the Sums for which Processes are issued out of that Court.

Upon Inspection of the several Parts of the said Goal, the Committee find that the said Goal is divided into two Divisions, *viz.* the Master's Side, and the Common Side, and that a part thereof is only fenced in with a few weak old Boards; That there are several Rooms on the Master's Side kept empty, some with but one or two Persons in them, and others at the same time crowded to that degree as even to make them unhealthy; particularly in one of the Rooms in a part of the Prison called the *Oake*, nine Men are laid in three Beds, and each Man pays 2s. 6d. per Week, so that Room singly produces 1l. 2s. 6d. per Week: But a more particular Account of the Numbers of Prisoners in each Room, and of the Sums they are to pay for Chamber Rent, will appear by the annexed Appendix (B.)

It appeared to the Committee that the Goaler of the said Prison, out of a view of Gain, hath frequently refused to remove Sick Persons, upon Complaint of those who lay in the same Bed with 'em; a particular Instance of which follows.

Mrs. *Mary Trapps* was Prisoner in the *Marshalsea*, and was put to lie in the same Bed with two other Women, each of which paid 2s. 6d. per Week Chamber Rent; she fell ill, and Languish'd for a considerable Time, and the last three Weeks grew so Offensive, that the others were hardly able to bear the Room; they frequently complained to the Turnkeys, and Officers, and desired to be removed, but all in vain; at last she smelt so strong that the Turnkey himself could not bear to come into the Room to hear the Complaints of her Bed-fellows, and they were forced to lie with her, or on the Boards, till she died.

And the Committee inspecting the various parts of the Goal, saw a Prisoner who kept his Bed with a Fistula, and two other Persons obliged to lie with him in the same Bed, tho' each paid 2s. 6d. per Week, yet they even submitted to such Rent and Usage rather than be turned down to the Common Side.

The Common Side is inclosed with a strong Brick Wall, in it are now Confined upwards of 330 Prisoners, most of them in the utmost Necessity; they are divided into particular Rooms called Wards, and the Prisoners belonging to each Ward are lock'd up in their respective Wards every Night, most of which are excessively Crowded, Thirty, Forty nay Fifty Persons having been locked up in some of them not Sixteen Foot Square; and at the same time that these Rooms have been so crowded, to the great endangering the Healths of the Prisoners, the largest Room in the Common Side hath been kept empty, and the Room over *George's Ward* was let out to a Taylor to work in, and no Body allowed to lye in it, tho' all the last Year there were sometimes Forty, and never less than Thirty Two Persons locked up in *George's Ward* every Night, which is a Room of Sixteen by Fourteen Feet, and about Eight Feet high; the Surface of the Room is not sufficient to contain that Number, when laid down, so that one half are hung up in Hammocks, whilst the other lie on the Floor under them; the Air is so wasted by the Number of Persons, who breathe in that narrow

Compass, that it is not sufficient to keep them from stifling, several having in the Heat of Summer perished for want of Air. Every Night at Eight of the Clock in the Winter, and Nine in the Summer, the Prisoners are locked up in their respective Wards, and from those Hours until Eight of the Clock in the Morning in the Winter, and Five in the Summer, they cannot upon any Occasion come out, so that they are forced to ease Nature within the Room, the Stench of which is noisome beyond Expression, and it seems surprising that it hath not caused a Contagion.

The crowding of Prisoners together in this manner is one great Occasion of the Goal Distemper; and tho' the unhappy Men should escape Infection, or overcome it, yet if they have not Relief from their Friends, Famine destroys them. All the Support such poor Wretches have to subsist on, is an accidental allowance of Pease given once a Week by a Gentleman, who conceals his Name, and about Thirty Pounds of Beef provided by the voluntary Contribution of the Judge and Officers of the *Marshalsea*, on *Monday, Wednesday* and *Friday*, which is divided into very small Portions of about an Ounce and an half, distributed with one fourth Part of an half penny Loaf; each of the Sick is first served with one of those Portions, and those that remain are divided amongst the Wards; but the Numbers of the People in them are so great, that it comes to the turn of each Man but about once in fourteen Days, and of each Woman, they being fewer, once in a Week.

When the miserable Wretch hath worn out the Charity of his Friends, and consumed the Money which he hath raised upon his Cloaths and Bedding, and hath eat his last Allowance of Provisions, he usually in a few Days grows weak for want of Food, with the Symptoms of a *Hectick Fever*; and when he is no longer able to stand, if he can raise 3 *d.* to pay the Fee of the common Nurse of the Prison, he obtains the Liberty of being carried into the Sick Ward, and lingers on for about a Month or two, by the assistance of the abovementioned Prison Portion of Provision, and then dies.

The Committee saw in the Women's Sick Ward many miserable Objects lying without Beds on the Floor, perishing with extream Want.

And in the Men's Sick-Ward yet much worse; for along the Side of the Walls of that Ward, Boards were laid upon Trestles like a Dresser in a Kitchen, and under them between those Trestles, were laid on the Floor one Tire of sick Men, and upon the Dresser another Tire, and over them hung a Third Tire in Hammocks.

On the giving Food to these poor Wretches (tho' it was done with the utmost Caution, they being only allowed at first the smallest Quantities, and that of liquid Nourishment) one died. The Vessels of his Stomach were so disordered and contracted for want of Use, that they were totally incapable of performing their Office, and the unhappy Creature perished about the time of Digestion. Upon his Body a Coroner's Inquest sate (a thing which tho' required by Law to be always done, hath for many Years been scandalously omitted in this Goal) and the Jury found that he died of Want.

Those who were not so far gone, on proper Nourishment given them recovered, so that not above Nine have died since the 25th of *March* last, the Day the Committee first met there; tho' before, a Day seldom passed without a Death, and upon the advancing of the Spring, not less than Eight or Ten usually died every 24 Hours.

The great Numbers who appeared to have perished for Want, induced the Committee to inquire what Charities were given for the Subsistance of the Prisoners in this Goal. They have as yet been only able to come at full Proof of 10 *l. per Annum*, left by Sir *Thomas Gresham*,[11] and One Pound *per Annum* paid by each County in *England*, commonly called Exhibition Money; but have Reason to believe there are many other Sums which the shortness of the Time prevented the Committee from being able fully to discover.

All the Charities belonging to the Prison were formerly received by a Steward chose by the Prisoners on the Common Side, and the said Prisoners had a Common Seal belonging to them, kept by their said Steward, and they were divided into Six Wards, each of which chose monthly a Constable, and the said Constables signing a Receipt, and sealing it with the said Common Seal, was a full Discharge to the Persons paying the Charities.

In 1722, *Matthew Pugh* was chosen Steward by the Prisoners, and at their Request approved by Sir *John Bennet*,[12] then Judge of the *Marshalsea* Court; *Pugh* discover'd several Charities which had been before concealed, and applied them to the Use of the Prisoners; and in 1725, he acquainted the then Constables, that *John Darby* and his Servants in the Lodge, had got Possession of the old Common Seal, and that *Edward Gilbourne*, Deputy Prothonotary of the said Court, had the Possession of another Seal with the same Impression, which he had reason to believe was made use of to affix to Receipts for Charity-Money, (to the great Fraud and Oppression of the poor Prisoners) upon which the said Constables agreed to be at the Expence of making a New Seal with this Addition, *MARSHALSEA PRISON* 1725, and they also bought a Chest with Seven different Locks and Keys, so that the Chest could not be opened without all the said seven Keys, one of which was lodged in the Hands of each Constable, and the seventh in the Hands of the Steward, and they fixed the Chest to the Wall in the Ward called the *Constable's Ward*, and locked up the Seal therein, and whenever any Receipt was to be sealed, the Six Constables and the Steward were all concurring, and the Money so received was publickly known and divided.

But this publick and just Manner of receiving and distributing the Charities was disliked by the Keeper and his Servants, and they complained to the Judge of the *Palace Court*, and gave Information that the said *Pugh* was a very turbulent Fellow, and procured a Rule, a Copy of which is hereunto annexed in the Appendix marked (*C*), by which it is ordered that *Matthew Pugh* shall be no longer permitted to have access to the said Prison or Court, and the Prisoners are allowed to chuse another Steward; and accordingly *John Grace*,[13] then Clerk to the Keeper, was chosen Steward by those in the Keeper's Interest. But the Constables in behalf of the Prisoners refus'd to deliver up the Keys of the Chest where their Seal was, insisting, that all Receipts should be sealed as usual in a Publick manner, that they might know what Money was received, and thereupon the said Chest was broke down and carried away by the said *William Acton* and the said *John Grace*.

The said *William Acton* in his Defence against this Charge did not deny this Fact, but said he did it by Order of the Court; and being required to produce such Order, he said it was a verbal Order, given him by the said *Edward Gilbourne*. And the said *Edward Gilbourne* being examined in the Presence of the said *William Acton*, denied that he gave any such Order.

This Transaction was about the Time the Act for Relief of Insolvent Debtors in 1725 took place;[14] and the Old Prisoners, who knew this Affair, being discharged by that Act, those who were newly committed, being ignorant of their Rights to Charities, were defrauded thereof under this abuse.

After the Time of taking by Violence Possession of the Prisoners Seal, as before mentioned, the said Seal was used in the *Lodge*, without the Privity or Consent of the Prisoners, and was affixed to Receipts for Legacies and Charities, which the said *Gilbourne* receiv'd, and disposed of as he pleased, in a very irregular and arbitrary Manner, until Complaint thereof was made to Sir *John Darnall*, Judge of the Court;[15] and then what was afterwards paid for the Prisoners was distributed regularly, but no Account was given to the Prisoners by *Gilbourne* of the Moneys he received.

Till the turning out of *Pugh*, and the violent breaking open the Prisoners said Chest, the Steward used to distribute the Charity Money among the Prisoners equally and indifferently without Favour or Affection, and accounted regularly to the Prisoners, and never received any Money without their Privity and Orders; but since the said Violence, nothing hath been regularly done in respect of the Charities; sometimes the said *Edward Gilbourne*, at other times the said *John Grace*, distributed them as they thought fit; and since the said *William Acton*, Butcher, hath rented the said Goal, there has been no Steward, nor any Account given of the said Charities, he having taken upon himself to act as Steward without the Choice or Consent of the Prisoners: And upon his Examination, he confessed, that from *May* 1728, to *May* 1729, he had received Charity Money for the poor Prisoners, amounting to above 115 *l.* of which he had kept no Account, and took no Notice thereof till this Committee was appointed to Enquire into the State of the Goals, not expecting to have been asked about it. He pretended he had distributed the Money among the Prisoners directly, but produced no sort of Vouchers for it.

The present extreme Want and Necessity of the Prisoners in the said Goal proceeds from the Charities being grossly perverted, and not laid out in proper Provisions, and divided into proper Portions. For if 115 *l.* a Year, which *Acton* himself acknowledges he had received, had been laid out in Bread only, it would have afforded each Prisoner two Pounds of Bread *per* Week, (supposing the Prisoners on the Common Side to have amounted, one Time with another, to Three Hundred) which Pittance, tho' very small, would have prevented the Starving to Death many miserable Wretches, who have perished in the said Goal with meer Hunger.

The Committee have Reason to believe That the Charities given by well-disposed Persons unknown have been sufficient for the Support and Maintenance of the poor Prisoners in this Goal: But the Modesty of the Donors concealing their Alms, This too great Fear of Ostentation hath enabled the Goaler and his Miscreants at the *Lodge* to pervert the Charity-Moneys, and defraud the poor miserable Prisoners thereof.

The Committee have discovered some private Charities, (*notwithstanding the Industry of the Donors to conceal them*) particularly that of *His Grace the Duke of Dorset*, the present Lord Steward of the Household,[16] who raised a Fund of Charity upon the Destruction of that pernicious Practice of Selling Offices.

The Custom of this Court formerly was to sell all the Places belonging thereto, and the very Council and Attorneys purchased the Liberty of

Pleading and Practising in this Court; for which the first gave as far as 1000 *l.* the latter as far as 1500 *l.* each. One Moiety of which Sums was for the Benefit of the Lord Steward, and the other Moiety for the Knight Marshal.

As the present Inquiry is not into the Nature and Practice of this Court, (*the Abuses of which well deserve a particular Inquiry*) The Committee do not enlarge upon the ill Consequences of such corrupt Sales, but cannot forbear to observe, that the first who stemmed this Tide of Corruption was His Grace the Duke of *Argyle*,[17] then Lord Steward, who disdaining to share the Spoils of the Unfortunate, scorned to take any Money arising from the Sale of Offices, and made an Excellent Precedent (*very much disliked by the Practising Part of the Court*) that of *appointing Officers for their Merit, not for their Money*: Upon the Death of Sir *John Bennet*, His Grace, without Fee or Reward, appointed Sir *John Darnall* Judge of the Court, and followed the same Method in disposing of the other Offices of the Court.

The Duke of *Dorset* (now Lord Steward) was very much importuned by the Officers of the Court to permit the Practice of Selling as formerly, but being resolved not to give way to it, yet willing to be eased of their Importunity, He let them know, that he would sell the Place of one of the Council, then vacant; the Sum he sold it for was One hundred Pounds only, to *George Ballard*, Esq; which His Grace ordered to be applied to discharge poor Prisoners, and at the same time expressly directed Mr. *Ballard* to give no other Money to any Person whatsoever.

The aforementioned *Edw. Gilbourne*, Deputy Prothonotary, received the said Money, and was two Years in disposing of it, discharging such only as he himself thought proper.

In that Time an *Act for Relief of insolvent Debtors* took place,[18] by Vertue of which many Persons were discharged out of the said Prison, and others were at several times also discharged by private Charities, from Persons unknown; but the Names of those thus released cannot now be discovered, or compared with the List delivered by the said *Gilbourne*, of the Names of the Prisoners which he pretends were discharged by the Duke of *Dorset's* said Charity.

It appeared to the Committee, That the Keepers in the *Lodge* have greatly imposed on the charitable Persons, who without discovering their Names, have released Prisoners by paying their Debts and Fees: These Keepers have a Set of idle Fellows imployed by them as Agents in carrying on their wicked Designs, and whom they indulge in Riot, and in abusing their Fellow-Prisoners, and allow to go out as Messengers. These Persons are voluntary Prisoners, and in the List given in by *John Darby*, he acknowledged 20 who choose rather to be confined, than at Liberty. These the Keepers generally produce, as proper Objects of Charity, when pious Persons unknown come to discharge poor Prisoners in Secret, and their pretended Debts and Fees being paid, as such Objects, They, in Form, go out of the Prison, but in *a little Time* return back again to the same wicked Practice, to the scandalous Abuse of such Pious and Excellent Charities, and to the great Fraud and Oppression of the Miserable, for whom they were intended.

The Abuse of the Begging-Box is another great Imposition.

The Prisoners have all along had a Right to nominate Persons to go about with Begging-Baskets and Boxes, and to give them Deputations under their Hands and their Common Seal, to make such Collections; but since that Seal has been violently taken away, and kept in the *Lodge* as aforesaid, these Deputations are countersigned and sealed by the Deputy-Marshal, or some of his Agents or Servants; and the Prisoners have been forced to submit to give to such Persons, for their Pains, all the Moneys collected by them, provided they bring in two Baskets only of broken Victuals *per* Week, or, in Lieu thereof, pay two Shillings; and even this disadvantageous Agreement is not complied with, for the Prisoners are Months together with hearing any thing at all of their Basket-Men.

So that the good and charitable Intentions of Mankind are wickedly perverted, and rendered useless, and of no Avail to the poor Prisoners, who can neither come out to be relieved, nor can Those who come to relieve, have easy Access to such poor Wretches, nor distinguish the Impostors from the Unfortunate.

The only effectual Way to distribute such Charity rightly seems to be, to see some Prisoner of each *Ward*, who is not in the Keeper's Interest, and from such Prisoner to know the most Necessitous.

The abovementioned Practice of Farming and Defrauding the Begging-Box, is not peculiar to this Prison of the *Marshalsea* only. The poor Prisoners in the *Fleet-Prison* are abused in the same Manner.

In this Prison of the *Marshalsea*, Pyrates are kept as well as Debtors; and the first, who are generally a very desperate and abandoned Sort of People, are suffered to mix with all the unhappy Debtors of the Common Side: which may be of dangerous Consequence, for this being a Prison for the poorer Sort, in which great Numbers of poor Sailors are commonly confined, the Conversation of these Pyrates, and their Boasts how riotously they lived whilst at Sea, may instil Inclinations of following the same wicked Practices: This Correspondence with these desperate People hath already had some Influence upon the poor Debtors, and was in part the Occasion of several of them attempting to escape, to which Hunger and extreme Want being added, some of them became so desperate, that after having fasted four Days, and seeing no Hope of Relief, they attempted to break thro' the Prison Wall, and were taken in the Attempt.

This gave the Gaolers a Pretence to exercise their greater Cruelties; All the Persons so attempting to escape, were called into the *Lodge* by the said *Acton*, one by one, and there examined. One of them was seen to go in perfectly well, and when he came out again, he was in the greatest Disorder, his Thumbs were much swoln and very sore, and he declared, that the Occasion of his being in that Condition, was that the Keeper, in Order to extort from him a Confession of the Names of those, who had assisted him and others in their Attempt to escape, had screwed certain Instruments of Iron upon his Thumbs so close, that they had forced the Blood out of them, with exquisite Pain; after this he was carryed into the Strong Room, where besides the other Irons which he had on, they fixed on his Neck and Hands an Iron Instrument, called a *Collar*, (like a pair of Tongs) and he being a large lusty Man, when they screwed the said Instrument close, his Eyes were ready to start out of his Head, the Blood gushed out of his Ears and Nose, he foamed at the Mouth, the Slaber run down, and he made several Motions to speak, but could not; after these Tortures, he was confined in the Strong Room for many Days with a very heavy pair of Irons, called *Sheers*, on his Legs.

It has been usual in this Prison for the Keepers unlawfully to assume to themselves a pretended Authority of Magistrates, and not only to judge and decree Punishments arbitrarily, but also to execute the same unmercifully: Numberless are the Instances of their immoderate Beating poor Debtors at their pleasure; insomuch that the very Name of the *Instrument* hung up in the *Lodge*, for beating the Prisoners, became a Terrour to them.

The various Tortures and Cruelties before mentioned not contenting these wicked Keepers in their said pretended Magistracy over the Prisoners, they found a Way of making within this Prison a Confinement more dreadful than the Strong Room itself, by coupling the Living with the Dead; and have made a Practice of Locking up Debtors, who displeased them, in the Yard with Humane Carcasses. One particular Instance of this Sort of Inhumanity was, of a Person whom the Keepers confined in that Part of the lower Yard which was then separated from the rest, whilst there were there two dead Bodies which had lain there Four Days; yet was He kept there with them Six Days longer, in which Time the Vermin devoured the Flesh from the Faces, eat the Eyes out of the Heads of the Carcasses, which were bloated, putrifyed, and turned green, during the poor Debtor's dismal Confinement with them.

The great Business depending in the House of Commons having often required the long Attendance of the Members of this Committee, the Committee have not been able to go thro' the Examinations which they had entered into, upon the various Complaints laid before them, of cruel Beating, Ironing, Torturing, and Murdering Debtors, too shocking and too numerous to be thoroughly examined in so short a Time, as the Remainder of this Session of Parliament allows.

One cruel and barbarous Instance, among others, which appeared to the Committee, they cannot omit, *viz.*

In the Year 1726, *Thomas Bliss*, a Carpenter,[19] not having any Friends to support him, was almost starved to Death in the Prison, upon which he attempted to get over the Prison by a Rope, lent him by another Prisoner: In the Attempt he was taken by the Keepers, dragged by the Heels into the *Lodge*, barbarously beaten, and put into Irons, in which he was kept several Weeks. One Afternoon, as he was quietly standing in the Yard with his Irons on, some of the said *Acton*'s Men called him into the *Lodge*, where *Acton* was then drinking and merry with Company; in about Half an Hour *Bliss* came out again, crying, and gave an Account, That when he was in the *Lodge*, they, for their Diversion (as they called it) fixed on his Head an Iron Engine, or Instrument (which appears to be an Iron Scull-Cap) which was screwed so close that it forced the Blood out of his Ears and Nose: And he further declared, That his Thumbs were at the same time put into a pair of Thumb-Screws, which were screwed so tight that the Blood started out of them; and from that time he continued disorder'd to the Day of his Death. He was let out of the Prison without paying his Debt, and at his going out *Acton* desired, *That all that was past might be forgot, and that he would not bear him any Ill Will.* This miserable Wretch was put into St. *Thomas*'s Hospital for Help, but dyed very soon.

The Committee observe;

That tho' in this Prison there are many Rooms entirely empty, yet in other Rooms the Prisoners are crowded together, to the utter Destruction of their Healths, and the endangering a General Infection.

That notwithstanding Thirty and Forty Prisoners were locked up together in one Room, yet the said *John Darby* (the Keeper) did certify to the Committee, That the said Prison of the *Marshalsea* was sufficient commodiously to contain the Number of Prisoners thereto committed.

That the Charities have not been accounted for, but have been scandalously perverted, while great Numbers have perish'd in the Prison thro' meer Want.

That many Prisoners have died daily in the said Prison, as well those in Execution as others, and no Coroner's Inquest hath sat upon their Bodies.

The said *William Acton* being examined, at first denied, but after being confronted with several Witnesses, acknowledged, that he had had Thumb-Screws in his Possession, and pretended he had given them to the Gaoler at *York*. He positively denied the having any Iron Instrument or Cap for the Head, and yet afterwards directed the Turnkeys where to find the Iron Scull-Cap before mentioned, and it was produced to the Committee.

The Committee also found several very heavy Iron Bars, Shackles, Fetters and Handcuffs for the miserable Prisoners in the said *Marshalsea* Prison.

The unwarrantable letting to Farm the Benefit of Keeping these Prisoners hath unjustifiably increased the Profits of the Prison, to the greater Oppression of the Prisoners: The said *William Acton* (to whom the Profits of the said Prison are Lett by the said *John Darby*) hath, in this First Year of his Farming the same, invented new oppressive Methods to make his Profits double those of the preceding Year.

If the Gaolers are not punished for these their wicked Devices, and due Care be not taken to prevent the like barbarous Practices for the future, the poor Prisoners, who may happen to survive these Cruelties, must be more miserable than can be expressed.

The Committee apprehending the Conclusion of this Session to be now so near as to prevent their proceeding to farther Enquiries, have thought it their Duty, at this time, to lay a State of these Facts before the House, hoping some Effectual Provision will be made, in the next Session of Parliament, for remedying the great Grievances before mentioned; for better Regulation of Goals; and for inflicting proper Punishments upon Goalers for Cruelties to their Prisoners.

And the Committee have come to the following Resolutions, *viz.*

Resolved, That it appears to this Committee, That *William Acton*, Clerk of the Prison of the *Marshalsea*, and Farmer of the same Goal,[20] and the Profits thereof, by Lease from Mr. *John Darby*, the Keeper of the said

Prison, hath been guilty of many High Crimes and Misdemeanours in the Execution of his Office; and hath arbitrarily and unlawfully loaded with Irons, Tortured and Destroyed, in the most Inhumane, Cruel, and Barbarous Manner, Prisoners for Debt under his Care, in high Violation and Contempt of the Laws of this Kingdom.

Resolved, That it appears to this Committee, That the Charities given by well-disposed Persons for the Relief and Sustenance of the poor Debtors, confined in the said Prison of the *Marshalsea*, are notoriously and scandalously misapplyed; and that the Keeper of the said Prison, and his Dependants and Agents, instead of distributing the said Charities to the said poor Debtors, have most unjustifiably possessed themselves thereof, and wickedly perverted the same to their own Uses, to the great Fraud and Oppression of the said poor Prisoners in general, and to the Starving many, who have perished in the said Prison for want thereof.

Resolved, That it is the Opinion of this Committee, That Mr. *John Darby*, Keeper of the said Prison of the *Marshalsea*, having contrary to, and in Defiance of the Law, Let to Farm his said Goal and Office, and the Profits thereof, unto the said *William Acton*; and having grosly neglected his Duty in not preventing or remedying the said Inhumanities, Cruelties, Frauds, and Abuses, is guilty of a High Misdemeanour in his Office, and a notorious Breach of his Trust, in Contempt of the Law, and to the great Oppression and Ruin of many of His Majesty's Subjects.

APPENDIX (*A.*)

A SCHEDULE *of such Fees as are Appointed and Established by the Judges of the Court of the* King's Palace *of* Westminister, *the* 17*th Day of* December 1675, Annoque RR. Car. 2^{di}27°, *to be from henceforth Taken and Received by the Keeper of the Prison belonging to the said Court, as followeth*, viz.

	l.	*s.*	*d.*
FOR the Knight Marshal's Fee upon the discharging of every Prisoner for the first Action only	0	1	8
For the Knight Marshal's Deputy upon the like Discharge,	0	0	3
For the Prothonotary upon the like Discharge	0	1	5

For his own Fee for his Care and safe Custody of every Prisoner, to be taken upon the Discharge of every such Prisoner for the first Action	0	4	8
For his Porter upon the like Discharge	0	1	6
For his own Fee upon every Discharge of such Prisoner for the Second Action	0	3	8
For his Porter upon the like Discharge	0	1	4
For his Clerk for entering the Charge against every Action, except that upon which he is first brought into Custody	0	1	0
For his said Clerk for entring every Discharge of a Prisoner for every Action	0	1	0

Edmond Wyndham.
Ja. Butler.

APPENDIX (B.)

An ACCOUNT of the Number of the Prisoners now lying for Debt in the MARSHALSEA PRISON, and of the *Chamber Rent.*

The *Master-side* is divided into five Parts, viz.			Number of Beds in each Room.	Number of Persons lying in each Room.	What each Prisoner pays per Week for his Lodging.	Total paid per Week.	Total paid per Annum.
	The *Horsepond*	3 Rooms					
	The *Oake*	8 Ditto					
	The *Nursery*	5 Ditto					
	The *Park*	11 Ditto					
	The *Long Gal.*	6 Ditto					
					s. d.	l. s. d.	l. s. d.
In the Horsepond Floor.							
In the first Room are two Persons			1	2	2 6	5 0	
In the Second Ditto one Man			1	1	2 6	2 6	
The Third is the Turnkeys							
Adjoyning is a Gallery consisting of 4 empty Rooms							
In the Chamberlain's House are 5 empty Rooms							
In the Oake Ground Floor.							
A small Coffee Room rented by a Woman at					2 6	0 2 6	
First Room has			2	3 Women	2 6 each	0 7 6	
Second Ditto			2	3 Ditto	2 6 Ditto	0 7 6	

REPORT RELATING TO MARSHALSEA PRISON

The *Master-side* is divided into five Parts, *viz.*		Number of Beds in each Room.	Number of Persons lying in each Room.	What each Prisoner pays *per* Week for his Lodging.	Total paid *per* Week.	Total paid *per Annum.*
	The *Horsepond* 3 Rooms					
	The *Oake* 8 Ditto					
	The *Nursery* 5 Ditto					
	The *Park* 11 Ditto					
	The *Long Gal.* 6 Ditto					
One pair of Stairs.						
A Room and Closet		2	2 Ditto	2 6 Ditto	0 5 0	
First Room		3	9 Men	2 6 Ditto	1 2 6	
Second Ditto		1	2 Ditto	1	0 2 0	
Third Ditto		2	6 Ditto	2 6 each	0 15 0	
Fourth Ditto		3	7 Ditto	2 6 Ditto	0 17 6	
Here is also a large Chamber let out for 3 Prisoners to work in at				1 0 Ditto	0 3 0	
In the Nursery.						
The Ground Floor is a Chandlers Room rented, at				6 0	0 6 0	
One pair of Stairs.						
First Room		1	2 Ditto	2 6 each	0 5 0	
Second Ditto		2	5 Ditto	2 6 Ditto	0 12 6	
Two pair of Stairs.						
First Ditto		1	3 Ditto	2 6 Ditto	0 7 6	
Second Ditto		2	6 Ditto	2 6 Ditto	0 15 0	
In The Park are two Stair Cases.						
In the first Stair Case are 5 Rooms.						
Ground Floor.						
One Room		1	2 Ditto	2 6 Ditto	0 5 0	
One pair of Stairs.						
First Room		1	1 Ditto	5 0	0 5 0	
Second Ditto		1	1 Ditto	5 0	0 5 0	
Two pair of Stairs.						
First Ditto		1	3 Ditto	2 6 each	0 7 6	
Second Ditto		1	3 Ditto	2 6 Ditto	0 7 6	
In the Second Stair Case are Six Rooms.						
Ground Floor						
First Room		1	3 Ditto	2 6 Ditto	0 7 6	
Second Ditto		1	3 Ditto	2 6 Ditto	0 7 6	
One pair of Stairs.						
First Ditto		1	2 Ditto	2 6 Ditto	0 5 0	
Second Ditto		3	7 Ditto	2 6 Ditto	0 17 6	
Two pair of Stairs.						
First Ditto		1	2 Ditto	2 6 Ditto	0 5 0	
Second Ditto		1	2 Ditto	2 6 Ditto	0 5 0	
In the Long Gallery					0 1 0	

Total paid *per* Week 10 13 6

Fifty two Weeks *per Annum* Amounts to 555 2 0

In the Long Gallery are six indifferent Rooms, two of them are taken up by a Prisoner and his Family, and a third by another Prisoner, paying One Shilling *per* Week; but this Building is in a very Ruinous Condition, and unsafe for the Confinement of other Prisoners than such as the Marshal is well assured of, the Walls being very weak, and lying next a Court which communicates with the *Borough* of *Southwark*.

On the Common Side are 3 Stair-Cases and 2 Wards. The first Stair-Case contains 5 Rooms or Wards.	Number of Persons lying in each Room.	Number of Beds or Hammocks in each Room.	What each Prisoner pays per Week for Lodging.	Total *per* Week.	Total *per Annum*.
On the Ground Floor.			*s. d.*	*l. s. d.*	*l. s. d.*
Is George's Ward, containing 32 Men and but 16 Hammocks	32	16			
One pair of Stairs.					
The Petitioning Room containing 13 Women, some lying on Beds, others on the Floor	13				
The Cook pays for a Chamber and Liberty to sell Provision to the Prisoners			4 0		
Two pair of Stairs.					
The Womens Sick Ward, 7 Women in a deplorable Condition	7				
New Room, 15 Women, some lying on Beds, others on the Floor	15				
At the Foot of this Stair-Case is a large empty Room kept (as we are informed) for Workmen, tho' the Wards being so extemely crowded it had been very proper to have placed some Prisoners in it					
The 2d Stair-Case contains 5 Rooms.					
On the Ground Floor.					
The Sick Mens Ward containing 11 miserable Men, in such Beds as they had, being some on the Floor and others on a Bulk over them, crowded in a small compass, in a very Melancholy and Affecting Condition	11				
One pair of Stairs.					
The Prince's Ward	36 Men	14 Ham.			
The Warrant Room for Lodging and Liberty of Working therein	7 Ditto		1 0 each	0 7 0	
Another Room containing two Prisoners having their own Furniture, who pay	2 Ditto		2 6	0 5 0	
Two pair of Stairs.					
The Charity Room, 13 Women with a few Beds on the Floor.	13				

On the Common Side are 3 Stair-Cases and 2 Wards. The first Stair-Case contains 5 Rooms or Wards.	Number of Persons lying in each Room.	Number of Beds or Hammocks in each Room.	What each Prisoner pays per Week for Lodging.	Total *per* Week.	Total *per Annum*.
Between the 2d and 3d Stair-Cases are two Ground Wards.					
First Pump Ward	25 Ditto	17 Ham.			
Second Constables Ward	38 Ditto	20 Ham.			
In the 3d Stair-Case are 5 Wards.					
On the Ground Floor.					
The King's Ward	38 Ditto	13 Ham.			
One pair of Stairs.					
The Duke's Ward	33 Ditto	20 Ham.			
The Queen's Ward	29 Ditto	18 Ham.			
Two pair of Stairs.					
The Dutchess's Ward, few Beds on the Floor	11 Wom.				
The Debtor Womens Ward, Ditto	9 Ditto				

16 0
The Amount of the Common Side   41 12 0
The Amount of the Master Side   555 2 0
Total Amount *per Annum*   596 14 0

APPENDIX (C.)

Palace Court, 30th *July* 1725.

UPON Information given to this Court by the Keeper of the Prison thereof, that one *Matthew Pugh* (who has for some time past received for the Prisoners of the said Prison, the Gifts and Legacies belonging to them) has under that Pretence very often behaved himself very turbulently in the said Prison, frequently occasioning Disturbances amongst the said Prisoners; and because of the impudent Behaviour of the said *Matthew Pugh*, as well in this Court as the Office of the Prothonotary thereof, It is this Day ordered that the said *Matthew Pugh* be no longer permitted to have Access to the Prison of this Court upon the Pretence aforesaid, and that the Prisoners of the said Prison be at Liberty to appoint another Person to receive the Gifts and Legacies belonging to them.

By the Court,
Gilbourne.

FARTHER IN
RELATION
TO THE
FLEET PRISON.

Farther in Relation to the
FLEET PRISON.

THE Dispatch which Your Committee found themselves obliged to give to their former Report (relating to the *Fleet* Prison) prevented their inserting several Facts, which in the Course of their Examination have since come to their Knowledge, in a fuller Light, and which they think proper to lay before the House, by way of Supplement to their said former Report, as followeth, *viz.*

It farther appeared to the Committee, that Mr. *Arne*, mentioned in the said former Report,[21] whilst he was in the Tap-House of the said *Fleet* Prison, during the Wardenship of *John Huggins* Esq; and behaving himself quietly, was suddenly seized by *John Barnes* (Agent for *Huggins*) and without any Reason given, was forced into the Strong Room or Dungeon on the Master's Side, which Dungeon being then but lately built, and so Damp that the Drops hung upon the Walls, was very nauseous and unwholesome. In this Place was this Unfortunate Man locked up, and never once permitted to go out; But by an Accident on a *Sunday*, the Door being opened, he ran into the Parlour adjoining to the Chappel, during the Time of Divine Service; he had then no Covering upon his Body but the Feathers of a Bed (which Bed was thrown in to him by a Prisoner) into which he crept, to defend himself from the Cold, and the Feathers stuck and were clotted upon him, by his own Excrements, and the Dirt which covered his Skin.

He was immediately seized and carried back into the said Dungeon, where thro' the Cold and the Restraint, and for want of Food, he lost his Senses, languished, and perished.

Notwithstanding the miserable Condition of this Man, and the Applications which were made to Mr. *Huggins*, the then Warden, who saw this miserable Object lying naked in the said Dungeon and unable to speak, but lifting up his Eyes to Mr. *Huggins*, the said *Huggins* had no Compassion on him, but caused the Door to be close locked upon him.

Oliver Reed,[22] another Prisoner in the *Fleet* Prison, was loaded with Irons, by the Directions of Mr. *Huggins*, who confessed to the Committee, That he sent for the Fetters and Manacles from *Newgate*, and ordered them to be put on the Hands and Leggs of this Unfortunate Debtor, who in *October* last was put into another Dungeon, (and was continued there till Your

Committee went to view the Goal) where he was forced to lye on a small Bed, with Chains of Forty Pounds Weight, which *even Bambridge* thought too heavy, and applyed to *Huggins* for Lighter. *Reed* had nothing but a thin ragged Blanket to cover his naked Body, in the most piercing Weather of the last hard Winter, and within three Yards of him was a Window trebled Barred, without Glass or Shutter, under which Window was a Heap of the most noisom Offalls to feed the Dogs there Kennelled, and the Place was the more unwholesome because of a Necessary-House in the same Room, the Stench whereof was so intollerable, that Your Committee could not continue in the Room six Minutes to examine this unhappy Person, whose great Sufferings under the Warden's cruel Usage of him, were far greater than Your Committee can express.

It appears also to the Committee, that the said Mr. *Huggins* hath, in Combination with *Richard Bishop* (his Tipstaff)[23] consented to let out several Prisoners, (whom they call by a Cant Name *Pidgeons*) to go into Foreign Parts, as well as into several distant Trading Counties at Home, and furnished them with a Sham Credit to buy Goods, which being consigned to the said *Bishop*, he took out Commissions of Bankruptcy against the Persons so let out of Prison, and fraudently employed as aforesaid, and thereby cheated the Creditors, who dealt with them, of their Goods, to a very considerable Value; And that a Waggon Load of Scarlet Cloth was brought away from the Owner, on such false Credit; but the Owner pursuing it, seized the Cloth as they were unloading it upon *Ludgate-Hill.*

And farther it appears to Your Committee, that during the said Mr. *Huggins*'s Wardenship, several Writs of *Habeas Corpus ad Testificandum* were surreptitiously taken out, by his Direction, to protect Prisoners, who desired to go to any Part of the Kingdom, on Pretence of giving Evidence at some Tryal, or at some Assizes; for which Liberty *Huggins* received large Sums of Money; and even those Writs have had Blanks left in them, to insert a pretended Cause: And to avoid Suspition of such Writs being Collusive, *Huggins* by Letter under his own Hand, and now in the Hands of Your Committee, pretended to caution his Servants not to be concerned in taking out such Writs, and by the said Letter it fully appears that this wicked Practice was for Lucre only, and such Liberty thus given was to Prisoners committed for very large Sums.

Your Committee, notwithstanding their Diligence and Zeal in the Premisses, have not been able to come at a true Account of the Charities given for Relief of the poor Prisoners in the *Fleet* Prison; but Your Committee have no Reason to believe there is in that Particular less Iniquity in the

Wardens Management, than in the other Practices; whereof the following may serve as an Instance.

Lieutenant *Robert Fitz-Simmonds* being discharged by the Plaintiff's Executors, on the 12th of *April* 1728, lay then in Prison for his Fees only, about which Time a Gentleman came to the *Fleet* Prison from an unknown Lady,[24] to discharge all such Prisoners as remained there for Fees only, provided the same exceeded not the Sum of three Guineas each, Or that the Warden would discharge such Prisoners of all Fees and Demands for that Sum; Upon which Mr. *Thomas Bambridge* (then Warden) sent for twelve Prisoners, and gave the said Gentleman a List of their Names, with his full Demands on them severally, which were considerably more than three Guineas each: However, *Bambridge, in Compliance with the Lady's great Charity, and in regard to the poor Prisoners*, consented to accept the Three Guineas for each Prisoner, in full Discharge of all Demands; assuring the said Gentleman, That they should be discharged on that Condition; whereupon he paid *Bambridge*, in the Presence of the said Twelve Prisoners, Thirty Six Guineas for their Discharge: But as soon as the Gentleman's Back was turned, *Bambridge* insisted on all his former Demands to the full, and would not suffer them to go out of Prison till they had given him Notes for what exceeded the Three Guineas.

Mr. *Fitz-Simmonds*, one of these Prisoners, was forced to sign a Note drawn by *Bambridge* himself, payable to *William Pindar* (one of his Accomplices)[25] or Order, for Twenty Seven Pounds Ten Shillings; and the other Eleven of the said Prisoners were forced to do in the same Manner.

It also appears to the Committee, that the first bringing of Soldiers to the *Fleet* Prison, to put in Fear, and to insult the poor Debtors, was in the Time when Mr. *Huggins* was Warden.

In Justice to his Majesty's Revenue, the Committee think it their indispensible Duty to lay before the House one particular Transaction of Mr. *Huggins* with Mr. *Thomas Perrin, of London*, Merchant, Debtor to the Crown in several Bonds to the Amount of 42057 *l.* (wherewith he was charged in the *Fleet* Prison, and was permitted to Escape from thence by Mr. *Huggins*, when Warden.) The Committee having come to a more particular Knowledge of this Affair, by the Papers which the said *Perrin* sent over from *Holland*, to the Treasury here, as his Case, the Committee crave leave to subjoin the same by way of Appendix to this Report; with this Observation, That at the Time when Mr. *Huggins* was examined before the Committee touching this Escape, He acquainted them, That he had got a *Quietus* for the same, in the late King's Reign, and also that the Commissioners of the Customs having put up to Sale *Perrin*'s Security to the Crown, He (*Huggins*) bought in the said Debt of 42057 *l*. for about 2000 *l*.

The Committee think it proper to lay before the House the Case of Sir *William Rich* Bart. a Prisoner for Debt in the *Fleet* Prison, *viz*.[26]

It appeared to the Committee, That Sir *William Rich* removed himself by *Habeas Corpus* from *Newgate* (where he lay for Debt) to the *Fleet* Prison; but instead of being admitted (as he desired) into that Prison, he was carried to and confined at *Corbett*'s Spunging-House for a Fortnight, at very great Expences: And tho' he often applied to be put into the Prison, it was refused, unless he would pay 5*l*. to the Warden, as a Commitment-Fee; and also 10*s*. *per* Week for his Lodgings, which exorbitant Demands he was obliged to comply with, not being able to support and pay the heavier Extortions of the said Spunging-House.

In about Ten Weeks after Sir *William*'s Removal, Mr. *Bambridge* became Deputy-Warden, to whom Sir *William* applyed for a Chamber at a less Rent, which he obtained at 3*s*. 6*d*. *per* Week, on Payment of Four Guineas. After Sir *William* had been in this New Chamber about Three Weeks, *William Pindar* the Chamberlain came to him and demanded the Rent of 3*s*. 6*d*. *per* Week, which was paid; but Sir *William* not being able to pay all the Arrears of the great Rent due for the former Chamber, a Message came from Mr. *Bambridge* that he wanted him in the *Lodge*; but Sir *William* conceiving it was the Part of Mr. *Bambridge* to come to him, if he had Business, answered to that Effect; thereupon *James Barnes, Corbett*, and others, Armed with Pikes and Halberts, required Sir *William* to go and wait upon Mr. *Bambridge*; But *Bambridge* immediately following his said Messengers, met Sir *William* upon the Stairs, seized him by the Collar, and, the rest of *Bambridge*'s Followers assisting, dragged Sir *William* into the *Lodge*, and soon after procured him to be removed by *Habeas Corpus* to the *King's-Bench* Prison, where he remained Twelve Months, and was afterwards brought back to the *Fleet* Prison, by another *Habeas Corpus*, and carried again to *Corbett*'s Spunging-House, in order to extort a farther 5*l*. as a Baronet's Fee, for his Commitment, tho' Sir *William* offered to pay the Fee settled by the *Court of Common-Pleas* of 2*l*. 4*s*. 8*d*.

After Ten Weeks Stay at *Corbett*'s, Sir *William*, late at Night, was ordered into the Prison, and by the Consent of one of the Prisoners, on the Master's Side, went into his Room, where the said Prisoner permitted him to have part of his Bed, and desiring his Stay, said he would raise Money to pay the Warden.

Soon after this, the said *Barnes* came into the Room to turn Sir *William* out by Force; and the Reason being asked, *Barnes* answered, shortly, He would not stand arguing with him, and then put a Red-hot Poker to Sir *William*'s Breast, and swore, *If he did not pay the Money, or go down immediately, he wou'd run the Poker into his Body.*

Then came in Two Men like Ruffians, armed with Muskets, and Bayonets fixed on them, and forcing the Standers-by out of the Room, *Barnes* run at Sir *William* with the said Red-hot Poker, which Sir *William* having the good Luck to put by, *Barnes*, on that Disappointment, ordered the said Ruffians to Fire on him; but being told by another, That if they killed him they would be hanged, they desisted to Fire; and *Barnes* being afterwards put out of the Room by some of the Prisoners who came to protect Sir *William* from the said Danger, Sir *William* went quietly down into the Ward on the Common-Side, called *Julius Caesar*'s Ward; and the next Morning intending to go again to the Master's Side, and being opposed by a Centinel placed by *Bambridge*, he returned, and went into a Room on the Common-Side, and staid by the Fire; and a Cobler being there at work, Sir *William* borrowed a Knife to cut a Piece of loose Leather from his Shoe, which being done, he laid down the Knife upon the Table.

Bambridge, with *Corbett*, and *John Everett*, and several others (his Accomplices) from *Newgate*, some with Muskets and Bayonets fixed on them, rushing together into the Room, to Sir *William*, *Bambridge* haughtily demanded of him, *How he durst use his Servants ill;* and instantly, without staying for any Answer, struck Sir *William* with a Stick, thicker than his Wrist; but in some measure Sir *William* put by the Blow, and in his Surprize caught up and struck *Bambridge* with the said Knife, which lay on the Table, near him; *Bambridge* ordering his Men to Fire, one of them snapt his Firelock at Sir *William*, and *Corbett* made a Stroke at him with a Hanger, which Stroke one *Langley* happening to receive, it gave him a great Wound in his Head, thro' his Hat and Wigg.

Immediately after this, Sir *William* was loaded with heavy Irons, and put into the Dungeon on the Common Side, for Two or Three Days, and was then removed to the Dungeon on the Master's Side, in which deplorable Situation, in the last hard Winter, he remained Ten Days, and could have no Fire but Charcoal, which (there being no Fire-place) the Closeness of the Dungeon, and the Fear of being suffocated, rendred more dangerous and intolerable than the Severity of the Weather.

Sir *William* applying to the *Court of Common Pleas* for Redress, a Rule was made for his Removal, and lighter Irons; (*Bambridge* being wounded) Sir *William* was accordingly removed, but the heavy Irons were kept on him; and in that Condition he suffered until the Committee visited the Prison, having been forced to lye in his Cloaths for a Month before, by reason of the said Irons.

One Application to the *Court of Common Pleas* for Redress, cost Sir *William* 14*l.*

The Expence of the meanest Prisoner, on the first Motion to the said Court for Redress, is as followeth, *viz.*

	l.	*s.*	*d.*
An Attorney to take Instructions for drawing the Affidavit	0	3	4
For drawing, according to the Length,	0	6	8
Stamps	0	1	1
To the Judge's Clerk to take the Affidavit	0	6	8
To Council to move	0	10	6
To the Prothonotary for the Rule, which is generally *Nisi*	0	2	0
Copy and Service on the Warden	0	2	2
The Attorney's Attendance in Court	0	3	4
The Council's second Fee, when the Warden shews Cause	0	10	6
The Attorney's Attendance	0	3	4
To the Prothonotary for the second Rule	0	2	0
Copy and Service	0	2	0
	2	13	7

The Committee in their former Report (relating to the *Fleet* Prison) spoke only in general of Exorbitant Fees paid at the Entry of Prisoners into that Prison; But having since obtained an Account of particular Articles paid on that head, the Committee have thought it proper to lay the same before the House, *viz. John Dudley* paid at his Entrance into the *Fleet* Prison as follows;

	l.	*s.*	*d.*
For four Surrenders at the Judge's Chambers to his Clerks	9	11	6
To the Tip-Staff	2	2	0
To the Warden	16	12	0
Taking up his Security Bond upon his Surrender	6	6	0

Turning him into the House and for Liberty again several times	10	10	0
	45	1	6
Samuel Siddale paid,			
For three Surrenders at the Judge's Chambers	3	8	0
To the Tip-Staff	0	10	6
Three Committment Fees to *Corbett*, the Tipstaff, who wou'd not admit him into Prison until paid	6	10	0
To the Chamberlain	0	3	0
To the Turnkey	0	2	0
	10	13	6
Walter Newbury paid,			
Fees at the Judge's Chambers on five Actions	7	12	10
To the Warden	11	4	0
To the Turnkey	0	2	6
To the Steward, or Chamberlain	0	5	0
	19	4	4

The former Report of the Committee, relating to the said *Fleet* Prison, having been under the Consideration of the House, and Directions having been given thereupon, the Committee propose nothing farther, at present, to the House in relation to the said Prison, in particular.

THE APPENDIX.

PERRIN's CASE,

As it relates to JOHN HUGGINS *Esq; Warden of the* FLEET.

THAT in *Easter* Term 1714, *John Huggins* Esq; Warden of the *Fleet*, for a Sum of Money, and upon a Security Bond, wherein the said *Thomas Perrin*, together with *Benjamin Robinson*, and Three other Persons, as his Securities, were bound for his Lodging without the said Prison, permitted him the Liberty aforesaid.

That the said Sureties were Persons of no Account or Substance. That the said *Perrin*, with the Privity and express Consent of the said *Huggins*, went often at large, out of the Rules, without any Day-Rule, or lawful Licence so to do.

That on the Twelfth of *August* 1714, the said *Perrin* went over to *Holland*, having first imployed the said Warden to sollicit a Matter then depending before the Commissioners of the Customs, upon a Reference on a Petition of the said *Perrin*, praying, That his Case might be considered with relation to the said Debts, and have his Liberty on giving Security to Return to Prison when required.

That the Warden undertook the Care and Negotiation of the said Business, and the better to carry on the same, corresponded with the said *Perrin* when in *Holland*, who on that Account, and for his Liberty, remitted by Bills, and otherwise, considerable Sums of Money which the Warden received.

That afterwards the said Warden, fearing a Prosecution for the Escape, sent over Mr. *Robinson* into *Holland*, to remind *Perrin* of his Promise to return to the said Prison of the *Fleet* before the next Term; promising him the said *Perrin*, by Letters, and upon Oath before a Master in *Chancery*, that he the Warden would not seize his Person, in the mean time, and that whatever the said *Robinson* undertook for him (the Warden) touching the Case and Favour of *Perrin*, he, the said *Robinson*, should see faithfully performed.

That in pursuance thereof it was agreed between the said *Robinson* and *Huggins*, *Perrin* should have Liberty to transact his Affairs, at large, so as he returned to Prison before next Term; and for his Security in that behalf, the Warden offered to trust *Perrin* entirely, not doubting *Perrin's* Honour; and gives, in one of his Letters, this Reason, *viz*. That *Perrin* came once before from *Holland*, to surrender himself to save his Bail; whereupon *Perrin* came back to *London*, without any Seizure, Recaption, Restraint, or Molestation of his Person, and for his Security on that Behalf, the Warden offered, and did give *Perrin* a General Release, and by this Deed, bearing Date 20th *October* 1714, released to *Perrin* all and all manner of Actions, Cause and Causes of Action, Suits, Bills, Bonds, Writings Obligatory, Debts, Dues, Duties, Accounts, Sum and Sums of Money, Judgments, Executions, Extents, Quarrels, Controversies, Trespasses, Damages and Demands whatsoever.

That on the 22d of *October* 1714, *Perrin* returned to the Rules of the Prison, goes under the Key, to save the Warden, as if in Execution for the said Debts, and for the pretended Damages, by means of the said Escape into *Holland*, altho' that was all settled betwixt *Perrin* and the Warden, and his Right of Seizure and Recaption released also.

That *Perrin* remained in the *Fleet* until on or about the Second of *April* 1716, but, some short time before, consults the Warden about a new intended Voyage to *Holland*, in order to raise more Money for the said Warden, by applying to Messieurs *Senserf* and Son, his old Correspondents, and by endeavouring to fall into Business, to exercise his Industry, for the Benefit of the Warden, which he so effectually brought about, that he remitted to the said Warden near 1000*l.* which came safe to the Warden's Hands.

That *Huggins*, to prevent his being sued, as he pretended, immediately proposed to the Commissioners of the Customs, that they would be pleased to say That the Crown had gained One Thousand Pounds more than if *Perrin* had not escaped; and after he had prevailed with the Sollicitor so to do, they drew up a Report, and transmitted it to the Treasury, Signed by the Commissioners of the Customs.

THE
AFFIDAVIT
Mentioned in the said
CASE.

JOHN HUGGINS, *Warden of the* Fleet, *maketh Oath, That* Thomas Perrin *of* London, *Merchant, shall Peaceably and Quietly, without Interruption or Molestation, Hold and Enjoy to himself the Liberty of the Rules of the Prison of the* Fleet, *without any future Charge whatsoever, and this Deponent will not permit or suffer the said* Thomas Perrin, *under any Pretence whatsoever (against his Will) to be Confined within the Walls of the said Prison, nor shall the said* Thomas Perrin *be removed to any other Prison, by or thro' the Means or Procurement of this Deponent, by* Habeas Corpus *or otherwise, to any of his Majesty's Prison or Prisons, Place or Places of Confinement, so far as to the utmost of his this Deponent's Power can be prevented; and in Case a* Habeas Corpus *be brought to Effect, so as that the said* Thomas Perrin *should be removed, he, this Deponent, will use his utmost Endeavours to bring him back to the Rules of the* Fleet, *that he may Enjoy the Liberty aforesaid, or to procure for him the*

Liberty of the Rules at this Deponent's own proper Charge and Expence, and so to be continued to him under Moses Cooke, Esq, *the present Marshal, or any other Marshal, so long as the said* Thomas Perrin *shall continue to be a Prisoner, so as that he may either at the* Kings Bench *or* Fleet-Prisons *enjoy the Liberty proposed, notwithstanding any Action or Actions, Judgment or Judgments, Declaration or Declarations, Extent or Extents, by means of his late or present Misfortunes, or any thing that may or shall happen to or arise therefrom: And that in Case this Deponent should sell, assign, or set over the Wardenship or Property in the* Fleet, *That then and in such Case, he this Deponent will, at his own Cost, use his Endeavours, so that he shall enjoy the Liberty aforesaid, and upon his single Security, and that he shall have Day-Rules to transact his Affairs in Term Time, as often as his Occasions require, without any Expence to him the said* Thomas Perrin; *and in Case of his consenting to be within the Walls of the Prison, shall be let into the Rules again whenever he shall require the same, by writing to Mr.* Samuel Blunt, *or any other Person immediately.*

Jur. 22. Oct. 1710.
Coram Will. Rogers.

John Huggins.

COPY of his General Release, upon Stamp Paper, in Form as followeth, *viz.*

KNOW *all Men by these Presents, That I* John Huggins, *of the Parish of St.* Martins in the Fields, *in the County of* Middlesex, *Esq; have remised, released and for ever quit Claim unto* Thomas Perrin *of* London, *Merchant, his Heirs, Executors and Administrators, all and all manner of Actions, Cause and Causes of Actions, Suits, Bills, Bonds, Writings Obligatory, Debts, Dues, Duties, Accompts, Sum or Sums of Money, Judgments, Executions, Extents, Quarrels, Controversies, Trespasses, Damages and Demands whatsoever, both in Law and Equity, or otherwise howsoever, which against the said* Thomas Perrin *I ever had, and which I, my Heirs, Executors and Administrators shall or may have, Claim, Challenge or Demand, for or by Reason, or Means of any Matter, Cause or Thing whatsoever, from the beginning of the World, unto the Day of the Date of these Presents. In Witness whereof I have hereunto set my Hand and Seal the 20th Day of* October, *in the First Year of the Reign of Our Sovereign Lord* GEORGE, *by the Grace of God, of* Great-Britain, France, *and* Ireland *King, Defender of the Faith* &c. Annoq: Dom. 1714.

Sealed and Delivered in the Presence of
   Sam. Blunt.
   Benja: Robinson.

                                        John Huggins.

THE Resolutions of the Committee being severally read a Second time, were, upon the Question severally put thereupon, agreed unto by the House, and are as follow, *viz.*

Resolved,
That *William Acton*, Clerk of the Prison of the *Marshalsea*, and Farmer of the same Goal, and the Profits thereof, by Lease from Mr. *John Darby*, the Keeper of the said Prison, hath been guilty of many High Crimes and Misdemeanours in the Execution of his Office; and hath Arbitrarily and Unlawfully loaded with Irons, Tortured and Destroyed, in the most Inhumane, Cruel and Barbarous manner, Prisoners for Debt, under his Care, in high Violation and Contempt of the Laws of this Kingdom.

Resolved,
That the Charities given by well-disposed Persons for the Relief and Sustenance of the Poor Debtors confined in the said Prison of the *Marshalsea*, are notoriously and scandalously misapplied; and that the Keeper of the said Prison, and his Dependants and Agents, instead of distributing the said Charities to the said Poor Debtors, have most unjustifiably possessed themselves thereof, and wickedly perverted the same to their own Uses, to the great Fraud and Oppression of the said Poor Prisoners in general, and to the Starving many, who have perished in the said Prison for want thereof.

Resolved,
That Mr. *John Darby*, Keeper of the said Prison of the *Marshalsea*, having, contrary to and in defiance of the Law, lett to Farm his said Goal and Office, and the Profits thereof, unto the said *William Acton*, and having grosly neglected his Duty in not preventing or remedying the said Inhumanities, Cruelties, Frauds and Abuses, is guilty of a High Misdemeanour in his Office, and a Notorious Breach of his Trust, in Contempt of the Law, and to the great Oppression and Ruin of many of His Majesty's Subjects.

Mr. *Oglethorpe* acquainted the House, That he was directed by the Committee to Move, That an humble Address be presented to His Majesty, That he will be graciously pleased to direct his Attorney-General forthwith to prosecute, in the most effectual manner, the said *William Acton*, and *John Darby*, for their said Crimes and Misdemeanours.

And Mr. *Oglethorpe* Moved the House accordingly.

Resolved, Nemine Contradicente,

That an humble Address be presented to his Majesty, That he will be graciously pleased to direct his Attorney-General forthwith to prosecute, in the most effectual manner, the said *William Acton* and *John Darby*, for their said Crimes and Misdemeanours.

Ordered,

That the said Address he presented to His Majesty by such Members of this House as are of His Majesty's most Honourable Privy-Council.

Ordered,

That the Report from the Committee appointed to Enquire into the State of the Goals of this Kingdom (this Day made to the House) in relation to the State of the Prison of the Court of *Marshalsea*, and of the King's Palace Court of *Westminster*; and also of a farther Progress which the Committee had made in their Enquiry into the State of the *Fleet* Prison, with the Appendixes, and the Resolution of the House thereupon, be Printed, and that Mr. *Speaker* do appoint the Printing thereof; and that no Person, but such as he shall appoint, do presume to print the same.

FINIS.

A Preliminary Report on the King's Bench Prison (1730)

As he showed from the outset of his investigations by reporting Bambridge for attempting to suppress testimony, Oglethorpe again demonstrated that he would brook no tampering with the witnesses summoned by the committee. With the backing of his committee, on March 6, 1730, he recommended to the House of Commons that George Gray, an attorney, be imprisoned for attempting to bribe a witness. Gray's incarceration seems to have been ignored in the newspapers.

I reprint from *Journals of the House of Commons*, 21:476, 480.

Veneris, 6° die Martii,

Anno 3° Georgii 2di Regis, 1729.

. . . .

Mr. *Oglethorpe,* from the Committee, appointed to enquire into the State of the Gaols of this Kingdom, acquainted the House, that the said Committee, having entered upon their Enquiry, into the State of the *King*'s *Bench* Prison, did find, that several indirect Practices had been used, to prevent, and elude, such Enquiry: And he made a Report thereof to the House; which he read in his Place, and afterwards delivered in at the Clerk's Table; where the same was read, and is as follows; *viz.*

That it appeared to the Committee, that *George Gray,* an Attorney at Law, wrote several Letters to *Richard Mullins,* Esquire, Marshal of the *King*'s *Bench,* dated the 2d, 21st, and 22d, of *February* last, demanding a Debt of 1 *l.* 8 *s.* on behalf of one *Richard Powell;* and suggesting, that if he would not pay the said Money, *Powell* could give Informations against him; and intimating, that he, *Gray,* could be of Service to Mr. *Mullins,* as he had been last Year to Mr. *Bambridge,* to whom he had given a full Account of the Measures to be taken against him, by means of his being then employed under one of the Solicitors, concerned against *Bambridge* and *Huggins.*

That *Gray* afterwards came, by Appointment, to Mr. *Mullins*'s House, and acquainted him, that *Powell* talked of informing the Committee of a Murder, committed by him the said *Mullins;* but that, if *Mullins* would give him Three Guineas, he would prevent *Powell*'s giving any Information against him to the Committee: That Mr. *Mackay* was employed in drawing up Informations,[1] to be laid before the Committee; and that, if he, *Mullins,* would place Five Guineas in proper Hands, it might be an Advantage to him, the said *Mullins,* in respect to *Mackay.*

That on the 23d of *February, Gray,* by a Letter, written by himself, but signed by him in the Name of *John Mackay,* acquainted the Committee, that *Richard Powell, Robert Elliott,* and other Persons, named in the Letter, could give an account of the Charities, and Usage, of the Prison, and also an Account of the Death and Murder of *Thomas Denham,* Mr. *Allen,* and others, through the Cruelty of the Marshals.

And *Gray* the same Day wrote a letter to Mr. *Mullins,* giving him an Account of the Contents of what he had laid before the Committee, and that he had taken *Powell* away, and prevented his giving Evidence before the

Committee; and advised Mr. *Mullins* to send Two Guineas, the Remainder of which, after letting *Powell* have 25 Shillings, he says, he, *Gray*, should soon expend in *Mullins*'s Service; and that he, *Gray*, designed that Evening to drink with *Elliott*, meaning the aforesaid *Robert Elliott*.

And by the general Tenure [Tenor] of all the Letters he undertakes to prevent Evidence being given to the Committee; and he did actually convey away the said *Richard Powell*, and suppressed his Evidence; and this, in order to get Money from the Marshal, and render the Enquiry of this Committee ineffectual.

The Marshal of the *King*'s *Bench* having laid the aforementioned Letters before the Committee, they ordered *Gray* to attend. He complied not with the Two first Orders; but wrote, the 26th of *February*, to the Marshal, that he had received them; and that the Party on the Morrow would lay the Matter before the Chairman of the Committee, if the Matter proposed was not complied with.

It appeared to the Committee, that the said *George Gray* had tampered with some Witnesses, in respect of their Evidence to be given to this Committee, and had hindered others from appearing, or giving Evidence; and the Committee ordered the said Transactions to be reported to the House.

Resolved, nemine contradicente, That *George Gray*, Attorney at Law, having tampered with some Witnesses, in respect of their Evidence to be given to the Committee, appointed by this House to enquire into the State of the Gaols of this Kingdom, and having hindered others from appearing, and giving Evidence to the said Committee, is guilty of a high Crime and Misdemeanor, in Breach of the Privilege of this House, and in Contempt of the Authority thereof.

Ordered, That the said *George Gray* be, for his said Offence, committed Prisoner to his Majesty's Prison of the *Gatehouse*; and that Mr. Speaker do issue his Warrants accordingly.

An Addendum to the Fleet Prison Report (1730)

Burdened by the expenses that he had undertaken toward purchasing Huggins's patent to the Fleet and the improvements that he had introduced there, James Gambier petitioned that the government pay twenty-five hundred pounds to purchase the patent and that it extend his wardenship to cover his own life, rather than expire with the death of Bambridge. Impressed by Gambier's improvements at the Fleet, Oglethorpe and his committee supported the petition, reported in its favor on March 24, 1730, and doubtless helped to expedite it through the House. Approved in advance by the king, the requisite resolution was passed on April 9, 1730 (*JHC* 21:468, 538).

My text is taken from *Journals of the House of Commons*, 21:511, 513.

Martis, 24° *die Martii*
Anno 3° Georgii 2ᵈⁱ Regis, 1729.

. . . .

Mr. *Oglethorpe* reported from the Committee, appointed to enquire into the State of the Gaols of this Kingdom, and to whom the Petition of *James Gambier,* Warden of the *Fleet* Prison, was referred; that the Committee had examined the Matter of the said Petition, and had directed him to report the same, as it appeared to them, to the House: And he read the Report in his Place, and afterwards delivered it in at the Clerk's Table; where the same was read, and is as follows; *viz.*

Dougal Cuthbert, Esquire, being called, and examined, said, that he had paid the Value of 1,300*l.* in Money, Stock, and Bonds, and had given a promissory Bond of 1,200*l.* and pledged certain Deeds and Writings, as a further collateral Security for the Payment of the said 1,200*l.* in all 2,500*l.* to *John Huggins,* Esquire, to induce him to surrender his Patent of Warden of the *Fleet,* and to procure, by his, the said *John Huggins*'s Interest, a Patent of the Reversion of the said Office for the said *Dougal Cuthbert,* to commence after the Decease of *Thomas Bambridge,* during his natural Life; which said Patent he accordingly procured: And, to support his said Evidence, he produced two Receipts, signed by *John Huggins.* And the said *Dougal Cuthbert* further said, that he had received 500*l.* of *James Gambier,* Esquire, on Account of an Agreement with him made for the said reversionary Patent.

That it appeared by an Act, intituled, "An Act to disable *Thomas Bambridge,*" &c. that he was disabled to hold the said Office of Warden, and the Crown was enabled to grant the same, during Pleasure, for the Life of the said *Bambridge.*

James Gambier, Esquire, being examined, said, that he last Year accepted of the Office of Warden of the *Fleet,* during Pleasure, for the Life of *Thomas Bambridge,* upon the Belief, that the Tenure would be altered to good Behaviour, removeable by Address from either House of Parliament: That he grounded this Belief on a Bill, that had passed the House of Commons last Year, *nemine contradicente,* by which the Sense of the House appeared to be, that it was for the publick Good, that the Office of the Warden of the *Fleet* should be grantable by the Crown, during good Behaviour only, and the future Wardens be removeable, upon Address from either House of Parliament; and the said *James Gambier* was induced to agree with the said *Dugald Cuthbert* for the Surrender of the said Patent, on the Payment of the Sum of 2,500 *l.* of which Sum he, the said *Gambier*, has already paid 500 *l.* to the end that such Regulation, as was intended, should be made by Parliament, believing, that the Publick would pay the said 2,500 *l.*

Thomas Brafield, being examined, said, that, since the said *Gambier* hath held the Office of Warden, he hath been obliged to several Expences, for Repairs, and other Matters, which were absolutely necessary; particularly, that he hath rebuilt Part of the Womens Ward on the common Side, and hath pulled down, and levelled with the Ground, the Dungeon on the Master Side, in which *Arne* perished: That he hath made several Reductions of Fees, and Chamber Rent; and that, from the former high Prices of Chamber Rent, he hath reduced the same to 2 *s.* 6 *d. per* Week for each Room, furnished by him, and half of that Sum for each unfurnished Room, whether there be one or more Prisoners therein; so that, if there be Four Prisoners in a Room, furnished by the Warden, each pays 7½*d. per* Week, and, if there be Four Prisoners in a Room, furnished by themselves, each pays the Half thereof; whereas formerly each Prisoner paid at the least 2*s.* 6*d. per* Head, though never so many lay in the same Room.

Ordered, That the said Report be referred to the Committee of the whole House, who are to consider further of the Supply granted to his Majesty.

A Report from the Committee appointed to Enquire into the State of the Goals of this Kingdom. Relating to the King's Bench Prison (1730)

When, on January 13, 1730, the House of Commons began its new session, it was for a while uncertain whether Oglethorpe's committee would be reactivated. Soon after Parliament reopened, Oglethorpe made a motion that might well have stopped all the committee's further inquiries, for it seemed an insult directed at Lawrence Carter, Baron of the Exchequer and a member of Parliament, who had presided at the trials of William Acton and had sat on the bench at several other trials of the accused wardens. As Knatchbull recorded in his diary for January 26, 1730,

> A motion by Oglethorpe and Vernon about having trials printed upon the prosecution order by Parliament last year for Bambridge and his officers, upon a supposition that they had not fair trials and that the House was now concerned in it, and hinted as if the judges had been partial, for that Carter had been desired by them to have them printed, and he answered he would not subject his judgment to the appeal of the people, for it was different from the judgment of the House, and so it might since the evidence was different, which might arise from the evidence, having swore one thing before the committee and another at the trial, so the House seemed no way to countenance it and it dropped.[1]

On February 15, however, Oglethorpe spoke to Sir John Percival

of restoring the Committee of Gaols, and said it was necessary for our reputations, being vilified in the world for proceeding so zealously last year, that the same oppressions continue, and the judges acted strangely in commanding Gambier, the new Warden of the Fleet, to restore the dungeon there, which Gambier had of his own accord pulled down; that there are several prisons remaining to visit, for which we had not time last year, and that we had not brought in a bill for regulating all the gaols of England, as we were directed by the House last year. I was not very willing [Percival commented] to revive the Committee, because I knew the ill will the Administration bore it, and the weight of the judges and Court against us.²

On February 16, finally, a group of some thirty members of the House met privately and "agreed to move to-morrow for reviving the Committee of Goals." On the following day a new committee of eighty-eight members was named.³ On February 21, twenty-one of these made their first visit to the King's Bench Prison. In late April and early May, however, the committee found itself entangled in investigating the conduct of Lord Chief Justice Sir Robert Eyre, on the charge of his visiting Bambridge in Newgate while the warden was awaiting trial, presumably before him.⁴ Only after Hughes had made his report exonerating Eyre did Oglethorpe finally present his report to the House.⁵

In its visitations the committee found at the King's Bench no such starvation and brutality as it had discovered in the Fleet and the Marshalsea. Apart from the possible mismanagement of charity monies, the warden received a clean bill of health and even the recommendation of being charitable and compassionate. What Oglethorpe and his committee did find and develop was collusion in the escape of some affluent debtors from the rules and thus from their creditors. Such was the complicated pattern of ownership and management of the King's Bench Prison that it was virtually impossible to establish financial responsibility for escapes. Neither Sir John Lenthall's heirs (the proprietors), their trustees, the marshal, the deputy marshal, or the deputy's deputy thought themselves financially responsible for any escapes; and it was actually in the interest of the acting deputy to promote them—to charge high fees for permitting debtors to live within the rules. Even the law of 8–9 William III, cap. 27, laid no restriction upon the marshal in giving this permission.

It was at the King's Bench particularly that Oglethorpe perceived that the state of the prisoners depended more upon the vigilance and integrity of the responsible judges who supervised the prison than upon the character of the warden. Thus the prisoners at the King's Bench "had heard of terrible Oppressions formerly," but none since the advent of Lord Chief Justice Robert Raymond, "who not accepting of any Presents, or Fees from the Marshal of the said Prison, hath kept the Marshal strictly to his Duty." Chief Justice Raymond's conduct, the committee thought, should set the standard. Not only should wardens be prohibited from accepting bribes for permitting prisoners to escape, but the judges and their clerks should be forbidden to accept any fees or gifts from the warden or his subordinates.

Oglethorpe did not spare even the decisions of the chief justices. One foolish ruling followed the action of Samuel Woodham, Justice of the Peace for Surrey, when he arrested two prisoners who were living within the rules, for their violent attack upon a woman. When they were unable to provide security, Woodham committed them to the county jail. For this action he was accused by the deputy warden of rescuing them from the King's Bench Prison and was forced by the court to pay more than thirty pounds in costs! In another ruling, the late Lord Chief Justice John Pratt had held that the justices could enlarge the rules—the boundaries—of the prison "in such Manner as they should think fit." Oglethorpe retorted, "If this be Law, all *England* may be made one extended Prison."

Although he later conducted another parliamentary investigation of the King's Bench, with this report Oglethorpe's penal investigations came to a virtual end. The exposure of brutal wardens was embarrassing enough to those who administered justice, but they could not tolerate revelations of the corrupt judicial supervision that was responsible for prison corruption. They could not permit more investigations and exposure of such eminent (and questionable) judges as Lord Chief Justice Sir John Eyre. Half a century later John Howard was to become known as the great philanthropist of prison reform. Oglethorpe, not Howard, deserves that reputation. He began the process of reform and understood and attacked the forces that stood in its way.

A

REPORT

FROM THE

COMMITTEE

APPOINTED TO

ENQUIRE

Into the State of the GOALS of this

Kingdom.

Relating to the King's-Bench *Prison.*

Publish'd by Order of the HOUSE of COMMONS.

[Printer's ornament.]
LONDON:
Printed for *Richard Williamson* near *Gray's-Inn-Gate* in *Holborn.* MDCCXXX.

By *Virtue of an Order of the House of Commons, I do appoint* Richard Williamson *to print this Report: And that no other Person presume to print the same.*

AR. ONSLOW, Speaker.

A REPORT FROM THE COMMITTEE

Appointed to enquire into the State of the GOALS *of this Kingdom.*

Veneris 8 *Die Maii* 1730.

MR. *Oglethorpe*, from the Committee appointed to enquire into the State of the Goals of this Kingdom, acquainted the House That they had agreed upon a Report of their Proceedings, to be made to the House, when the House will please to receive the same.

Ordered, That the Report be received upon *Monday* Morning next.

Lunæ 11 *Die Maii* 1730.

Mr. *Oglethorpe*, from the Committee appointed to enquire into the State of the Goals of this Kingdom, made a Report (according to Order) of the Progress the Committee had made in their Enquiry into the State of the *King*'s-*Bench* Prison; with the Resolutions of the Committee thereupon, and he read the Report in his Place, and afterwards delivered the same in at the Table, together with an *Appendix* to it, containing at large those Examinations and Papers which are referred to in the Report.

Ordered, That the Report be taken into Consideration to Morrow Morning.

Martis 12 *Die Maii* 1730.

The Order of the Day being read, for the House to take into Consideration the Report from the Committee appointed to enquire into the State of the Goals of this Kingdom:

The Report was read, and is as followeth, *viz.*

The Committee appointed to enquire into the State of the Goals of this Kingdom, having entred into an Examination of the State of the King's-Bench *Prison, have thought it proper to lay their Proceedings before the House, viz.*

It appeared to the Committee That the Prison of the *King's-Bench* doth belong to the Court of the *King's-Bench*, and the Keeper of the said Prison is styled Marshal of the *Marshalsea* of our Sovereign Lord the King, before himself being; which Office of Marshal formerly belonged to the Earl Marshal of *England*, as appears by an Inquisition taken in the Eleventh Year of *Henry* the Sixth, on the Death of *John Mowbray*, Duke of *Norfolk*, which sets forth, That it had been separated from the Office of Earl Marshal,[6] but in the Twentieth Year of *Richard* the Second, by Letters Patent, confirmed by Parliament, was reunited to the Office of Earl Marshal, and granted to *Thomas Mowbray*, then Earl of *Nottingham*, afterwards Duke of *Norfolk*, and the Heirs Male of his Body, to be held in *Capite*;[7] and that the yearly Value of the Office of Marshal of the *King's-Bench* was Ten Marks.

That the Heirs Male of the said Duke failed, and the Office devolved to the Crown.

That *William Lenthall* Esq; mortgaged certain Manors and Lands for Seven Thousand Pounds, to Sir *John Cutler* Knight, and for the further securing of the said Seven Thousand Pounds, and the additional Sum of Three Thousand Pounds, he, by Indenture bearing Date the Twenty fourth Day of *February* One Thousand Six Hundred and Eighty Four, mortgaged the Office of the Marshal of the *King's-Bench* Prison, to the said Sir *John Cutler*,[8] by a bare Covenant to stand seized of the said Office, subject to the Payment of the said Ten Thousand Pounds and Interest.

Whether the said *William Lenthall* Esq; had any or what Title to the said Office, and under what Limitation it was granted from the Crown, doth not appear to this Committee.[9]   *Appendix.* (A)

That the frequent Escapes of Prisoners from the *King's-Bench*, and the *Fleet*, occasioned an Act to be passed, 8 & 9 *Gulielmi Tertii*, (intitled, *An Act for the more effectual Relief of Creditors, in Cases of Escapes, and for preventing Abuses in Prisons, and pretended priviledged Places.*)[10]

In which Act it is recited, *That divers great Sums of Money and other Rewards were received by the Marshal of the* King's Bench, *and Warden of the* Fleet, *to assist or permit Prisoners to escape; For preventing which, it is enacted, That if any Marshal or Warden of the said Prisons, or their respective Deputy or Deputies, whatsoever, shall take any Sum of Money, Reward or Gratuity whatsoever, or Security for the same, to procure, assist, connive at or permit any such*   8 & 9 Gul. Cap. 26. Sect. 4.

Escape, and shall be thereof lawfully convicted; the said Marshal or Warden, or their respective Deputy or Deputies, shall for every such Offence forfeit five hundred Pounds and his said Office, and be for ever after incapable of Executing such Office.

That by a subsequent Clause, it is in the said Act *provided, That nothing in the said Act contained shall extend to prejudice, impeach or lessen any Security or Securities for any Sum or Sums of Money made or given by, or out of the said Office of Marshal of the Marshalsea of the Court of King's Bench, or the Profits thereof, by William Lenthall, Esq; to Sir John Cutler Bart, deceased, or to Edmund Boulter, Esq; Executor of the said Sir John Cutler,*[11] *or to any other Person or Persons in Trust for them or either of them, or to subject the said Office or the Profits thereof, or the Person or Persons in whom the same are or shall be vested, to any of the Forfeitures or Penalties in the said Act contained, other than such as they are or may be liable unto before the making of the said Act, until such Sum or Sums secured thereby shall be fully satisfied and paid, any thing in the said Act contained to the contrary thereof notwithstanding.*   Sect. 1.

That this Exemption is only from the Penalties imposed by the said Act, and not from any Forfeitures or Penalties to which the said Office was otherwise lyable:

And the Heirs of *Lenthall* are not allowed to nominate a Marshal, without the Consent of the Mortgagees, as appears by the following Clause: *viz.*

That all and every Deputation or Deputations, Grant or Grants at any time heretofore made, or executed by William Lenthall Esq; of the said Office of Marshal of the Marshalsea of the said Court of King's-Bench, is and are hereby declared void and of none Effect, and that all and every succeeding Marshal shall, from Time to Time and at all Times hereafter, be constituted and appointed by the said William Lenthall, his Heirs and Assigns, by and with the Consent in Writing under the Hand and Seal of Edmund Boulter Esq; his Executors, Administrators and Assigns, until the Debt owing by the said William Lenthall to the said Edmund Boulter, Executor of Sir John Cutler Baronet, deceased, be satisfied.   Sect. 2.

That in *July* 1708, the Manors and Lands which were mortgaged with the said Office, for securing the said Ten Thousand Pounds, were sold for the Sum of Eight Thousand Seven Hundred Pounds: Seven Thousand Six Hundred Pounds whereof was paid, towards the discharging the Principal and Interest of the said Mortgage.

That in the Year One Thousand Seven and Eighteen *Charles Bodvile*, Earl of *Radnor*,[12] claiming under the said Sir *John Cutler*, and his said Executor, *Edmund Boulter*, did by Indenture, bearing Date the twentieth Day of *September* 1718, assign to *Joseph Studley* his Executors Administrators and Assigns,[13] in Consideration of a competent Sum, all his Right and Title to the Money secured upon the said Office, which in the said Deed he mentions to amount to 19,284*l*. 2*s*. 4*d*. which is said to have arisen to that Sum by the adding of Interest, Repairs and other Charges.

That on Examination of Witnesses, it appeared, that the said compe- (B) tent Sum was 10,500*l*. which was all the Money that was paid by the said *Studley*, to the said Earl.

That the said *Studley* purchased these Securities in Trust for other Per- (C) sons, and divided them into Shares, which, being sold at various Prices, by divers mesne Assignments and Transfers came into the Hands of the present Mortgagees, *viz*.

Twentieth Parts.

Mr. *John Preston*	4
Mr. *Thomas* and *John Martin* in Trust, *&c*.	4
Mr. *Studley*	1
Mr. *Thomas Martin* in his own Right	7
Mr. *John Martin* in his own Right	4

That the said Mortgagees have received the Rents and Profits of the said Office, and the Profits arising from the Sale and Alienation of the Offices in the Disposition of the Marshal, whereby they have received a much greater Sum than the Interest of the said 10,500 *l*. to this time amounts to.

That *Lenthall's* Claim to the Freehold of the said Office hath been con- (D.1.) veyed to and kept in Trustees, and these Trustees have, generally, been Men of mean Circumstances, and nominated at the Request of the Mort- (D.2.) gagees.

The present Trustees are *James Slann*, a Footman to one of the Mortgagees, and *John Wildey*, a Scrivener, which said Trustees, in Pursuance of a verbal Order of four of the Mortgagees, did, by Lease dated the fourteenth Day of *January* One Thousand Seven Hundred Twenty Nine, let to *Richard Mullens* Esq;[14] the Office of Marshal and Keeper of the Prisoners in the *King's-Bench* Prison, for three Years, which Prisoners (as appears by the Commitment Books) are in Number Six Hundred Fifty Seven, and are charged with One Hundred Twenty Six Thousand, Four Hundred Thirty Four Pounds, Twelve Shillings; besides great Numbers who are charged without Specification of the Sums; they being charged on Surrenders to Actions, the Number of which Actions amount to Three Hundred Ninty Eight, and the Sums due may probably be very great.

The Committee do not find that any Security (except their own personal Security) hath been taken or required from any Marshal of the *King's-Bench*, for the safe keeping of the Prisoners, either by the Trustees or by any other, and the Marshals, as well as the Trustees, have generally been Men of very mean Circumstances; and the Mortgagees, having thus screened themselves behind Trustees nominated at their own Request, deem themselves not answerable for Escapes; So the Creditor hath no Person of any Substance to have recourse to, in case of an Escape; The Consequence of which, amongst many other Examples, appeared very evidently in the (E.) Case of Mr. *Poulter*. He was indebted to Mr. *William Wilson*, in the Sum of Eighteen Thousand Pounds, for which he was charged in Execution, in the *King's-Bench* Prison, and chose rather to make the Marshal a large Present, than to pay his own Debts; Mr. *Machen*, who was then Marshal, accepted of the Money, *Poulter* went to *Holland*, and *Wilson* sued and recovered Judgment against *Machen*, the Marshal, who (being an Insolvent) remained a Prisoner in his own Goal, and *Wilson* applied to the Court of *King's-Bench*, that the Profits of the Office might be sequestered, for his Debt, but the Mortgagees made such a Claim as to protect them; So that *Wilson*, having a Right, but no Remedy, and being by this Sleight of Law entirely ruined, shot himself, in Despair.

The Office of Marshal of the said Prison was let to the said *Richard Mullens*, by a Trustee, by the Consent and Direction of the Mortgagees, in *January* One Thousand Seven Hundred Twenty Four, for the annual Rent of Seven Hundred Pounds, he being over and above obliged to pay the annual Sum of Twenty Two Pounds Ten Shillings, as a Fee-Farm Rent, and also an annual Sum of Thirty Pounds to the Chamberlain, nominated by the Mortgagees; the whole amounting to 750 *l. per Annum.*

His Lease was renewed in *January* last, and by Indenture, bearing Date the fourteenth Day of the said Month, he covenants with *James Slann* and *John Wildey*, to pay them 700 *l. per Annum.* clear of all Taxes, besides which to pay the Fee-Farm Rent, *&c.* although all the open, and legal Profits, of which the said *Mullens* could give any Account to the Committee, amounted to about Three Hundred and Fifty Pounds *per Annum*, and no more.

The high Rents of the said Office cannot be made up, without great Oppression, much less can the other Fees, with which it is loaded, be complied with, insomuch that the Marshals generally continue but a short time in that Office, there having been fifteen from the Year 1668 to the Year (F.) 1724; and sometimes on a Prisoner's being committed for a considerable

Sum, the Marshal accepts of Money to grant him the Rules, and suffers him to escape; and if the Plantiff recovers against the Marshal, he turns himself a Prisoner into his own Goal, which is accompanied with a kind of Goal-Delivery: The Insolvent Marshal, being in this Condition, generally refuses to give his Successors any Account of the Prisoners, to whom he gave the Liberty of the Rules, and by this Proceeding the new Marshal does not apprehend himself to be charged, or chargeable with them.

On this Occasion a Rule of Court is sometimes granted, for the new Marshal to take all the Prisoners in the Rules, and Persons who have escaped. But the Marshal does not think himself obliged to retake them, and it gives the new Marshal a Pretence to squeeze great Sums of Money, out of such Prisoners as enjoy the Rules. (G.)

Over and above the aforementioned exorbitant Rents, on a New Marshal's being sworn, it hath been usual for him to pay One Hundred Guineas to the Lord Chief Justice of the *King's-Bench*, and Fifty Guineas to each of the Puisne Judges of that Court. The present Marshal, when he was sworn Marshal (in Pursuance of a Lease granted to him in 1724) gave a Purse of One Hundred Guineas into the Hands of Sir *John Prat* Knight, then Lord Chief Justice of the *King's-Bench*; and one other Purse containing Fifty Guineas, to Mr. Justice *Fortescue*; and the like Sum to Mr. Justice *Powis*; and he offered the like Sum to Sir *Robert Raymond* Knight,[15] then one of the Puisne Judges of that Court, who refused the same, saying, he did not know any such Fee was due, and that if it was not a legal Fee, he would not take it, but that he would inform himself of the Lord Chief Justice, and the other Judges; and, some Days after, he accepted the same Sum, having seen the Lord Chief Justice, and the other Judges of the said Court. *Vide* (D.2.)

The said *Richard Mullens* was again sworn into the said Office on the twenty fifth Day of *January* One Thousand Seven Hundred Twenty Nine, (his former Lease being then expired, and a new one obtained) on which Occasion Sir *Robert Raymond* Knight, Lord Chief Justice of the *King's-Bench*, and the other Judges of the said Bench, did not accept of any Fee, whatsoever, from the said Marshal.

Over and above these Fees or Presents paid by the Marshals, on their being sworn into the said Office, they used to pay, every *Christmas*, to the Lord Chief Justice of the *King's-Bench* twenty Guineas; and to each of the Puisne Judges ten Guineas; until such Time as the present Sir *Robert Raymond* came to be Lord Chief Justice; He then generously refused to accept of any such Presents, and would never receive any Gratification, whatsoever, from the said Marshal; and he was imitated in this by Mr. Justice

Reynolds,[16] who, though he accepted the Ten Guineas, sent the same, by his Clerk, to be distributed amongst the Prisoners of the said Prison; and all the Judges of the said Court have now followed this Example: At *Christmas* 1729, they all refused to accept any Presents, from the said Marshal.

Not only the Marshals, but the Deputy Marshals usually made Presents, (on their Admittance) to the Lord Chief Justice of the said Court; Mr. *John Morris*, who is now Deputy Marshal, on his buying that Office, besides the Purchase Money paid by him for the said Office, made a Present to the Lord Chief Justice *Holt* of twenty Guineas,[17] which, as far as he remembers, he gave to him with his own Hands. (H.)

That upon Inspecting the said (*King's-Bench*) Prison, it appears to be in very bad Repair, and not capable of containing a third Part of the Number of Prisoners, even now in the Marshal's Custody, who amount to six hundred and fifty seven, which Number is much less than used to be in that Custody, before the late Acts of Parliament against frivolous Arrests, and for relief of insolvent Debtors: And it is remarkable that not one Person discharged by the said late Act (for relief of Insolvent Debtors) hath been recommitted for any new Debt.

The common Side of this Prison is divided into little Cabins or Lodges, the Floors of many of which are six or eight Feet below the Level of the Ground, the Master's Side is in very bad Condition; and the whole in no Way adequate to the vast Rent paid for it.

Many Complaints were laid before the Committee of Cruelties committed by former Marshals of the said Prison, particularly of a Murder of one *Allen*, a Prisoner in the said Prison, in the Year 1723,[18] when *Machen* was Marshal; and also Complaints of exorbitant Sums having been taken for the Liberty of the Rules:

But the requisite Attendances on other Services of the House have made it impracticable to go through the Examinations of these Complaints, before the Conclusion of this Session.

However the Committee having examined all the Prisoners on the common Side, and many of those on the Master's Side (who are, mostly, new Prisoners, committed since the Beginning of the late Parliamentary Inquiries into the State of the Goals) It appeared, by their Examinations, that no Violence or Cruelty hath been used to them by the present Marshal, but, on the contrary, that he hath done many Acts of Compassion, and Charity towards those on the common Side; by which, and by his free Confessions, and satisfactory Answers given to the Committee, upon his several Examinations before them, he hath rather intituled himself to Favour, than Blame.

The said Prisoners also declared, that they had heard of terrible Oppressions formerly, none of which have happened of late, the Ears of the present Lord Chief Justice of the Court of *King's-Bench*, being always open to the Complaints of the Prisoners, and he having, with great Patience, heard all their Petitions.

Their chief Complaints, at present, are the great Distress they are reduced to; the Charities not being sufficient for Maintenance of the poor Prisoners; and that the being admitted on the common Side, (and thereby intituled to the Benefit of the Charities, which are confined to that Side) is granted as a particular Favour, and not as a general Right, and that it is with great Difficulty a poor Wretch on the Master's Side, though never so miserable, can be admitted on the Common Side, to share in these Charities.

The Marshal is chiefly enabled to pay his Rent, by permitting Prisoners, on Security, to live out of the Prison, any where within the Rules. The Streightness of the Prison, and it's Incapacity to contain the Numbers thereto usually committed, occasioned the Prisoners Application to the Court of *King's-Bench*, for more Room: Who took upon them to impower the Marshal to suffer his Prisoners to live out of the Walls of the Prison, he being answerable for their Forth-Coming; The Limits within which such Prisoners were allowed to be, were fix'd by the Court of *King's-Bench*, and that Space of Ground is called the Rules, and now deemed Part of the Prison: The Court of *King's-Bench* hath taken on them to enlarge the said Space, particularly in the Time when Sir *John Prat*, Knight, was Lord Chief Justice, the Court then declared, that it was in their Power to extend the Rules, in such Manner as they should think fit. *Vide* (E.)

If this be Law, all *England* may be made one extended Prison.

The Prisoners make large Presents to the Marshal for the Liberty of these Rules, and being under his Protection, and in his Favour, may take Houses or Lodgings within the Rules, and live in a very easy Manner, whilst the poor honest Debtor, who hath paid away all his Substance to satisfy his Creditors, is a close Prisoner, within the Prison: Thus the Debtor who will not pay his Creditors lives at Ease, and he who cannot pay, suffers.

The Prisoners enjoying the Liberty the Rules are, by the present Usage of the Court of *King's-Bench*, in some Manner, protected, even in Criminal Cases; For if they are guilty of the greatest Crimes, or Disorders, they cannot (by the Opinion of that Court) be committed by any Authority, but that of the Judges of the said Court (of *King's-Bench*.) So that if a Murder, Riot or Mutiny should happen whilst the said Judges are on the Circuits, or otherwise absent, there is no Power to commit to the County Goal any (I.)

Prisoner in the Rules, who shall be concerned therein; For should a Justice of the Peace, on Complaint made, commit a Prisoner in the Rules, to the County Goal, he would, it seems (by a late Opinion of the said Court) be deemed guilty of a Rescue and Escape, and be liable to the Debts of the Prisoner, whom he had so committed: For,

It appears that a Complaint was made, in *December* 1728, to *Samuel Woodham* Esquire,[19] one of His Majesty's Justices of the Peace for the County of *Surry*, against *Humphrey Heybord* and *Joseph Allen* (two Prisoners in the Rules) for violently assaulting a Woman, and other Misdemeanors, and they not being able to find Security for their Appearance at the next Quarter Sessions, for the said County, Mr. *Woodham* committed them to the said County Goal: On this, the Marshal moved the Court of *King's-Bench* for an Attachment against Mr. *Woodham;* And the Matter being brought before the Court, the Court declared that Mr. *Woodham,* in committing the said *Heybord* and *Allen,* (Prisoners in the Custody of the Marshal) to the County-Goal, upon any Pretence whatsoever, (notwithstanding the County Goal was within the Rules of the Prison of the *King's-Bench*) was guilty of a Rescue: After which the Court interposed, and prevailed with the said *Mullens* (the Marshal) to make up the Matter, on Mr. *Woodham's* paying Thirty One Pounds, Costs; (for committing two Prisoners who had broke the Peace, and could not find Security.)

The high Rent paid by the Marshal, occasions exorbitant Fees, Extortions and many other Inconveniences.

The Marshal hath One Shilling, *per* Night, for every Prisoner who lies in a Spunging House, which may be a great Inducement to him to keep Prisoners from coming into the Prison.

The Prison-Fees are exorbitant; and the Judges having met together, and proceeding to take the same into their Consideration, in Order to their making a Reduction thereof, (pursuant to the late Act) a Doubt arose, Whether they could or ought to reduce the said Fees, because of the Property of the Mortgagees: And this Matter remains for the further Consideration of Parliament.

That no Security being given for the safe Custody of the Prisoners, and the artful Confusion of the Title between the Trustees for *Lenthall,* and the Mortgagees, render the Custody of the said Prison unsafe and precarious.

It appeared to the Committee, That notwithstanding the Inconveniency arising from the Claim of the Mortgagees, and the high Rent paid by the Marshal, yet this Prison (of the *King's-Bench*) is much better regulated, than any other Prison the Committee hath enquired into; Which they cannot but ascribe to the Care of the Lord Chief Justice *Raymond*, who not accepting of any Presents, or Fees from the Marshal of the said Prison, hath kept the said Marshal strictly to the Performance of his Duty; and his Lordship hath heard and redressed the Complaints of the Prisoners.

It appeared to the Committee, That there are now in being some Books, and Lists of Charities belonging to this Prison; and also that there have been other Books relating to the said Charities; which Books are not now Forth-Coming.[20]

There is a Charity collected from the several Counties, and another of Monies collected in the Courts of *Westminster-Hall*, called High-Barr- (K.) Money. In the collecting the first of the said Charities there is some Difficulty, full Powers not being given for the raising thereof. And it hath been represented to the Committee, That the latter (tho' Charity Money) doth belong to the Lord Chief Justice, and that he hath a Right to dispose of the same as he thinks fit.

And it appeared to the Committee, That, out of the small Charity which (L.) yet remains unimbezled, an Attempt was lately made to deduct Monies to repair the Wards for receiving the Furniture given to the sick Rooms by the present Lord Chief Justice *Raymond:* And that these poor Creatures, besides their great Fees, pay also for repairing Rooms in the Goal, and they were induced to sign a Common Seal for this Purpose.

That the poor Prisoners suffer greatly by the applying of the Charity Money to Repairs, or to any other Uses, than dividing it amongst them, and by their not being admitted to the Common Side, and the sharing the Charities.

That the prosecuting Justices of the Peace for acting in Cases of Breaches of the Peace committed by Prisoners of the *King's-Bench* Prison, or within the Rules thereof, greatly tends to the Encouraging of Disorderly, Riotous and Dangerous Practices there.

By inspecting the Lists of Prisoners for Debt, transmitted from the various Goals of this Kingdom, and the Gazettes, and other Authorities, The Committee find, That near Six Thousand Persons have been discharged out of the said Goals, by Vertue of the Act passed in the last Session of Parliament (*For Relief of Insolvent Debtors*)[21] and that Six Hundred of his Majesty's Subjects, Fugitives for Debt, have returned and reaped the Benefit of that Act; and by the Returns of the Lists from the County Goals, it appears, that many hundred Persons are still confined there, who were Prisoners for Debt, before the Twenty Ninth Day of *September* 1728; from which Time the said Act took Place.

The Committee came to the following Resolutions, *viz.*

Resolved, That it is the Opinion of this Committee, That effectual Provision be made to prevent the Judges, their Clerks and Servants from receiving any Fees, Gifts, Presents, or any Gratuities whatsoever from the Goaler, or Keeper of any Prison, or from any Officer Intrusted with the Custody of the Prisoners, or any Person impowered by them.

Resolved, That it is the Opinion of this Committee, That it is necessary to make further Provision for the Discovering, Collecting, Distributing, and Accounting for the Charities belonging to the *King's-Bench* Prison.

Resolved, That it is the Opinion of this Committee, That it is necessary to make further Provision for Creditors, for their more easy and effectual Recovery of Debts and Damages, on the Escapes of Prisoners from the *King's-Bench* Prison.

Resolved, That it is the Opinion of this Committee, That it is necessary to make further Provision for the better Preservation of the Peace, within the *King's-Bench* Prison, and the Rules thereof.

APPENDIX.

Examination of John Wildey.

JOHN WILDEY being examined the 11th Day of *March* 1729, saith, That he this Examinant hath searched the Records at the *Tower*, and also at the Chapel of the *Rolls*, for the Original Grant from the Crown of the Office of Marshal and Prison of the *King's-Bench*, but could not find the same, or any other Deed or Conveyance relating to the said Office, either to Mr. *Lenthall* or the Duke of *Norfolk*, and that he this Examinant doth not know what Title the said *Lenthall* had thereto. (A.)

Examination of John Jones *Esq;*

JOHN JONES Esq, being examined the 16th Day of *March* 1729, saith, That he was concerned for the late Earl of *Radnor* in the Sale of the said Earl's Interest in the Office of Marshal and Prison of the *King's-Bench*, And that (B.)

he this Examinant remembers the Payment of the Consideration Money for the same, and that upwards of 10,000 *l.* was paid to the said Earl in this Examinant's Presence; and this Examinant believes that the whole Consideration Money being 10,500 *l.* was then paid to the said Earl.

Examination of Mr. Jasper Blythman.

JASPER BLYTHMAN Gent. being examined the 13*th* Day of *March* 1729, saith, That he saw the late Earl of *Radnor* sign the Receipt (now produced to him this Examinant) for 10,500 *l.* and that his this Examinant's Name, subscribed as a Witness to the said Receipt, is of this Examinant's proper Hand-writing, and this Examinant further saith, That he cannot at this Distance of Time say whether the Money was paid at the Time of Signing the said Receipt, But doth believe that the same was then paid, for that otherwise the said Earl would not have signed the said Receipt, nor should this Examinant have witnessed the same, and also for that by the Sale of the Office of Marshal and Prison of the *King's-Bench*, and of an Estate in *Wales*, the said Earl rendred his Circumstances (which before that Time were very uneasy and unsettled) entirely easy.

Lord Radnor'*s Receipt for* 10,500 *l.*
(*produced by Mr.* Wildey, 13 March 1729.)

I The Right Honourable *Charles Bodville* Earl of *Radnor*, do hereby acknowledge that I have, this twentieth Day of *September* One Thousand Seven Hundred and Eighteen, received of *Joseph Studley* of *London* Gent. the Sum of Ten Thousand and Five Hundred Pounds, of lawful Money of *Great Britain*, being the Consideration of and for my assigning to him (by an Indenture bearing equal Date herewith, and made or expressed to be made between me the said Earl of the one Part, and the said *Joseph Studley* and *Hall Loader* and *John Allen* of *London* Gent. of the other Part) the Debt remaining due to me upon several Securities made by *William Lenthall* Esq; deceased, to Sir *John Cutler* Knt. and Bar. deceased, and secured by the Office of Marshal of the *Marshalsea* of the *King's-Bench*, the Consideration of which Assignment is in the said Indenture mentioned to be a compenent Sum of Money, paid by him the said *Joseph Studley* to me, and therefore of and from the said Consideration Money, and every Part thereof, and all Demands concerning the same, I do hereby acquit and discharge the said *Joseph Studley*, Witness my Hand the Day and Year abovesaid.

Witness
    Jas. Blythman,   RADNOR.
    John Martin.
    William Batty.

An Account of the Shares of the several Proprietors of the King's-Bench. (C.)
(*delivered by Mr.* John Wildey, 13 March 1729.)

LORD Radnor assigns to Mr. *Studley* for 1050*l*.	20 *Sept.* 1718.
Mr. Studley declares That the 1050*l*. was the Money of *Richard Houlditch* and *Robert Knight*, Esquires, *Thomas Martin* and *William King*, Goldsmiths, and *William Martin* Gent. and by them paid in equal Shares, *viz.* 210*l*. apiece.	24 *Sept.* 1718.
Mr. *King* sold his Fifth Part to Mr. *Crull* for 2178*l*. 15*s*.	4 *Dec.* 1718.
Mr. *Crull* assigned to *Surman* for 2775*l*.	31 *Mar.* 1720.
Note, Upon *Surman*'s Forfeiture it became vested in the Trustees of the *South-Sea* Company.	
The Trustees assign'd to *Richard Bishop*, *Surman*'s Share for 1555*l*.	1727.
Mr. *Bishop* assigned his Share to Mr. *Preston* for 1821*l*.	21 *Mar.* 1728.
Mr. *Houlditch* sold his Fifth Part to *Richard Capper* for 2200*l*.	4 *Dec.* 1718.
Note, Mr. *Capper* acknowledged that he was only a Trustee for Mr. *Bowman*.	20 *Feb.* 1720.
Note, Mr. *Bowman*, by Will, gave his Fifth to Mr. *Thomas* and *John Martin*, in Trust, *&c.*	
Mr. *Thomas Martin* sold one Fourth of his Fifth Part to Mr. *Studley* for 525*l*.	4 *Apr.* 1720.
Mr. *Knight*'s Fifth Part became forfeited to the Trustees of the *South Sea* Company.	1721.
The Trustees of the *South-Sea* Company assigned Mr.	

Knight's Fifth Part to Mr. *Thomas Martin* for 1605 *l.*   1727.
Mr. *William Martin* assign'd one Moiety of his Fifth
Part to Mr. *John Martin* for 1200*l.*   8 *Apr.* 1721.
And afterwards the said Mr. *William Martin* assigned
the other Moiety to said *John Martin.*

Examinations of Mr. Joseph Studley, *the* 9th, 11th, *and* 13th March 1729. *At the Committee appointed to enquire into the State of the Goals of this Kingdom.*

JOSEPH STUDLEY being examined the 9th Day of *March* 1729, saith, That he is intitled to one twentieth Part of the Office of Marshal and Prison of the *King's-Bench*, and that he hath had such Share ever since the Year 1718, and that he paid for the same 525 *l.* at two Payments, in or about *October* 1718, to the Use of Mr. *William Martin:* And this Examinant further saith, That the whole Debt due to the Earl of *Radnor*, on the said Premises, was assigned to this Examinant; and that he this Examinant has all along received the Rents and Profits of the said Premises, for all the Proprietors thereof, and hath from Time to Time accounted with Mr. *Martin* and Mr. *Wildey*, who have all such Accounts, as also all the Title Deeds and Writings relating to the said Office of Marshal and Prison of the *King's-Bench*, in their or one of their Custody, and that he this Examinant hath been allowed 5*l.* a Term, for his Trouble; And this Examinant further saith, That the Book now produced by this Examinant doth contain a true Account of all Alienations of Offices, Fines and other Profits of the said Office of Marshal and Prison of the *King's-Bench* which have come to the Hands or Knowledge of this Examinant; And the said Examinant being asked whether he doth not apprehend himself lyable to make good Escapes, he this Examinant saith that he is not liable thereto, it having been so determined, upon a Tryal at Law, in *Poulter*'s Case; And this Examinant further saith, That both *Machen*, the late Marshal, and Mr. *Mullens* the present Marshal of the *King's-Bench*, were appointed Marshals since this Examinant's said Purchase, and with this Examinant's Consent, and that both the said Marshals gave Security for Payment of the Rent, but that no Security was taken from either of them to answer, or make good Escapes, or for good Behavoiur. And the said *Joseph Studley* being again examined, on the 11th Day of *March* 1729, saith, That he was present at the Execution of the Purchase Deeds, dated the 20th of *September* 1718, by the late Earl of *Radnor;* and then saw the said Earl sign the Receipt for 10500*l.* Consideration Money, and did then also see Mr. *William Martin* pay unto the said Earl several Bank Notes at Mr. *Blythman's* Chambers, in the *Temple,* but how much in the Whole was paid to the said Earl this Examinant doth not know: And the said Examinant being again examined, on the 13th Day of *March* 1729, saith, That he hath used his best Endeavours to find out *Lenthall's* Title to the Office of Marshal and Prison of the *King's-Bench,* but hath not been able to discover the same, nor can give any other Account thereof, than that he this Examinant hath been informed by Mr. *Martin,* that the Title Deeds of the said Office were lodged in the House of Lords, upon the passing of an Act of Parliament, relating to the said Prison in the 8th and 9th Years of the Reign of King *William* the Third.²²

Examination of James Slann.

JAMES SLANN, Footman to *Thomas Martin* Esq; being examined the 6th Day of *March* 1729, and asked what Property he has in the Prison of the *King's-Bench,* says, That he is a Nominal Trustee for the Heirs of Mr. *Lenthall:* And this Examinant being asked what he means by a Nominal Trustee, and by whom he was appointed such Trustee: He says, he does not know what a Nominal Trustee is, nor by whom he was appointed such. And being asked how he knows he is a Nominal Trustee, he says, he is informed that he is such, but does not know by whom he was so informed. (D.1.

And this Examinant being asked whether he Signed and Sealed the Deed now shewn to him, and by whose Order he so executed the same: he says, he did Sign and Seal the said Deed, by the Order of his Master, Mr. *Martin;* And the said Examinant being asked how long it is since he executed the said Deed, and who was present when he executed the same, he says, he does not know how long it is since he executed the said Deed, nor who was present at such Execution, except Mr. *John Wildey,* who was then present. And the said Examinant being asked, whether he ever read or heard read the said Deed, or knows the Contents thereof, saith, That he never did read or hear read the said Deed, nor knows the Contents thereof, and that he this Examinant hath Signed and Sealed several Deeds, without reading or hearing the same read, or knowing the Contents of the same.

And this Examinant being asked, whether at the Time of his executing the said Deed he apprehended he should reap any Benefit by his executing the same, or that he was thereby lyable to answer any Escapes, and whether he was able to make good Escapes that might happen, or to pay

REPORT RELATING TO KING'S BENCH PRISON 145

Four or Five Thousand Pounds on that Occasion, he this Examinant saith, that he knew not whether he was to reap any Benefit by his signing the said Deed, and that he did not apprehend, by his signing the same, he was lyable to make good any Escapes that happened, and saith, That if any Escapes should happen, he is not able to make good or pay for the same.

Examination of Mr. John Wildey.

JOHN WILDEY being examined the 6th Day of *March* 1729, and being asked (D.2.) what Property he has in the *King's-Bench* Prison, saith, that he is a Trustee for the Heirs of *Lenthall*, and was nominated such Trustee, at the Request of *John Martin* Esq; in a Deed now shewn to this Examinant, and that he this Examinant, by the verbal Order of the said Mr. *Martin*, and of Mr. *Thomas Martin*, Mr. *Studley*, and Mr. *John Preston*, did execute the other Deed, now also shewn to this Examinant.

And this Examinant being asked, whether he does not apprehend himself liable to answer Escapes, or who is liable to make good the same: He this Examinant saith, That he doth not apprehend himself, or any of the Proprietors of the *King's-Bench* Prison answerable for Escapes, but that the Marshal of the said Prison is liable to make good the same, and that he this Examinant was never put to any Trouble upon Account of Escapes: And this Examinant being asked, whether the said Marshal has given any, and what Security, to answer Escapes: This Examinant saith, that the said Marshal has given no other Security for that Purpose, than his own personal Security by a Covenant contained in the said last mentioned Deed; but this Examinant apprehends, that if any Escapes shall happen, which the said Marshal shall not be able to make good, the Heirs of *Lenthall* will be liable to make good the same: And this Examinant further saith, that he doth not, nor ever did receive any Rent whatsoever from the Marshal of the *King's-Bench*, nor ever sign any Receipt for Rent: And the said Examiant being asked whether he ever received any Surplus Money for the Heirs of *Lenthall*, he this Examinant saith, that he never did receive any such Surplus Money.

Examination of Mr. John Preston.

MR. *John Preston* being examined the 9th Day of *March* 1729, saith, That he this Examinant is entituled to one fifth Part (the Whole into five equal

Parts being divided) in the Office of Marshal of the *King's-Bench* and the Prison thereof, with the Buildings and Appurtenances thereto belonging, and that he purchased the same in *May* last, of *Richard Bishop*, to whom this Examinant paid eighteen Hundred and twenty one Pounds for the said Share; and that the said *Richard Bishop* thereupon assigned to this Examinant all the Estate and Interest of him the said *Richard Bishop* in the said Premisses; the Profits whereof, being usually accounted for by *Joseph Studley*, the Receiver thereof, every Term, this Examinant saith that he hath received for his Share of the said Profits Eight and Twenty Pounds, each Term, or thereabouts.

And the said Examinant being asked, whether he does not think himself liable to make good Escapes of Prisoners that may happen: saith, he hath been advised, and doth apprehend that he is not liable thereto, being only a Mortgagee.

And the said Examinant being asked, whether Mr. *Mullens*, was made Marshal of the *King's-Bench*, since this Examinant's said Purchase, and with this Examinant's Consent, and whether the said *Mullens* had given Security to answer, or make good Escapes, this Examinant saith, that the said *Mullens* was made Marshal since the Purchase, and with the Consent of this Examinant; and that he this Examinant doth not know that any Security has been given by the said *Mullens*, to answer or make good any Escapes.

The further Examinations of Mr. Richard Mullens, (Marshal of the King's-Bench *Prison) taken before the Committee of the House of Commons, appointed to inspect the Goals of this Kingdom, this* 21st *Day of* February 1729. *and* 9th *of April* 1730.

THIS Examinant saith, That he is Marshal of the *King's-Bench* Prison, and appointed by the Proprietors, *viz. Thomas Martin, William Martin, John Martin, John Preston,* and *Joseph Studley* Esquires, That the said Proprietors have a Right to present a Marshal of the said Prison, to the Court of *King's-Bench,* who are to approve and confirm the said Marshal, and after he is sworn in, before the said Court, he is then in full Possession of the said Office. This Examinant further saith, that, in the Year 1724, he applied to the said *Joseph Studley*, in order for to get the Office of Marshal to the *King's-Bench* Prison, and by Means of the said *Joseph Studley* was introduced to the other Proprietors, whom he (*Mullens*) met at *Garraway*'s Coffee-House, towards the End of the Year 1724, when the said Proprietors, *viz. Thomas Martin, John Martin,* and *Joseph Studley* Esquires (and as he thinks *William Martin*) were present, who proposed to the said Examinant, That they the said Proprietors would present him to the Court of *King's-Bench,* as Marshal of the said Prison, and grant him (*Mullens*) a Lease of the said Office, and Prison, for the Space of five Years, with a Right of Renewal for three Years, after the Expiration of the said Term, on Condition of paying to the said Proprietors the annual Sum of Eight Hundred Pounds; and also the further annual Sum of about Twenty Pounds as a quit Rent, and to allow to the Chamberlain of the said Prison, appointed by the Proprietors, the usual Profits of the said Office, which he hath since compounded with the said Chamberlain, for the yearly Sum of thirty Pounds; and that the said Proprietors further told him, that over and above the said Sums, he (the Marshal) before he was approved of; and sworn into the said Office, must pay One Hundred Guineas to the Lord Chief Justice of the *King's-Bench,* and a further Sum of fifty Guineas, to each of the three Puisne Judges of the said Court; That he this Examinant objected to all these Demands, as too exorbitant, from the Impossibility of fairly raising the said Sums; to which the said Proprietors answered, that if he (*Mullens*) refused to take the said Office on these Conditions, many others would gladly accept of this Offer, and that the former Marshals had made a great deal of Money of the said Office, and particularly Mr. *Machen* had got between two and three Thousand Pounds by it: This Examinant replied, that no Person could make such a Profit honestly, and if any one got so much Money in the said Office, it must be by giving Liberty to some of the Prisoners, and running away with them; to which the said *John* and *Thomas Martin,* or one of them, answered, that he (*Mullens*) must take his Chance for that, for he took the said Office with his Eyes open: And this Examinant further saith, that he agreed with the said Proprietors for the said Office, and Prison, and a Grant of the same was made to him, and executed on the 14th Day of *January* 1724, by *Richard Wellman,* a Hackney Writer to the said *John Martin,* or one of them, with the Consent of the said *Joseph Studley,* and that on or before the twenty Third Day of the said Month of *January,* he (*Mullens*) gave a Purse, containing One Hundred Guineas, into the Hands of Sir *John Prat,* the then Lord Chief Justice of the *King's-Bench;* and one other Purse, containing Fifty Guineas, to Mr. Justice *Fortescue;* and the like Sum to Mr. Justice

Powis; and he offered the like Sum to Sir *Robert Raymond*, then one of the Puisne Judges of the said Court, who refused the same, saying he did not know any such Fee was due, and that if it was not a legal Fee he would not take it, but that he would inform himself of the Lord Chief Justice and the other Judges; and some Days after, the said Sir *Robert Raymond* did accept of the said Sum, having, as he informed this Examinant, seen the Lord Chief Justice, and the other Judges of the said Court; and this Examinant has heard and believes that no Marshal was ever approved of, and sworn into the said Office, without making the said Presents, except himself, who, on the Renewal of his Grant of the said Office and Prison, was sworn into the said Office, on the Twenty Fifth Day of *January* last 1729, without making the said Presents to the Judges: And he (*Mullens*) further saith, that the Marshal usually gave, every *Christmas*, Twenty Guineas to the Lord Chief Justice of the *King's-Bench*, and Ten Guineas to each of the Puisne Judges of the said Court; but that Sir *Robert Raymond*, the present Chief Justice, has always refused the said Sum, but desired he would not mention such Refusal, least his Successors should think he lessened their Perquisites; And further saith, that Mr. Justice *Reynolds* did accept of the Ten Guineas, but sent the said Sum by his Clerk, to be distributed among the Prisoners of the said Prison: And further saith, that all the Judges of the said Court refused to take the said Presents, last *Christmas*.

R. MULLENS.

At the Committee appointed to enquire into the State of the Goals of this Kingdom.

The said *Richard Mullens* being examined, this Ninth Day of *April* 1730, in the most solemn Manner, saith that, the above written Examination, and every Part thereof is true.

R. MULLENS.

The said *Richard Mullens* further saith, That the Lease, by which he agreed to pay Eight Hundred Pounds *per Annum* to the said Proprietors, was, by the Interposition of the Lord Chief Justice *Prat*, cancelled, and a new Lease granted of the same Date, which is the Lease last expired.

R. MULLENS.

Examination of Mr. Richard Mullens, (*Marshal of the* King's-Bench *Prison*) 21 February 1729.

ABOUT five Months ago all the Judges of the *King's-Bench* ordered Mr. *Mullens* to give the Proprietors Notice, to attend them at the Lord Chief Justice's Chambers, and they all met accordingly; my Lord Chief Justice then told the Proprietors, the Occasion of sending for them, was to acquaint them, that they (the Judges) were of Opinion, that there would be a Parliamentary Enquiry into their Prison, as there had been of others, and though they apprehended they had no direct Right to make any Order upon them, (the Proprietors) yet they recommended it to them (the Proprietors) to alter the exorbitant Rent they now let it at, and though they imagined they were secure, under an Act of Parliament, yet it was their Opinion, that the Parliament would construe it, that by their letting it at such exorbitant Rents, and to People without sufficient Security, and obscure People permitted to covenant for it, that Escapes would be deemed voluntary in them, as if they had acted themselves, as Marshal; That they themselves would be liable to make good the Escapes and forfeit their Office.

R. MULLENS.

At the Committee appointed to enquire into the State of the Goals of this Kingdom.

The said *Richard Mullens* being examined this ninth Day of *April* 1730, in the most solemn Manner, saith, That the above-written Examination, and every Part thereof is true.

R. MULLENS.

The fourth Examination of Mr. Mullens, *in the most solemn Manner,* 9 April 1730. *At the Committee appointed to enquire into the State of the Goals of this Kingdom.*

RICHARD MULLENS, Marshal of the *King's-Bench* Prison, being examined, (E.) this ninth Day of *April* 1730, in the most solemn Manner, saith, That he this Examinant hath lived within the Rules of the said Prison, and been conversant therein, for the Space of ten or eleven Years, and that in or about the Year One Thousand Seven Hundred Twenty Three, one *Poulter* was committed to the Custody of *Richard Machen*, then Marshal, in Execution for 18000 *l.* and upwards, at the Suit of *William Wilson*, and that soon afterwards the said *Machen* gave the said *Poulter* the Liberty of the Rules, for 260 Guineas or thereabouts, and took a Bond from the said *Poulter's* Brother for 1000 *l.* (as the said *Machen* informed this Examinant) and in about ten Days, after the said *Poulter* obtained the Liberty of the Rules, he escaped to *Holland*, and there continues, as this Examinant is also informed; and thereupon the said *Wilson* brought an Action, in the Court of *King's-Bench* against the said *Machen*, for the said Escape, and recovered Judgment for the said Debt; and afterwards the said *Wilson* moved the said Court, that the Profits of the Office of Marshal and Prison of the *King's-Bench*, might be sequestered for the said Debt; and the Court referred it to the Master of the *King's-Bench* Office to state the Account of the Mortgagees; and the said Master reported due to them 18000*l.* and the said *Wilson* could not obtain any Satisfaction, and soon afterwards shot himself, in Despair, at an Inn, in *Barnaby-Street*, which this Examinant believes was called *St. Christopher's*; and this Examinant further saith, that the said *Machen* is now a Prisoner, in the Custody of this Examinant, at the Suits of *Elizabeth* and *Ann Wilson*, the Administratrixes of the said *William Wilson*, and also at the Suits of *Benjamin Arnold* and *Christopher Thwaites*; and that several other Prisoners besides the said *Poulter* did escape during the Time that the said *Machen* was Marshal; and that the Rent of the Office and Prison is so exorbitant, that no Person of good Substance would take the said Office, and that it has been customary for former Marshals to suffer Escapes, to enable them to raise Money to pay their Rent, and get their Livelihood.

R. MULLENS.

The Examinations of Mr. Richard Mullens (*Marshal of the* King's-Bench *Prison*) taken 23 Feb. 1729. *and* 9 April 1730.

THIS Examinant saith that *Knight* and *Surman*, being posessed of two Fifths of the Office of Marshal of the Prison of the *King's-Bench*, as he is informed, *Thomas Martin* Esq; and *Richard Bishop*, (Tipstaff of the Court of *Common-Pleas*) purchased those two Fifths, of the Trustees of the *South-Sea* Company, for the Sum of Sixteen Hundred Pounds each, as this Examinant is also informed, and some time, about twelve Months since, Mr. *Preston* (Clerk of the *Vintner's* Company) purchased Mr. *Bishop's* said Fifth, but knows not what Sum of Money was paid for it; That he computes the Fees, which he has actually received, as Marshal of the Prison, to amount to about Fifty Pounds, annually, before they were lately reduced, and that he expects very little will arise from those Fees, for the future, That what induced him to take a new Grant of the said Office and Prison, at a Rent of Seven Hundred and Fifty Pounds was, from an Assurance given him by Mr. *Studley*, one of the Proprietors, of an Intention of the Proprietors to reduce his Rent to Four Hundred Pounds, the Judges having recommended such Reduction, and in further Hopes, that if the Government should take the Goal into their Hands, he (*Mullens*) might be appointed Marshal of it; That the Profit chiefly arises from giving the Liberty of the Rules to the Prisoners; which were greatly enlarged by the late Chief Justice *Prat*, by the Addition of St. *George's-Fields* to the Rules, on Application of the Prisoners to the Court of *King's-Bench*, But having kept no Account of these Profits, he can't say what they annually produce; that he believes there are generally upwards of One Hundred and Twenty Prisoners, who enjoy the Liberty of the Rules, but that he will deliver in a particular Account of them to the Committee; That, on his being admitted Marshal, he had no Prisoners delivered to him, but such as were within the House, under the Key, which did not exceed Seventy Seven, but that he had no Account given him of all the Prisoners, that had the Liberty of the Rules, granted them by his Predecessor, *Machen*, nor does he apprehend himself to be charged or chargeable therewith; he is informed and believes, that great Numbers of those Prisoners, who then enjoyed the Rules, made their Escape when *Machen* run away; and believes he has an Authority by Virtue of a Rule of Court (the Copy of which is delivered to the Committee) to retake, and lock up any of those Prisoners, if he thinks fit, but that he is not by such Rule obliged to retake them, and thereby make himself liable; and believes this has been the Practice of all former Marshals, for many Years, since the Office has been in the Hands of particular Proprietors; That his other Profits arise to him by Groats out of the Judgments, and Bails in the Court of *King's-Bench* paid him by the Master of the *King's-Bench* Office, which he computes at about One Hundred Pounds, annually; that he lets the Profit of his Tap and Sutlerage, to one *Metcalf* (a Brewer of *Greenwich*) for One Hundred Guineas Fine, and One Hundred Guineas, yearly: That he has one Shilling out of every Day Rule, which he computes to be worth to him about Thirty Five Pounds *per Annum*, That he has One Shilling for every Night that a Prisoner lies in a Spunging-House, which he computes to be worth about Thirty Pounds, yearly; And these he declares are the only Methods by which he makes any Profits.

R. MULLENS.

At the Committee appointed to enquire into the State of the Goals of this Kingdom.

The said *Richard Mullens* being examined, this ninth Day of *April* 1730, in the most solemn Manner, saith, that the above written Examination and every Part thereof is true.

R. MULLENS.

A LIST *of the Names of the several Persons who have executed the Office of Marshal of the Court of* King's-Bench *(from the Year* 1668) *the Dates of their several Admissions, and how long they respectively continued in the said Office, as appears* per *the several books of Entry which are now in Custody of Mr.* Richard Mullens, *present Marshal of the said Court.*
Delivered by the said Mr. MULLENS.[23]   (F.)

Marshals Names.	Admitted.	How long continued.	
Mr. *Steph. Mosdell*	*Feb.* 12th 1668	To *Apr.* 23d 1672	
Mr. *Thomas Meney*	*April* 24th 1672	To *Oct.* 21st 1675	
From the Year	—— 1675	To the Year 1684	Books wanting
Mr. *Hen. Glover*	*May* 20th 1684	To *April* 12th 1687	
Mr. *Coke*	*April* 15th 1687	To *Nov.* 9th 1688	
Mr. *Philpot*	*Nov.* 23d 1688	To *May* 31st 1690	
Mr. *Will. Briggs*	*June* 2d 1690	To *Oct.* 3d 1693	
From the Year	—— 1693	To the Year 1696	Books wanting
Mr. *George Taylor*	*May* 2d 1696	To *Feb.* 23d 1698	
Mr. *Godfrey Gimbert*	*Dec.* 29th 1698	To *Mar.* 29th 1701	
Mr. *William. Sutton*	*Mar.* 15th 1700	To *Nov.* 10th 1703	
Mr. *Fr. Southward*	*Nov.* 11th 1703	The Continuance uncertain	Book cut
Mr. *Will. Broughton*	*May* 6th 1706	To *Feb.* 13th 1711	
Mr. *Moses Cook*	*Feb.* 14th 1711	To *Feb.* 7th 1715	
Mr. *David Crawford*	*Feb.* 9th 1715	To *Mar.* 8th 1721	
Mr. *Richard Machen*	*Mar.* 24th 1721	To Jan. 20th 1724	
Mr. *Rich. Mullens*	*Jan.* 24th 1724	Present Marshal	

Copy of a Rule of Court, for the new Marshal to retake such *Prisoners as had* (G.)
the Liberty of the Rules granted by his Predecessors.

*Die Mercurii in Quinden' S*ᵈ*. Hillarii Anno* 11° *Georgii Regis.*

Ordinat' est quod Marr' Maresc' hujus Cur' recapiat omnes Prisonar' ad largum existen' necnon omnes Prisonar' qui secer' escap' e Prison' Marr', & non legitime exonerantur e Prison' pr', & ducat eos in Prison' pr'.

*Ex motione M*ʳⁱ*.* KETLEBY, *per Cur'.*

Examination of Mr. John Morris.

JOHN MORRIS, Deputy Marshal of the *King's-Bench* Prison, being examined (H.)
this 21st Day of *February,* 1729, says, That he was appointed Deputy-Marshal of the *King's-Bench,* by *Charles* Earl of *Radnor,* above twenty Years ago (but hath not the Grant now with him) and paid fifty Pounds to *Thomas Cook* for the said Earl, by Way of Alienation, and a considerable Sum to him the said *Cook* (who was then Deputy-Marshal, and is since dead) for his surrendring to this Examinant; and that he paid a further Sum of Ten Guineas to one *Broughton,* the then Marshal, and Twenty Guineas to the Lord Chief Justice *Holt,* which, as far as this Examinant remembers, he gave to him with his own Hands.

Being asked, in what Manner the Office was surrendred, says, that *Cook* surrendred the Office to Lord *Radnor,* two Days before Lord *Radnor* granted the Office to the Examinant.

Being asked, what was the Business of Deputy-Marshal, says — That now the Business of Deputy-Marshal is to attend the Court of *King's-Bench,* with the Lord Chief Justice, wheresoever he goes, but formerly the Offices of Deputy-Marshal, and Clerk of the Papers were annexed; and now the Fees are given in jointly together.

Being asked if he ever gave any Thing, by Way of *Christmas* Box, to the Judges, or any Officers under them: — Says, that there was a Table kept in the Lord Chief Justice *Holt*'s Time, and now he sometimes eats at the Lord Chief Justice's Table, and he has given at *Christmas,* half a Crown, or so, to each Servant.

23ᵈ *February* 1729. JOHN MORRIS Deputy Marshal.

Examination of Samuel Woodham *Esq*; 7 April 1730. *At the Committee appointed to enquire into the State of the Goals of this Kingdom.*

SAMUEL WOODHAM Esq; one of his Majesty's Justices of the Peace for the County of *Surry*, being examined the 7th Day of *April* 1730, in the most solemn Manner, saith, That he this Examinant having, in the Month of *December* 1728, committed, for want of Sureties, to the County Goal of *Surry*, *Humphry Heybord* and *Joseph Allen*, for violent Assaults committed by them; And *Richard Mullens*, Marshal of the Court of *King's-Bench*, having threatned to move the said Court, against this Examinant, for so doing, he the said *Mullens* alledging that the said *Heybord* and *Allen* were then Prisoners in the Custody of him, (the said *Mullens*) this Examinant, together with Sir *John Gonson*,[24] did, about Three Weeks before the then next Term, wait upon the Lord Chief Justice of the said Court, and acquaint him therewith, To which his Lordship answered, That what this Examinant had done, was very right, and that this Examinant should proceed, in the same Manner, against all Offenders in the like Cases, and that he would support or protect this Examinant therein, or to that Effect: And this Examinant further saith, That the said *Mullens*, as he had before threatned, did accordingly, in *Hilary* Term 1728, move the Court of *King's-Bench*, that an Attachment might be awarded against this Examinant, for this Examinant's having committed the said *Heybord* and *Allen* to the said County Goal, as aforesaid, (although such County Goal is within the Rules of the *King's-Bench* Prison) and thereupon a Rule having been granted by the said Court, for this Examinant to shew Cause, why such Attachment should not be awarded against him, he this Examinant did attend with his Council, eight Days or thereabouts, in order to shew Cause against such Attachment, and to represent to the said Court (as he had before done to the said Lord Chief Justice) the Reasons why this Examinant had committed the said *Heybord* and *Allen* to the said County Goal, (which Reasons are contained in an Affidavit made by this Examinant, in the said Court) and this Examinant saith, That before this Examinant's Council could be heard, The said Court declared that this Examinant, in committing the said *Heybord* and *Allen* (being Prisoners in the Custody of the said Marshal) to the said County-Goal, upon any Pretence whatsoever, and notwithstanding that such County Goal was within the Rules of the Prison of the *King's-Bench*, was guilty of a Rescue, or to that Effect; and the Council for the said *Mullens* then moving; that he the said *Mullens* might be at Liberty to sue this Examinant, for the Rescues or Escapes of the said *Heybord* and

(I.)

Allen, This Examinant was asked by the said Court, whether he, this Examinant, was willing to pay unto the said *Mullens* his Costs, to which this Examinant (by the Advice of his Council, and to avoid further Prosecutions) answered, that he was willing to pay the same, and this Examinant saith, that thereupon a Bill of Costs was delivered, by the Attorney for the said *Mullens*, to this Examinant, amounting to Thirty one Pounds and upwards; in which was included one Article of 8 *l*. and upwards, for Expences, which the said *Mullens* alledged he had been at, in removing into the Crown Office several Indictments, which had been preferred against the said *Allen* and *Heybord* for Misdemeanors, they had been guilty of; no Ways relating to those for which they had been committed by this Examinant, as aforesaid; and the said Bill of Costs being referred to Mr. *Clark* (Master of the *King's-Bench* Office) for a Taxation, and a Dispute arising touching the said Article of 8 *l*. and upwards, so charged for removing the said Indictments, as aforesaid, this Examinant did attend the said Lord Chief Justice, for his Opinion, whether this Examinant ought to pay the same, and his Lordship then declared to this Examinant, he apprehended the said Court did not mean, or intend that this Examinant should pay those Costs, or to that Effect; which Declaration of his Lordship's this Examinant did communicate to Mr. *Marriot*, his, this Examinant's Attorney, who, thereupon, insisted before the said Mr. *Clark*, that the said Article should be disallowed; but the said Mr. *Clark*, not being satisfied therewith, did attend the said Lord Chief Justice alone, for his Directions therein; and the said Mr. *Clark*, at his Return from the said Lord Chief Justice, did declare that his Lordship directed, that this Examinant should pay all Costs, as well the 8 *l*. and upwards, as other the Costs contained in the said Bill; and this Examinant hath been obliged to pay the same accordingly.

SAMUEL WOODHAM.

Examination of Sir John Gonson, *in the most solemn Manner. At the Committee appointed to enquire into the State of the Goals of this Kingdom.*

SIR *John Gonson* Knight, being examined, the Ninth Day of *April* One Thousand Seven Hundred and Thirty, in the most solemn Manner, saith, That about sixteen or eighteen Months since, *Samuel Woodham* Esquire, one of his Majesty's Justices of the Peace, for the County of *Surry*, desired this Examinant to accompany him to the Lord Chief Justice of the *King's-Bench*, to inform him, that he the said Mr. *Woodham* had been threatned with Trouble, for having executed his Office, in committing Persons, who were Prisoners within the Rules of the *King's-Bench*, (on Account of Misdemeanors by them committed) to the County-Goal of *Surry* (which County-Goal this Examinant believes to be within the Rules of the *King's-Bench* Prison) That they found the said Chief Justice at his Chambers, in *Serjeant's-Inn*, and that there passed a long Conversation between the said Lord Chief Justice, Mr. *Woodham* and this Examinant, all the Particulars whereof this Examinant cannot take upon him to remember, but, upon the Whole, the said Lord Chief Justice received them with great Civility, and did not then seem to blame the said Mr. *Woodham*; but this Examinant very well remembers, that the said Lord Chief Justice then said, That he would support the said Mr. *Woodham*, and the Gentlemen in the Commission of the Peace, as far as he could by Law; or used Words to that Effect.

J. GONSON.

Examination of Mr. Joseph Mason.

MR. *Joseph Mason*, Clerk to the Lord Chief Justice of the Court of *King's-Bench*, being examined the 16th Day of *March* 1729, saith, That he this Examinant hath always received the Exibition Money belonging to the *King's-Bench*, and also the said Lord Chief Justice's Share of the High-Bar Money, which High-Bar Money has been given away by the said Lord Chief Justice to Charitable Uses; and this Examinant further saith, he believes that the High-Bar Money doth belong to the said Lord Chief Justice, and that he hath a Right to dispose of the same, as he thinks fit.

(K)

Examination of Thomas Backhouse, *Steward to the Common Side*, &c. *At the Committee appointed to enquire into the State of the Goals of this Kingdom.*

THOMAS BACKHOUSE being examined the 7th Day of *April* 1730, in the most solemn Manner, saith, That last *Michaelmas* Term the *Lord Chief Justice of the Court of King's-Bench gave Furniture for the Sick Wards* of the *King's-Bench* Prison, upon which *the Marshal* of the said Prison *told this Examinant* that the Wards were not in a fit Condition to receive the Furniture, and that *they ought to be repaired*, which this Examinant understood to be at the Expence of the Prisoners; *and accordingly this Examinant ordered the said Sick Wards* or Rooms to be *repaired*, and called the Prisoners together, and

(L.)

told them that the Marshal said it was fitting the Sick Rooms should be repaired, before the Lord Chief Justice's Furniture should be put up; and asked them whether they were consenting it should be done, and *William Watson* and *Thomas Maund*, and others, said they were consenting, and this Examinant doth not remember that any Person refused to be consenting, and that this Examinant ordered Workmen to repair the said Rooms, and when the Workmen demanded Money of him, he went to the Marshal, and desired him to send this Examinant some Moneys, To which the Marshal told him he might get the Common Seal; and this Examinant accordingly applied to the Prisoners to sign a Common Seal, and some of them refused to sign the same, particularly *William Lucas*, (who afterwards upon Persuasion did sign) and *William Moore* who then refused, and hath not yet consented to sign the said Common Seal; notwithstanding which this Examinant did obtain a Common Seal, which the said Marshal signed; and this Examinant did present the said Seal to *Joseph Mason* Gent. Clerk to the said Lord Chief Justice, in order to receive 4 *l.* 14 *s.* 5 *d.* for the said Repairs, out of the County Moneys designed for the Subsistance of the poor Prisoners, on the Common Side in the *King's-Bench*, which the said *Mason* refused to comply with, as not having any Moneys in his Hands; And this Examinant further saith, That he never knew any Money raised upon the Prisoners, nor taken out of the Charities, for Repairs; But, on Recollection, saith, That he paid for the mending of the Windows, out of the said County-Moneys, designed for the Subsistance of the said poor Prisoners, and that he did this but once, about one Year since or upwards; And this Examinant further saith, That he is Steward of the Common Side of the said Prison, and was chose such by the Prisoners, about two Years since, with the Approbation of the said Marshal.

T. BACKHOUSE.

Seal, for 4*l.* 14s. 5d. *dated* 21 March 1729. *Produced by* Tho. Backhouse, 7 April 1730.

WE the present Assistants of the Common Side of the *King's-Bench* Prison, by and with the Consent of the rest of our Fellow Prisoners, having examined the Accounts of Mr. *Thomas Backhouse*, our Steward, in respect to the Repairs in and about the Sick Rooms in the said Prison, do find that there is due to him, on that Account, the Sum of Four Pounds Fourteen Shillings Five Pence; and we do hereby desire *Samuel Clark* Esq; to affix hereto our

House-Seal, and Mr. *Joseph Mason* to pay to our said Steward the said Sum of 4*l.* 14*s.* 5*d.* out of our County-Money, as it is or shall become due to us; as witness our Hands this 21st Day of *March* 1729.

    R. Mullens, Marshal.   *Will. Watson,*
               Robt. Greenwood, Assistants.
               Will. Lucas,
               J. Howell,
               John Giles,
               Joseph Mott,
               Edward Russett,
               Rich. Whittaker.

THE Resolutions of the Committee being severally read a Second Time, were, upon the Question severally put thereupon, agreed unto by the House, and are as follow, *viz.*

Resolved,

That effectual Provision be made to prevent the Judges, their Clerks and Servants from receiving any Fees, Gifts, Presents or any Gratuities whatsoever from the Goaler or Keeper of any Prison, or from any Officer intrusted with the Custody of the Prisoners, or any Person impowered by them.

Resolved,

That it is necessary to make further Provision for the Discovering, Collecting, Distributing and Accounting for the Charities belonging to the *King's-Bench* Prison.

Resolved,

That it is necessary to make further Provision for Creditors, for their more easy and effectual Recovey of Debts and Damages on the Escapes of Prisoners from the *King's-Bench* Prison.

Resolved,

That it is necessary to make further Provision for the better Preservation of the Peace with the *King's-Bench* Prison, and the Rules thereof.

Ordered,

That the said Report, with the *Appendix*, be printed, And that Mr. *Speaker* do appoint the Printing thereof, and that no Person but such as He shall appoint do presume to print the same.

FINIS.

An Appeal for the
Georgia Colony (1732)

This anonymous and untitled request for contributions toward the proposed Georgia colony appeared in the *London Journal* for July 29, 1732.[1] From several quotations, some of them extended ones, from Oglethorpe's then unpublished *Some Account of the Design of the Trustees for establishing Colonys in America*, it seems obvious that this appeal was by Oglethorpe himself.[2] He was, after all, the designated publicist for the Trustees, with the specific responsibility of assuring favorable publicity in the newspapers. Although the parallels of generous Greeks and Romans with contemporary Englishmen may now seem somewhat confusing, Oglethorpe's readers were familiar with the classical models and their English parallels. From the introductory statement that English readers are "of the same nation" with the models, we know that these models are contemporary rather than classical; various anachronisms confirm contemporary times; and the tenses gradually shift from past to present. Such parallels—the use of Greek and Roman models and names for contemporary Englishmen—were prominent in the poetry of Alexander Pope and indeed generally in the literature of the time. Apparently Oglethorpe found this sort of parallel useful for praising friends and colleagues without embarrassing them and perhaps convenient for praising several under one name.

I reprint from the *London Journal*.

To the Author of the LONDON JOURNAL.

SIR,

As you often express a tender Compassion for the Miseries of your Fellow-Creatures; I hope you'll give the following Letter a Place in your Journal, because its chief Aim is to relieve the Distressed.

THE thinking of the Misfortunes of others, and giving Succour to the afflicted, even before they ask, is the most glorious Action that can be performed by a mere human Creature; and if we consider this as flowing from the Christian Motive Charity, it meets with a Reward even in this Life, and secures a present internal Happiness, by the Assurance of a perpetual one hereafter.

Separate from that greater Motive of a future Reward, things are so ordered by Nature, that as *Philanthropia,* or the Love of Mankind, prevails more or less, the State flourishes or declines. In the Time of *Scipio* the *African,*[3] the whole *Roman* People had a noble Tenderness for the Miseries of others. A Latin Audience was not then led away by a loose Jest, or idle Song; but a tender and generous Sentiment affected uncorrupted *Romans.* When *Chremes* says, *Homo sum: humani nihil a me alienum puto,* the crowded Theatre wept and applauded.[4] A City so sensible of what was right, so touched with the Miseries of their Fellow-Creatures, could not fail of Success; they were worthy of the Empire of the World, and they soon acquired it.

In a State where this Spirit prevails, the People multiply wonderfully; for this is the very opposite to sordid Self-love, Oppression, and Cruelty. Where this Love of Mankind prevails, there is no need of Laws to force Humanity, and prevent the Oppression of the Powerful; Good-nature there makes the Great a Law to themselves. When this Disposition is general, the selfish Wretch, even when authorized by Law, is afraid of oppressing his Inferiors; since such a Proceeding would draw upon him Contempt and Infamy[.] The Usurer is ashamed to profit of the elapsed Day. The Colonel will no more wear Lace purchased by the off Reckonings, than he will wear the old Clothes of the Soldier. The Lawyer will not keep a poor Man's Fee, on a Cause broke off undetermined. The Gentleman will not take the Advantage of the Mortality of a Family, and refuse to renew an expired Lease, because the Orphan's Father and Mother died together. The Physician will not write twice a Day in a House,[5] where Want is perhaps a greater Ill than the Distemper, at least equally sure to destroy.

The reciting the Weakness of Mankind is very disagreeable, but it is pleasant to dwell upon Instances that set human Nature in a beautiful Light. Who can help rejoicing, that he is of the same Nation and Species with *Hippocrates, Decius, Messala,* and *Cornelius?* The brave *Leostenes* left *Evadne* with a numerous Family of Children in strait Circumstances. *Hippocrates* was her Physician in a dangerous Illness;[6] he refused to receive the Fees which his frequent Attendance intitled him to: She seemed to be uneasy under this Generosity: *Hippocrates* perceived it, and then received Fees constantly, but sent a Bank Note from an unknown Hand, of much more Value than the Fees he received.

Decius was Colonel of a Regiment for some Years,[7] and in those Times when there was Money saved by Clothing, he regularly divided the Profits amongst the Widows and Orphans of the Officers of his Regiment.

Messala fills the Bench with the Applause of Mankind.[8] The Prisoners, in a Jurisdiction of which he had the Care, petitioned him against the Oppression of their Keeper; he sat Three whole Days to hear their Complaints; and finding that their Adversaries hoped, from the Necessities of the Accusers, to stifle Truth, he gave them Money sufficient to bring their Cause to a full Hearing.

Cornelius,[9] descended from a Race of Heroes and Patriots, has successfully commanded Armies; he makes Frugality and OEconomy the great Foundation of Generosity: by this he can do Justice to all, pay his Debts, be generous to those who deserve it, and serve his Country without fear of losing his Employments: He declines Expence; but if an Officer, who had served his Country well, had not wherewithall to buy a Commission which of Right belonged to him, *Cornelius* lent him Money, without Interest, without Security. When the Estates of a great Number of his Countrymen, (hereditary Foes to his Family) by Forfeiture, fell into his Hands; to his hereditary Enemies he gave back their Fortunes, and became a prevalent Solicitor for the Lives of those his Sword had vanquish'd. The Employments under him, which, by his Predecessors, used to be sold, and made no inconsiderable Part of the Perquisite or Income of the Office, he gives some as a Reward to the Veterane Soldier, when discharged; some to the Orphans of Officers, who by employing all their Time and Blood in the Service of the Publick, could not provide for the future Support of their Families; yet the undiscerning Multitude blames the Frugality of *Cornelius*, and call *Thraso* generous.[10]

Alphus is called covetous;[11] had he not been frugal, he would not be the rich *Alphus*. By Industry and Frugality he has got and saved a great Estate: He has purchased Lands large enough to make an *Italian* Principality, but has not raised the Rents of one of his Tenants; he envies them not the Comforts earned by the Sweat of their Brow; he is glad to have his Tenants live well; he looks on them as Men, and as such rejoices in their Enjoyment of the Comforts of Life. When Lives drop, he puts in the next Relation at the ancient moderate Fine; and, in Cases of great Compassion, he abates, or even remits that. Such Men, when their Duty or their Country calls for it, can be generous; whilst the extravagant Prodigal, who gives and owes, may be unjust, but can't be generous.

A compassionate Feeling of the Miseries of others, a kind Striving to relieve them, strikes with Love even those who do not receive the Benefit. When one gives to a wretched Object in the Streets, the poor Passers-by frequently bless you, for that which they have in their Will, but not in their Power to do. I, like these, applaud the generous and good-natur'd Acts; which, since I have not the Power to do, I must beg your Assistance to commend[.] Nor can I quite despair of our Times, tho' bad enough, since I see not only particular Instances of Good-nature, but Numbers associated to carry on the common Cause of Humanity. I read the other Day a little Book, containing an Account of the persecuted *Saltzburghers*,[12] with a more melancholy Pleasure than I should a good Tragedy. The Concern for the wretched Multitude raised Compassion; and the Satisfaction to find that in *England* there is still left a Number of Gentlemen, who make the Afflictions of their distressed Protestant Brethren their own, pleased wonderfully.[13] I believe there is not a thinking Man whose Heart has not yearned for their Sufferings; and yet how impotent was that Compassion? Men of large Fortunes, and generous open Hearts, might feel severely for them; but they knew not which way to succour them. But now that these Gentlemen have offered their Assistance, every one in *England*, that has Money and Inclination, can, by their Means, convey Relief to Men distressed in the utmost Parts of *Germany*. The poor Wanderer, banished for his Religion, with his starving Babes crying round him, will, in the suburbs of *Frankfort* and *Ausburgh*, be preserved from perishing, by Charity perhaps given in some Inland County of *England*. Whomsoever God has blessed with Wealth, has now an Opportunity to relieve them; and if he neglects it, he is as much guilty of their Sufferings, as if he saw them perish, and would not assist them.

There is another Society, of whose Intentions I have seen something in the News-Papers, heard much in Conversation, and yet learn but little perfectly. They seem to me the most luxurious of People, and are providing for themselves the most exquisite and delicate kind of Entertainment, that of making the Miserable happy; and being blessed by all the lower Degrees and Ranks of People; I cannot help envying them. I never repined at the Narrowness of my Fortune till now, that it renders me incapable of giving Assistance to such a Design: Yet since Gold nor Silver I have none, I will, by your Assistance, give them what I have, the Fruits of several Years Experience and Reading. We know where it said, a poor Man saved a City;[14] why may not a poor Man's Advice be useful in founding one?

Want of Property is now called the greatest Misfortune, and by many deemed the only one. He who has no Money, nor Means of getting a Livelihood, is now in *England* an Outcast of the Society; and a Leper amongst the *Jews* was not more miserable, nor more abandoned. Without paying, he cannot have Food; he cannot have a Shed to cover him: If he begs, the Beadle raises a Tax upon him, or whips him, for taking the Liberty of asking without his Licence; if he can find Credit, and takes up upon Trust, he loses Light and Air, and rots in a Dungeon, instead of starving at large;[15] and yet these are at least Fellow-Creatures, if not Christian Brethren, *for whom we believe Christ died.* And tho' some may be brought into these Circumstances by Vices, yet many are so by their Folly, many by inevitable Misfortunes, and many even by a strict Adherence to Virtue.[16] It seems odd to say the last; but (not to mention scrupulous Consciences about Religion and Government) how many are ruined by being indulgent Parents, kind Brethren, pious Children, or generous Friends? How many themselves become Bail, rather than see a Father, a Brother, a Child, or (which is much dearer) a Friend, torne away to Prison, and buried forever within a Jayl? Much worse than buried; for in the Grave there is Rest; but here they are intombed alive, and mixed with shameless Profligates; forced to hear the most horrid Converse, and subject to the Passions of the most absolute, rapacious, and abandoned of Men! What noble Temper, but, to prevent them from suffering, will expose himself? What generous Man, when urged on by Nature and Friendship, can help plunging into the Pit-fall of the Law, and becoming Security? The Unfortunate, fallen from better Circumstances into extreme Want, are very numerous. Stocks, Trade, Law-Suits, Guardians, Fires, Servants, Bubbles, and other numberless Accidents, reduce good Families from flourishing, into miserable Circumstances. Numberless are the lower Sort of People who, drawn to *London* by the Hopes of high Wages, cannot get Employment; each Trade is so over-stock'd, that Masterly Hands only can earn Bread. The want of Friends, want of Credit, or a false Shame of working in a lower Degree, prevents several honest Men from being useful in *England;* and makes them perish for Want, fly their Country, or seek for Bread by unlawful Means. Want first reduces them to Sickness, or Prison; and when the Man's Industry is useless, the Wife and wretched Children must either perish, or ask Relief of their Parish, which perhaps disowns them, perhaps allows them enough to prevent their being famished to Death, but not enough to prevent Sickness, the constant Companion of Famine.[17] I have heard, at a moderate Computation, that 2000, not including Prisoners, (of whom are computed double that Number) perish yearly of this kind of Distemper, tho' the Name of it is hardly found in the Weekly Bills. To avoid it, the unfortunate *Richard Smith* not only destroyed himself, but, out of a dreadful Fondness to free his Wife and Child from a wretched World, killed them also.[18] Nor is this now a thing unusual; how frequent mention is there in the Prints of those, who, to avoid Want, fall Self-murder'd? How generous and Christian an Action would it be, to preserve such Multitudes? And as most good Actions do, it carries with it a consequential Reward, and Six Thousand Subjects yearly saved; and their natural Increase would, in the Age of a Man, augment the Wealth and Power of a State beyond what is easily conceived. These Trustees then intend to save these wretched People, and give them once again an Opportunity of using their Industry, once again a Chance of living comfortably; they will *deserve* that unutterable Pleasure, which they cannot but reap from such an Action.

I have often wondered, that no Use was made of those vast Tracts of waste Lands subject to the Crown of *Great Britain* in *America*. It was generally held by the old Civilians,[19] that it was unjust for one Nation to keep vast Quantities of Land uncultivated; they esteemed this so wrong a thing, that they mentioned it as one of the just Causes of War. If this be to neighbouring Nations, how much more is it so to our own Subjects, whilst you let them perish for want of those Lands to exercise their Industry upon, which you suffer to be the Receptacle of wild Beasts only. *Rome, Athens*, and the glorious Republicks of the ancient World, thought it of as much Consequence to preserve their Citizens, and build Towns, as to conquer them from Enemies: They, at the Publick Expence, defrayed the Charge of establishing their necessitous People in Colonies.

If I understand it right, the Trustees for the Colony of *Georgia* are to take the same Care, of sending forth and maintaining those whom Misfortunes forced to quit their native Country. But for to defray this Expence there is no Tax, nor is any one obliged to pay towards it, the Good-nature and Humanity of each Man is the Assessor. If the Trustees intend to employ the Money collected to relieve the Prisoner, to give Bread to the

Hungry, Clothes to the Naked, Liberty of Religion to the Oppressed for Conscience sake; to rescue deluded Youth, or helpless Orphans, from the Temptations Want or idle Company may expose them to; and of these to form well-regulated Towns, and to give them Houses, Cattle, and Lands of Inheritance; to instruct them how to raise all those good Things which make Life comfortable; and how to enjoy them under such Laws as tend to make them virtuous and happy both here and hereafter.[20] If these are their Intentions, these Motives will be the most active Tax Gatherers. Not a Good-natur'd Man of any Substance in *England*, but what will give something towards it; and a very little given by each Man, amounts to a great Sum.[21]

If they give Liberty of Religion, establish the People free, fix an *Agrarian* Law, prohibit within their Jurisdiction that abominable and destructive Custom of Slavery, by which the labouring Hands are rendered useless to the Defence of the State. In fine, if they go upon the glorious Maxims of Liberty and Virtue, their Province, in the Age of a Man, by being the Asilum of the Unfortunate, will be more advantagious to *Britain* than the Conquest of a Kingdom.

With respect to Trade, as it is now in their Power without Injustice, to order that as they please, they should prohibit the making any Manufactures, but give the People Encouragement to raise such gross Produces as may enable them to buy all they want to better Advantage than if they made them. This may be done there by having the People instructed in raising Silk, Wine and Oil. *London* pays to *Italy* only for Raw Silk 300,000 l. a Year, and that is the kind of Silk which thrives in *Carolina*.[22] The *English* Plantations in *America* pay 115,000 l. to the *Portugueze* at the *Maderas* for Wine, and Oil is no inconsiderable Article. If Men can earn 30 or 40 l. a Year by their Labour on these rich Commodities, they will never attempt to make Woolen Goods, Iron Work, Stockings, or any other Manufactures, which they can buy from *England*, where they are made by Men who work for 15 or 20 l. a Year.[23]

In a few Years these Things may be brought to much greater Perfection, than one would now venture to say. About the Year 1690, the first Rice was carried to *Carolina* in One Hundred Pound Bag; and in 1722, 24000 Barrels of Rice was imported from thence to Europe.[24] So that *England*, which used to buy Rice from Abroad, now furnishes Foreign Markets, and does the same in Pitch and Tarr.

The Profit and Gain that will arise from this Design, if it is well executed, is the meanest Motive; therefore I shall not dwell upon that, but the relieving Thousands, who, in the Anguish of their Souls, curse their very Being; and the saving them from Destruction here, and perhaps hereafter, are Motives that would sway every tender, generous and christian Soul, to give their utmost Assistance to so noble a Work.

I have thus thrown in my little Mite. If I knew more of the Intentions of the Trustees, I could write better upon the Subject. If the Hints I have given should be of Use to them in directing their Measures; or if what I have said should incline any one Person to be a Benefactor to so good a Work, I have attained my End, and done that by my Pen which my Circumstances would not allow me to do with my Purse.

Select Tracts
Relating to Colonies (1732)

elect Tracts Relating to Colonies appeared on or about November 7, 1732, when it was advertised in the *London Evening Post* as published "This Day." Although copies of this edition have been conjecturally dated as early as 1700 and as late as 1741, there was only one impression in the century. It was reprinted, without attribution, by Trevor B. Reese in *The Most Delightful Country of the Universe: Promtional Literature of the Colony of Georgia, 1717–1734* (Savannah, 1972), 76–112.

Although Oglethorpe's editorship has been questioned,[1] it seems established in a letter that Thomas Coram wrote on November 20, 1732, to Henry Newman, secretary of the SPCK: "If you have not one of the Stitchd Books containing about 40 or [4]5 pages which Mr. Oglethorpe had printed entitled Select Tracts relating to Colonys I will inclose one of them to you if you will pleas to permit me."[2] Oglethorpe's editorship is confirmed by the bibliographer John Nichols, who in his *Literary Anecdotes of the Eighteenth Century* asserted that both *Selects Tracts* and *A New and Accurate Account of the Provinces of South-Carolina and Georgia* were "the production of James-Edward Oglethorpe."[3] There is also considerable internal evidence that Oglethorpe edited the little anthology, for the excerpts there seem to have been taken from books that Oglethorpe owned,[4] and he had already briefly sketched his mercantile thinking in his *Some Account of the Design of the Trustees*.

Since Oglethorpe's design for a charitable colony grew out of his concern for relocating London debtors, he must have realized early in his planning that support for his colony would depend not only upon private contributions, but upon parliamentary subventions; and he knew that many members of Parliament felt that emigration drew off Britain's most valuable resource—its citizenry. To counter this feeling, Oglethorpe edited and reprinted some of the mercantile classics that argued the benefits of emigration.

In editing his selections, Oglethorpe took considerable liberties, mainly those of omission. Only the first selection, Francis Bacon's "Essay on Plantations," is printed entire, apparently from Oglethorpe's copy of the 1696 edition of the *Essays*, pages 92–95. From the others, Oglethorpe selected only what was apt for his purpose. All the excerpts from Machiavelli, apparently reprinted from Oglethorpe's copy of *The Works* (London, 1680), are fragments. The third selection, supposedly written by Jan de Witt, is actually chapter 26 of Pieter de la Court's *Het Interest van Holland* (Amsterdam, 1662), printed from Oglethorpe's copy of *The True Interest and Political Maxims of the Republick of Holland . . . Written by John de Witt* (London, 1702).[5] Here Oglethorpe reprinted most of the chapter, but omitted the footnotes and side notes and skipped from page 146 to page 153. From *Some Account of the Province of Pennsilvania* (London, 1681), by William Penn, Oglethorpe used only the first four pages of the text. From Sir Josiah Child's "Discourse concerning Plantations," which he took from a copy of *A New Discourse concerning Trade* (London, 1692), he reprinted the first half. Where he omitted text, he usually, but not always, indicated these omissions by long dashes.

Some of the omissions that he did not indicate are quite interesting. Thus in the selection from Child, in the second answer to the fourth proposition, "every Person sent abroad with the *Negroes* and Utensils" becomes "every Person sent abroad with Utensils"; and in the same sentence Oglethorpe omitted "it being customary in most of our *Islands* in *America*, upon every Plantation, to employ eight or ten Blacks for one white Servant." On rare occasions Oglethorpe also altered his original. Since Machiavelli was rarely concerned with colonies, but established political principles that the economic mercantilists developed, Oglethorpe sometimes altered his original in order to make the author's comments more pertinent to the colonial situation. For example, in chapter 10 of *The Prince*, where the author was concerned with "principalities," the editor substituted, in the chapter title, "*Cities* or *Colonies*"; and in the opening sentence he altered "free" to "safe." In the opening sentence of chapter 11 of the *Discourses upon Titus Livius*, Machiavelli's "Commonwealth" becomes "virtuous City." Apart from such infrequent substantive changes as these, there seems to be no reason why we should regard the accidental changes as Oglethorpe's: he probably sent marked copies of the books and pamphlets along to the printer; and in the eighteenth century the compositor sometimes adapted his copy to his own printing house style.

Select Tracts is here reproduced from the first, undated impression of 1732.

SELECT TRACTS RELATING TO COLONIES.

CONSISTING OF

I. An Essay on Plantations. By Sir FRANCIS BACON Lord Chancellor of *England*.

II. Some Passages taken out of the *History of Florence*, &c.

III. A Treatise. By JOHN DE WITT Pensioner of *Holland*.

IV. The Benefit of Plantations or COLONIES. By WILLIAM PENN.

V. A Discourse concerning Plantations. By Sir JOSIAH CHILD.

[Printer's ornament]

LONDON,

Printed for J. ROBERTS at the *Oxford-Arms* in *Warwick-Lane*.

Price Six-pence.]

THE INTRODUCTION.

NOTHING *so much improves the Mind, and directs the Judgment to right Determinations as Experience and the Opinions of wise Men. As new* Colonies *are now so much talked of,*[6] *it may be agreeable to the Publick, to see what has been writ upon that Subject by Philosophers, Statesmen, and Merchants, Men of different Professions, living in different Ages and Countreys, who could have no common View in deceiving. To save the Reader therefore the Trouble of hunting their Opinions out in many Books, the following Tracts are collected and published.*

The first is by one whose great Genius was not only an Ornament to the Nation and Age he lived in, but an Honour to Mankind. It is by Tradition deliver'd down, that he writ his Treatise on Plantations upon the following Occasion.

Sir Walter Raleigh *the excellent Historian, Soldier, Statesman, and Philosopher,*[7] *made many Attempts to settle in* America, *went twice in Person to* Guiana *and once to* Virginia, *the latter of these was granted to him by Queen* Elizabeth, *who loved great Designs, carried her Views far, and studied the Welfare of* England *in future Generations as well as in her own Age. Under her Countenance he settled the first* Colony *in* Virginia, *so nam'd in Compliment to her Majesty. The Queen died, and with her expired all Encouragement to noble Undertakings.* Raleigh *not fit for a weak Mixture of timorous and arbitrary Measures was disgraced, condemned, imprisoned; the Plantation neglected, and all Thoughts of* America *given over by the Court.*

But tho' Sir Walter *was destroyed, his Spirit survived**, and "many worthy Patriots, Lords, Knights, Gentlemen, Merchants, and others held Consultation and procured a Patent establishing a Council and Company, whereby* Colonies *to* Virginia *should be deduced, and the Affairs of that Plantation should be governed."*[8] *The Earl of* Southhampton *and* Sir Edwin Sandys, *among many other very considerable Men, were of that Council, and they being intimate Friends of* Sir Francis Bacon, *prevailed with him to write Instructions concerning the new Colony. This was afterwards printed amongst his Essays, and is here annexed.*[9]

The next consists of Passages taken out of different Parts of the Florentine Historian.[10] *He treats of* Colonies *as a Politician, and therefore mentions them as they may be useful or prejudicial towards the preserving or increasing the Power*

---

*See a short Collection of the most remarkable Passages from the Beginning to the Dissolution of the *Virginia* Company, p. 2. printed 1651.

of the Prince or State. Being thoroughly conversant with the Ancients, he from the Roman *Maxims chalks the Outlines of a Plan for peopling a whole Countrey in a regular Manner, and by that Means remedying the Inconveniencies of Climate, Air, and Soil. He shews the Difference between supporting Conquests by Garrisons of* Colonies, *and supporting them by mercenary Troops, and just sketches out the only Plan upon which he seems to think they can be successfully founded, viz. Religion, Liberty, good Laws, the Exercise of Arms, and Encouragement of Arts. It is much to be lamented, that he did not write upon this Subject professedly, but only took it up cursorily; this makes him very short, but yet he who reads with Attention will find great Depth in what he writes, and many excellent Things to be learnt.*

The third Tract was writ by John De Witt *the famous Pensionary of* Holland, *who being both a Statesman and a Merchant mixes political with trading Considerations. This Piece was first published single, but afterwards some small Additions made and printed in his political Maxims.*

The fourth Tract is writ by William Penn *Proprietary of* Pensilvania. *It was printed in the Year* 1680,[11] *about the Time that he began to settle that* Colony, *and given amongst his Friends, but never sold; so that the Copies of it are exceeding scarce. These were the Maxims upon which he acted, and which he so successfully pursued, that he peopled the Province of* Pensilvania, *where he laid out the City of* Philadelphia. "*Foreseeing the Effects of Justice, Liberty, and wise Regulations, he formed the Plan to admit of great Increase; he chose a Situation between two navigable Rivers, and designed a Town in Form of an oblong Square, extending two Miles in Length from one River to the other. The long Streets eight in Number, and two Miles in Length, he cut at right Angles by others of one Mile in Length and sixteen in Number, all strait and spacious; he left proper Spaces for Markets, Parades, Keys, Wharfs, Meeting-houses, Schools, Hospitals, and other future publick Buildings. In the Province there is now eighty Thousand Inhabitants and in the Town of* Philadelphia, *a great Number of Houses. It increases every Day in Buildings, which are all carried on regularly according to the first Plan.*"[12]

The fifth Tract is a Discourse by Sir Josiah Child.[13] *He writ with an excellent Intention, that of undeceiving the People, by exposing several vulgar Errors, the twelfth of which vulgar Errors, and which in this Discourse he labours to confute is,* "*That our Plantations depopulate, and consequently impoverish England.*" *He did this so effectually, that whereas before he wrote, the generality of the World believed that Plantations depopulated the Kingdom, and consequently strove to hinder them; all wise Men have since the publishing of his Book been undeceived, and the Plantations have been continually encouraged by Parliament, to the great Increase of the Wealth, Trade, and People of the Kingdom.*

AN
ESSAY
ON
PLANTATIONS
BY
Sir FRANCIS BACON Ld. *Verulam.*

PLANTATIONS are amongst Ancient, Primitive, and Heroical Works. When the World was young, it begat more Children; but now it is old it begets fewer: For I may justly account new Plantations to be the Children of former Kingdoms. I like a Plantation in a pure Soil, that is, where People are not displanted, to the end, to plant others; for else it is rather an Extirpation, than a Plantation. Planting of Countries is like planting of Woods; for you must make account to lose almost twenty Years profit, and expect your Recompense in the End. For the principal Thing that hath been the Destruction of most Plantations, hath been the base and hasty drawing of Profit in the first Years. It is true, speedy Profit is not to be neglected, as far as may stand with the good of the Plantation, but no farther. It is a shameful and unblessed Thing, to take the Scum of People, and wicked condemned Men, to be the People with whom you plant: And not only so, but it spoileth the Plantation; for they will ever live like Rogues, and not fall to work, but be lazy, and do mischief, and spend Victuals, and be quickly weary; and then certify over to their Countrey to the Discredit of the Plantation.[14] The People wherewith you plant, ought to be Gard'ners, Plowmen, Labourers, Smiths, Carpenters, Joiners, Fishermen, Fowlers, with some few Apothecaries, Surgeons, Cooks, and Bakers. In a Countrey of Plantation, first look about what kind of Victual the Countrey yields of it self to hand; as Chesnuts, Wallnuts, Pine-Apples, Olives, Dates, Plumbs, Cherries, Wild-honey, and the like, and make use of them. Then consider what Victual, or esculent Things there are, which grow speedily, and within the Year; as Parsnips, Carrots, Turnips, Onions, Radish, Artichoaks of *Jerusalem*, Maiz, and the like. For Wheat, Barley and Oats, they ask too much labour: But with Pease and Beans you may begin, both because they ask less labour, and because they serve for Meat as well as for Bread. And of Rice likewise cometh a great Increase, and it is a Kind of Meat. Above all, there ought to be brought store of Bisket, Oat-meal, Flour, Meal, and the like in the Beginning, till Bread may be had. For Beasts and Birds, take such as are least subject to Diseases, and multiply fastest; as Swine, Goats, Cocks, Hens, Turkeys, Geese, House-Doves, and the like. The Victual in Plantations ought to be expended almost as in a besieged Town, that is, with a certain Allowance; and let the main Part of the Ground employed to Gardens or Corn, be to a common Stock, and to be laid in, and stored up, and then delivered out in Proportion, besides some Spots of Ground that any particular Person will manure for his own private Use. Consider likewise what Commodities the Soil, where the Plantation is, doth naturally yield, that they may some way help to defray the Charge of the Plantation: So it be not, as was said, to the untimely Prejudice of the main Business; as it hath fared with Tobacco in *Virginia*. Wood commonly aboundeth but too much, and therefore Timber is fit to be one. If there be Iron-Ore, and Streams whereupon to set the Mills, Iron is a brave Commodity where Wood aboundeth. Making of Bay-Salt, if the Climate be proper for it, should be put in Experience. Growing Silk likewise, if any be, is a likely Commodity. Pitch and Tar, where Store of Firs and Pines are, will not fail. So Drugs and Sweet-Woods, where they are, cannot but yield great Profit. Soap-Ashes likewise, and other Things that may be thought of. But moil not too much under Ground; for the Hope of Mines is very uncertain, and useth to make the Planters lazy in other Things. For Government, let it be in the Hands of one assisted with some Counsel; and let them have Commission to exercise martial Laws with some Limitation. And above all, let Men make that Profit of being in the Wilderness, as to have God always, and his Service before their Eyes. Let not the Government of the Plantation depend upon too many Counsellors and Undertakers in the Countrey that planteth,[15] but upon a temperate Number; and let those be rather Noblemen and Gentlemen, than Merchants; for they look ever to the present Gain. Let there be Freedoms from Customs, till the Plantation be of Strength; and not only Freedom from Customs but Freedom to carry their Commodities, where they may make the best of them, except there be some special Cause of Caution. Cram not in People, by sending too fast, Company after Company, but rather hearken how they waste, and send Supplies proportionably; but so, as the Number may live well in the

Plantation, and not by Surcharge be in Penury. It hath been a great endangering to the Health of some Plantations, that they have built along the Sea and Rivers in marshy and unwholesome Grounds.[16] Therefore, tho' you begin there to avoid Carriage and other like Discommodities, yet still build rather upwards from the Streams, than along. It concerneth likewise the Health of the Plantation, that they have good Store of Salt with them, that they may use it with their Victuals, when it shall be necessary. *If you plant where Savages are, do not only entertain them with Trifles and Gingles*, but use them JUSTLY *and graciously*, with sufficient Guard nevertheless; and do not win their Favour by helping them to invade their Enemies,[17] but for their Defence it is not amiss. And send oft of them over to the Countrey that plant, that they may see a better Condition than their own, and commend it when they return.[18] When the Plantation grows to Strength, then it is time to plant with Women as well as with Men, that the Plantation may spread into Generations, and not be ever pieced from without. It is the sinfullest Thing in the World to forsake or destitute a Plantation once in forwardness; for besides the Dishonour, it is Guiltiness of Blood of many commiserable Persons.

Some Passages taken out of the History of Florence, *Book II.*[19]

AMongst the great and admirable Orders of former Kingdoms and Common-wealths (tho' in our Times it is discontinued and lost) it was the Custom upon every Occasion to establish Colonies and build new Towns and Cities; and indeed nothing is more worthy and becoming an excellent Prince, a well dispos'd Common-wealth, nor more for the Interest and Advantage of a Province, than to erect new Towns, where Men may cohabit with more Convenience both for Agriculture and Defence. For besides the Beauty and Ornament which followed upon that Custom, it render'd such Provinces as were conquer'd more dutiful and secure to the Conqueror, planted the void Places, and made a commodious Distribution of the People; upon which living regularly and in Order, they did not only multiply faster, but were more ready to invade, and more able for Defense. But by the Negligence and Omission of Common-wealths and Principalities this Method of establishing Colonies being at present disused, the Provinces are become weaker and some of them ruined. For (as

I said before) it is this Order alone that secures a Countrey and supply's it with People. The Security consists in this, that in a new Contrey a Colony placed by Authority, is a Fortress and Guard to keep the Natives in Obedience; neither without this can a Province continue inhabited, or preserve a just Distribution of the People, because all Places being not equally fertile or healthful, where it is barren they desert; where unwholesome they die; and unless there be some Way to invite or dispose new Men to the one as well as the other, that Province must fail; the abandoning some Places leaving them desolate and weak, and the thronging to others, making them indigent and poor. And forasmuch as these inconveniencies are not to be remedied by Nature, Art and Industry is to be applied; and we see many Countries which are naturally unhealthful, much better'd by the Multitude of Inhabitants; the Earth being purifi'd by their Tillage, and the Air by their Fires, which Nature alone could never have effected. Of this *Venice* is an Instance sufficient; for tho' seated in a sickly and watrish Place, the Concourse of so many People at one Time made it healthful enough. *Pisa* by reason of the Malignity of the Air was very ill inhabited till the Inhabitants of *Genoa* and its Territories, being defeated and dispossessed by the *Saracens*,[20] it followed that being supplanted all of them at once, and repairing thither in such Numbers, that Town in a short Time became populous and potent. But the Custom of sending Colonies being laid aside, new Conquests are not so easily kept, void Places not so easily supplied; nor full and exurberant Places so easily evacuated. Whereupon many Places in the World, and particularly in *Italy*, are become desolate and deserted in respect of what in former Ages they have been, which is imputable to nothing but that Princes do not retain their ancient Appetite of true Glory, nor Commonwealths the laudable Customs of the Ancients.

The PRINCE.

CHAP. III. *Speaking of the Methods by which distant Provinces may be kept in Subjection, he says,*[21]

THERE is another Remedy rather better than worse, and that is to plant *Colonies* in one or two Places, which may be as it were the Keys of that State, and either that must be done, or of Necessity an Army of Horse and

Foot be maintain'd in those Parts, which is much worse; for Colonies are of no great Expence; the Prince sends and maintains them at a very little Charge, and intrenches only upon such as he is constrained to dispossess of their Houses and Land for the Subsistence and Accomodation of the new Inhabitants, who are but few, and a small Part of the State; they also who are injured and offended, living dispersed and in Poverty, cannot do any Mischief, and the rest being quiet and undisturbed, will not stir, lest they should mistake, and run themselves into the same Condition with their Neighbours.

I conclude likewise, that those Colonies which are least chargeable, are most faithful and inoffensive, and those few who are offended are too poor and dispersed, to do any hurt, as I said before.——But if instead of Colonies an Army be kept on foot it will be much more expensive, and the whole Revenue of that Province being consumed in the keeping it, the Acquisition will be a Loss, and rather a Prejudice than otherwise. ——In all Respects therefore, this Kind of Guard is unprofitable, whereas on the other Side Colonies are useful.——The *Romans* in their new Conquests observ'd this Course, they planted their Colonies, entertained the inferior Lords into their Protection without increasing their Power, they kept under such as were more potent, and would not suffer any Foreign Prince to have Interest among them.

CHAP. X. *In the following Paragraph, he gives an Example from the* Germans *how Cities or* COLONIES *may be safe, where the Friendship of the neighbouring Inhabitants is doubtful.*[22]

THE Towns in *Germany* are many of them safe, tho' their Countrey and District be but small.——Because they are all so well fortified, every one looks upon the taking of any one of them as a Work of great Difficulty and Time, their Walls being so strong, their Ditches so deep, their Works so regular, and well provided with Cannon, and their Stores and Magazines always furnished for a Twelvemonth. Besides which, for the Aliment and Sustenance of the People, and that they may be no Burthen to the Publick, they have Work-houses, where for a Year together the Poor may be employed in such Things as are the Nerves and Life of that City, and sustain themselves by their Labour. Military Discipline and Exercises are likewise in much request there, and many Laws and good Customs they have to maintain them.

DISCOURSES *upon* TITUS LIVIUS. Book I. Chap. I.²³

ALL Cities are built either by Natives born in the Countrey where they were erected, or by Strangers. The first happens when, to the Inhabitants dispersed in many and little Parties, it appears their Habitation is insecure, not being able apart (by Reason of their Distance or Smallness of their Numbers) to resist an Invasion (if any Enemy should fall upon them) or to unite suddenly for their Defence without leaving their Houses and Families exposed, which by Consequence would be certain Prey to the Enemy. Whereupon to evade those Dangers, moved either by their own Impulse, or the Suggestions of some Person among them of more than ordinary Authority, they oblige themselves to live together in some Place to be chosen by them for Convenience of Provision and Easiness of Defense. — The second Case, when a City is raised by Strangers, it is done either by People that are free, or by those who are depending (as Colonies) or else by some Prince or Republick to ease and disburthen themselves of their Exuberance, or to defend some Territory, which being newly acquired, they desire with more Safety and less Expence to maintain of which Sort of Colonies several were built by the People of *Rome* all over their Empire — And because Men build as often by Necessity as Choice, the Judgment and Wisdom of the Builder is greater where there is less Room and Latitude for his Election; it is worthy our Consideration, whether it is more advantageous building in barren and unfruitful Places, to the end that the People being constrain'd to be industrious, and less obnoxious to Idleness might live in more Unity, the Poverty of the Soil giving them less Opportunity of Dissension. Thus it fell out in *Raugia*,²⁴ and several other Cities built in such Places; and that Kind of Election would doubtless be most prudent and profitable, if Men could be content to live quietly of what they had, without an ambitious Desire of Command. But there being no Security against that, but Power, it is necessary to avoid that Sterility, and build in the fruitfulest Places can be found, where their Numbers increasing by the Plentifulness of the Soil, they may be able not only to defend themselves against an Assault, but repel any Opposition shall be made to their Grandeur: And as to that Idleness to which the Richness of the Situation disposes, it may be provided against by Laws and convenient Exercise joined, according to the Example of several wise Men, who having inhabited Countreys pleasant, fruitful, and apt to produce such lazy People improper for Service; to prevent the Inconvenience which might follow thereupon, enjoined such a Necessity of Exercise to such as were intended for the Wars, that by Degrees they became better Soldiers than those Countreys which were mountainous and barren could any where produce. Among whom may be reckoned the Kingdom of *Egypt*, which notwithstanding that it was extremely pleasant and plentiful, by the Virtue and Efficacy of its Laws, produced excellent Men, and perhaps such, as had not their Names been extinguished with Time, might have deserved as much Honour as *Alexander* the Great, and many other great Captains whose Memories are so fresh and so venerable among us. And whoever would consider the Government of the *Soldan*, the Discipline of the *Mamalukes*, and the rest of their Militia before they were extirpated by *Selimus* the *Turk*,[25] might find their great Prudence and Caution in exercising their Soldiers, and preventing that Softness and Effeminacy to which the Felicity of their Soil did so naturally incline them.

For these Reasons I conceive best to build in a fruitful Place, if the ill Consequences of that Fertility be averted by convenient Laws. *Alexander* the Great being desirous to build a City to perpetuate his Name, *Dinocrates* an Architect came to him,[26] and undertook to build him one upon the Mountain *Athos*, and to recommend and enforce his Proposal besides the Goodness of the Soil he persuaded him it should be made in the Shape and Figure of a Man a Thing which would be new, wonderful and suitable to his Greatness. But when *Alexander* enquired whence it was to be supplied, the Architect replied he had not consider'd of that; at which *Alexander* laugh'd very heartily, and leaving him and his Mountain to themselves, he built *Alexandria*, where People might be tempted to plant by the Richness of the Soil, the nearness of the Sea, and Convenience of the River *Nile*.

CHAP. X.[27]

AMONG all excellent and illustrious Men, they are most Praise-worthy who have been the chief Establishers of Religion and of the Worship of the Deity. In the second Place are they who have laid the Foundations of any Kingdom or City; in the third, those who having the Command of great Armies have enlarged their own or the Dominion of their Countrey; in the next Place learned Men of all Sciences, according to their several Studies and Degrees; and last of all (as being infinitely the greatest Number) come the Artificers and Mechanicks; all to be commended as they are ingenious or skillful in their Professions. On the other Side they are infamous and detestable, who are contemners of Religion, Subverters of Governments, Enemies of Virtue, of Learning, of Art, and in short of every Thing that is useful and honourable to Mankind; and of this Sort are the Prophane, the Seditious, the Ignorant, the Idle, the Debauch'd, and the Vile. And altho' Nature has so order'd it, that there is neither wise Man nor Fool, nor good Man, nor bad, who if it were propos'd to him which he would chuse of these two Sorts of People, wou'd not prefer that which was to be preferr'd, and condemn the other; yet the Generality of Mankind deluded by a false Impression of Good, and vain Notion of Glory, leaving those Ways which are excellent and commendable, either wilfully or ignorantly wander into those Paths which lead them to Dishonour; and whereas to their immortal Honour they might establish a Commonwealth or Kingdom as they please, they run headlong into a Tyranny, not considering what Fame, what Glory, what Affection, what Security, what Quiet and Satisfaction of Mind they part with; nor what Reproach, Scandal, Hate, Danger and Disquiet they incurr. It is impossible but all People (whether of private Condition in the Common-wealth, or such as by their Fortune or Virtue have arriv'd to be Princes) if they have any Knowledge in History, and the Passages of old, would rather chuse (if private Persons) to be *Scipios* than *Caesars:* and (if Princes) to be *Agesilaus, Timoleon* and *Dion,* than *Nabis, Phalaris,* or *Dionysius;*[28] because they must find one highly celebrated and admired, and the other as much abhor'd and condemn'd; they must find *Timoleon* and the rest to have as much Interest and Authority in their Countries as *Dionysius* or *Phalaris* had in theirs, and much more Security. Nor let any Man deceive himself in *Caesar*'s Reputation, finding him so exceedingly eminent in History, for those who have cry'd him up, were either corrupted by his Fortune, or terrified by his Power, for whilst the Empire continued, it was never permitted that any Man should speak any Thing against him, and doubtless had Writers had their Liberty they could have said as much of him as of *Cataline;*[29] and *Caesar* is so much the worse of the two, by how much it is worse to effect and perpetrate an ill Thing, than to design it;

CHAP. XI.[30]

HE that would establish a virtuous City at this Day, would find it more easy among the rude People of the Mountains, who have not been acquainted with Civility, than among such as have been educated in Cities, where their Civility was corrupted; like rude unpolish'd Marble, which is more readily carved into a Statue, than what has been mangled already by some bungling Workman. So that all Things consider'd, I conclude that

Religion being introduced by *Numa*,[31] was one of the first Causes of that City's Felicity, because Religion produced good Laws, good Laws good Fortune, and good Fortune a good End in whatever they undertook. And as strictness in divine Worship, and Conscience of Oaths, are great Helps to the Advancement of a State, so Contempt of the one and Neglect of the other are great Means of its Destruction. Take away Religion, and take away the Foundation of Government.

CHAP. XXI. *The Author in the following Passage proves, that any Kind of Men may be made Soldiers; from whence may be drawn, that there is no need of having regular Soldiers, if the Men who form a* COLONY *be disciplin'd.*[32]

THERE is scarce any Body ignorant, that of late Years the *English* invaded *France*, and entertain'd no Soldiers but their own; and yet tho' *England* had had no Wars of thirty Years before, and had neither Officer nor Soldier who had ever seen a Battle, they ventured to attack a Kingdom, where the Officers were excellent, the Soldiers good, having been trained up for several Years together in the *Italian* Wars. This proceeded from the Prudence of the Prince, and the Excellence of the Government, in which (though in Times of Peace[)] the Exercise of Arms is not intermitted. *Pelopidas* and *Epaminondas* having relieved *Thebes*, and rescued it from the Tyranny of the *Spartans*,[33] finding themselves in the Middle of a servile and effeminate People, they so order'd it by their Virtue and Discipline, that they brought them to the Use of Arms, took the Field with them against the *Spartans*, and overthrew them. From whence that Historian infers, that there are Soldiers not only in *Lacedemon*, but wherever there are Men, if there be any Body to exercise and train them; which *Tullus* perform'd most exquisitely among the *Romans*,[34] as is most excellently express'd by *Virgil*, in these Words;

———— *Desidesque movebit*
Tullus *in arma viros.*[35]

BOOK II. CHAP VI.[36]

WE shall now speak of the *Roman* Customs, —— by which it will appear with what Wisdom they deviated from the common Ways of the World, and by what easy Methods they arriv'd at their Supremacy and Grandeur. He who makes War at his own Choice and is under no Constraint, or else by Ambition has doubtless this End, to get what he is able, and keep it whilst he can, and rather to enrich than impoverish his own Countrey: For such a one it is necessary to have Regard to his Charge, and to see that neither the conquering nor maintaining are more expensive to him than will consist with his Revenue. — And whoever consi[ders] their Wars from the Beginning of *Rome* to the Siege of the *Vei*,[37] will find that they were determined in a very short Time, some in six, some in ten, and some in twenty Days. For their Custom was upon the first Appearance of a War, immediately to draw out their Army, and seeking out the Enemy they did what they could to bring him to a Battle. Having beaten him by Reason of the Surprize; the Enemy, that his Countrey might not wholly be harrass'd, for the most Part proposed an Agreement, in which the *Romans* were sure to insist upon some Part of their Territory; which either they converted to their particular Profit, or consigned to some *Colony*, which was to be placed there for the Security of their Frontiers; by which means the Wars being ended in a short Time, their Conquests were kept without any considerable Expence; for the *Colony* had that Countrey for their Pay, and the *Romans* had their *Colonies* for their Security. Nor could there be any Way more advantageous and safe; for whilst there was no Enemy in the Field, those Guards were sufficient; and when any Army was set out to disturb them, the *Romans* were always ready with another in their Defence, and having fought them, they commonly prevail'd, forced them to harder Conditions, and return'd when they had done: by which Means they gain'd daily upon the Enemy, and grew more powerful at Home: And in this Manner they proceeded till their Leaguer before *Veij*. — From that Time they maintain'd War at greater Distance, whereby they were obliged to continue longer in the Field, yet they left not their old Custom of dispatching it as soon as they could, with respect to the Circumstances of Place and Time; for which Reason they continued their *Colonies*. — And then for continuing their *Colonies*; the great Advantage and Convenience that resulted from them, was sufficient to prevail. This Practice therefore was observed perpetually among the *Romans* in the Management of their Wars, only they varied something about the Distribution of the Prey. — —They thought convenient, that the Publick should have its Share; that upon any new Enterprize they might not be constrain'd to lay new Taxes upon the People; and by this Way their Coffers were fill'd in a short Time. So that by these two Ways, by the Distribution of their Prey, and the Settling of *Colonies* Rome grew rich by its Wars, whereas other Princes and States (without great Discretion) grow poor.

CHAP. VII. *What Proportion of Land the* Romans *allow'd to every Man in their* COLONIES.[38]

I Think it no easy Matter to set down the exact Proportion of Land which the *Romans* assign'd to every single Person in their *Colonies*; for I believe they gave more or less, according to the Barrenness or Fertility of the Soil; and that in all Places they were sparing enough. And the first Reason that induces me, is, that thereby they might send more Men, and by Consequence their Frontiers be better guarded: Another is, because living at Home indigent themselves, it is not to be supposed they would suffer those whom they sent abroad to grown too opulent and rich: And in this I am much confirm'd by *Livy*, where he tells us that upon the taking of *Veij*, the *Romans* sent a *Colony* thither, and in the Distribution of the Land alotted every Man no more than three Acres, and a little more according to our Measure.[39] They might consider likewise that their Wants would not be supplied by the Quantity so much as the Improvement and Cultivation of their Land. Yet I do not doubt but they had publick Pastures and Woods to sustain their Cattle, and supply themselves without firing, without which a *Colony* could hardly subsist.

CHAP. XIX.[40]

THESE false Opinions are so rooted in the Minds of Men, and so confirm'd with ill Examples, that no Body thinks of reforming our late Errors, or restoring the old Discipline of the *Romans*. — Which if Princes and Commonwealths could be persuaded to believe, they would commit fewer Faults, be more strong against the Insults of the Enemy, and those who had the Government of any civil State, would know better how to conduct and manage themselves, either as to the Enlargement, or Conservation of their Dominion, and find, that Leagues and Confederacies, rather than absolute Conquests; sending *Colonies* into what they had conquer'd; making publick Funds of the Spoils of the Enemy; to infest and perplex the Enemy rather with Excursions, and Battles, than Sieges; to keep the Publick rich, and the Private poor, and with all possible Caution to keep up a well Disciplined and orderly Militia are the Ways to make a Commonwealth formidable and great.

JOHN DE WITT

A

TREATISE

Proving that it would be very advantageous for the Rulers and People of Holland, *and for Traffick and Commerce, as well as Navigation, to erect* Dutch COLONIES *in Foreign Countries. By* John De Witt, *Pensioner of* Holland.[41]

Supposing all the Expedients which the wisest of Men could invent to attract or allure Foreigners to become Inhabitants of *Holland* were practised, and those Inhabitants made to subsist by due Administration of Justice, yet would there be found in *Holland* many old and new Inhabitants, who for want of Estate and Credit, live very uneasily, and therefore would desire to remove thence. It is evident first as to Persons and Estates, that the Inhabitants here are not only exposed to the ordinary Misfortunes of Mankind, of not foreseeing future Events, Weakness, and Want; but besides, they make very uncertain Profit by Manufactures, Fishing, Trading, and Shipping. And on the other side by Sickness, Wars, Piracies, Rocks, Sands, Storms, and Bankrupts, or by the Unfaithfulness of their own Masters of Ships they may lose the greatest Part of their Estates, whilst in the Interim they continue charged with the natural Burdens of *Holland*, as great House-Rent, Imposts, and Taxes; nor have they any reformed Cloisters to provide creditable Opportunities for discharging themselves by such Losses of maintaining their Children, or according to the Proverb to turn Soldier or Monk; so that by such Accidents falling into extreme Poverty, they consequently lose their Credit and Respect among Men: For to have been Rich is a double Poverty, and nothing is less regarded than a poor Man's Wisdom; In such Cases he would find himself in the most lamentable Condition that can befal a Man in this World.

And secondly, as to Reputation: It is well known that in this Republick the Government consists of very few Men in Proportion to the Number of Inhabitants; And that the said Government is not by Law annexed or restrained to any certain Family, but is open to all the Inhabitants; so that they who have been eight or ten Years Burgers, may be chosen to the Government in most Cities, and have the most eminent Employments of *Scheepen* or Burgomaster. Whence we may infer, that many that were of the Offspring of those that were heretofore made use of in the Government, and also many others, who by reason of their ancient Stock, and great Skill in Polity and extraordinary Riches, thro' natural Self-love and Ambition, conceive themselves wronged, when other new Ones of less Fitness and Estate, are chosen to the Government before them; and therefore thinking themselves undervalued, seek a Change, and would be induced to transport themselves to other Countries, where their Qualifications, great Estate, and Ambition, might produce very good Effects. Whereas on the other Side, whilst they continue to dwell in these Lands, they speak ill of the Government and Rulers in particular. And if by this or any other Accident, Tumults should be occasioned against the Rulers in particular, or the Government itself, they, being Persons of Quality, might become the Leaders of the Seditions, who to obtain their End, and to have such Insurrections tend to their Advantage, would not rest till they had displaced and turned out the lawful Rulers, and put themselves in their Places, which is one of the saddest Calamities that can befal the Republick, or Cities: Seeing Rulers who became such by Mutiny, are always the Cause of horrible Enormities before they attain the Government, and must commit many Cruelties e'er they can fix themselves on the Bench of Magistry.

And seeing we have already made many Conquests of Countries in *India*,[42] and finding how hardly (and that with great Charge of Soldiers) they must be kept; and that *the Politicians of old have taught us, that there is no better Means, especially for a State which depends on Merchandize and Navigation, to preserve Foreign Conquests, than by setling* COLONIES *in them:* We may easily conclude, that the same Method would be very useful and expedient for our State.

Thirdly, it is well known, that the poorest People of all the Countries round about us, come to dwell in *Holland* in Hope of earning their Living by Manufactury, Fisheries, Navigation, and other Trades; or failing that, that they shall have the Benefit of Alms-Houses and Hospitals, where they will be better provided for than in their own Countrey. And altho' in this Manner very many poor People have been maintained; yet in bad Times it could not last long; but thence might easily arise a general Uproar, with the Plunder and Subversion of the whole State: To prevent which, and other the like Mischiefs, and to give discontented Persons and Men in

Straits an open Way, the Republicks of *Tyre, Sidon, Carthage, Greece,* and *Rome, &c,* in ancient Times, having special Regard to the true Interest of Republicks, which were perfectly founded on Traffick, or Conquests of Lands, did not neglect to erect many *Colonies:* Yea even the Kings of *Spain, Portugal,* and *England, &c.* have lately very profitably erected divers *Colonies,* and continue so doing in remote and uncultivated Countries; which formerly added an incredible Strength, to those ancient Republicks, and do still to *Spain, Portugal,* and *England, &c.* producing besides their Strength the greatest Traffick and Navigation. So that it is a wonderful Thing that *Holland* having these old and new Examples before their Eyes; and besides by its natural great Wants, and very great Sums of Money given yearly for Charity to poor Inhabitants, and being yearly press'd by so many broken Estates, and want of greater Traffick and Navigation, hath not hitherto made any free *Colonies* for the Inhabitants of *Holland;* tho' we by our Shipping have discovered and navigated many fruitful uninhabited, and unmanured Countries, where if *Colonies* were erected, they might be free, and yet subject to the Lords the States of *Holland,* as all the open Countries and Cities that have no Votes amongst us are; and it might cause an incredible great and certain Traffick and Navigation with the Inhabitants of *Holland.*

It is well worth Observation, that these Colonies would no less strengthen the Treasure and Power of the States in Peace and War, than they do those of *Spain, Portugal,* and *England,* which during the manifold intestine Dissensions and Revolutions of State, have always adhered to their ancient native Countrey against their Enemies. And by this Means also many ambitious and discontented Inhabitants of *Holland* might conveniently *sub Specie honoris,* be gratified, by having some Authority in and about the Government of the said *Colonies.* But some may object, that heretofore the Rulers of *Holland* in the respective Grants or Charters given to the East and *West-India* Companies, have given them alone the Power of navigating their Districts, with Exclusion of all other Inhabitants, which extend so far, that out of them the whole World hath now no fruitful uninhabited Lands, where we might erect new *Colonies;* and that those Districts are so far spread, because our Rulers trusted, that the said Companies could, and would propagate and advance such Colonies: Tho' supposing those *Colonies* must indeed in Speculation be acknowledged singularly profitable for this State, yet nevertheless those respective Districts and Limits Bounds of the said Companies, were purposely extended so far by the States General, and especially by the States of *Holland,* effectually to hinder the making of those Colonies, since our Nation is naturally averse to Husbandry, and utterly unfit to plant Colonies, and ever inclined to merchandizing.

To which I answer, that it's likely the first Grants or Charters, both of the East and West, and other copious Districts, were probably made upon mature Deliberation; but that the Rulers perceiving afterwards how very few Countries the said Companies do traffick with, and what a vast many Countries and Sea-Ports in their Districts remain without Traffick or Navigation, they cannot be excused of too great Imprudence in that they have, notwithstanding the Continuance of such Districts to this Day, kept their common trading Inhabitants, consisting of so great Numbers, from those uninhabited Countries by our Companies: So that by Reason of the Want of trafficking Countries or new Colonies in little *Europe* and its Confines, the *Hollanders* are necessitated to overstock all Trade and Navigation, and to spoil and ruin them both, to the great Prejudice of such Merchants and Owners of Ships on whom it falls, altho' *Holland*, during that Time of their Trades being overstock'd had a greater Commerce, and deterred the Traders of other Countries from that Traffick, which the *Hollanders* with the first Appearance of Gain do, and must reassume, if they will continue to live in *Holland*; where all Manner of Foreign Trade since the erecting the said Companies was necessitated to be driven, notwithstanding the Uncertainty of Gain, and Fear of over-trading our selves.

And that the said Companies neither have nor do endeavour to make new Colonies for the Benefit of the Lands, and the Inhabitants thereof, hath hitherto abundantly appeared, and we must not lightly believe that they will do otherwise for the future; which I suppose will also appear, if we consider, that the Directors from whom this should proceed, are advanced and privately sworn to promote the Benefit of the Subscribers of the respective Companies; so that if the Colonies should not tend to the Benefit of the Subscribers in general, we cannot expect the Companies should promote them. Yea, supposing such Colonies should tend to the greatest Profit of the said Subscribers in general, yet such is the common Corruption of Man, that those Plantations should not be erected unless such Directors or Governors can make their own Advantage by them.

And seeing all new Colonies in unmanured Countries, must for some Years together have Necessaries carried to them, till such Plantations can maintain themselves out of their own Product, begin to trade and go to Sea, and then there is some small Duty imposed on the Planters and their Traffick, or Navigation, whereby the Undertakers may be reimbursed: Yet the Partners having expended so much, are not assured, that their Grant or Lease of Years shall be prolonged and continued to them on the same Terms. Moreover, in regard of these new Colonies, the Directors ought therefore to have less Salary, seeing by this free Trade of the Planters and Inhabitants, they may be eased of the great Pains they take about their general Traffick and Equipage of Ships, which concerns them much in particular for many considerable Reasons not here to be mention'd.

And as concerning our People in the East and West, they being hitherto of so loose a Life, are so wasteful, expensive, and lazy, that it may thence seem to be concluded, that the Nation of *Holland* is naturally and wholly unfit for new Colonies; yet I dare venture to say it is not so: But certain it is, that the Directors of the said Companies their Mariners and Soldiers, and likewise their other Servants are hired on such strait-laced and severe Terms, and they require of them such multitude of Oaths, importing the Penalty of the Loss of all their Wages and Estate, that very few Inhabitants of *Holland*, unless out of mere Necessity, or some poor ignorant slavish-minded and debauched Foreigners, will offer themselves to that hard Servitude.[43] It is also true that all such as are in the *Indies*, especially the *East-Indies*, do find that not only while they serve, but after they have served their Time for which they are bound, they are under an intollerable compulsive Slavery; insomuch, that none can thrive there but their great Officers, who being placed over them, to exact the Oaths of the Mercenaries or Hirelings, and to put in Execution the Companies Commands, and being without Controul, to accuse or check them, they commonly favour one another, and afterwards coming Home with great Treasures are in Fear that they will be seized and confiscated by the Directors.[44] So that it is no Wonder that so few good, and so many ignorant, lazy, prodigal, and vicious People take Service of the *East-India* Company. But it is doubly to be admired, that any intelligent, frugal, diligent, and virtuous People, especially *Hollanders*, unless driven by extreme Necessity, should give up themselves to that slavish Servitude.

All which being true, let none think it strange, that the Scum of *Holland* and of most other Nations having by their Service become Freemen there, and yet not permitted to drive any Trade by Sea, or with Foreign People, are very unfit, and have no Inclination at all to those forced Colonies, do always thirst after their own sweet and free native Countries of *Holland*: Whereas notwithstanding on the contrary, the ingenious, frugal, industrious *Hollanders*, by those Virtues which are almost peculiar to them, are more fit than any Nation in the World to erect Colonies and to live on them, when they have the Liberty given them to manure them for their own Livelihoods. And those that doubt thereof, let them please to observe, that the *Hollanders* before and since these two licens'd Companies, even under Foreign Princes, have made many new Colonies;[45] namely, in *Lyfland, Prussia, Brandenburgh, Pomerania, Denmark, Sleswick, France, England, Flanders, &c.* and moreover have not only manured unfruitful unplanted Lands, but also undertaken the chargeable and hazardous Task of draining of Fenlands. And it is observable that in all the said Places their Butter, Cheese, Fruits, and Product of the Earth, are more desired, and esteemed than those of their Neighbours. And if we farther observe, that no Countries in the World, whether the Land be for Breeding, or Feeding, are so well order'd as those of our plain Lands in *Holland;* and that no others, Boors or Husbandmen, do travel so many Countries as ours do; we shall be convinced, that no Nation under Heaven is so fit for setting up of new Colonies, and manuring of Ground as our People are. And if in our Nation there is also to be found (which however is unjustly and unwisely denied by the Opposers of these new *Holland* Colonies) a very great Aptness and Inclination to Merchandising and Navigation, then we may in all Respects believe, that we under our own free Government might erect very excellent Colonies when it shall please the State to begin and encourage the same on good Foundations, and to indulge them for a short Time with their Favour and Defence.

The Benefit of Plantations, or COLONIES. By William Penn.[46]

COLONIES are the Seeds of Nations, begun and nourish'd by the Care of wise and populous Countries; as conceiving them best for the Increase of humane Stock, and beneficial for Commerce.

Some of the wisest Men in History, have justly taken their Fame from this Design and Service: We read of the Reputation given on this Account to *Moses, Joshua,* and *Caleb,* in Scripture Records; and what Renown the *Greek* Story yields to *Lycurgus, Theseus,* and those *Greeks* that planted many Parts of *Asia.* Nor is the *Roman* Account wanting of Instances to the Credit of that People; they had a *Romulus,* a *Numa Pompilius;*[47] and not only reduc'd, but moraliz'd the Manners of the Nations they subjected; so that they may have been rather said to conquer their Barbarity than them.

Nor did any of these ever dream it was the Way of decreasing their People or Wealth: For the Cause of the Decay of any of those States or Empires was not their Plantations, but their Luxury and Corruption of Manners: For when they grew to neglect their ancient Discipline that maintain'd and rewarded Virtue and Industry, and addicted themselves to Pleasure and Effeminancy, they debased their Spirits and debauch'd their Morals, from whence Ruin did never fail to follow to any People. With Justice therefore I deny the vulgar Opinion against Plantations, that they weaken *England*; they have manifestly inrich'd, and so strengthen'd her, which I briefly evidence thus.

First, Those that go into a Foreign Plantation, their Industry there is worth more than if they stay'd at Home, the Product of their Labour being in Commodities of a superiour Nature to those of this Countrey. For Instance, what is an improv'd Acre in *Jamaica* or *Barbadoes* worth to an improv'd Acre in *England?* We know 'tis three times the Value, and the Product of it comes for *England*, and is usually paid for in *English* Growth and Manufacture. Nay, *Virginia* shews, that an ordinary Industry in one Man produces three Thousand Pound Weight of Tobacco, and twenty Barrels of Corn yearly: He feeds himself, and brings as much of Commodity into *England* besides, as being return'd in the Growth and Workmanship of this Countrey, is much more than he could have spent here: Let it also be remembered, that the three Thousand Weight of Tobacco brings in two Thousand Two-pences by Way of Custom to the King, which makes twenty-five Pounds; an extraordinary Profit.

Secondly, More being produc'd and imported than we can spend here, we export it to other Countries in *Europe*, which brings in Money, or the Growth of those Countries, which is the same Thing; and this is the Advantage of the *English* Merchants and Seamen.

Thirdly, Such as could not only not marry here, but hardly live and allow themselves Cloaths, do marry there and bestow thrice more in all Necessaries and Conveniences (and not a little in ornamental Things too) for themselves, their Wives and Children, both as to apparel and household Stuff; which coming out of *England*, I say 'tis impossible that *England* should not be a considerable Gainer.

Fourthly, But let it be consider'd, that the Plantations imploy many Hundreds of Shipping, and many Thousands of Seamen; which must be in divers Respects an Advantage to *England*, being an Island, and by Nature fitted for Navigation above any Countrey in *Europe*. This is follow'd by other depending Trades, as Shipwrights, Carpenters, Sawyers,

Hewers, Trunnel-makers, Joyners, Slop-sellers, Dry-salters, Iron-workers, the East-land Merchants, Timber-sellers, and Victuallers, with many more Trades which hang upon Navigation: So that we may easily see the Objection (that the *Colonies* or Plantations hurt *England*) is at least of no Strength, especially if we consider how many Thousand *Blacks* and *Indians* are also accomodated with Cloaths and many Sorts of Tools and Utensils from *England*, and that their Labour is mostly brought hither, which adds Wealth and People to the *English* Dominions. But 'tis further said, they injure *England*, in that they draw away too many of the People; for we are not so populous in the Countries as formerly. I say there are other Reasons for that.

First, Countrey People are so extremely addicted to put their Children into Gentlemens Service, or send them to Towns to learn Trades, that Husbandry is neglected; and after a soft and delicate Usage there, they are for ever unfitted for the Labour of a farming Life.

Secondly, The Pride of the Age in its Attendance and Retinue is so gross and universal, that where a Man of a Thousand Pounds a Year formerly kept but four or five Servants, he now keeps more than twice the Number; he must have a Gentleman to wait upon him in his Chambers, a Coachman, a Groom or two, a Butler, a Man Cook, a Gardner, two or three Lacques, it may be an Huntsman, and a Faulkner; the Wife a Gentlewoman and Maids accordingly: This was not known by our Ancestors of like Quality. This hinders the Plough and the Dairy from whence they are taken, and instead of keeping People to manly Labour, they are effeminated by a lazy and luxurious Living; but which is worse, these People rarely marry, tho' many of them do worse; but if they do, it is when they are in Age; and the Reason is clear, because their usual keeping at their Masters is too great and costly for them with a Family at their own Charge, and they scarcely know how to live lower; so that too many of them chuse rather to vend their Lusts at an evil Ordinary than honestly marry and work. The Excess and Sloth of the Age not allowing of Marriage, and the Charge that follows; all which hinders the Increase of our People. If Men, they often turn Soldiers, or Gamesters, or Highwaymen; if Women, they too frequently dress themselves for a bad Market, rather than know the Dairy again, or honestly return to Labour; whereby it happens that both the Stock of the Nation decays, and the Issue is corrupted.

Thirdly, Of old Time the Nobility and Gentry spent their Estates in the Countrey, and that kept the People in it: And their Servants married and sat at easy Rents under their Masters Favour, which peopled the Place:

Now the great Men (too much loving the Town and resorting to *London*) draw many People thither to attend them, who either don't marry, or if they do, they pine away their small Gains in some petty Shop; for there are so many, they prey upon one another.

Fourthly, The Countrey thus neglected, and no due Ballance kept between Trade and Husbandry, City and Countrey, the poor Countrey man takes double Toil, and cannot (for Want of Hands) dress and manure his Land to the Advantage it formerly yielded him; yet must he pay the old Rents, which occasions Servants, and such Children as go to Trades, to continue single, at least all their youthful Time, which also obstructs the Increase of our People.

Fifthly, The Decay of some Countrey Manufactures (where no Provision is made to supply the People with a new Way of Living) causes the more Industrious to go abroad to seek their Bread in other Countries, and gives the lazy an Occasion to loiter and beg, or do worse; by which Means the Land swarms with Beggars. Formerly 'twas rare to find any asking Alms but the Maim'd or Blind, or very aged; now Thousands of both Sexes run up and down, both City and Countrey, that are sound and youthful, and able to work, with false *Pretences* and *Certificates*; nor is there any Care taken to employ or deter such *Vagrants*, which weakens the Countrey as to People and Labour.

To which let me add, that the great Debauchery in this Kingdom has not only render'd many unfruitful when married, but they live not out half their Time, through Excesses, which might be prevented by a vigorous Execution of our good Laws against Corruption of Manners. These and the like Evils are the true Grounds of the Decay of our People in the Countrey, to say nothing of Plague and Wars. Towns and Cities cannot complain of the Decay of People, being more replenish'd than ever, especially *London*, which with Reason helps the Countrey-Man to this Objection. And tho' some do go to the Plantations, yet numbering the Parishes in *England*, and computing how many live more than die, and are born than buried, there goes not over to all the Plantations a fourth Part of the yearly Increase of the People; and when they are there, they are not (as I said before) lost to *England*, since they furnish them with much Cloaths, Household-stuff, Tools, and the like Necessaries, and that in greater Quantities than here their Condition could have needed, or they could have bought; being there well to pass, that were but low here, if not poor; and now Masters of Families too, when here they had none; and could hardly keep themselves; and very often it happens that some of them after their Industry and Success there have made them wealthy, they return and empty their Riches into *England,* one in this Capacity being able to buy out twenty of what he was when he went over.

A Discourse concerning Plantations. By Sir JOSIAH CHILD, Published 1692.[48]

THE Trade of our *English* Plantations in *America* being now of as great Bulk, and employing as much Shipping as most of the Trades of this Kingdom, it seems not unnecessary to discourse more at large concerning the Nature of Plantations, and the good or evil Consequences of them, in Relation to this and other Kingdoms; and the rather because some Gentlemen of no mean Capacities, are of Opinion, that his Majesty's Plantations abroad have very much prejudic'd this Kingdom, by draining us of our People; for the Confirmation of which Opinion they urge the Example of *Spain*; which they say is almost ruin'd by the Depopulation which the *West-Indies* hath occasion'd. To the End therefore a more particular Scrutiny may be made in this Matter, I shall humbly offer my Opinion in the following Propositions; and then give those Reasons of Probability which presently occur to my Memory, in Confirmation of each Proposition.

First, I agree that Land (tho' excellent) without Hands proportionable, will not enrich any Kingdom.

Secondly, That whatever tends to the depopulating of a Kingdom, tends to the Impoverishment of it.

Thirdly, That most Nations in the civiliz'd Parts of the World, are more or less rich or poor proportionably to the Paucity or Plenty of their People, and not to the Sterility or Fruitfulness of their Lands.

Fourthly, I do NOT *agree that our People in* England *are in any considerable Measure abated by Reason of our* FOREIGN PLANTATIONS, *but propose to prove the* CONTRARY.

Fifthly, I am of Opinion, that we had immediately before the Plague, many more People in *England,* than we had before the inhabiting of *Virginia, New-England, Barbadoes,* and the rest of our *American* Plantations.[49]

The first PROPOSITION, That Lands, tho' in their nature excellently good, without Hands proportionable, will not enrich any Kingdom.

This first Proposition I suppose will readily be assented to by all judicious Persons, and therefore for the Proof of it, I shall only alledge a Matter of Fact.

The Land of *Palestine*, once the richest Countrey in the Universe, since it came under the *Turk's* Dominion, and consequently unpeopled, is now become the poorest.

Andaluzia and *Grenada*, formerly wonderful rich, and full of good Towns, since dispeopled by the *Spaniard* by Expulsion of the Moors, many of their Towns and brave Countrey-Houses are fallen into Rubbish, and their whole Countrey into miserable Poverty, though their Lands naturally are prodigiously fertile.

A Hundred other Instances of Fact might be given to the like Purpose.

The second PROPOSITION, Whatever tends to the populating of a Kingdom, tends to the Improvement of it.

The former Proposition being granted, I suppose this will not be denied, and the Means is good Laws, whereby any Kingdom may be populated and consequently enriched.[50]

The third PROPOSITION, That most Nations in the civiliz'd Parts of the World, are more or less rich or poor, proportionable to the Paucity or Plenty of their People.

This third is a Consequent of the two former Propositions: And the whole World is a Witness to the Truth of it. The seven united Provinces are certainly the most populous Tract of Land in Christendom, and for their Bigness undoubtedly the richest. *England* for its Bigness, except our Forests, Wastes, and Commons, which by our Laws and Customs are barred from Improvement, I hope it yet a more populous Countrey than *France*, and consequently richer; I say in Proportion to its bigness; *Italy* in like Proportion more populous than *France*, and richer, and *France* more populous and richer than *Spain*, &c.

The fourth PROPOSITION, *I do* not *agree that our People in* England *are in any considerable Measure abated, by Reason of our Foreign Plantations*, but *propose to prove the* contrary.

This I know is a controverted Point, and do believe where there is one Man of my Mind there may be a Thousand of the contrary; but I hope when the following Grounds of my Opinion have been thoroughly examin'd, there will not be so many Dissenters.

That very many People now go, and have gone from this Kingdom almost every Year for these sixty Years past, and have and do settle in our

Foreign Plantations, is most certain. But the first Question will be, whether if *England* had no Foreign Plantations for those People to be transported unto, they could or would have stay'd and liv'd at Home with us?

I am of opinion they never would nor could.

To resolve this Question we must consider what Kind of People they were, and are, that have and do transport themselves to our Foreign Plantations.

New-England (as every one knows) was originally inhabited, and hath since successively been replenish'd, by a Sort of People call'd *Puritans*, which could not conform to the Ecclesiastical Laws of *England*; but being wearied with Church Censures and Persecutions, were forc'd to quit their Father's Land, to find out new Habitations, as many of them did in *Germany* and *Holland*,[51] as well as *New-England*; and had there not been a *New-England* found for some of them, *Germany* and *Holland* probably had receiv'd the rest: But old *England* to be sure had lost them all.

Virginia and *Barbadoes* were first peopled by a Sort of loose vagrant People, vicious and destitute of Means to live at Home (being either unfit for Labour, or such as could find none to employ themselves about, or had so misbehav'd themselves by Whoring, Thieving, or other Debauchery, that none would set them on work) which Merchants and Masters of Ships by their Agents (or Spirits as they were call'd) gather'd up about the Streets of *London* and other Places, cloath'd and transported to be employ'd upon Plantations; and these, I say, were such as, had there been no *English* Foreign Plantation in the World, could probably never have liv'd at Home to do Service for their Countrey, but must have come to be hang'd or starv'd, or died untimely of some of those miserable Diseases, that proceed from Want and Vice; or else have sold themselves for Soldiers, to be knock'd on the Head, or starv'd, in the Quarrels of our Neighbors, as many Thousands of brave *Englishmen* were in the low Countries, as also in the Wars of *Germany*, *France*, and *Sweden*, &c. or else if they could by begging, or otherwise, arrive to the Stock of half a Crown to waft them over to *Holland*, become Servants to the *Dutch*, who refuse none.

But the principal Growth and Increase of the aforesaid Plantations of *Virginia* and *Barbadoes* happen'd in, or immediately after, our late Civil Wars, when the worsted Party by the Fate of War being depriv'd of their Estates, and having some of them never been bred to Labour, and others made unfit for it by the lazy Habit of a Soldier's Life, there wanting Means to maintain them all abroad with his Majesty, many of them betook themselves to the aforesaid Plantations, and great Numbers of *Scotch* Soldiers of his Majesty's Army, after *Worcester* Fight,[52] were by the then prevailing Powers voluntarily sent thither.

Another great Swarm, or Accession of new Inhabitants to the aforesaid Plantations, as also to *New-England, Jamaica,* and all other his Majesty's Plantations in the *West-Indies,* ensued upon his Majesty's Restauration; when the former prevailing Party being by a divine Hand of Providence brought under, the Army disbanded, many Officers displac'd, and all the new Purchasers of publick Titles dispossest of their pretended Lands, Estates, *&c.* many became impoverish'd, destitute of Employment; and therefore such as could find no Way of living at Home, and some which fear'd the Re-istablishment of the Ecclesiastical Laws, under which they could not live, were forc'd to transport themselves or sell themselves for a few Years, to be transported by others to the Foreign *English* Plantations: The constant Supply that the said Plantations have since had, hath been such vagrant loose People, as I have before mention'd, pick'd up, especially about the Streets and Suburbs of *London* and *Westminster,* and Malefactors condemn'd for Crimes, for which by the Law they deserv'd to die; and some of those People call'd Quakers, banish'd for meeting on Pretences of religious Worship.

Now if from the Premises it be duly consider'd what Kind of Persons those have been, by which our Plantations have at all Times been replenish'd: I suppose it will appear that such they have been, and under such Circumstances, that if his Majesty had had no Foreign Plantations, to which they might have resorted, *England* however must have lost them.

To illustrate the Truth whereof a little further, let us consider what Captain *Graunt* the ingenius Author of the Observations upon the Bills of Mortality saith, *p.* 76. and in other Places of his Book concerning the City of *London;* and it is not only said, but undeniably prov'd, *viz.* that the City of *London,* let the Mortality be what it will, by Plague or otherwise, repairs its Inhabitants once in two Years. And *p.* 101. again, if there be encouragement for a hundred Persons in *London* (that is, a way how a hundred may live better than in the Countrey) the evacuating of a fourth or third Part of that Number must soon be supplied out of the Countrey, who in a short Time remove themselves from thence hither so long, until the City, for want of Receipt and Encouragement, refuses them.[53]

First, What he hath prov'd concerning *London,* I say of *England* in general; and the same may be said of any Kingdom or Countrey in the World.

Such as our Employment is for People, so many will our People be; and if we should imagin we have in *England* Employment but for one Hundred People, and we have born and bred amongst us a Hundred and fifty People; I say the fifty must away from us, or starve or be hang'd to prevent it, whether we had any Foreign Plantations or not.[54]

Secondly, If by Reason of the Accomodation of living in our Foreign Plantations, we have evacuated more of our People than we should have done if we had no such Plantations, I say with the aforesaid Author in the Case of *London*; and if that Evacuation be grown to an Excess (which I believe it never did barely on the Account of the Plantations) that Decrease would procure its own Remedy; for much Want of People, if our Laws gave Encouragement, would procure us a Supply of People without the Charge of breeding them, as the *Dutch* are, and always have been supplied in their greatest Extremities.

Object. I. But it may be said, Is not the Facility of being transported into the Plantations, together with the enticing Methods customarily us'd to persuade People to go thither, and the Encouragement of living there with a People that speak our Language, strong Motives to draw our People from us; and do they not draw more from us than otherwise would leave us, to go into Foreign Plantations where they understand not the Language?

I answer first, it is not much more difficult to get a Passage to *Holland*, than it is to our Plantations.

Secondly, Many of those that go to our Plantations, if they could not go thither, would and must go into foreign Countries, tho' it were ten times more difficult to get thither than it is; or else, which is worse (as hath been said) would adventure to be hang'd, to prevent begging or starving, as too many have done.

Thirdly, I do acknowledge that the Facility of getting to the Plantations, may cause some more to leave us, than would do if they had none but Foreign Countries for Refuge: But then if it be consider'd, that our Plantations spending mostly our *English* Manufactures, and those of all Sorts almost imaginable, in egregious Quantities, and employing near two Thirds of all our *English* Shipping, do therein give a constant Sustenance to, it may be, two Hundred Thousand Persons here at Home; then *I must needs conclude upon the whole Matter, that we have not the fewer, but the more People in* England *by Reason of our* English *Plantations in* America.

Object. II. But it may be said, is not this inferring and arguing against Sense and Experience? Doth not all the World see that the many noble Kingdoms of *Spain*, in *Europe*, are almost depopulated and ruinated, by Reason of their Peoples flocking over to the *West-Indies*? And do not all other Nations diminish in People after they become possess'd of Foreign Plantations.

Answ. I. I answer with Submission to better Judgments, that in my Opinion contending for Uniformity in Religion hath contributed ten Times more to the depopulating of *Spain* than all the *American* Plantations: What was it but that, which caused the Expulsion of so many Thousand *Moors*, who had built and inhabited most of the chief Cities and Towns of *Andaluzia, Granada, Aragon,* and other Parts? What was it but that and the Inquisition, that hath and doth daily expel such vast Numbers of rich *Jews* with their Families and Estates into *Germany, Italy, Turky, Holland,* and *England?* What was it but that, which caus'd those vast and long Wars between the King and the low Countries, and the Effusion of so much *Spanish* Blood and Treasure, and the final Loss of the seven Provinces; which we now see so prodigious rich, and full of People, while *Spain* is empty and poor, and *Flanders* thin and weak, in continual Fear of being made a Prey to their Neighbours?

Secondly, I answer, we must warily distinguish between Countrey and Countrey; for tho' Plantations may have drain'd *Spain* of People, it does not follow that they have or will drain *England* or *Holland;* because where Liberty and Property are not so well preserv'd, and where Interest of Money is permitted to go at twelve *per Cent.* there can be no considerable Manufactures, and no more of Tillage and Grazing, than, as we proverbially say, will keep Life and Soul together; and where there is little Manufacturing, and as little Husbandry of Lands, the Profit of Plantations, *viz.* the greatest Part thereof, will not redound to the Mother Kingdom, but to other Countries, wherein there are more Manufactures and Productions from the Earth; from hence it follows, Plantations thus manag'd, prove Drains of the People from their Mother Kingdom; whereas Plantations belonging to Mother-Kingdoms or Countries, where Liberty and Property is better preserv'd, and Interest of Money restrain'd to a low Rate, the Consequence is, that every Person sent abroad with the Utensils he is constrain'd to employ, or that are employ'd with him;[55] I say in this Case we may reckon, that for Provisions, Cloaths, and Household-goods, Seamen, and all others employ'd about Materials for Building, Fitting, and Victualling of Ships, every *Englishman* in *Barbadoes* or *Jamaica* creates Employment for four Men at Home.

Thirdly, I answer, That *Holland* now sends as many, and more People, to reside yearly in their Plantations, Fortresses, and Ships in the *East-Indies* (besides many into the *West-Indies*) than *Spain;* and yet is so far from declining in the Number of their People at Home, that it is evident they do monstrously increase: And so, I hope, under the next Head to prove that *England* hath constantly increas'd in People at Home, since our Settlement upon Plantations in *America*, altho' not in so great a Proportion as the *Dutch*.

The fifth PROPOSITION, *I am of Opinion, that we had immediately before the late Plague, more People in* England, *than we had before the inhabiting of* NEW-ENGLAND, VIRGINIA, BARBADOES, *&c.*

The Proof of this at best, I know, can but be conjectural; but in Confirmation of my Opinion, I have, I think, of my Mind, the most industrious *English* Calculator this Age has produc'd in publick, *viz.* Captain *Graunt* in the aforemention'd Treatise, *p.* 88. his Words are "Upon the whole Matter we may therefore conclude, that the People of the whole Nation do increase, and consequently the Decrease of *Winchester, Lincoln,* and other like Places, must be attributed to other Reasons than that of refurnishing *London* only."[56]

Secondly, It is manifest by the aforesaid worthy Author's Calculations, that the Inhabitants of *London,* and Parts adjacent, have increas'd to almost double within these sixty Years; and that City hath usually been taken for an Index of the whole.

I know it will be said, that altho' *London* have so increas'd, other Parts have so much diminish'd, whereof some are named before; but if to answer the Diminution of the Inhabitants in some particular Places, it be consider'd how others are increas'd, *viz. Yarmouth, Hull, Scarborough,* and other Ports in the North; as also *Liverpool, Westchester* and *Bristol, Portsmouth, Lime,* and *Plimouth;* and withal, if it be consider'd what great Improvements have been made these last sixty Years upon breaking up and inclosing of Wastes, Forrests, and Parks, and draining of the Fens, and all those Places inhabited and furnish'd with Husbandry *&c.* then I think it will appear probable, that we have in *England* now, at least had before the late Plague, more People than we had before we first enter'd upon Foreign Plantations, notwithstanding likewise the great Numbers of Men which have issued from us into *Ireland;* which Countrey, as our Laws now are, I reckon not among the Number of Plantations profitable to *England,* nor within the Limits of this Discourse, tho' peradvanture something may be picked out of these Papers, which may deserve Consideration in Relation to that Countrey.

But it may be said, if we have more People now than in former Ages, how came it to pass that in the Times of King *Henry* IVth and Vth, and other Times formerly, we could raise such great Armies, and employ them in Foreign Wars, and yet retain a sufficient Number to defend the Kingdom, and cultivate our Lands at Home.

I answer, First the Bigness of Armies is not always a certain Indication of the Numerousness of a Nation, but sometimes rather of the Nature of the Government, and Distribution of the Lands: As for Instance: Where the Prince and Lords are Owners of the whole Territory, altho' the People be thin, the Armies upon Occasion may be very great, as in *East-India*, *Turky*, and the Kingdoms of *Fesse* and *Morocco*, where *Taffelet* was lately said to have an Army of one Hundred and Fifty or two Hundred Thousand Men,[57] altho' every Body knows that Countrey hath as great a Scarcity of People as any in the World: But since Freeholders are so much increas'd in *England* and the servile Tenures alter'd, doubtless it is more difficult, as well as more chargeable, to draw great Numbers of Men into Foreign Wars.

Since the Introduction of the new Artillery of Powder, Shot, and Fire-Arms into the World, all War is become rather an Expence of Money than Men; and Success attends those that can most and longest spend Money, rather than Men; and consequently Princes Armies in *Europe* are become more proportionable to their Purses than to the Number of their People.

FINIS.

A New and Accurate Account of the Provinces of South-Carolina and Georgia (1732)

New and Accurate Account of the Provinces of South-Carolina and Georgia appeared on or about December 14, 1732, when it was advertised in the *London Evening Post* as published "This Day." Oglethorpe had left on the *Anne* almost a month earlier.

Although in 1924 the authorship of this tract was brought into doubt when Verner W. Crane contended that it was written by Benjamin Martyn,[1] the first secretary of the Georgia Trustees, it is clearly the work of James Oglethorpe. Like *Select Tracts*, it was attributed to Oglethorpe by the bibliographer John Nichols in 1812–15. Both "An Essay on Plantations; or, Tracts relating to the Colonies" and "An Account of the Colony in Georgia," which he listed under 1732, were, he asserted, "the production of James-Edward Oglethorpe, Esq."[2] Nichols's assertion that the editor of *Select Tracts* was also author of *A New and Accurate Account* is strengthened by the author's "puff," in his preface, of the editor's tract; and that, as Captain Coram made clear, was the work of Oglethorpe. There is additional evidence of Oglethorpe's authorship in his *Some Account of the Design of the Trustees for establishing Colonys in America*,[3] for when on February 4, 1732, the Bray Associates failed to approve this 110-page manuscript, which the general had written at their direction, and subsequently approved, instead, Martyn's short and uncontroversial version, Oglethorpe was left with considerable promotional material on his hands. Some of this he utilized in his newspaper appeal to potential benefactors and in his two colonial tracts of 1732, publishing both at his own expense.

There is still more evidence. Because proof copy was evidently not ready before the author left England, or because he was too busy to read it, the pamphlet incorporated some embarrassing blunders. Thus the reader is assured that after the ten-year period of grace, the South Carolinian immigrants, and presumably the Georgians as well, would have to pay only fourpence per acre for their grants, rather than the actual four shillings; and the benevolent society that was assisting foreign Protestants to immigrate to Georgia was identified as the Society for the Propagation of the Gospel in Foreign Parts, rather than the Society for the Promotion of Christian Knowledge. Had Martyn written the tract, he would have submitted it to the Georgia Trustees, as he did all his other promotional pamphlets; and they would have revised and corrected it. If he had then read proof, he would have corrected any remaing blunders.[4]

In writing *Some Account* Oglethorpe had been torn between diverse purposes. He was trying to secure, from Parliament and private charity, approval and funds for the colony and the colonists. He was also advertising for colonists. Finally he was offering advice and directions to the "overseer" who would accompany the first transport and help establish the first township. After he decided to go with the first colonists himself, he no longer needed to offer such advice; and in *Some Account of the Designs of the Trustees for Establishing Colonies in America* Benjamin Martyn had taken care of the advertisement to prospective emigrants and the appeal to private donors. Thus in *A New and Accurate Account* Oglethorpe had a more unified purpose and audience: to argue, addressing himself primarily to Parliament, that colonization was a salutory endeavor for Great Britain, and to demonstrate that the new province of Georgia would be especially important and valuable.

After sketching the history of the region, Oglethorpe first demonstrated that the English held a legal title to the territory and that although in the past the region had been subjected to some crippling attacks by hostile Indians, it was now safe from their inroads. In his subsequent chapters he developed his thesis: colonies, and especially Georgia, were essential to the prosperity of Great Britain.

Here Oglethorpe utilized all the mercantilist arguments that he had employed in his *Some Account*, those of Sir William Petty, Charles Davenant, Sir Josiah Child, and Joshua Gee; and he added some of the arguments of Jean Pierre Purry: the colonies would provide inexpensive raw materials that would enable Britain to compete favorably in the world market, and the mother country would thus enjoy a favorable balance of trade. The colony would increase trade for British goods and help to build up the merchant marine and increase the number of British sailors, on whom Britain relied to control shipping lanes and the colonies as well. They would serve as outlets for surplus population that would prove only a burden upon the mother country, but a benefit to the colonies. Georgia, particularly, would protect the southern frontier and provide important raw materials, such as silk, which the more northern colonies were unable to produce. Oglethorpe handled his arguments soundly. According to Klaus E. Knorr, "considering the usual demographic notions of his age, Oglethorp's ideas on the value of population were founded on solid economic insights."[5]

Oglethorpe's mercantilism was tempered by his concern for the colony and the colonists. The destitute Britons would become productive Georgians, and the persecuted foreign Protestants would bring to the new colony their productive skills and their Christian virtues. On their behalf Oglethorpe became, as David S. Shields has maintained, "a pioneer in the resistance to the restrictive pattern of trade imposed upon the empire" and "laid out the arguments on behalf of free trade." Indeed Knorr named the general the earliest of the five "notable Englishmen who, anterior to the American War of Independence, uttered opinions precursory to the later evolution of the idea of a British Commonwealth of Nations."[6]

In his account of Georgia and its potentialities, Oglethorpe was surer than he had been in *Some Account*. His expectations for the region, based as they were upon Purry's fallacy that similar latitudes produce similar vegetation, were far too sanguine. But his grasp of its geography had improved. In *Some Account* he had relied for his description of the region principally upon John Oldmixon's *British Empire in America* (1708), quoting long excerpts from this source, including passages from John Archdale's *New Description of Carolina* (1707).[7] Since writing that first tract, Oglethorpe had acquired a copy of Archdale's work, had acquired also the enlarged edition of Jean Pierre Purry's *Description Abregée de l'Etat présent de la Caroline Meridionale* (1732), and had talked with Purry at some length about the region. In fact on December 4, 1731, the general acquired a fourth interest in Purry's colony across the Savannah River in South Carolina.[8] Doubtless Purry's conviction that similar latitudes guaranteed the success of similar products fed Oglethorpe's illusion that silk and grapes would flourish in Georgia.[9]

Of the first edition there was only one impression, but two issues: that of the second differs from the first only in bearing the date 1733 rather than 1732.[10] There have been two subsequent printings: the first in 1840, in *Collections of the Georgia Historical Society*, where a few of the notes were shortened or omitted; the second in 1972, in *The Most Delightful Country of the Universe*, where editor Trevor R. Reese attributed the work to Martyn, to Oglethorpe, and to both.[11]

Oglethorpe's own copy of the 1733 issue has never been properly identified. Now housed in the De Renne Collection of the Hargrett Rare Book and Manuscript Library of the University of Georgia,[12] it is there listed as a work "*attributed to* Oglethorpe," "With manuscript annotations, possibly by the author." Citing Crane, however, Librarian Leonard Mackall added, "It is very doubtful if Oglethorpe wrote this tract."[13] He evidently thought that the annotator's hand might be that of Benjamin Martyn, but it is certainly not his. It appears to be that of James Oglethorpe.

Nor are the markings accurately described as "annotations," for they are not comments, but directions to the printer, or compositor. There are almost a hundred directions, one in pencil, the rest in ink. They call for corrections and improvements in typography, spelling, punctuation, style, and fact. Forty-four consist of short horizontal lines in the margin. Half of these apparently call for the elimination of hyphens; the rest seem to point out defective type, uneven spacing, and uneven lineation. Such directions would have been functional only if the passages could have been improved typographically when the type pages were taken from the warehouse, untied, and prepared for a new impression. Even in a page-for-page and line-for-line reprint, the compositor would not have needed to be warned about uneven lineation or defective type. Apparently Oglethorpe made the corrections when he returned to England in 1734 with Tomochichi and the other Indians and was encouraged by their popularity to hope that supplies of the first impression would be exhausted and that a second impression would be called for. With this hope in mind, he advertised *A New and Accurate Account* in the *Daily Advertiser* on September 5, 1734, as "Lately publish'd" and evidently corrected a copy of the 1733 issue so that an improved, second impression could be run off. Unfortunately the supply of the 1733 issue proved adequate to satisfy buyers.

Whether the stylistic and substantive changes—six in spelling, twenty in punctuation, and twenty-one in wording—are corrections or improvements, it is impossible to state, for in most printing shops the compositor was expected to correct the author's spelling and often to adapt his punctuation to printing-house style. Thus in his directions to the printer, Oglethorpe may have been restoring his original as often as he was improving it. Especially interesting are the corrections in quotations from Sir Edward Coke and from Edmund Waller; for the first group suggests that the corrector was back in his own library; the second, that the corrector was indeed the author. In correcting the punctuation and spelling in the quotation from Coke's *Fourth Report*, the corrector restored "*ominantium*" to "*dominantium*" and "*ego*" to "*ago*," though he failed to notice and correct "*eum*" to "*eam*," perhaps because of the slight difference between the italic *u* and *a* in such small type. These corrections might have been made from memory, for Oglethorpe's memory was excellent, and he long retained his grasp of Latin. But more likely he was back in his own library. There was then no British Library, and most reprints of Coke's *Reports* did not contain the prefaces.

In the quotation from Waller's "Battle of the Summer Isles," the corrector duly placed a comma after "*The Prince of* Trees," and he altered "*Plantines*" to "*Plantanes.*" But he failed to correct "*lusty Swine*" to "*wanton Swine*," the invariable reading in all the editions of Waller that I have been able to locate and the reading in Oldmixon's *British Empire* (2:379–81), from which Oglethorpe quoted in the tract and which may have suggested the quotation. The word "lusty" may have come from some poetic miscellany or from some volume of travels, but whether it came from such a source or from Oglethorpe's inaccurate recall, the fact that the corrector left it unchanged suggests that the corrector was indeed the author.

My text is that of the first, 1732 isssue, but I have incorporated the changes that Oglethorpe called for in his copy of the 1733 issue. I have bracketed my conjectural readings, necessitated by the binder's cropping some of Oglethorpe's corrections in the margins, and I have called attention in the notes to all the substantive changes and to many examples of Oglethorpe's heavier punctuation.

A

New and Accurate ACCOUNT

OF THE

PROVINCES

OF

SOUTH-CAROLINA

AND

GEORGIA:

With many curious and useful Observations on the Trade, Navigation and Plantations of *Great-Britain*, compared with her most powerful maritime Neighbours in antient and modern Times.

[Printer's ornament]

LONDON:

Printed for J. WORRALL at the *Bible* and *Dove* in *Bell-Yard* near *Lincoln*'s *Inn;* and Sold by J. ROBERTS near *Oxford-Arms* in *Warwick-Lane.* 1732.

(Price One Shilling.)

THE PREFACE.

THERE *have been several Accounts of the Provinces of* Carolina *publish'd formerly; among which, Mr.* Archdale's *Description of* South-Carolina *is of most undoubted Credit.*[14] *Another Account in the Form of a Letter, (first printed in the Year* 1710*) was lately re-printed by Mr.* Clarke *near the Royal-Exchange.*[15] *I could shew many Faults in this Piece, both as to Facts and Reasoning, but shall only mention a few that are obvious to almost every Reader who has ever heard any Thing of that Province. The Author is fawningly Partial to the then Administration of Government there. He praises its great Blemishes. He finds a Beauty in their Attack upon St.* Augustino; *an Expedition improvidently projected, and unsuccessfully attempted. He applauds their Paper Currency,*[16] *which was a wretched Expedient to salve up the Wounds their little Republick had received in that unhappy War: A Remedy like those which our profligate young Fellows frequently meet with at the Hands of Quack-Doctors, who have just Skill enough in Drugs to remove a Clap by establishing a Pox in the Room of it.*[17] *If that Writer had any Knowledge of Commerce, or History, he must have known that a* forced Paper Credit *is* incompatible with Trade, and never held up to Par *in any Age or Country in the World; much less could it suit the Commerce of an Infant-Colony, whose very Existence (in the Notion of People at a Distance) was at that Time precarious. I shall no farther pursue the Crudities of that Author, it is sufficient to observe, That if his Account had been as just and accurate as Mr.* Archdale's, *it could not answer the Expectations of the Publick at this Time. Those Treatises tell us of Twenty Sail of Shipping, but now we can truly say that there are yearly Two Hundred freighted at* Charles-Town.[18] *The wide Extent of their Rice Trade; the amazing Encrease of their Stock of Negroes and of Cattle; and the encouraging Essays they have made in Wine and Silk, render* South-Carolina *a new Country to the Geographers. Neither of these Writers is copious enough on the Topick of the Benefits which may arise to* Great-Britain *by Peopling this fruitful Continent: That Argument is therefore handled the more largely in the following Pages. About Two Years ago, Captain* Purry, *a* Swiss Gentleman, *wrote* *an authentick Account of that Country in French, which was printed at* Neufchattel *in* Switzerland: *And to shew that he*

---

*This is entitled, *Description Abregee de l' Etat present de la Caroline meridionale.*[19]

believ'd himself when he gave a beautiful Description of South-Carolina, *he is gone to settle there with six Hundred of his Countrymen.*

And he that hangs, or beats out's Brains
The Devil's in him if he feigns. *Hud.*[20]

Mr. Archdales's *Veracity will hardly be question'd by any but Bigots, when the Publick shall be inform'd of his remarkable Integrity in his own Principles. He, being a Quaker, was chosen into Parliament by the Town of* Colchester *in* Essex, *but chose to relinquish his Seat rather than violate his Conscience with regard to Oaths and the Test-act.*[21] *He governed* South-Carolina *with that Moderation, that the Colony blesses his Memory; and their latest Posterity will have cause to bless it; for, under Providence, they owe to him their very Being.*

An Anonymous Author ought to have Vouchers for his Facts. I make an impartial Judgment of the Incorrectness of my Style, and therefore can't resolve to prefix my Name to this Piece: But by proper References to Mr. Archdale *and Mr.* Purry, *I shew that they concur with me in the Geography and natural History of the Country. The Reasonings and Observations are the Result of various Reading and Conversation in many Years: Let these therefore stand, or fall by themselves.*

Since the following Chapters were prepared for the Press, I have read a curious Pamphlet, entitled, Select Tracts relating to Colonies, &c. Sold by Mr. Roberts, *the Publisher of this Essay.*[22] *Those Tracts were written by the most knowing Men of their Respective Generations, and the Style and Matter of the Introduction to them sufficiently evince the eminent Abilities of the Person (whoever he was) that collected them. Had I seen them earlier, they would have been of singular Use to me in many of my Observations and Arguments in the following Sheets: I now must be content to pride my self in having accidentally fallen into the same Way of Reasoning with the great Authors of those Tracts.*

I designed to have added a Chapter, containing the Scheme for settling the new Colony of Georgia: *But, upon a Revisal of an Elegant Piece which was published in the* Craftsman *to that effect,*[23] *I thought proper to desist, for my own Sake. I shall only take Leave here to mention a Precedent of our own for planting Colonies, which, perhaps, in Part, or in the Whole, may be worthy our Imitation.*

England *was more than four Hundred Years in Possession of a great Part of* Ireland *before the Whole was compleatly conquer'd: The Wars there, and Loss of* English *Blood were infinite, the Invaders mixed and intermarried with the Natives throughout the Provinces, and degenerated in Habit, Language, Customs and Affections. In the Days of K.* James *the First, the* Londoners *were at* the Charge of sending into the most dangerous Part of that Kingdom more than four Hundred poor Families.[24] There were a City, and a Town built, as had been agreed on: The City of London-derry contained three Hundred, the Town of Colerain a Hundred Houses; these were fortified with Walls and Ditches, and established with most ample Privileges. They send two Members each to the Parliament of that Kingdom, and the Mayor of London-derry is always the First in the Commissions of Oyer and Terminer and Assise. That City chooses two Sheriffs as our London does, and they are of Course Sheriffs of the County at large, as the Sheriffs of London are Sheriffs of the County of Middlesex. The Salmon Fisheries were given to the City of London who generally receive more than a Thousand Pounds per Ann. from them. What the present House-Rents of their City and Town amounts to, I shall not pretend to say, but believe they make a considerable Yearly Sum, because the Tenants have lately been too brisk Bidders for each others Bargains. The City of London-derry, and its Liberties, (which I think are three Miles round it) the Town of Colerain and the Fisheries, belong to the Twelve Companies of London consider'd as one aggregate Body. There are two Men chosen out of each Company to make up this Corporation, and, I think, they are called the London Society for the Plantation of Ulster.[25] Besides this great Estate belonging to them in one Body, each Company, in its own Right, and by itself, has, or lately had, a large and rich Manor belonging to it. One of them was lately sold for Twenty Thousand Pounds, and I think a Quit Rent of a Hundred a Year reserved upon it to the Company for ever. The Londoners have drawn above a Hundred Thousand Pounds from that Colony within Ten Years last past, and 'tis not probable that the first Settlement ever cost them Eight Thousand Pounds, which made Four Hundred Families of their poor Freemen happy, at the same Time that it purchased so good an Estate and strengthened the English Interest in that Kingdom. No other Part of Ireland is now so perfectly free from the native Irish as are those two Towns and their Districts. The Populace of London-derry and of the adjoyning Country were so vigorous at the Revolution as to endure a Siege which has made that English Colony memorable to latest Posterity.

'Tis needless to expatiate in the just Commendation of the Trustees for establishing the Colony in Georgia. They have, for the Benefit of Mankind, given up that Ease and Indolence to which they were entitled by their Fortunes and the too prevalent Custom of their Native Country. They, in some Degree, imitate their Redeemer in Sympathizing with the Miserable, and in Labouring to Relieve them. They take not for their Pattern an Epicurean Deity: They set before their Eyes the Giver of all good Gifts, who has put it into their Hearts, (and may he *daily more and more enable their Hands) to save Multitudes of his living Images from Perdition.*

A New and Accurate
ACCOUNT
OF THE
PROVINCES
OF
South-Carolina and *Georgia,* &c.

CHAP. I.

The Situation of Carolina, *the Historical Account of it; how far the Right to a new Country is acquir'd by the first Discovery; by Occupancy; lost by Dereliction.*

THE Great and Beautiful Country of *Carolina* is bounded on the *North* between 35 and 36 Deg. of *N.* Latitude with *Virginia* and the *Apalatian* Mountains, on the *East* with the *Atlantick* Ocean, on the *South* about 30 Deg. *N.* Latitude,[26] with Part of the *Atlantick,* or *Gulph* of *Florida,* and with *Florida, and on the *West* its Extent is unknown. All the Charters, or Patents of our Kings that describe its Bounds, have carried it *Westward* in a direct Line as far as the *South* Seas.[28]

THE *Spaniards* formerly included it all under the general Name of *Florida,* and pretended a Right to it by Virtue of the Pope's Donation,[29] as indeed they did to all *America.* The *French,* in the Days of their *Charles* the IXth, made a little Settlement there by the Countenance and Encouragement of Admiral *Coligny;* but the civil Wars in *France* prevented him from taking due Care of it, and it came to nothing. He made a Second, but almost all his Men were murdered by the *Spaniards* after Quarter given; and the

---

*Florida is a Country to the *South* of *Carolina,* claim'd by the *Spainards,* who have a little Fort there call'd St. *Augustino,* about 150 Miles from the Borders of *Carolina,* or rather of the new Province of *Georgia.*[27]

French King did not resent it, probably because they were Protestants. 'Tis not unlikely that the Admiral's View in sending these Colonies was to secure a Retreat for himself and the rest of the Reformed in case they were conquered in *France*.[30]

THE *Spaniards* by Injustice and Cruelty provoked the *Indians*, and prepared them for the Arrival of a Third Body of *French*, who put all the *Spaniards* to the Sword. The Commander of this Third Expedition contented himself with making a Tour in the Country; he made no Settlement there, nor did the *Spaniards* seek to recover it; so that from the Year 1567 it lay deserted by all *European* Nations, 'till the Days of our King *Charles* the IId, when the *English* effectually settled there, by Virtue of His Majesty's Grant to certain Lords Proprietors, and compleated that Right, which his Predecessor, K. *Henry* the VIIth, had acquired by the first Discovery of this Part of the Continent. 'Tis true, indeed, the *Spaniards* were acquainted with this Country so early as the Year 1512, under the Conduct of *John Ponce de Leon*, but Sir *Sebastian Cabot*, or *Cabota*, born at *Bristol*, of *Venetian* Parents, had first discover'd it in the Year 1497,[31] under the Commission, at the Costs, and in the Name of our K. *Henry* the VII, as appears by foreign Writers of that Age of great Repute in the learned World, and some of them are *Spanish* Authors.

I think the *Civilians* are not all agreed upon sure Canons, or Maxims concerning the best Method of acquiring the Dominion of Countries, nor how far the first Discovery can vest, or establish a Right. Some *Romish* and *Spanish* Lawers have been so fond as to fancy that the Pope's Donation is the best Title imaginable; yet (I know not how it happens) not only the Hereticks of *England*, but even the most Christian King,[32] the eldest Son of the Church, has contravened that Title, has taken Possession of large Countries in *America* and grasps at more.

I believe the Doctrine most generally received is this: That Occupancy is the most unquestionable Title by the Law of Nature; and that touching at a Coast for Fuel and Water; erecting a Cross, or the Arms of a Prince, or State, and trapanning away two or three of the Savage Natives into Captivity, are not such an Occupancy as can reasonably acquire the Dominion of a Country; for at that rate *Cain*, who was a Vagabond on Earth, might have claimed universal Monarchy, and have left no Room for the Children of *Seth*. The common Sense of Mankind could not fail to establish a Rule, that Dereliction should be as certain a Method of waving, or giving up Property, as the true and genuine Occupancy is of acquiring it; and for a like Reason; for if I am entitled to take a Thing out of the Common of

Nature, and make it my seperate Property by using it, my not using it any longer is the most natural Waiver and Abdication of that Property, and justly throws that Thing into the Common again, to be possess'd by the next Occupant. This Occupancy then consists in a Settlement of People, dwelling in fixed Habitations and tilling the Earth; and this is what Princes and States would prefer to all other Rights, let Declarations and Manifestoes swell with never so many historical Claims of the earliest Discovery, when Sovereigns are disposed to quarrel. And this Right, like all other Rights, must at all Times be accompanied with a sufficient Force to defend it,[33] for Reasons too obvious here to be enlarg'd on.

UNDER this rational Notion of acquiring Dominion, an Extent of the antient *Florida* of Three Hundred Miles in Length by the Ocean Coast, became the Property of *England* more than Sixty Years ago. For King *Charles* the IId having by his *Letters Patents granted the same to several Lords Proprietors by the Name of *Carolina*, they Peopled it with a Colony which has ever since subsisted, tho' frequently check'd in its Growth by heavy Difficulties and Discouragements.

THIS Colony had a very promising Beginning; there were a great Number of Laws, or Constitutions agreed to by the Lords Proprietors, which gave a general Toleration for tender Consciences, and contain'd many other wholesome Regulations. These had been drawn up by the great Lawyer and famous Politician the Earl of *Shaftsbury*, with the Assistance of Mr. *Lock* the Philosopher,[34] but were not duly observ'd when the Lords Proprietors came to exercise their Jurisdiction over Numbers of People: There was a natural Infirmity in the Policy of their Charter, which was the Source of many of the Misfortunes of the Colony, without any Imputation on the noble Families concern'd. For the Grantees, being Eight in Number, and not incorporated, and no Provision being made to conclude the whole Number by the Voices of the Majority, there could not be the timely Measures always agreed on, which were proper, or necessary for the Safety and good Government of the Plantation. In the mean Time the Inhabitants grew unruly, and quarrelled about Religion and Politicks; and while there was a meer Anarchy among them, they were expos'd to the Attacks and Insults of their *Spanish* and *Indian* Neighbours, whom they had imprudently provok'd and injur'd; and to discharge the Debts contracted by their unsuccessful Attempts, they unskilfully forced a Paper-Currency upon the Subject, by an Act of their Parliament, which naturally put an

---

*The Letters Patents to the Earl of *Clarendon*, &c. bore Date the 29th Day of *March*, 1663.

End to Credit and suspended their Commerce; and as if they had conspir'd against the Growth of the Colony, they repealed their Laws for Liberty of Conscience, tho' the Majority of the People were Dissenters, and had resorted thither under the publick Faith for a compleat Indulgence, which they considered as Part of their *Magna Charta*. Their strict Conformity-Law was indeed repealed long before the Lords Proprietors surrendered their Patent, but it was long enough in Force to do abundance of Mischief.

And yet such are the natural Advantages of this happy Climate, that even under these Discouragements, the Colony grew so considerably, that *Charles-Town* has now near *Six Hundred good Houses, and the whole Plantation has above Forty Thousand Negroe Slaves, worth at least a Million of Pounds *Sterling*, besides an infinite Number of Cattle. Tho' it was only within these Four Years that an End was put to their Sorrows; for about that Time, the Lords Proprietors and Planters (who long had been heartily tired of each other) were, by the Interposition of the Legislature, fairly divorced forever, and the Property of the Whole vested in the Crown.

Chap. II.

Of the Air, Soil, Climate, and Produce of South-Carolina *and* Georgia. *Reasons why this Country is not well-peopled with* Indians. *The Natives describ'd.*

FROM what was said in the foregoing Chapter it can't be a Matter of Wonder, That a great Part of *Carolina* should have hitherto remain'd uninhabited. The Whole is divided into Two distinct Governments, by the Names of *North-Carolina* and *South-Carolina*. I shall confine my self to treat of the Latter. The new Province of *Georgia* is taken out of it, and divided from it on the *North* by the River *Savannah*, equal to the *Rhine*; its *Southern* Boundary is the River *Alatamaha*; it lies about the 30th and 31st Degree, North-Latitude, in the same Climate with *Barbary*, the *North* Part of *Ægypt*, the *South* Part of *Natolia*, or *Asia-Minor*, and the most temperate Parts of *Persia* and *China*.

†The Air is Healthy, being always serene, pleasant and temperate, never

---

*See Descrip. Abreg. Page 8.
†*Archdale*'s Descrip. p. 7, 8. and Descrip. Abreg. p. 16.

subject to excessive Heat or Cold, nor to sudden Changes; the Winter is regular and short, and the Summer cool'd with refreshing Breezes; and tho' this Country is within Three Hundred Miles of *Virginia*, it never feels the cutting *North-West-Wind* in that uneasy and dangerous Degree that the *Virginians* complain of. This Wind is generally attributed to those great Seas of fresh Water which lie to the *Northwest* beyond the *Apalachean* Mountains. It seems, a Journey of an Hundred Leagues in that warm Climate, blunts the Edge which the Wind gets in its Passage over those prodigious Lakes. Nor on the other Hand doth this Country ever feel the intense Heats of *Spain, Barbary, Italy,* and *Ægypt*; probably because, instead of the scorching Sands of *Africk* and *Arabia*, it has to the *Southward*, the spacious Bay of *Mexico*, which is much more temperate in its effect upon the Winds, than are those burning sandy Desarts.

*The Soil of this Country is generally Sandy, especially near the Sea; but 'tis impregnated with such a fertile Mixture that they use no Manure, even in their most antient Settlements, which have been under tillage these Sixty Years. It will produce almost every Thing in wonderful Quantities with very little Culture. Farther up the Country the Land is more mixed with a blackish Mould, and its Foundation generally Clay good for Bricks. They make their Lime of Oystershells, of which there are great Quantities on Banks near the Shore. All Things will undoubtedly thrive in this Country that are to be found in the happiest Places under the same Latitude. Their Rice, the only considerable Staple which requires many of their Hands at present, is known to be incomparably better than that of the *East Indies;* their Pitch, Tar and Turpentine (of which they export great Quantities) are the Rewards of their Industry in clearing the Land of superfluous Timber. †Mulberries both Black and White, are Natives of this Soil, and are found in the Woods, as are many other Sorts of Fruit-Trees of excellent Kinds, and the Growth of them is surprizingly swift; for a Peach, Apricot, or Nectarine, will, from the Stone, grow to be a bearing Tree in four or five Years Time. All Sorts of Corn yield an amazing Increase, an Hundred Fold is the common Estimate, tho' their Husbandry is so slight, that they can only be said to scratch the Earth and meerly to cover the Seed. ‡All the best Sorts of Cattle and Fowls are multiplied without Number, and

---

*Descr. Abreg. p. 6. *Archd.* Descr. p. 8.
†Descrp. Abreg. p. 13.
‡Descr. Abreg. p. 11, 12, 13.

therefore almost without a Price; you may see there more than a Thousand Calves in the same Inclosure belonging to one Person. *The Vine is also a wild Native here, Five or Six Sorts grow wild in the Woods; it has been said that the Stone of the Grape is too large, and the Skin too thick, but several who have tried, find all imaginable Encouragement to propagate the different Kinds from *Europe;* nor is it doubted that by proper Culture this wild Grape may be meliorated, so as well to reward the Care of the Planter.

The wild Beasts are Deer, Elks, Bears, Wolves, Buffaloes, Wild-Boars, and abundance of Hares and Rabbits: They have also the Cata-mountain, or small Leopard; but this is not the dangerous Species of the *East Indies.* Their Fowls are no less various; they have all the Sorts that we have in *England,* both wild and tame, and many others either useful or beautiful. It would be endless to enumerate their Fishes, the River *Savannah* is plentifully stock'd with them of many excellent Kinds: No Part in the World affords more Variety or greater Plenty. They have Oak, Cedar, Cypress, Fir, Walnut and Ash, besides the Sassafras. They have Oranges, Lemons, Apples and Pears, besides the Peach and Apricot mention'd before; some of †these are so delicious, that whoever tastes them will despise the insipid watry Taste of those we have in *England;* and yet such is the Plenty of them, that they are given to the Hogs in great Quantities. *Sarsaparilla, Cassia,* and other Sorts of Trees grow in the Woods, yielding Gums and Rosin, and also some Oyl excellent for curing Wounds.

‡THE Woods near the *Savannah* are not hard to be clear'd, many of them have no Underwood, and the Trees do not stand generally thick on the Ground, but at considerable Distances asunder. When you fell the Timber for Use, or to make Tar, the Root will rot in Four or Five Years, and in the mean Time you may pasture the Ground. But if you would only destroy the Timber, 'tis done by half a Dozen Strokes of an Ax surrounding each Tree a little above the Root; in a Year or two, the Water getting into the Wounds, rots the Timber, and a brisk Gust of Wind fells many Acres for you in an Hour, of which you may then make one bright Bonfire. Such will be frequently here the Fate of the Pine, the Walnut, the Cypress, the Oak, and the Cedar. Such an Air and Soil can be fitly describ'd only by a Poetical Pen,[35] because there's but little Danger of exceeding the Truth. Take there-

*Ib. 10.
†*Archdale*'s Descrip. p. 7.
‡Descr. Abreg. p. 7.

fore Part of Mr. *Waller's* Description of an Island in the Neighbourhood of *Carolina* to give you an Idea of this happy Climate.

> *The lofty Cedar which to Heav'n aspires,*
> *The Prince of Trees, is fuel for their Fires.*
> *The sweet Palmettaes a new* Bacchus *yield,*
> *With Leaves as ample as the broadest Shield.*
> *Under the Shadow of whose friendly Boughs*
> *They sit carousing where their Liquor grows.*
> *Figs there unplanted thro' the Fields do grow,*
> *Such as fierce* Cato *did the* Romans *show:*
> *With the rare Fruit inviting them to spoil*
> Carthage, *the Mistress of so rich a Soil.*
> *With candid Plantanes and the juicy Pine,*
> *On choicest Melons and sweet Grapes they dine,*
> *And with Potatoes fat their lusty Swine.*
>
> —— *The kind Spring, which but salutes us here,*
> *Inhabits there and courts them all the Year.*
> *Ripe Fruits and Blossoms on the same Trees live,*
> *At once they promise, what at once they give.*
> *So sweet the Air, so moderate the Clime,*
> *None sickly lives, or dies before his Time.*
> *Heav'n sure has kept this Spot of Earth uncurst,*
> *To shew how all Things were created first.*[36]

The Thought of the Poet in the last Couplet is adopted by the Ingenious Dr. *Burnet* in his Theory of the Earth, with fine Improvements of it. The Dr. seems fully convinced that the Temperament of the Climate of *Bermudas* approaches very near to that of the Antediluvian World,[37] in which he fancies that Spring and Autumn were continual and universal over the Face of the Earth, 'till the Almighty (as *Milton* has it) turned the Poles askance:[38] And by physical Reasoning he duduces the Longævity of the Antediluvians from this happy Equality of Seasons, uninterrupted by the shocking Vicissitudes of Heat and Cold,[39] which tear the human Frame asunder. He thinks that a Person born in *Bermudas*, and continuing there all his Life-Time, has a moral Probability of living Three Hundred Years. This Conjecture seems to be supported by what we are told in *Purchas* his Pilgrimage of one of the *Indian* Kings of *Florida*, who was Three Hundred Years old, and his Father was Fifty Years older, and then living.[40]

The Father is describ'd as a Skeleton cover'd with Skin; his Sinews, Veins and Arteries, and other Parts appear'd so clearly through his Skin, that a Man might easily tell and discern them the one from the other. His Son shewed five Generations descended from himself. 'Twas such a Figure as this *Indian* King, which induc'd the Antients to feign that *Tithonus* being very old was chang'd into a Grasshopper.[41]

Longa Tithonum *minuit senectus.* Hor.[42]

Now *Georgia* is just about the Middle of *Purchas* his *Florida*. But not to go too far with the Poet, *Theorist*, and Old Historian; 'tis probable those *Indians* divided the solar Year into two Years as the *Virginian Indians* did. Let us rely upon what we know at this Day; it must not be concealed, that in this Country, as almost in every new Climate, Strangers are apt to have a Seasoning; an Ague, or Sort of a Fever, but then 'tis very slight: And for the rest, People very seldom want Health here but by Intemperance, (which indeed is too common) And notwithstanding their several Skirmishes with the *Spaniards* and *Indians*, and that the Plague was imported thither in the Year 1706;[43] yet there are now several aged Persons living at *Charles Town*, who were of that little Number that first settled there and hewed down Timber above Sixty Years ago.

By the Healthiness of this Climate, and some Accounts of *Spanish* Expeditions hither in early Times, which were vigorously repulsed by great Armies of the Natives, one would expect to find the Country by this Time fully peopled with *Indians*. It is indeed probable that they were much more numerous in those Days than they are at present, or else they could not have defended themselves against the *Spaniards* as they did. But if their Numbers were formerly considerable they have since greatly decreased; and that might easily happen in a Century, even tho' the Country be naturally fertile and healthy, for the *Indians* in all the Continent of North *America*, near the *Atlantick* Ocean, have been discovered to have this Resemblance in common: They are small Tribes of Huntsmen, exceedingly apt to make War upon each other, as our 5 Nations of *Iroquois* beyond New-*England* and New-*York*, have within these Forty Years driven many other Nations from fertile inland Countries, of the extent of many Millions of Acres; and that not without incredible Slaughter. Add to which, that these poor Creatures, living with hardly any Husbandry, or Stores of Provisions, must perish in Heaps if the Fruits of the Woods, or their Hunting should once fail them; one scanty Season would infallibly famish whole Nations of them. Another great Cause of their Destruction was the Small-pox, the *Europeans* brought this Distemper among them: Now their common Cure in all Fevers is to sweat plentifully, and then to stop that Evacuation at once by plunging instantly into a River.[44] They can't be persuaded to alter this Method in the Case of the Small-pox, and it certainly kills them. Rum also has been a fatal Liquor to them, many of them have been inclined to drink it to such an Excess as we sometimes hear of at Home in the Abuse of Geneva, and sometimes they are so little Masters of their Reason, when intoxicated, as to be too apt to commit Murders; but there are many sober Men among them who abhor the Abuse of this Liquor. Thus Mr. *Archdale* relates, that, when he was Governour, he order'd an *Indian* to be executed, who being drunk with Rum had murder'd an *Indian* of another Tribe. The King of his Tribe came to him and reminded him how often he had warned him of the Dangers attending Excesses in that Liquor, but exhorted him (since Death was unavoidable) to die like a Man, which the unhappy Man performed with Firmness and Gallantry.[45] I have mentioned this Story because a vulgar Error prevails, as if the *Indians* were all addicted to this Vice. But to return to the Opposition against the *Spaniards*. 'Tis also probable that many Tribes were leagued together in the Common Cause, and that the *Spaniards* were thence induced to think the People of this Part of the Continent much more numerous than in Truth they were. 'Tis most certain that the Nations of *Carolina* in our Days have exactly answer'd in all Respects the Descriptions we have of the Inhabitants of *Virginia*, when we first got footing there in the Beginning of the last Century. Captain *Smith* (next to Sir *Walter Rawleigh*) the most indust'rous and resolute Planter of *Virginia* in those Days, computed that all the Tribes in a Country much more fertile and little less in Extent than *England*, could not draw into the Field above Five Thousand fighting Men, tho' the Tract of Land is sufficient to maintain more than Ten Millions of People.[46]

—— *Sane populus numerabilis, utpote parvus.* Hor.[47]

THIS is confirmed and illustrated by the well-attested Story that one of their little Kings instructed his Minister, who was coming hither, to number our Tribe; the Minister, at his Arrival, attempted to execute his Commission by making Notches on a Stick, but soon grew tir'd of his Arithmetick, and at his Return express'd the Multitude of our Fore-Fathers by pointing to the Stars, and to the fallen Leaves of a Wood in Autumn.[48] And here I can't omit saying, that it is a Policy of considerable Benefit to our Colonies, and an Expence well laid out, at proper Distances of Time to persuade some of the chiefest Savages, both for Authority and Understanding, to visit *Great Britain*: That awed with the high Idea which our Metropolis gives them of the Grandeur of this Empire, and propagating that Idea among their Tribes, our Planters in their several Neighbourhoods may enjoy uninterrupted Peace and Commerce with them, and even Assistance from them, for at least one Generation. Such was the Journey of the *Irroquois* Chiefs in the Reign of Queen *Anne*, and such was lately the Visit from our *Indian* Neighbours of *Carolina*.[49] The good Effects of these Visits are well known to the Planters of those Colonies respectively, and probably will be felt with Pleasure for an Age to come.

THE Description of the *Carolina-Indians* in their present State of Nature, is as follows, *They are tawny or olive-Coloured,[50] occasioned chiefly by oyling their Skins, and by exposing themselves naked to the Rays of the Sun. They are generally streight-body'd, comely in Person, quick of Apprehension, and great Hunters, by which they are not only serviceable by killing Deer to procure Skins for Trade with us, but our People that live in Country Plantations procure of them the whole Deer's Flesh, and they bring it many Miles for the Value of Six Pence Sterling, and a wild Turkey of Forty Pound Weight for the Value of Two Pence.

CHAP. III.

Persons reduc'd to Poverty are not Wealth to the Nation, may be happy in Georgia, *and profitable to* England; *they are within the Design of the Patent.*

SINCE the Time that the Lords Proprietors sold their Rights in *Carolina* to the Crown, the Governour there, has been ordered and instructed to assign liberally Portions of Land to every new Planter according to his Ability to occupy it; to erect Towns and Parishes of Twenty Thousand Acres of Land in each District; and to grant to each Parish the Privilege of sending two Members to the Assembly of the Province, as soon as One Hundred Masters of Families shall be settled in it. Neither will the Planters be confin'd to the Ground first allotted them, their Lots are to be augmented as they become able to cultivate a larger Quantity. These Lands are to be granted in Fee-simple under the Yearly Rent of Four Shillings

*Arch. Descr. p. 7.

for every Hundred Acres:⁵¹ But this Rent is not to be charged for the first Ten Years; during that Time the Lands shall be entirely Free.

BUT all this Encouragement was not sufficient to People this Country.⁵² They who can make Life tolerable here are willing to stay at Home, as 'tis indeed best for the Kingdom that they should, and they who are oppress'd by Poverty and Misfortunes are unable to be at the Charges of removing from their Miseries. These were the People intended to be relieved, but they were not able to reach the friendly Arm extended for their Relief, something else must be done, of which more shall be said in a proper Place. Let us in the mean Time cast our Eyes on the Multitude of unfortunate People in the Kingdom of reputable Families, and of liberal, or at least, [hon]est reputa[b]le Education:⁵³ Some undone by Guardians, some by Law-Suits, some by Accidents in Commerce, some by Stocks and Bubbles, and some by Suretyship;⁵⁴ But all agree [in thin]king in this one Circumstance, that they must either be Burthensome to their Relations, or betake themselves to little Shifts for Sustenance, which ('tis ten to one) do not answer their Purposes, and to which a well-educated Mind descends with the utmost Constraint. What various Misfortunes may reduce the Rich, the Industrious, to the Danger of a Prison, to a moral Certainty of Starving! These are the People that may relieve themselves and strengthen *Georgia*, by resorting thither, and Great *Britain* by their Departure.

I appeal to the Recollection of the Reader (tho' he be Opulent, tho' he be Noble) does not his own Sphere of Acquaintance? (I may venture to ask) Does not even his own Blood, his Set of near Relations furnish him with some Instances of such Persons as have been here describ'd? Must they Starve? What honest Mind can bear to think it? Must they be fed by the Contributions of Others? Certainly they must, rather than be suffered to perish. Are these Wealth to the Nation? Are they not a Burthen to themselves, a Burthen to their Kindred and Acquaintance? A Burthen to the whole Community?

I have heard it said (and 'tis easy to say so) let them learn to work; let them subdue their Pride, and descend to mean Employments, keep Alehouses, or Coffee-houses, even sell Fruit, or clean Shoes for an honest Lively-hood. But alas! These Occupations, and many more like them, are overstock'd already by People who know better how to follow them, than do they whom we have been talking of. Half of those who are bred in low Life, and well versed in such Shifts and Expedients, find but a very narrow Maintenance by them. As for Labouring, I cou'd almost wish that the Gentleman, or Merchant who thinks that another Gentleman, or Merchant in want, can thresh, or dig, to the Value of Subsistence for his Family, or even for himself; I say I could wish the Person who thinks so, were obliged to make trial of it for a Week, or (not to be too severe) for only a Day: He would find himself to be less than the Fourth Part of a Labourer, and that the Fourth Part of a Labourer's Wages could not maintain him. I have heard it said, that a Man may learn to labour by Practice; 'tis admitted: But it must also be admitted that before he can learn, he may starve. Suppose a Gentleman were this Day to begin, and with grievous toil found himself able to earn Three Pence, how many Days, or Months, are necessary to form him that he may deserve a Shilling, *per diem?* Men, whose Wants are importunate, must try such Expedients as will give immediate Relief. 'Tis too late for them to begin to learn a Trade when their pressing Necessities call for the Exercise of it.

HAVING thus described (I fear, too truly) the pityable Condition of the better Sort of the Indigent, an Objection rises against their Removal upon what is stated of their Imbecility for Drudgery. It may be asked, if they can't get Bread here for their Labour, how will their Condition be mended in *Georgia?* The Answer is easy; Part of it is well attested, and Part self-evident. They have Land there for nothing, and that *Land is so fertile that (as is said before) they receive an Hundred Fold increase for taking very little Pains. Give here in *England* Ten Acres of good Land to One of these helpless Persons, and I doubt not his Ability to make it sustain him, and this by his own Culture, without letting it to another: But the Difference between no Rent, and Rack-Rent, is the Difference between eating and starving. If I make but Twenty Pound of the Produce of a Field, and am to pay Twenty Pound Rent for it; 'tis plain I must perish if I have not another Fund to support me: But if I pay no Rent, the Produce of that Field will supply the mere Necessities of Life.

WITH a View to the Relief of People in the Condition I have described, His Majesty has this present Year incorporated a considerable Number of Persons of Quality and Distinction, and vested a large Tract of *South-Carolina* in them, by the Name of *Georgia*, in Trust to be distributed among the Necessitous. These Trustees not only give Land to the Unhappy who go thither, but are also impower'd to receive the voluntary Contributions of charitable Persons to enable them to furnish the poor Adventurers with all Necessaries for the Expence of the Voyage, occupying the Land, and supporting them 'till they find themselves comfortably settled. So that now

---

*Descr. Abreg. p. 13.

the Unfortunate will not be obliged to bind themselves to a long Servitude, to pay for their Passage, for they may be carried *gratis* into a Land of Liberty and Plenty; where they immediately find themselves in Possession of a competent Estate, in an happier Climate than they knew before, and they are Unfortunate indeed if there they can't forget their Sorrows.⁵⁵

CHAP. IV.

England *will grow Rich by sending her Poor Abroad. Of Refugees, Conversion of* Indians, *small Offenders,* Roman *Colonies.*

BESIDES the Persons described in the preceding Chapter, there are others whom it may be proper to send Abroad for the Reasons hereafter given, which Reasons will also shew at whose Expence these other Sorts of indigent People ought to be removed. I think it may be laid down for a Rule, that *we may well spare all those, who having neither Income, nor Industry, equal to their Necessities, are forced to live upon the Fortunes, or Labours of others;* and that they who now are an heavy *Rent-charge* upon the Publick, may be made an immense *Revenue* to it, and this by an happy Exchange of their Proverty for an Affluence.

BELIEVING it will be granted that the People described in the last Chapter ought in Prudence to go Abroad; and that we are bound in Humanity and Charity to send them: There arises a Question, whether our aiding their Departure be consistent with good Policy? I raise this Objection on purpose to answer it, because some who mean very well to the Publick have fancy'd that our Numbers *absolutely taken,* without a Distinction, are real Wealth to a Nation. Upon a little Examination, this will appear to be a mistaken Notion. It arises from a Mis-Application of Sir *William Petty's* Political Arithmetick, and of Sir *William Temple's* Observations on the united *Netherlands.*⁵⁶ But when these great Men esteem People as the Wealth of a Nation, surely they can only mean such as labour, and by their Industry add yearly to the Capital Stock of their Country, at the same Time, that they provide the Necessaries or Comforts of Life for themselves. Perhaps the Rasp-houses may be reckoned Part of the Riches of *Holland,* because the Drones are made to work in them:⁵⁷ But is an Infirmary of Incurables Wealth to a Community? Or (which is worse, because 'tis remediable and is not remedied) are Hundreds of Prisons filled with Thousands of *English* Debtors, are they a Glory, or a Reproach, a Benefit, or a Burthen, to the Nation? Who can be so absurd as to say that we should be enriched by the Importation of a Multitude of Cripples, who might be able perhaps to earn a Fourth Part of what is necessary to sustain them? If Ten Thousand of these would be an Addition to our Wealth, Ten Millions of them must add a Thousand Times as much to it. Did the Fire of *London* add to the Wealth of the Nation? I am sure it gave abundance of Employment to the Poor, just as People are employed in Trade to feed and cloath the Inhabitants of Prisons. But these are also a slow Fire, an Hectick Fever to consume the Vitals of the State. The true State of National Wealth is like that of private Wealth, 'tis comparative. The Nation, as well as Individuals, must work to save and not to spend. If I work hard all Day and at Night give my Wages to the next Cripple I see, it may be profitable to my Soul, but my worldly Fortune is in the same Condition as if I had stood idle. If the Produce of the Nation be in Moveables Land and Labour Fifty Millions in a Year, and only Forty Eight Millions are expended to maintain the People: Now has the Nation added Two Millions to its Capital, but if it spends Fifty One Millions, then is that to be made good by sinking Part of the Personal Estate, or Mortgaging the real. And upon a *par, plus* a Million, and *minus* a Million in Earnings and Expences will operate nothing towards encreasing the National Wealth, if you proceed in *infinitum,* tis only impoverishing the Rich to maintain the Poor; it seems indeed to have something of Levelling in it: to prevent which, I think our Men of Fortune would act wisely once for all; to put these poor People on a Footing of their own, and shake off the perpetual Incumbrance by a single Act of prudent Beneficence.

ONE of the Gentlemen would have *Scotland, Ireland* and *Wales* sunk under Water, but all the People saved and settled in *England.*[58] He certainly deceived himself with a View of the *artificial Strength of the *Dutch,* when their Fishery was at the highest Pitch, and when they were Carriers for Mankind. But they have not been able to preserve these Branches of Trade entire, and their Numbers must decrease as do the Means of maintaining them. †Therefore instead of taking it for granted, that Numbers of People

*See the 6th Chapter.
†To illustrate the Doctrine laid down in this Sentence, take the following Part of a Description of a neighbouring Country by a celebrated Author.

"I met in my Days Journey, nine Cars loaden with old musty shrivel'd Hides, one Carload of Butter, one Cow and Calf driven by a Man and his Wife. A Colony of one Hundred and Fifty Beggars, all repairing to People our Metropolis, and by encreasing the Number of Hands, to encrease its Wealth; upon the old Maxim, that People are the Riches of a Nation. And therefore one Thousand Mouths with hardly Ten Pair of Hands, or any Work to employ necessarily create a Traffick; we may invert the Proposition, and safely hold, that an extensive Traffick will infallibly be attended with sufficient Numbers of People.

AND yet these unhappy People, who are not able to earn above a Fourth Part of their Sustenance at Home, and as we have shewn are a Load on the Fortunes and Industry of others, may in the new Province of *Georgia* well provide by their Labour a decent Maintenance, and at the same Time enrich their Mother Country.

UPON what has been said, the Reader may be desirous to see a State of the Difference (with respect to the Interests of the Industrious and Wealthy Part of the Nation,) between a poor Person here, earning but Half his Sustenance, and the same Person settled in a Freehold, of a fertile Soil without Tithes or Taxes: And in this Computation let us remember that of the many Thousands of poor Debtors, who fill our Prisons, few earn any Thing at present; and this Colony is chiefly intended for the Unfortunate, there being no Danger of the Departure of such as are able to maintain themselves here.

A Man who is equal in Ability, only to the Fourth Part of a Labourer, (and many such there are,) we will suppose to earn Four Pence *per Diem*, or Five Pounds *per Annum*, in *London;* his Wife and a Child of above Seven Years Old, Four Pence *per Diem* more: Upon a fair Supposition (because 'tis the common Case) he has another Child too Young to earn any Thing. These live but wretchedly at an Expence of Twenty Pounds *per Ann.* to defray which they earn Ten Pounds; so that they are a Loss to the Rich and Industrious Part of the Nation of Ten Pounds *per Ann.* for there are but three general Methods of supplying the Defect of their Ability. Whatever they consume more than they earn, must be furnished, First, either by the Bounty, or Charity of others; or Secondly, by Frauds, as by running

---

them, will infallibly make us a rich and flourishing People. Secondly, Travellers enough, but Seven in Ten wanting Shirts and Cravats; Nine in Ten going barefoot and carrying their Broagues and Stockings in their Hands. One Woman in Twenty having a Pillion, the rest Riding bare back'd. Above Two Hundred Horsemen, with Four Pair of Boots amongst them all, Seventeen Saddles of Leather, (the rest being made of Straw,) and most of their Garranes only shod before. I went into one of the Principal Farmers Houses out of Curiosity, and his whole Furniture consisted of Two Blocks for Stools, a Bench on each side the Fire-Place made of Turf, six Trenchers, one Bowl, a Pot, six Horn-spoons, three Noggins, three Blankets (one of which served the Man and Maid-Servant; the other Two, the Master of the Family, his Wife and five Children,) a small Churn, a wooden Candlestick, a broken Stick for a pair of Tongs. In the publick Towns, one third of the Inhabitants walking the Streets barefoot, *&c.*[59]

in Debt to the Ruin of the Industrious, &c. Or, Thirdly by what our Law calls Force and Felony, as Theft and Robbery, &c. They must be supplied at some of these Rates, therefore (as I said before,) this Family is a Loss to the Rich and Industrious of Ten Pounds *per Ann.* and if the Particulars of their Consumption, or an Equivalent for them could have brought Ten Pounds from any Foreign Market, then has the whole Community lost Ten Pounds by this Family.

Now this very Family in *Georgia*, by raising Rice and Corn sufficient for its Occasions, and by attending the Care of their Cattle and Land (which almost every one is able to do for himself in some tolerable Degree) will easily produce in the gross Value, the Sum of Sixty Pounds *per Ann.* nor is this to be wonder'd at, because of the valuable Assistance it has from a fertile Soil and a Stock given *gratis*, which must always be remembred in this Calculation.

THE Lots to be assigned to each Family, as 'tis said, will be about Fifty Acres. The usual *Wages of a common Labourer in *Carolina* is Three Shill. *per Diem*, *English* Value, or Twenty Shillings of their Money. Therefore our poor Man, (who is only equal to the Fourth Part of a Man,) at about Nine Pence *per Diem*, earns about Twelve Pounds *per Ann.* his Care of his Stock on his Land in his Hours of Resting from Labour, (amounting to one Half of each Day) is worth also Twelve Pounds *per Ann.* his Wife and eldest Child may easily between them earn as much as the Man; So that the Sum remaining to be raised by the Wealth of the Soil and the Stock thereon (abstracted from the Care and Labour of the Husbandman) is only Twelve Pounds *per Ann.* it must be observed that 'tho this Family, when in *London*, was dieted but meanly, yet it could afford very little for Cloaths out of the Twenty Pounds it then expended, but now it will fare much better in *Georgia*, at the same Expence, because Provisions will be cheap, and it will also pay Forty Pounds a Year to *England* for Apparel, Furniture and Utensils of the Manufacture of this Kingdom. Behold then the Benefit the Common Weal receives by relieving her famishing Sons. Take it stated only upon One Hundred such Families as follows,

In *London* an Hundred Men earn	500 *l.*
An Hundred Women and an Hundred Children	500 *l.*
Total	1000 *l.*

*Descr. Abreg. p 9.

In *Georgia* an Hundred Families earn
An Hundred Men for Labour 1200 *l.*
Ditto for Care 1200 *l.*
An Hundred Women and an Hundred Children 2400 *l.*
Land and Stock in themselves 1200 *l.*

      Total 6000 *l.*

In *London* an Hundred Families consume 2000 *l.*
Supplied by their Labour 1000 *l.*
By the Wealth of others 1000 *l.*

In *Georgia* an Hundred Families consume of
 their own Produce 2000 *l.*
Of *English* Produce 4000 *l.*

 Thus taking it that we gained One Thousand Pounds *per Ann.* (which was the Value of their Labour) before their Removal, and that we now gain Four Thousand Pounds,[60] we have got an Addition of Three Thousand Pounds *per Ann.* to our Income; but if, (as the Truth is) we formerly lost One Thousand Pounds *per Ann.* and the Nation now gains Four Thousand Pounds *per Ann.* the Rich and Industrious are now profited to the Value of Five Thousand Pounds *per Ann.* I might also shew other great Advantages in the Encrease of our Customs, our Shipping, and our Seamen. It is plain that these Hundred Families, thus removed, employ near Two Hundred Families here to work for them, and thus by their Absence they encrease the People of *Great Britain,* for Hands will not be long wanting where Employment is to be had: If we can find Business that will feed them, what between the Encouragement of and Encrease by Propagation on the one Hand,[61] and the Preservation of those who now perish for Want on the other: We should quickly find we had strengthened our Hive by sending a Swarm away to provide for themselves.[62]

 It is also highly for the Honour and Advancement of our holy Religion to assign a new Country to the poor *Germans,* who have left their own for the Sake of Truth. It will be a powerful Encouragement to Confessors of this Kind to hold fast their Integrity, when they know their case not to be desperate in this World. Nor need we fear that the King of *Prussia* will be able to engross them all,[63] we shall have a Share of them if we will contribute chearfully to their Removal. The Society for Promo[ting]

Christian [Know]legde h[as] gloriously exerted itse[lf] on this Occasion:[64] They have resolv'd to advance such a Sum of Money to the Trustees for the Colony of *Georgia*, as will enable them to provide for Seven Hundred poor *Salzburghers*. This is laying a Foundation for the Conversion of the Heathen, at the same Time, that they snatch a great Number of poor Christians out of the Danger of Apostacy. 'Tis to be hoped this laudable Example will be followed by private Persons, who may thus at once do much for the Glory of God, and for the Wealth and Trade of *Great Britain*. Subjects thus acquir'd by the impolitick Persecutions, by the superstitious Barbarities of neighbouring Princes, are a noble Addition to the capital Stock of the *British* Empire. If our People be Ten Millions, and we were to have an Access of Ten Thousand *useful* Refugees, every Stock-jobber in *Exchange-Alley* must allow that this would encrease our Wealth and Figure in the World, as one added to a Thousand, or, as $1/10$ *per Cent*. This would be the Proportion of our Growth compar'd with our Neighbors, who have not been the Persecutors; but as against the Persecutor, the Increase of our Strength would be in a double Ratio, compounded as well of negative as of positive Quantity. Thus if *A* and *B* are worth One Thousand Pounds each, and a Third Person gives Twenty Shillings to *A*, now *A* is become richer than *B* by $1/10$ *per Cent.* but if *A* gains Twenty Shillings from *B*, then *A* is become richer than *B* by about $2/10$ or $1/5$ *per Cent.* for *A* is worth One Thousand and One Pounds, and *B* is worth only Nine Hundred and Ninety Nine Pounds.[65]

The Encrease of our People, on this fruitful Continent, will probably, in due Time, have a good Effect on the Natives, if we do not shamefully neglect their Conversion: If we were moderately attentive to our Duty on this Head, we have no Reason to doubt of Success. The *Spaniard* has at this Day as many Christians, as he has Subjects in *America*, Negroes excepted. We may more reasonably hope to make Converts and good Subjects of the *Indians* in Amity with us, by using them well, when we grow numerous in their Neighbourhood, than the *Spaniards* could have expected to have done by their inexpressible Cruelties, which raised the utmost Aversion in the Minds of the poor *Indians* against them and their Religion together. One of their own Friers who had not relinquish'd his Humanity,[66] tells us of an *Indian* Prince, who just as the *Spaniards* were about to murder him, was importuned by one of their Religious to become a Christian; the Priest told him much of Heaven and Hell, of Joy and Misery eternal; the Prince desired to be informed which of the two Places was allotted for the *Spaniards?* Heaven, quoth the Priest; says the Prince, I'm resolved not to go there. How different from this was the Reflection of an *Indian* Chief in *Pensilvania:* *What is the Matter, says he, with us that we are thus sick in our own* Air, *and these Strangers well? 'Tis as if they were sent hither to inherit our Land in our steads; but the Reason is plain, they love the Great God and we do not.* Was not this *Indian* almost become a Christian? *New-England* has many Convert-*Indians,* who are very good Subjects, 'tho no other Colony had such long and cruel Wars with its *Indian* Neighbours.

THE pious Benefactions of the People of *England* have in all Ages equall'd, if not surpassed, all Instances of the Kind in other Countries. The mistaken Piety of our Ancestors gave a third Part of the Kingdom to the Church: Their Intentions were right, tho' they erred in the Object. Since the Statutes against *mort-main* and superstitious Uses,[68] our great and numerous Foundations of Hospitals and Alms-houses are the Wonder of Foreigners. Some of these, especially of the largest, are doubtless of great Use, and excellently administered. And yet, if the Numbers in this Nation, who feel the Woes of others and would contribute to relieve them, did but consider the Cases of the People describ'd in the last Chapter, of the *German* Emigrants, and even of the poor *Indians;* they would be apt to conclude that there ought to be a Blessing in Store for these also. About Eight Pounds allowed to an indigent Person here, may poorly support him, and this must be repeated yearly; but a little more, than double that Sum, relieves him for Life, sends him to our new World, gives Plenty there to him and his Posterity; putting them in Possession of a good Estate, of which, they may be their own Stewards.

BUT this is not all, that Sum which settles one poor Family in the Colony does not end there; it in Truth purchases an Estate to be applied to like Uses, in all future Times. The Author of these Pages is credibly inform'd that the Trustees will reserve to themselves square Lots of Ground interspers'd at proper Distances among the Lands, which shall be given away: As the Country fills with People, these Lots will become valuable, and at moderate Rents will be a growing Fund to provide for those whose melancholy Cases may require Assistance hereafter: Thus the Settlement of Five Hundred Persons will open the Way to settle a Thousand more afterwards with equal Facility. Nor is this Advance of the Value of these Lots of Land a chimerical Notion; it will happen certainly and suddenly. All

Brit. Emp. Vol. I. p. 162.[67]

the Lands within Fifty Miles of *Charlestown* have within these Seven Years encreas'd near Four-Fold in their *Value, so that you must pay Three or Four Hundred Pounds for a Plantation, which Seven Years ago you could have bought for a Hundred Pounds, and 'tis certain that Fifty Years ago you might have purchas'd at *Charlestown* for Five Shillings a Spot of Land which the Owner would not sell at this Day for Two Hundred Pounds Sterling.

THE Legislature is only able to take a proper Course for the Transportation of small Offenders, if it shall seem best, when the Wisdom of the Nation is assembled; I mean only those who are but Novices in Iniquity. Prevention is better than the Punishment of Crimes, it may reform such to make them Servants to such Planters as were reduc'd from a good Condition. The Manners and Habits of very young Offenders would meliorate in a Country not populous enough to encourage a profligate Course of Life,[69] a Country where Discipline will easily be preserv'd. These might supply the Place of Negroes, and yet (because their Servitude is only to be temporary) they might upon Occasion be found useful against the *French*, or *Spaniards*; indeed, as the Proportion of Negroes now stands, that Country, South Carolina,[70] would be in great Danger of being lost, in Case of a War with either of those Powers. The present Wealth of the Planters in their Slaves too probably threatens their future Ruin, if proper Measures be not taken to strengthen their Neighbourhood with large Supplies of Free-men. I would not here be understood to advance, that our common Run of *Old-Baily* Transports wou'd be a proper Beginning in the Infancy of *Georgia*. No, they would be too hard for our young Planters, they ought never to be sent any where but to the Sugar Islands, unless we had Mines to employ them.

THE Poverty of the Publick, with regard to its immense Debt, and the Anticipation of Taxes attending that Debt, will probably be a Reason to many worthy Patriots, not to afford a large *pecuniary* Assistance in Parliament, tho' they give all other furtherance to this Settlement, and yet powerful Reasons might be offer'd, why the Commons of *Great Britain*, with Justice to those that send them,[71] might apply a large Sum of publick Money to this Occasion. Let us suppose that Twenty Five Thousand of the most helpless People in *Great Britain* were settled there at an Expence of half a Million of Money; the Easiness of the Labour in winding

---

*Descr. Abreg. p. 9.

off the Silk and tending the Silk Worm would agree with the most of those who throughout the Kingdom are chargeable to the Parishes. That Labour with the Benefit of Land stock'd for them *gratis*, would well subsist them, and save our Parishes near Two Hundred Thousand Pounds directly, in their annual Payments;[72] not to compute wh[at] would also be saved indirectly, by the Unwillingness of many pretended Invalids to go the Voyage, who would them betake themselves to industrious Courses to gain a Livelyhood.

I shall consider the Benefit of employing them in raising Silk when I come in the Fifth Chapter, to treat of the Commerce of *Carolina*. I shall only here observe that the Number of Poor, last mention'd, being thus dispos'd of, would send us Goods, at least to the Value of Five Hundred Thousand Pounds annually, to pay for their *English* Necessaries; and that would be somewhat better than our being oblig'd to maintain them at the Rate of Two Hundred Thousand Pounds a Year here at Home.

I can't dismiss this Enquiry concerning the proper Persons to plant this Colony, without observing that the Wisdom of the *Roman* State discharged not only its ungovernable distressed Multitude, but also its Emeriti, its Soldiers, which had served long and well in War, into Colonies upon the Frontiers of their Empire. 'Twas by this Policy that they elbow'd all the Nations round them. Their Military Hospital went a Progress, we can trace its Stages *Northward* from the *Tiber* to the *Po*, to the *Rhone*, to the *Rhine*, to the *Thames:* The like Advances they made on all Sides round them, and their Soldiers were at least as fond of the Estates thus settled on them as ours can be of their Pensions.

WHAT I said before in this Chapter, with regard to the encreasing Fund, to arise by reserved Lots of Ground interspersed among the Lands that will be distributed to the Planters, will hold good in the same Manner in such Settlements as might be made at a national Expence, so that Twenty Thousand People, well settled, will raise the Value of the reserved Lands, in such Measure as will bring *Great Britain* to resemble the present *Carolina* in one happy Instance, *viz.* That there is not a *Beggar, or very poor Person in the whole Country. Then should we have no going to Decay, no complaining in our Streets.

---

*Descr. Abreg. p. 6.

Chap. V.

Of the present and (probable) future Trade of South-Carolina *and* Georgia. *Rice, Silk, Cotton, Wine,* &c.

THE present State of *South-Carolina* and its Commerce may give us an Idea of the Condition of the early Settlements in the new Colony of *Georgia*. Their first Essays in Trade and Husbandry will doubtless be in Imitation of their nearest Neighbours. We shall therefore consider these Colonies together, the Difference in their Air and Soil being hardly discernable, and the same Traffick being proper for them both.

WE are not to imagine that either the present Branches of Trade in that Country, will be perpetual, or that there is not room to introduce others of more Importance than any they have hitherto been acquainted with. Thus it will necessarily fall out that their present Exports of Lumber and of Deer Skins will decrease, or rather wholly cease when the Country grows populous: And this for an obvious Reason, the Land will be better employ'd, it will be dis-afforrested, and no longer left vacant to the Growth of great Woods, and the Sustenance of wild Herds of Deer. But the very Reason why these Branches of Trade will cease will also be the Cause of their taking up others, or improving them to such a Degree, as must put these Colonies in a Condition to vie with the most flourishing Countries of *Europe* and *Asia:* And that without Prejudice to their Dependance on *Great Britain*. We shall *by their Growth* in People and Commerce have the Navigation and Dominion of the Ocean *establish'd* in us more firmly than ever. We shall be their Market for great Quantities of *Raw-silk, and perhaps for Wine, Oyl, Cotton, Drugs, Dying-Stuffs, and many other lesser Commodities. They have already tried the Vine and the Silkworm, and have all imaginable Encouragement to expect that these will prove most valuable Staple-Commodities to them. And I have been credibly inform'd, That the Trustees for *Georgia* furnish proper Expences for a skilful *Botanist* to collect the Seeds of Drugs and Dying-Stuffs in other Countries in the same Climate,[73] in order to cultivate such of them as shall be found to thrive well in *Georgia*. This Gentleman could not be expected to proceed at his own Charges, but he's the only Person belonging to the Management of that Trust who does not serve *Gratis*.

THE Raw-silk, which *Great Britain* and *Ireland* are able to consume,

---

*Descr. Abreg. p. 13. *Archd.* Descr. p. 30.

will employ Forty or Fifty Thousand Persons in that Country, nor need they be the strongest, or most industrious Part of Mankind; It must be *a weak Hand indeed that cannot earn Bread where Silk-worms and White Mulberry-trees are so plenty. Most of the Poor in *Great Britain*, who are maintain'd by Charity, are capable of this, tho' not of harder Labour: And the Planters may be certain of selling their Raw-silk to the utmost Extent of the *British* Demand for that Commodity; because a *British* Parliament will not fail to encourage the Importation of it from thence, rather than from *Aliens*, that the Planters may be able to make large Demands upon us for our Home Commodities: For this will be the Consequence of their employing all their People in producing a Commodity, which is so far from rivalling, that it will supply a rich Manufacture to their Mother-Country.

THE present Medium of our Importation of Silk will not be the Measure hereafter of that Branch of Trade when the *Georgians* shall enter into the Management of the Silk-worm. *Great Britain* will then be able to sell Silk-Manufactures cheaper than all *Europe* besides, because the *Georgians* may grow rich, and yet afford their Raw-silk for less than half the Price that we now pay for that of *Piedmont:* The Peasant of *Piedmont*, after he has tended the Worm, and wound off the Silk, pays half of it for the Rent of the Mulberry-trees, and the Eggs of the Silk-worm; but in *Georgia* the working Hand will have the Benefit of all his Labour. This is Fifty in a Hundred, or *Cent per Cent* difference in favour of the *Georgians*, which receives a great Addition from another Consideration, *viz.* the *Georgian* will have his Provisions incomparably cheaper than the *Piemontese*, because he pays no Rent for the Land that produces them; he lives upon his own Estate. But there is still another Reason why *Great Britain* should quickly and effectually encourage the Production of Silk in *Georgia*; for, in effect, it will cost us nothing; it will be purchased by the several Manufactures of *Great Britain*, and this, I fear, is not our present Case with respect to *Piedmont*: Especially (if as we have been lately told) they have prohibited the Importation of Woollen Goods into that Principality.

THAT this little Treatise might be the more Satisfactory to the Reader,[74] I could wish I had been minutely informed of the present State of our Silk Trade; of the medium Value of Silk *per* Pound; to what Amount it is imported; of its Duty, Freight, Commission and Insurance; and Lastly, by what returns in Commerce it is purchased. I'm persuaded, these Estimates would afford plentiful Matter for Observations in favour of this Position,

Arch. Descr. p. 30.

viz. that *Great Britain* ought vigorously to attempt to get this Trade into her own Hands. I shall however aim at a Computation, upon my Memory of Facts, which I have heard from those who understand that Commerce.

1. *GREAT BRITAIN* imports Silk from *Piedmont*, near the Yearly Value of Three Hundred Thousand Pounds.
2. THE medium Price is about Twelve Shillings *per* Pound in Piedmont.
3. THE Duty here is about Four Shillings *per* Pound.
4. THE Price of Raw-Silk in *London*, is generally more than Half of the Price of the wrought Goods in their fullest Perfection.

1*st Observ.* IF the *Piemontese* paid no Rent for the Mulberry-Tree and Silk-worm, he might afford Silk at Six Shillings *per* Pound.

2*d Observ.* IF Silk were bought in *Piedmont* at Six Shillings *per* Pound, and imported Duty-free, it might be sold in *London* at Seven Shillings *per* Pound. For, the Commission, Insurance and Exchange, or Interest of Money would be but Half what they are at present, and there must be some Allowance for the Interest of the Money that was usually applied to pay the Duty.

3*d Observ.* THEREFORE, *Great Britain*, by encouraging the Growth of Silk in *Georgia*, may save above a Hundred Thousand Pound *per Ann.* of what she lays out in *Piedmont*.

4*th Observ.* THE *Georgian* (without taking the Cheapness of his Provisions into Question) may enable *Great Britain* to under-sell all her Rivals in *Europe* in the Silk-Manufacture in a Proportion resembling what follows.

	l.	*s.*	*d.*
France, Raw-silk, One Pound Weight	0	14	0
Workmanship	0	16	0
Total	1	10	0
Great Britain Raw-silk, One Pound Weight	0	7	0
Workmanship	0	16	0
Total	1	3	0

The Difference of these is Seven Sh[illings] in Thirty,[75] which is near Twenty Five Pound in an Hundred, and is above Thirty *per Cent.* The Reader is desired to consider these Computations as stated by guess. But the same Reasoning will hold in a considerable Degree upon the more exact State of the several Values.⁷⁶

*RICE is another Growth of this Province that doth not interfere with *Great Britain*. But we reap their Harvests; for when they have sold the Rice in a foreign Market, they lay out the Money in our Manufactures to carry Home with them. They have already made an handsome Progress in *Carolina*, in cultivating this Grain. They have exported above †Ten Thousand Tuns of it by Weight in a Year already, all produced in a few Years from so small a Quantity as was carried thither in a Bag, fit to hold only a Hundred Pound Stirling in Silver; they have sold Cargoes of it in *Turkey*. They have all the World for their Market. A Market not easily glutted.

THE Indulgence of the *British* Legislature to *Carolina* in this Branch of their Trade, shews our new *Georgians* what Encouragement they may expect from that *August* Body, as soon as they shall learn the Management of the Silk-worm. The Law for the Ease of the Rice-Trade, is alone sufficient to enrich whole Provinces:⁷⁷ They are now at Liberty to proceed in their Voyages directly to any Part of *Europe*, South of *Cape Fenesterre*, or to *Asia* and *Africk* before they touch at *Great Britain*. The Difference of the Charge of Freight is not Half the Benefit they receive from this Act of Parliament; they arrive at the desired Ports time enough to forestal the Markets of *Spain*, *Portugal*, and the *Levant*. It now frequently happens that Cargoes arrive safe, which, as the Law stood formerly, would have been lost at Sea, by Means of the Deviation homew[ard].⁷⁸ This new Law, in a Manner, forces them into the *Spanish*, *Portuguese*, and *Levant* Trades, and gives them Two Returns of Commerce instead of One. They may now dispose of their *American* Grain in the first Place, and then come loaden to *Great Britain* with the most profitable Wares of the Countries where they traded; and lastly, buy for ready Money such *British* Manufactures as they have Occasion to carry Home.

WHEN I speak of the future Trade of these happy Provinces, I might expatiate upon many valuable Branches of it besides the Silk and Rice: Branches which it must ‡ enjoy as certainly as Nature shall hold her Course in the Production of Vegetables, and the Revolution of Seasons. But because I would not swell this Treatise to too expensive a Bulk, I shall content my self with acquainting the Reader that they have no Doubt of the kindly

---

*Descr. Abreg. p. 13.
†Descr. Abreg. p 7.
‡Descr. Abreg. p. 25, 26.

Growth of Cotton, Almonds, Olives, &c. And in short, of every Vegetable that can be found in the best Countries under the same Latitude.

I FORESEE an Objection against what is here laid down: It may be said that all the Countries under the same Latitude do not produce the same Commodities; that some of them are incapable of raising choice Vegetables, which others of them nourish with the utmost Facility. For Answer to this Objection, what was said in the second Chapter shou'd be consider'd: The intemperate Heats of *Barbary*, *Ægypt* and *Arabia* are there accounted for, from the Vicinity of boundless sandy Desarts; on the other Hand, near Mount *Caucasus* in *Asia*, and particularly in the Kingdom of *Kaschmere*, or *Kasimere*, (which is entirely surrounded by prodigious Mountains) their Seasons are almost as Cold as ours in *England*, tho' they lie in the same Latitude with *Tangier*, or *Gibraltar*.

THESE Instances of the Temperature in Countries equidistant from the *Æquator*, are very opposite to each other, the Medium between them is the happy Portion of *Georgia*; which therefore must be productive of most of the valuable Commodities in the Vegetable World.

CHAP. VI.

Observations on the Commerce, Navigation, and Plantations of Great Britain, compared with those of some of her Neighbours.

WHOEVER would be fully informed concerning the Figure which *England* has made in all Ages, in Maritime Affairs, may find abundance of curious Matter in *Selden*'s *Mare Clausum*, and from his Time to ours may learn Facts from the *Gazettes*, or read a faithful Transcript of both in *Burchet*'s Naval History.[79] I shall take notice of Two remarkable Periods of our antient Maritime Story, because some useful Observations may be made in comparing them, both with other Nations, and with ourselves in our present Situation.

WE are told that *Edgar*, King of this Island, had Four Thousand Ships, by the Terrour of which he subdued *Norway*, *Denmark*, all the Islands of the Ocean, and the greatest Part of *Ireland*. These Instances of his Power are specified in a *Record cited by that great Lawyer, *Sir Edward Coke*, in the

---

*Altitonantis Dei largiflua Clementia, qui est Rex Regum & Dominus dominantium, ego Edgarus Anglorum Basileus, *omniumque [rerum] Insularum Oceani quæ* Britanniam *circumjacent, cunc-*

Preface to his Fourth Report. This Monarch made a Naval Progress yearly round this Island, and once took it in his Head to cause eight conquer'd Kings to row his Barge on the River *Dee*. But it seems that some of his Successors have had such *pacifick Ministers,* as either neglected to keep our Fleets in repair, or were *afraid* to make use of them: For, at several Periods of Time, since the Days of King *Edgar,* we find that this Kingdom has been *miserably insulted* on the Seas, and even succesfully invaded by other Nations.

THE *British Neptune* slept, or slumbered, most Part of the Time, from the Reign of King *Edgar* to that of Queen *Elizabeth:* In her Days he sprung up with Vigour, being rous'd by *Spain,* which was then the greatest maritime Power on Earth. From Queen *Elizabeth* to our Time, our naval Strength has gradually encreased, insomuch that at this Day, the *Spanish* Fleets opposed to ours, would make a very contemptible Figure on the Ocean: We now have it in our Power to Lord it over the watry World. It may be worth our Enquiry to know how these Fluctuations have happened in the Dominion of the Seas? And in the Issue, that Enquiry will be found pertinent to the Project now on Foot for planting a new Colony in *Georgia*.

THE Tasks and Course of Life of Sea-faring Men are not to be learned in an Instant; their Employment is a laborious Trade, To be acquired only by Application and Industry. Money will buy all naval Stores except Mariners, but unless a Succession of them be preserv'd, no Wealth will be able to purchase them. The surest, the cheapest, I may justly call it, the only *profitable* Method of supporting such a Succession, is to have perpetual Occasion for a Multitude of Seamen in a Course of Trade. 'Tis indeed probable that *Edgar's* amazing Power at Sea was, for the most Part, owing to his own great Genius, attended with indefatigable Industry in training up, and Year by Year augmenting the Number of his Mariners; for in those Days, *England* had no great Share of foreign Traffick, People generally contenting themselves with the Produce of their native Country. This great Prince must therefore have grievously oppress'd his Vassals to

---

tarumque Nationum quæ infra eum includuntur, Imperator & Dominus, gratias ago ipsi Deo omnipotenti Regi meo, qui meum imperium sic ampliavit & exaltavit super Regnum patrum meorum, qui licet Monarchiam totius Angliæ *adepti sunt a tempore* Athelstani *qui primus regum* Anglorum *omnes Nationes quæ Britanniam incolunt sibi armis subegit, nullus tamen eorum ultra fines imperium suum dilatare agressus est, mihi tamen concessit propitia Divinitas cum* Anglorum *Imperio, omnia Regna Insularum Oceani cum suis ferocissimis Regibus usque Norvegiam, maximamque partem* Hiberniæ *cum sua noblissima civitate de* Dublina Anglorum *regno Subjugare.* Pref. to 4th Co.[80] See also *Rapins* History of *England,* in the Life of *Edgar*.[81]

enable him to keep up so great an Armament; and 'tis no Wonder that it dwindled in succeeding Reigns because it had not that *solid* Aliment, *Trade*, to nourish it.

THE *Spanish* Successes in *America* caus'd their Shipping to encrease beyond all their Neighbours; they had Occasion in their Beginnings there, for great Numbers of Transports, to carry not only Men, but also Horses and other Cattle, and Stores, to their new Conquests. Add to which, that *Sicily* and a great Part of *Italy* belonged to them at that Time. The Communication with these Places last mentioned, was by Sea, so that they had a considerable Part in the Encrease of the *Spanish* naval Power. In this flourishing Condition they continued for a great Part of the long Reigns of their *Philip* the 2d, and of our *Elizabeth*. She had not a Fleet able to give their *Armada* Battle: Her Ships indeed were light and nimble, the *Spanish*, tho' larger and more numerous, were unwieldly; therefore the lighter Vessels being in no Danger of a Chace, fought, or stood off, as they saw Occasion. But this Advantage would not have been sufficient, if *Providence* had not interposed a *Tempest*, for the Protection of *England*.

THE Queen knew to what Causes she ow'd her *Danger* and her *Deliverance*, and became more attentive than ever to plant *Colonies in* America. Death prevented her from executing her great Designs; but some of her *best* and *wisest* Subjects, and boldest Seamen, had enter'd so deeply into the Plan, and laid it so nearly to their Hearts, that what she had intended in the Settlement of *Virginia* was in a good Measure effected in the Reign of King *James* the 1st, tho' the Undertaking was a great *Difficulty upon his *timerous* Councils, because the *Spaniards*, of whom he stood in *servile* Awe, did not approve of it. But his Shame, *with much Debate*, barely got the better of his Fears, and that Mine of Treasure was opened to *Great Britain*.

THIS, with what else has since been executed in favour of *England*, both on the Continent, and in the Islands of that new World, has added such a Weight of maritime Force to the natural Strength which we owe to our Situation, that we are able to give Law to the Ocean. *Spain*, indeed, has greater Countries and more Subjects in *America* than we have, and yet does not navigate in that Trade a *Tenth Part* of the *Shipping* that we do. By a *lucky Kind of Poverty* our Dominions there have no Mines of Gold, or Silver: We must be, and ought to be contented to deal in Rum, Sugar, Rice, Tobacco, Horses, Beef, Corn, Fish, Lumber, and other Commodities that

---

*See a short Collection of the most remarkable Passages from the Original to the Dissolution of the *Virginia* Company.[82]

require great Stowage; the Carriage of these employs Millions of Tuns of Shipping. The Value of Five Thousand Pounds in these Wares loads a Vessel, which in the *Spanish* Trade would be freighted Homeward with Half a Million of Pounds Sterling. Thus has the Almighty placed the true Riches of this Earth on the Surface of it; our Rice and Tobacco are more *real* and *permanent Wealth* than their richest Minerals. They are *Wealth* which create a *Power* to defend our Possession of them: And without a sufficient *Force* to defend it, the Possession of all *Wealth is precarious*. Should not *Great Britain* therefore be attentive to the new Settlement of *Georgia?* What an Addition will it quickly make to the Tunnage of our Shipping? And what a seasonable Support will it prove to our *Island Colonies*, who stand in need of so near a Neighbourhood of their Brethren.

THE *Dutch* were esteemed all the last Century the only Match for *England* on the Seas; but as a great Part of their Strength was meerly *Artificial*, it subsides like the Vivacity of a Wretch who has raised his Spirits with a Dose of *Opium.* Commerce and that Wealth and Power which attend it, may be either *absolutely* in the Power of a State, or Empire, consider'd *in* and by *itself*, without Regard to it's Neighbours, which I call *natural* Wealth, Power and Commerce; or they may depend upon Treaties with other States, or be owing to their Connivance, which *pro tempore* amount to a *tacit* Agreement; these latter Species I call *Technical* Wealth, *&c.* Such was the Fishery of the *Dutch*, which they enjoyed by the *Inactivity* of some of our *English* Kings: And this must decline of Course, because of our superiour Treasures of this Kind on the Banks of *Newfoundland.* Another Branch of their artifical Strength was, that by the Indolence of all Nations they were for a Time the *Carriers of the Universe:* But the World is grown *wiser*, other Nations begin to *work* for themselves, and the *Netherlands* will sadly find that this *temporary Fund* of Strength must also fail them. Their only natural foreign Wealth and Strength is their *East-India* Trade; Part of this is truly their own, because the Land that produces Spices is in their *Possession:* But when the two former Branches shall be cut off, they will find that *Possession* every Day more and more *precarious.*

THUS The *British* Empire has a *natural* Wealth in itself and in its dependent Members; but it has also for many Years past enjoy'd an *adventisious*, or *artificial* Traffick. We have been employ'd by all the World in the *Woollen Manufacture*, but other Nations have begun of late to cloath themselves and their Neighbours too. 'Tis a fond Fancy in us to imagine that there are no fleecy Sheep in the World but our own, or that the Rest of Mankind will not learn the Mystery of Working in Wooll. We feel this Trade decreasing Daily, and yet there are those among us who wou'd argue against Demonstration. But when they hope, by any Laws of *Great Britain* to hinder *foreign Nations* from falling into the *Woollen-Manufacture*, they may as well sollicit an Act of Parliament to prevent their *Grass to grow*, and to *intercept* their *Sun-shine*. I will consider one Objection before I leave this Point, because some imagine that we are secure in this Trade, against the Endeavours of all Foreigners; say they, we make *better* Goods than can be made with any foreign *Wool*, unless it be mixed with ours. Be it so. But then, does our great Wealth and Income by that Trade consist only in our *finest* Goods? Do not our Merchants complain that *Ireland* under-sells us in *coarse* Goods at *Lisbon;* that because their Wares are *coarse*, they can be afforded *cheap*, therefore they have a *ready Market*, while ours that are *finer*, but *dearer*, may rot in the Ware-house? What says our *Russia-Company?* Has not *Prussia* supplanted us in the Cloathing of the *Muscovite Army?* Who is ignorant of the Extensiveness of the Undertaking at *Abbeville* in *Picardy?*[83] We are sending some armed Sloops to check the *Irish*,[84] but *who will restrain the French and Germans?* The Multitude don't much value the *Fineness* of their Garments, they only desire to be *warm;* '*tis the Cloathing of the Millions that produces Millions of Money;* and this is what other Countries will certainly have their Share in.

Is not this a Time to cast our Eyes upon our *natural Wealth*, and to augment it as fast as possible? If *Muscovy* supplies its own woollen Goods, or is supplied by any other *Foreigner*, it ought to make us resolve to bring our Naval Stores from *North America;* if *Spain* and *Italy* refuse our Drapery, we may reject their Silk, their Raisins, Oyl, Wine, Olives, and Divers other Merchandizes, and be supplied from *Carolina* and *Georgia*. I have been credibly informed that a Gentleman, now living in this Kingdom, was the *first* Person who made *Pitch* in *America*, about Thirty Years ago;[85] the People whom he conversed with then, look'd on his Experiment as a Chimæra, but it has prov'd so real as to reduce that Commodity, I think, four Fifths in its Value: So that we now buy for Twenty Pounds what was formerly worth a Hundred Pound.

FRANCE has not the same Advantage as *Great Britain* in it Situation, for maritime Affairs: That Country is extended wide within Land, and has not the Benefit of being penetrated by many deep Creeks, or navigable Rivers; on Half its Borders 'tis bounded with the Continent; and the good Harbours of *France* are but few, compared with the Numbers of ours. These Reasons of our Superiority over them in maritime Affairs in General, served to prevent their encreasing in *North-America* as fast as we did, and there is another special Reason, *viz.* We have had the *Navigation* of *North-America* in us by the *large Traffick* of our early Settlements, and even of the *French Sugar-Colonies*, which we supply with Lumber, Horses and Provisions. We have five Souls on the Continent for one of theirs; their principal Settlement is in a Climate too cold and not very fruitful: And yet they contrive all imaginable Methods of augmenting their Numbers. They *intermarry* with the Natives and convert them; and the *French* King supplies Two Thousand *Persons* Yearly with Money to enable them to go thither, without being afraid that he shall *drain his Country* of People.

'Tis easy to demonstrate that we can afford to send People Abroad better than *France* and *Spain*. They have in each of those Kingdoms more than One Hundred Thousand *Cloyster'd Females*, not permitted to *propagate* their Species, and the Number of Males in a State of *Celibacy* is still abundantly greater as it comprehends their *Secular* and *Regular* Clergy, and a considerable Part of their great Armies who resolve against Marriage, because of the uncomfortable Prospects they have, with regard to their Progeny. It may be said indeed, that these don't marry, yet many of them get Children: But it must be admitted that the usual Fate of that Kind of Propogation is to be destroyed secretly, either before, or after the Birth; and the Former of these Crimes frequently procures Barrenness in the Woman. I have entered into the Consideration of the Loss by the Celibacy of their Males, that no Body may imagine the Computation of their Deficiencies should be made upon their cloyster'd Females only.

AND yet let us take a short View of their Losses upon that Calculation, allowing a Monk, or a Priest, for an Husband to each immur'd Woman. The most exact Rules in this Kind of Arithmetick are as follows,

1st. The People who go on in an ordinary Course of Propagation and Mortality, and are not visited with some extraordinary destructive Calamity, grow *double* in their Number in One Hundred *Years*.

2d, Thirty Three *Years*, are a sufficient Allowance for a Generation, or Three Generations to an Hundred Years. Now,

Since the Reformation, near Two Hundred Years are elapsed, at which Time Celibacy was abolish'd in *England*.

Therefore, in that Time *France* has lost more than Five Generations, *Principal* of its Inhabitants, at the Rate of Two Hundred Thousand in each Generation, besides the accumulated Numbers of *Cent per Cent*, for each Hundred Years, which Loss must be reckon'd upon the Second Century as *Interest* upon *Interest;* so that the Two Hundred Thousand individual Persons who were under the Vow in *France*, an Hundred and Eighty Years ago will Twenty Years hence be a *Negative* upon their Numbers to the Value of Eight Hundred Thousand People.

They who understand a little Arithmetick, may divert themselves by computing the Amount of all the Parts of this Loss of People in the Five Generations: To those who do not relish Numbers, I fear, I have here and elsewhere been too tedious.

My aim in this Chapter is to rectify the Notions of some of my Countrymen, upon an Affair so important as our Commerce; to point out the Differences between a *natural* and an *artificial* Trade; to instance them in our Neighbours compared with ourselves; to shew the Industry of the *French* to rival us in *America*, in spite of their Geography and their Religion; and to inculcate that our Strength depends on our *Shipping*, and our *Shipping* on our wide extended *Colonies*, which have neither Gold nor Silver, and *for that very Reason*, confirm us the more Powerfully in the *Dominion of the Seas*.

If what has been offer'd to the Publick in the foregoing Sheets meets a favourable Reception, the Author will add some farther Observations hereafter on the same Subject.[86] At present he only wishes that any Thing here laid down, whether Fact or Observation, may be of use to *Great Britain*.

FINIS.

A Description of the Indians in Georgia (1733)

Oglethorpe's description of the Georgia Indians was first published in Richard Hooker's *Weekly Miscellany* for August 11, 1733.[1] Oglethorpe apparently dispatched this account to the Georgia Trustees along with his separate letter of June 9, 1733.[2]

He evidently designed it to serve several purposes: to diminish the fears of potential emigrants concerning the Indians and to promote instead the notion that most of them were Noble Savages, certainly to encourage the sending of missionaries to Christianize them, and perhaps to justify the subsequent edicts and law banning the sale of rum in Georgia.

Although the letter of June 9, 1733, is still extant, the account itself now exists only in its printed versions. It is here reprinted from the *Weekly Miscellany*.

Part of a Letter from James Oglethorpe, *Esq; at* Georgia, *to the Hon.*
────── *in* London. *Dated the* 9th *of* June *last.*

THERE seems to be a Door opened to our Colony towards the Conversion of the *Indians.* You will see by an Account printed in the inclosed Gazette* that they are desirous of Instruction, which they have hitherto always refus'd to receive. I have had many Conversations with their chief Men, too long here to recite, the whole Tenour of which shews that there is nothing wanting to their Conversion, but one, who understands their Language well, to explain to them the *Mysteries* of Religion; for as to the *moral* Part of Christianity they understand it and assent to it. They abhor *Adultery,* and do not approve of *Plurality* of *Wives.*[3] *Theft* is a Thing not known among the *Creek* Nation, tho' frequent, and even honourable, amongst the *Uchees.*[4] *Murder* they look upon as a most abominable Crime, but do not esteem the killing of an *Enemy,* or one that has injur'd them, Murder. The Passion of *Revenge,* which they call *Honour,* and *Drunkenness,* which they learnt from our Traders, seem to be the two greatest Obstacles to their being truly Christians: But upon both these Points they hear Reason; and with respect to drinking of *Rum,* I have weaned those near me a good deal from it. As for *Revenge,* they say, as they have no executive Power of Justice amongst them, they are forced to kill the Man who has injured them, in order to prevent others from doing the like; but they do not think that any Injury, except *Adultery,* or *Murder,* deserves Revenge. They hold, that if a Man commits *Adultery,* the injur'd Husband is oblig'd to have Revenge, by cutting off the Ears of the *Adulterer,* which if he is too sturdy and strong to submit to, then the injured Husband kills him the first Time that he has an Opportunity so to do with Safety. In Cases of *Murder,* the *next in Blood* is obliged to kill the Murderer, or else he is looked upon as infamous in the Nation where he lives; and the Weakness of the executive Power is such, that there is no other way of Punishment but by the Revenger of Blood, as the Scripture calls it. For there is no coercive Power in any of their Nations. Their Kings can do no more than *perswade.* All the Power that they have is no more than to call their old Men and their Captains together, and to propound to them, without Interruption, the Measures they think proper. After *they* have done speaking, all the others have Lib-

---

* *Which was inserted at large in our last* MISCELLANY.

erty to give their Opinions also; and they reason together till they have
brought each other into some unanimous Resolution. These Conferences
in Matters of great Difficulty have sometimes lasted two Days, and are
always carried on with great Temper and Modesty. If they do not come
into some unanimous Resolution upon the Matter, the Meeting breaks up;
but if they are Unanimous (which they generally are) then they call in the
young Men, and recommend to them the putting in Execution the Resolution, with their strongest and most lively Eloquence. And, indeed, they
seem to me, both in Action and Expression, to be thorough Masters of
true Eloquence; and, making Allowances for what they suffer thro' bad-
ness of Interpreters, many of their Speeches are equal to those which we
admire most in the *Greek* and *Roman* Writings. They generally in their
Speeches use *Similies* and *Metaphors*. Their *Similies* were quite new to me,
and generally wonderful proper and well carried on. But in the *Conferences* among their chief Men they are more *Laconick* and concise. In fine,
in speaking to their young Men they generally address to the Passions; in
speaking to their old Men they apply to Reason only. For Example, *Tomo
chi-chi*, in his first set Speech to me, among other Things, said, *Here is a
little Present;* and then gave me a *Buffalo's Skin*, painted on the Inside, with
the Head and Feathers of an *Eagle*.[5] He desired me to accept it because the
Eagle signified *Speed*, and the *Buffalo's*, Strength. That the *English* were as
swift as the Bird, and as strong as the Beast; since, like the first, they flew
from the utmost Parts of the Earth over the vast Seas; and, like the second,
nothing could withstand them. That the *Feathers* of the Eagle were *soft*, and
signified *Love;* the Buffalo's Skin *warm*, and signified *Protection;* therefore
he hoped that we would Love and Protect their little Families. One of the
Indians of the *Cherichee* Nation being come down to the Governor upon the
Rumour of the War, the Governor told him that he *need fear nothing, but
might speak freely*. He answer'd smartly, "I always speak freely, what should
I fear? I am now among my Friends, and I never feared even amongst my
Enemies." Another Instance of their short manner of speaking was, when
I ordered one of the *Carolina* Boatmen, who was drunk; and had beaten an
Indian, to be tied to a Gun till he was sober in order to be whipped; *Tomo-
chi-chi* came to me to beg me to pardon the Boatman, which I refused to
do unless the *Indian*, who had been beaten, should also desire the Pardon
for him. *Tomo chi-chi* desired him to do so, but he insisted on Satisfaction
by the Punishment of the Man; upon which *Tomo chi-chi* said, "O *Fonseka*
(for that was his Name) this *Englishman* being drunk, has beat you; if he
is whipt for so doing, the *Englishmen* will expect, that, if an *Indian* should

insult them when drunk, the *Indian* should be whipt for it. When you are drunk you are quarrelsome, and you know you love to be drunk, but you don't love to be whipt." *Fonseka* was convinced, and begged me to pardon the Man, which as soon as I granted, *Tomo chi-chi* and *Fonseka* run and untied him; which I perceived, was done to shew that he owed his Safety to their Intercession.

An Account of Carolina and Georgia (1739)

"An Account of Carolina and Georgia," so titled by Thaddeus Mason Harris, appeared in April 1739, in the three supplementary volumes that Thomas Salmon published through Bettesworth and Hitch to bring his *Modern History* up to date.[1] In 1841 Harris reprinted it, editing it rather heavily, omitting about a fifth, and incorrectly identifying the provenance as Salmon's "fourth" edition.[2] Oglethorpe apparently wrote his account in late 1737 or early 1738, while he was back in England and had time to respond to Salmon's request. Salmon prefaced the account with the acknowledgment: "The following pages are an answer from General OGLETHORPE, to some enquiries made by the author, concerning the state of Carolina and Georgia."[3]

In this his third description of the region, Oglethorpe utilized a good deal of what he had already written in his *Some Account* and had published in his *New and Accurate Account*; but here for the first time he enjoyed the advantage of first-hand knowledge. Perhaps the most remarkable part of the piece, a section omitted by Harris, is his description of the Gulf Stream. It had been mentioned by various navigators for more than two centuries, beginning with Ponce de Leon's pilot Antonio de Alaminas in 1513, and had been charted, though inaccurately, by Athanasius Kircher in 1665. Most striking is Oglethorpe's measurement of its velocity at three miles an hour; for although the path was well known, the velocity seems to have been rarely measured and recorded. The earliest known published figure seems to have been Antoine François Laval's estimate of a league an hour, in his *Voyage de la Louisiane* (1728). If Oglethorpe did not borrow his estimate from Laval, whose account the Oglethorpe booksale catalog shows (item 883), he may have taken it from Captain John Gascoigne, who had in 1729, in his log of the *Alborough*, remarked on the velocity.[4] On the other hand, Oglethorpe could have made his own estimate.

I reprint from the Bettesworth and Hitch edition of 1739.

A Continuation of the present state of Carolina.

Carolina is part of that territory which was originally discovered by Sir Sebastian Cabot. The English now possess the sea-coast, from the river St. John's, in 30 degrees 21 minutes north latitude. Westward the King's charter declares to to be bounded by the Pacifick Ocean.

Carolina is divided into North Carolina, South Carolina, and Georgia; the latter is a province which his Majesty has taken out of Carolina, and is the southern and western frontier of that province, lying between it, and the French, Spaniards, and Indians.

The part of Carolina that is settled, is for the most part a flat country: all near the sea, is a range of islands, which breaks the fury of the ocean: within is generally low-land for twenty or twenty five miles, where the country begins to rise in gentle swellings. At seventy or eighty miles from the sea, the hills grow higher, till they terminate in mountains.

The coast of Georgia is also defended from the rage of the sea by a range of islands. Those islands are divided from the main by canals of salt water, navigable for the largest boats, and even for small sloops. The lofty woods growing on each side the canals, make very pleasant landscapes. The land at about seven or eight miles from the sea, is tolerably high; and the farther you go westward the more it rises, till at about 150 miles distance from the sea, to the west, the Cherikees or Apellachean mountains begin, which are so high that the snow lies upon some of them all the year.

This ridge of mountains runs in a line from north to south, on the back of the English colonies of Carolina and Virginia; beginning at the great lakes of Canada, and extending south, it ends in the province of Georgia, at about two hundred miles from the bay of Appellachee, which is part of the gulph of Mexico. There is a plain country from the foot of these mountains to that sea.

The face of the country is mostly covered with woods; the banks of the rivers are in some places low, and form a kind of natural meadows, where the floods prevent trees from growing. In other places, in the hollows, between the hillocks, the brooks and streams being stopt by falls of trees, or other obstructions, the water is penn'd back: these places are often covered with canes and thickets, and are called in the corrupted American dialect, swamps.[5] The sides of the hills are generally covered with oaks and hiccary, or wild walnuts, cedar, sassafras, and the famous laurel tulip, which is esteemed one of the most beautiful trees in the world:[6] the flat tops of the hillocks are all covered with groves of pine-trees, with plenty of grass growing under them; and free from underwood, that you may gallop a horse for forty or fifty miles an end. In the low grounds, and islands of the river, there are cypress, bay-trees, poplar, plane, frankincense, or gum-trees, and other aquaticks. All parts of the province are well watered; and in digging a moderate depth, you never miss of a fine spring.

What we call the Atlantic Ocean, washes the east and south-east coasts of these provinces. The gulph stream of Florida sets with a tide in the ocean to the east of the province; and it is very remarkable, that the banks and soundings of the coast extend twenty or twenty-five miles to the east of the coast. To explain this, we will mention the manner of the voyage from Europe. You set out with variable winds, and having got enough to the west of Europe, you stand southerly till you meet with the trade winds; which you do, on this side the 20th degree north latitude. Those winds blowing generally eastwardly, and moderately brisk, soon drive you over the greatest part of the Atlantick ocean: you keep the same latitude, till you think you are near the Bahamas, and then you steer northwardly, to avoid falling in with them, till you come into 29 degrees, and then you run in to make the shore. You cross the gulph stream of Florida, which is a rapid tide, that sets out from between the island of Cuba and Bahama, on the one side, and Florida on the other. It is upwards of twenty leagues wide, and so rapid that it runs to the northward, at the rate of three miles an hour.[7] When you are past the gulph stream, you throw the lead, and if you find the ground at twenty five leagues of the coast of Georgia or Carolina, these they call the banks, and the water shoals gradually to shore, till you come within two leagues, where the banks are so shoaly that they bar all further passage, excepting in the channels which lie between the bars. These bars are the defence of the coast against enemies fleets, and the reason that it has laid so long undiscovered; for without good pilots you cannot come into any harbour, the shoaliness of the coast frightened ships so from coming to make discoveries upon it: till Mr. OGLETHORPE had the entries on the coast of Georgia sounded in the year 1733, no ship attempted to go into ports in Georgia, nor did the merchants believe there were any ports upon that coast. Though now they find the river Savannah an excellent harbour; and upon the worst of the bar, three fathom at dead low water. There is also a noble harbour to the southward, called Teky-Sound,[8] where there is anchoring for a large squadron in ten or fourteen fathom water land-locked, and a good and safe entry through the bar.

Between these harbours on the one side, and the Bahamas on the other, the Spanish ships must come home with all the treasures of Mexico; and a squadron here in time of war, can hardly miss intercepting them, and at the same time have safe harbours under their lee, and a healthy climate; have all Georgia, Carolina, and North-America, a plentiful country, to supply them with fresh provisions; so that they would be under none of those inconveniences from want and sickness, which those squadrons suffered who lay at Porto Bello.[9]

The tides upon this coast flow generally seven foot: the soundings are sand, or ooze, and some oyster banks, but no rocks: the coast appears low from the sea, and covered with woods.

Cape Fear is a point which runs with dreadful shoals far into the sea from the mouth of Clarendon river, in North Carolina. Sulivan's Island,[10] and the Coffin-land, are the marks of the entry into Charles-Town harbour: Hilton-head upon Trenches Island, shews the entry into Port-Royal; and the point of Tybee Island, marks the entry of the Savannah river.[11] Upon that point the trustees for Georgia have erected a noble final or lighthouse, 90 foot high, and 25 foot wide; it is an octagon, and upon the top there is a flag-staff 30 foot high.[12]

The province of Georgia is watered by three great rivers, which rise in the mountains, viz. the Alatamaha, the Ogechee, and the Savannah, the last of which is navigable six hundred miles for canoes, and three hundred miles for boats. The British dominions are divided from the Spanish Florida by a noble river called St. John's. These rivers fall into the Atlantick ocean; but there are besides them, the Flint, the Catooche, and even the Missisippi river, which pass through part of Carolina, or Georgia, and fall into the gulph of Apellachee or Mexico.

All Carolina is divided into three parts: North Carolina, which is divided from South Carolina by Clarendon river, and of late by a line marked out by order of the council: South Carolina; which on the south is divided from Georgia by the river Savannah. Carolina is divided into several counties; but in Georgia there is but one yet erected, viz. the county of Savannah: it is bounded on the one side by the river Savannah, on the other by the sea, on the third by the river Ogechee, on the fourth by the river Ebenezer, and a line drawn from the Ebenezer to the Ogechee. In this country are the rivers of Vernon, Little Ogechee, and of Westbrook.[13] There is the town of Savannah, where there is a seat of judicature, consisting of three bailiffs and a recorder. It is situated upon the banks of the river of the same name. It consists of about two hundred houses, and lies upon a plain of about a mile wide, the bank steep to the river, forty five foot perpendicularly high: the streets are laid out regular. There are near Savannah, in the same country, the villages of Hampstead, Highgate, Skydoway, and Thunderbolt; the latter of which is a translation of a name: their fables say, that a thunderbolt fell, and a spring thereupon arose in that place, which still smells of the thunder. This spring is impregnated with a mixture of sulphur and steel, and from this smell probably the story arose. In the same county is Joseph's Town, and the town of Ebenezer, both upon the river Savannah, and the villages of Abercorn and Westbrook. There are saw-mills erecting on the river Ebenezer,[14] and the fort Argyle lies upon the pass of this county over the Ogechee. In the southern divisions of the province lies the town of Frederica, with its district, where there is a court with three bailiffs and a recorder. It lies on one of the branches of the Alatamaha. There is also the town of Darien, upon the same river, and several forts, upon the proper passes, some of four bastions, some are only redoubts; besides which there are villages in different parts of Georgia. At Savannah there is a publick store-house built of large square timbers; there is also a handsome court-house, guard-house, and work-house: the church is not yet begun, but materials are collecting, and it is designed to be a handsome edifice. The private houses are generally sawed timber, framed and covered with shingles; many of them are painted, and most have chimneys of brick. At Frederica, some of the houses are built of brick; the rest of the province is mostly wood. They are not got into luxury yet in their furniture, hewing only what is plain and needful; the winters being mild, there are yet but few houses with glass-windows.

The Indians are a manly well-shaped race; the men tall, the women little: they, as the antient Grecians did, anoint with oil, and expose themselves to the sun, which occasions their skins to be brown of colour. The men paint themselves of various colours, red, blue, yellow and black: the men wear generally a girdle, with a piece of cloth drawn through their legs, and turned over the girdle both before and behind, so as to hide their nakedness. The women wear a kind of petticoat to their knees. Both men and women in the winter wear mantles, something less than two yards square, which they wrap round their bodies, as the Romans did their toga, generally keeping their arms bare: they are sometimes of woollen, bought of the English; sometimes of furs, which they dress themselves. They wear a kind of pumps, which they call morgisons, made of deer skins, which they dress for that purpose. They are a generous good-natured people, very humane to strangers; patient of want and pain; slow to anger, and not easily provoked; but when they are thoroughly incensed, they are implacable; very quick of apprehension, and gay of temper. Their publick conferences shew them to be men of genius, and they have a natural eloquence, they never having had the use of letters. They love eating, and the English have taught many of them to drink strong liquors, which, when they do, they are miserable sights. They have no manufactures but what each family makes for its own use; they seem to despise working for hire, and spend their time chiefly in hunting and war; but plant corn enough for the support of their families, and of the strangers that come to visit them. Their food, instead of bread, is flour of Indian corn boiled, and seasoned like hasty-pudding; and this is called homminy. They also boil venison and make broth: they also roast or rather broil their meat. The flesh they feed on is buffaloe, deer, wild-turkeys, and other game; so that hunting is necessary, to provide flesh, and planting for corn. The land belongs to the women, and the corn that grows upon it; but meat must be got by the men, because it is they only that hunt. This makes marriage necessary, that the women may furnish corn, and the men meat. They have also fruit-trees in their gardens, viz. peaches, nectarines and locusts, melons and water-melons; potatoes, pumpkins, and onions, &c. in plenty, and many wild kinds of fruits; as parsimonies, grapes, chinquepins, and hickary-nuts, of which they make oil. The bees make their combs in the hollow trees, and the Indians find plenty of honey there, which they use instead of sugar. They make what answers salt of wood-ashes, and long-pepper which grows in their gardens; and bay-leaves supply their want of spice. Their exercises are a kind of ball-playing, hunting, and running; and they are very fond of dancing: their musick is a kind of a drum, as also hollow cocoa-nut shells. They have a square in the middle of their towns, in which the warriors sit, converse, and smoke together; but in rainy weather they meet in the King's house.

They are very healthy people, and have hardly any diseases, except those occasioned by the drinking of rum, and the small pox: those who do not drink rum are exceeding long-lived. Old BRIM, Emperor of the Creeks, who died but a few years ago, lived to one hundred and thirty years;[15] and he was neither blind nor bed-rid, till some months before his death. They have sometimes pleurisies and fevers, but no chronical distempers. They know of several herbs that have great virtues in physick, particularly for the cure of venomous bites and wounds.

The native animals are, first the urus or zorax, described by CAESAR, which the English very ignorantly and improperly call the buffaloe.[16] They have deer of several kinds, and plenty of roe-bucks and rabbits. There are bears and wolves, which are very small and timerous; and a brown wild-cat, without spots, which they very improperly call a tyger;[17] otters, beavers, foxes, and a species of badgers, which they call racoons. There is great abundance of wild fowls, viz. the wild turkey, the partridge, doves of various kinds; wild geese, wild ducks, teal, cranes, herons of many kinds, not known in Europe: there are great variety of eagles and hawks, and great numbers of small birds, particularly the rice bird,[18] which is very like the ortelan. There are also some rattle snakes, but not near so frequent as is generally reported. There are several species of snakes, some of which are not venomous. There are crocodiles, porpoises, sturgeon, mullets, cat-fish, bass, drum, devil-fish, and many species of fresh water fish, that we have not in Europe; oysters upon the sea islands in great abundance. But what is most troublesome there, is flies and gnats, which are very troublesome near the rivers; but as the country is cleared, they disperse and go away. Besides the animals that are natives, there are all the same animals as in Europe, cows, sheep, hogs, &c.

The vegetables are innumerable; for all that grow in Europe grow there; and many that cannot stand in our winters thrive there.

An Account of the Negroe Insurrection in South Carolina (1740)

The following narrative of the Stono rebellion in South Carolina in September 1739 is the fullest contemporary account available of the most violent black uprising on the continent during the colonial period.[1] It is also Oglethorpe's most effective response to the pleas of the Georgia malcontents that the Trustees should alter their policy and allow the use of black slaves in the colony—a change to which most of the Trustees and Oglethorpe in particular were adamantly opposed. These malcontents had been represented in England since early 1740 by Thomas Stephens, son of the Trustees' secretary in Georgia; and he had delivered their yet unpublished protest to members of Parliament.[2] The continued funding of the Georgia colony was in doubt.

The Stono rebellion, followed within a year by two others in the province, provided the evidence that Oglethorpe needed. As Peter H. Wood remarks, "For several years after the outbreak in St. Paul's Parish, the safety of the white minority, and the viability of their entire plantation system, hung in serious doubt for the first time since the Yamasee War."[3] Phinizy Spalding aptly asks: "Could Georgia have survived a Stono?"[4]

Although Oglethorpe has apparently not been credited with this account, there can be little question of his authorship or his intent to publish it. He enclosed it in a letter that he wrote to Verelst on October 9, 1739, and he added the postscript: "I [desire] you would have the Inclosed account [of the] Insurrection of the Carolina Negroes inserted in some News papers."[5] Four days after Verelst received the letter, the account appeared in the *London Daily Post, and General Advertiser* on March 17, 1740.[6] In order to reproduce the account as Oglethorpe wished it to appear, I use his original.[7]

An Account of the Negroe Insurrection in South Carolina

Sometime since there was a Proclamation published at *Augustine*, in which the King of *Spain* (then at Peace with Great Britain)[8] promised Protection and Freedom to all *Negroes Slaves* that would resort thither. Certain Negroes belonging to Captain Davis escaped to *Augustine*, and were received there.[9] They were demanded by General Oglethorpe who sent Lieutenant Demeré to *Augustine*,[10] and the Governour assured the General of his sincere Friendship, but at the same time showed his Orders from the Court of Spain, by which he was to receive all Run away Negroes. Of this, other Negroes having notice, as it is believed, from the Spanish Emissaries, four or five who were Cattel-Hunters, and knew the Woods, some of whom belonged to Captain Mackpherson,[11] ran away with His Horses, wounded his Son and killed another Man. Those marched thro Georgia, and were pursued, but the Rangers being then newly reduced, the Countrey people could not overtake them, though they were discovered by the Saltzburghers, as they passed by *Ebenezer*. They reached *Augustine*, one only being killed and another wounded by the Indians in their flight. They were received there with great honours, one of them had a Commission given to him, and a Coat faced with Velvet. Amongst the Negroe Slaves there are a people brought from the Kingdom of *Angola* in *Africa*, many of these speak Portugueze (which Language is as near Spanish as Scotch is to English,) by reason that the Portugueze have considerable Settlements, and the Jesuits have a Mission and School in that Kingdom and many Thousands of the Negroes there profess the Roman Catholick Religion. Several Spaniards upon diverse Pretences have for some time past been strolling about Carolina, two of them, who will give no account of themselves have been taken up and committed to Jayl in Georgia.[12] The good reception of the Negroes at *Augustine* was spread about, Several attempted to escape to the Spaniards, & were taken, one of them was hanged at Charles Town. In the latter end of July last Don Pedro, Colonel of the Spanish Horse,[13] went in a Launch to Charles Town under pretence of a message to General Oglethorpe and the Lieutenant Governour.

On the 9th. day of September last being Sunday which is the day the Planters allow them to work for themselves. Some *Angola* Negroes assembled, to the number of Twenty; and one who was called *Jemmy* was their Captain, they surprized a Warehouse belonging to Mr. Hutchenson at a place called Stonehow;[14] they there killed Mr. Robert Bathurst, and Mr. Gibbs, plundered the House and took a pretty many small Arms and Powder, which were there for Sale. Next they plundered and burnt Mr. Godfrey's house, and killed him, his Daughter and Son. They then turned back and marched Southward along Pons Pons, which is the Road through Georgia to *Augustine*, they passed Mr. Wallace's Tavern towards day break, and said they would not hurt him, for he was a good Man and kind to his Slaves but they broke open and plundered Mr. Lemy's House, and killed him, his Wife and Child. They marched on towards Mr. [Thomas] Rose's resolving to kill him, but he was saved by a Negroe, who having hid him went out and pacified the others. Several Negroes joyned them, they calling out Liberty, marched on with Colours displayed, and two Drums beating, pursuing all the white people they met with, and killing Man Woman and Child when they could come up to them. Collonel Bull Lieutenant Governour of South Carolina, who was then riding along the Road, discovered them, was pursued, and with much difficulty escaped & raised the Countrey. They burnt Colonel Hext's house and killed his Overseer and his Wife,[15] They then burnt Mr. Sprye's house, then Mr. Sacheverell's,[16] and then Mr. Nash's house, all lying upon the Pons Pons Road, and killed all the white People they found in them. Mr. Bullock got off, but they burnt his House; by this time many of them were drunk with the Rum they had taken in the Houses. They increased every minute by new Negroes coming to them, so that they were above Sixty, some say a hundred, on which they halted in a field; and set to dancing, Singing and beating Drums, to draw more Negroes to them, thinking they were now victorious over the whole Province, having marched ten miles & burnt all before them without Opposition, but the Militia being raised, the Planters with great briskness pursued them and when they came up, dismounting, charged them on foot. The Negroes were soon routed, though they behaved boldly, several being killed on the Spot, many ran back to their Plantations thinking they had not been missed, but they were there taken and Shot.[17] Such as were taken in the field also, were after being examined, shot on the Spot, and this is to be said to the honour of the Carolina Planters, that notwithstanding the Provocation they had received from so many Murders, they did not torture one Negroe, but only put them to an easy death. All that proved to be forced & were not concerned in the Murders & Burnings were pardoned. And this sudden Courage in the field, & the Humanity afterwards hath had so good an Effect that there hath been no farther Attempt, and the very Spirit of Revolt seems over. About 30 escaped from the fight, of which ten marched about 30 miles Southward, and being overtaken by the Planters on horseback, fought stoutly for some time and were all killed on the Spot, The rest are yet untaken. In the whole action about 40 Negroes and 20 whites were killed. The Lieutenant Governour sent an account of this to General Oglethorpe,[18] who met the advices on his return from the Indian Nation. He immediately ordered a Troop of Rangers to be ranged, to patrole through Georgia, placed some Men in the Garrison at Palichocolas, which was before abandoned, and near which the Negroes formerly passed, being the only place where Horses can come to swim over the River Savannah for near 100 miles, ordered out the Indians in pursuit, and a Detachment of the Garrison at Port Royal to assist the Planters on any Occasion, and published a Proclamation ordering all the Constables &ca. of Georgia to pursue and seize all Negroes, with a Reward for any that should be taken. It is hoped these measures will prevent any Negroes from getting down to the Spaniards.

A Thanksgiving for Victory (1742)

Oglethorpe's celebration of victory over the Spaniards was surely intended for publication. He had it read, on July 25, to the citizens of Frederica, and later to those of Savannah and Ebenezer;[1] and he apparently dispatched it north for publication. It appeared on November 29, in the *Boston Evening-Post*, which serves as my text, and on December 21, in Benjamin Franklin's *Pennsylvania Gazette*.[2]

The thanksgiving represents doubtless both a genuine expression of gratitude for what seemed to Oglethorpe a miraculous deliverance from the Spaniards and at the same time a vindication of his generalship, which since 1740 had been impugned by the South Carolina legislature.[3]

"Almighty GOD hath in all Ages shewn his Power and Mercy in the miraculous and gracious Deliverance of his Church, and in the Protection of righteous and religious Kings and States professing his holy and eternal Truths, from the open Invasions, wicked Conspiracies and malicious Practices of all the Enemies thereof. He hath by the manifestation of his Providence, delivered us from the Hands of the *Spaniards*, They with 14 sail of small Gallies and other Craft, came into *Cumberland* Sound, but Terror and Fear from the Lord came upon them, and they fled. The *Spaniards* also with another mighty Fleet of 36 Ships and Vessels came into *Jekyl* Sound, and after a sharp Fight became Masters thereof, we having only four Vessels to oppose their whole Strength, and God was the Shield of our People, since in so unequal a Fight, which was stoutly maintain'd for the Space of four Hours, not one of ours was kill'd, tho' many of theirs perish'd, and five were kill'd by one Shot only. They landed 4500 Men upon this Island, according to the Accounts of the Prisoners, and even of *Englishmen* who escaped from them.[4] The first Party march'd up thro' the Woods to this Town, and was within Sight thereof, when God deliver'd them into the Hands of a few of ours, they fought and were dispersed and fled. Another Party which supported them also fought, but were soon dispersed. We may with Truth say, that the Hand of the Lord fought for us, for in the two Fights more than 500 fled before 50, and yet they for a Time fought with Courage, and the Grenadiers particularly charg'd with great Resolution, but their Shot did not take Place, insomuch that none of ours were then kill'd, but the Enemy were broken and pursued with great Slaughter, so that by the Reports of the Prisoners since taken, upwards of 200 never return'd to their Camp. They also came up with their half Gallies towards this Town, and retir'd without so much as firing one Shot, and then Fear came upon them and they fled, leaving behind them some Cannon, and many Things they had taken. Twenty eight sail attack'd Fort *William*, in which were only fifty Men, and after three Hours fight went away and left the Province, they having been pursued as far as St. *John*'s; so that by this whole Expedition and great Armament, no more than two of ours were taken and three kill'd. Therefore with Truth we may say, the Lord hath done great Things for us, who hath delivered us out of the Hands of our numerous Enemies, who had already swallowed us up in their Thoughts, and boasted that they would torture and burn us; but the Lord was our Shield, and we of a Truth may say, that it was not our Strength nor Might that deliver'd us, but that it was the Lord; therefore it is meet and fitting that we should return Thanks to GOD, our Deliverer.

"*Having taken the Premises into Consideration, I do hereby Order, that Sunday the 25th Instant be observed as a Day of publick Thanksgiving to Almighty GOD, for his great Deliverance in having put an End to the* Spanish *Invasion, and that all Persons do solemnize the same in a Christian and Religious Manner, and abstain from Drunkenness and any other wicked and dissolute Testimonies of Joy.* Given under my Hand and Seal this 24th Day of *July*, at *Frederica*, in *Georgia*, Annoque Domini, 1742. JAMES OGLETHORPE."

The King's Bench Prison Revisited (1752)

In February of 1752 Oglethorpe again headed a parliamentary committee appointed to investigate prison conditions at the King's Bench Prison. On March 24 in his report to the House, he recommended that the prison, "inconvenient, dangerous, and unhealthy," should be rebuilt and, more important, that the government should purchase the mortgage of the prison, so that the recommended reforms could be more effectively implemented. For as long as the Lenthall mortgage lasted, it was virtually impossible to hold anyone responsible for the deplorable conditions that persisted there. Since Parliament was prorogued before Oglethorpe could read his report a second time, this report died. When Parliament revived the committee in 1753, Oglethorpe was not named chairman, probably because he had failed to establish the validity of the mortgage that he recommended purchasing. In the subsequent report, read on March 16, 1753, Sir William Calvert made the same recommendations and included much of the material from Oglethorpe's report, but also established the legality of the Lenthall title, though this was apparently subject to legal challenge. Calvert's report was adopted and was given royal assent on April 6, 1753. Ironically enough, on November 18, 1754, Oglethorpe himself would have been imprisoned for debt in the King's Bench had the Moravians not come to his assistance.[1]

I have reproduced Oglethorpe's report as printed in *The Journals of the House of Commons* (26:504–13), but have omitted appendix 1. It occupies four times the space devoted to the text of the report and would require foldout pages for proper reproduction, yet it sheds no light upon prison conditions at the King's Bench. It merely presents financial data upon which to estimate the amount which the heirs of Lenthall, Cutler, and Radnor could claim for the settlement of the title. Oglethorpe had already included much of these data in the appendixes to his 1730 report on the King's Bench.

Martis, 24° *die Martii*; Anno 25° Georgii II^{di} Regis, 1752.

Lieutenant General *Oglethorpe* reported for the Committee to whom the Petition of the Prisoners in the *King's Bench* Prison was referred, That the Committee had examined the Matter of the said Petition; and had directed him to report the same, as it appeared to them, to the House; and he read the Report in his Place; and afterwards delivered the same, together with an Appendix thereto, in at the Clerk's Table: Where the Report was read, and is as followeth; *viz.*

Your Committee thinks proper to reduce the Evidence, brought in Support of the said Petition, under Three Heads.

First, That which tended to prove the present incommodious, unhealthy, and insecure State of the said Prison.

Secondly, The Nature of the Mortgage, under which the Marshalship of the said Prison is now possessed and exercised.

Thirdly, The Inconveniencies arising, not only to the Petitioners, but to the Court, and Suitors in the *King's Bench*, and to the Publick in general, from the said Mortgage.

Upon the first Head, your Committee examined the Reverend Doctor *Howard*,[2] Rector of *St. George*'s Parish, within which the Prison is situated; Mr. *Isaac Stapleton*, Surgeon and Apothecary, who lives near the Prison, and has attended there for Twenty Years past; *William Tew, Joseph Wingrove, William Bishop, John Lloyd*, and others, who are, or have been, Prisoners within the Prison-house; and *John Ashton* Esquire, the present Marshal, with Mr. *John Chapman*, His Clerk and head Turnkey, and Messieurs *Steere* and *Poultney*, Surveyors and Master Builders, who have surveyed the Prison-house and Walls.[3]

By the concurrent Testimony of all the above Persons, it appears to your Committee, That the said Building is old and ruinous; that, in its present State, the Prisoners are in the most miserable Situation for Want of Room; Seventeen being sometimes crouded into one Room, not above Fourteen or Fifteen Foot square; and that the Common Side is often overflowed with the Common Sewer, which occasions noisome Stenches: And the Reverend Doctor *Howard* said, That he once attended a Person in the Cells of *Newgate*, which he thought preferable to the Cabbins in which the Prisoners, upon the Common Side of this Prison, are lodged.

It further appeared to your Committee, from the Evidence above, That in the Summer Time infectious Diseases are apt to break out, for Want of Room and Air, amongst the Prisoners; that last Summer, particularly, Six or Seven Prisoners died of a Pestilential Fever; several have died of the Small Pox, and several of Spotted Fevers, within the Prison; and that, if the Marshal's own Brother was confined a close Prisoner therein, he could give to him no Relief more than to the other Prisoners; and there is no Conveniency for separating the Sound from the Diseased, but One small Room, fit to contain One Person; and, that if the Prison should be suffered to remain the ensuing Summer in its present State, it may produce an Infection amongst the Prisoners, and may be of the most fatal Consequence.

After this general Representation of the inside State of the Prison, your Committee will not trouble the House with a great Variety of affecting Circumstances, that came out in the Course of this Evidence; which all concurred in proving the Place to be inconvenient, dangerous, and unhealthy.

And the said Mr. *Poultney* and Mr. *Steere* were of Opinion, that the same cannot be repaired.

Mr. *William Soame*, being examined, said, That there is a House and Garden, belonging to one Mr. *Lyddal*, near the said Prison, and within the Precincts thereof, which is very capable of being made an Infirmary; and may be made strong, and fit for the safe keeping of Prisoners, at the Expence of about £.100; that there are Eight large Rooms, and Four small ones, in it; and may be fitted up to contain Thirty-two Beds; and which the said Mr. *Lyddal* is willing to let at £.25 a Year.

Under the Second Head of your Committee's Inquiry, they examined Mr. *Brigstock*, Mr. *Blackwell*, and Mr. *Langmore*, Agents for the Mortgagees; by whom it appeared, That in *February* 1684, *William Lenthall* Esquire mortgaged certain Lands, and the Fee-simple of the said Marshalship, for a Sum of Money, to Sir *John Cutler* Knight,[4] till the same, and Interest, should be discharged; and that there are Clauses in an Act of the 8th and 9th of King *William* (intituled, An Act for the more effectual Relief of Creditors, in Cases of Escapes; and for preventing Abuses in Prisons; and pretended privileged Places) relating to the said Mortgage.

And the said Sir *John Cutler's* Executor, *Edmund Boulter* Esquire, his Heirs, Assigns, Administrators and Executors, are to have, by that Act, the Nomination of Marshals of the said Prison, till the said Mortgage, and Interest, is paid off; and that the Right of the said Mortgage devolved upon the Earl of *Radnor*, who, in the Year 1719, sold all his Right therein to

Joseph Studley, and others, in Trust, for the present Mortgagees, or those from whom they derive their Title; and that the Sum then charged by the Earl of *Radnor* upon the Mortgage was upwards of £. 19,000; and that the Sum of £. 10,500 was, *bona fide*, paid for the same.

And the said Mr. *Blackwell* delivered to your Committee, a General Account of Debtor and Creditor, hereto annexed, in the Appendix, N°.1; and leaves the Consideration of their Demand to the Judgment of the House.

Upon the strictest Inquiry, your Committee could not discover where the Original Grant or Patent, upon which the Conveyance of the Fee-simple of the said Marshalship was made, by *Lenthall*, to Sir *John Cutler*, was to be found:[5] And,

Mr. *Guthrie*, being examined, said, That, by certain Evidences, on Record, the said Office formerly appertained to the Office of Earl Marshal of *England*; but by Forfeitures, and Failures of Heirs Male, the said Office often reverted to the Crown; and that he apprehended, when the said Marshalship was in the Earl Marshal, he was obliged to maintain and repair the said Prison.

Mr. *Owen*, Clerk to Lord Chief Justice *Lee*,[6] being examined, said, That he had heard one Mr. *Long*, at *Pershore*, in *Worcestershire*, talk as if a Client of his was in Possession of the Original Patent: And Mr. *Owen* wrote to the said *Long*; and he (the said *Long*) wrote a Letter in Answer, which is hereto annexed, in the Appendix, N°.2.

Under the Third Head of Evidence, already mentioned, your Committee begs Leave to refer to a Paper laid before them by the said Mr. *Owen*, with the Authority and Approbation of the Lord Chief Justice of the *King*'s *Bench*, which is annexed, in the Appendix, (N°.3.) by which it appears to your Committee, That that Court has long looked upon the present Exercise of the Marshalship of the said Prison, under a Mortgage, as a Shame and Scandal to the Publick, because of the Hardships and Dangers arising therefrom, not only to the Prisoners, their Creditors, and that Court, but to the Subjects in general; and that Application ought to be made to Parliament thereon.

This Representation, from so great and good an Authority, naturally led your Committee to inquire, in the most strict Manner, into the Conduct and Behaviour of the present Marshal, Mr. *Ashton*, and likewise into the Fees, Perquisites, and Profits of his Place.

And, First, It appeared, by the concurring and unanimous Testimony of the above Witnesses, and likewise by that of Baron *Stein* and Mr. John *Upsdale*, Prisoners in the said Prison, that the said Marshal's Behaviour and Conduct in his Office, has been very humane, and that he omitted no Opportunity in his Power of alleviating and relieving the Hardships of the Prisoners in his Custody.

Touching the Fees of his Office, he produced a Table of them, by Order of your Committee; which is annexed, in the Appendix N°.4.

Touching the Perquisites and Profits of the same, he produced before your Committee his Books of Accounts, and likewise Abstracts from the same, distinguishing Year by Year; which Abstracts your Committee checked with the Particulars in his Books; and the whole of his said Fees, Perquisites, and Profits, do not, upon an Average, one Year with another, amount to the Sum which he is yearly obliged by Lease to pay for his Office to the Mortgagees, which is £. 500 a Year, besides Taxes.

And by an Abstract of his Accounts for the Years 1747, 1748, 1749, and 1750, it appears, that, within that Time, the Total of his Receipts amounts to £.3,092. 6. 5. and his Disbursements to £.3,218. 18. 4.; which Abstract is annexed, in the Appendix, N°.5.

The said Mr. *Poultney* and Mr. *Steere*, Surveyors, One of whom had been ordered by the Lord Chief Justice to survey the said Prison, produced to your Committee Plans, and an Elevation, for rebuilding the said Prison; and said, That to build it according to those Plans, including the external Walls round the Garden, making convenient Shores, Drains, *&c.* will amount to the Sum of about £.6,500, as estimated by them.

. . . .

APPENDIX, N°. 2.

Pershore, March 9th 1752.

Sir,

ON *Thursday* last I went to *Worcester* Assizes, and on *Friday* was taken ill with the Gout; which occasioned my not returning till Yesterday in the Afternoon, when I found yours at my House, of the 5th instant.

I have some Grants and other Deeds, now in my Custody, belonging to the Office of Marshal of the King's *Marshalsea;* most of which are wrote in *Latin* Abbreviations, in the old Court-hand, and most of them contain Three or Four Large Skins each; so that it was impossible, had I been at home, when your Letter came on *Saturday*, to have sent you up Copies by that Night's Post, as you desired, or even by the Post To-night.

And as I am now laid up, exceedingly bad with the Gout, and confined to my Room, I am not at present able to peruse those Deeds, to give you any Satisfaction relating thereto; but I hope in a few Days I may be in a Capacity for the Purpose.

These Writings was delivered to me by a Client of mine, who claimed the Office of Marshal, with Intent to prefer a Bill in the Court of Chancery against the Mortgagees, in Possession of the Profits of the Office, to account and deliver up the same; my Client being fully convinced that the Mortgagees had, many Years since, not only been fully paid, but that a considerable surplus Sum of Money was in their Hands to be accounted for; but my Client, soon after I had received the Writings, died, so that the Affair dropt: But the Writings now belong to his Widow, to whom he, by his Will, devised all his Estate, either in Possession, Reversion, Remainder, or Expectancy. I am, Sir,

Your most obedient humble Servant,

Hen. Long.

To Mr. *Thomas Owen* Attorney at Law, over against the End of *Plough-court, Carey-street, Lincoln's Inn, London.*

APPENDIX, N°. 3.

THOMAS *Owen*, Clerk to the Right Honourable the Lord Chief Justice *Lee*, pursuant to Order, attended the Committee; and, being examined, declareth as followeth:

That about Thirteen Years ago, and for several Years before, he was Deputy Marshal of the Court of *King's Bench*; and as such, and since he hath been Clerk to his Lordship, hath been acquainted with the State and Condition of the *King's Bench* Prison.

Saith, The same is a very ancient Building, and was, as he hath heard, and believes, the Stables of King *John*; and saith, the said Prison is very incommodious for the Purpose to which it is now converted.

Saith, That Prisoners, from all Parts of the Kingdom, are committed thereto, either for criminal or civil Matters, cognizable in the Court of *King's Bench*; and, that the said Prison ought to be more commodious than it is at present, for the Reception of the Unfortunate; and a Place of much greater Strength and Security, for the safe Custody of the Guilty: Saith, the Walls thereof are so thin, old, rotten, and crazy, that there hath not been a remarkable high Wind, for many Years past, that hath not blown down many Parts of the Wall of the said Prison; and would have made a general Gaol Delivery of the Prisoners therein, was not the greatest Care and Diligence used by the Marshal and his Officers to prevent it.

Saith, That in the Time of the late unnatural Rebellion, when all the Prisons about this Capital were full of Prisoners, the Prison of the *King's Bench* (the most proper Prison for such a Purpose) was deemed a Place of so little Safety, and so insecure, that not One State Prisoner was confined therein.

Saith, He hath oftentimes heard the late Marshal, *Mullins*, declare (who was a very humane good-natured Man), that when he was first appointed Marshal, he used weekly to order Beef, Pork, Broths, and other Victuals, to be distributed among such of his Prisoners as he thought were the greatest Objects of Charity; but was soon obliged to leave off those Donations, having found that the annual Rent, Taxes, and Outgoings, which, at that time, amounted to Eight or Nine hundred Pounds *per Annum*, was actually more than the Fees, Profits, and Perquisites, arising from the said Office.

Saith, He knows, that during the Time the late Lord *Raymond* presided as Chief Justice of the said Court, that great and many Complaints were then made to his Lordship, of the Inconveniences arising to the Prisoners, by the Payment of so large an annual Rent, by the Marshal of the said Prison; and he hath oftentimes heard his Lordship declare, it was a Shame, and a Scandal to the Publick, that the Affairs of the Prison were permitted to remain in such a Situation.

Saith, He is also well assured, that my Lord *Hardwicke*,[7] during the time his Lordship was Chief Justice of the said Court, was of the same Opinion, that the said Mortgage ought to be paid off and discharged.

Saith, That for the Space of Twelve Years last past, he hath been Clerk to the present Lord Chief Justice of the said Court; during which time many Petitions have been presented to the said Court and his Lordship, complaining, that Three, Four, or more Prisoners, were put into One Room; which the Judges (who are always ready to hear the Complaints of the meanest Prisoner) would have prevented, had it been in their Power; but, from the Straightness of the Prison, have found it impossible to redress the Grievance complained of.

Saith, That many Petitions have also been presented to his Lordship, praying, to be discharged without Payment of their Fees; several of whom, on his Lordship's Pleasure being signified to the Marshal, have been, accordingly, discharged; as many others would have been, had not his Lordship well known, that by a too frequent Compliance with such Requests, it would be impossible for the Marshal and his Officers, who all purchase their Places, to pay the Rent that is even now paid for the said Office.

Saith, That from the time of this Examinant's first coming into his Lordship's Service, until now, it hath been his Lordship's Opinion, that it was very detrimental to the Prisoners and the Publick that the Office of the Marshal was let to Sale; and the said Court so far interposed with the Proprietors and Mortgagees of the said Office, as he hath heard, and believes, that the Rent is much less now than was formerly paid for the said Office; and his Lordship was so desirous that proper Methods should be taken, in relation to the Discharge of the said Mortgage, that he ordered this Examinant, about Three Years ago, as near as he can recollect as to the Time, to give Notice to the said Proprietors and Mortgagees, to deliver in a stated Account of their Demands on the said Office; which this Examinant then did, on Mr. *Langmore*, their Attorney or Agent, in the Words, or to the Effect, mentioned in a Paper Writing, signed by this Declarant, marked with the Letter (A).

Saith, That in pursuance of such Notice, said Mr. *Langmore* delivered to his Lordship the Account marked Letter (B).

Saith, That since this Examinant's Order to attend this honourable Committee, he hath acquainted his Lordship thereof; who hath authorized this Examinant to acquaint the said Committee, that it is with his Lordship's Consent, Concurrence, and highest Approbation, that Application hath been made to the House to rebuild the said Prison, and pay off the said Mortgage; and that his Lordship hopes it will meet with such immediate Dispatch, as the Nature of the Case shall require.

Thos. Owen.

(A) In Appendix N°. 3.

To *William Martin* Esquire, and the rest of the Mortgagees of the Office or Place of Marshal of the King's *Marshalsea*.

Gentlemen,

You are desired, within One Week from the Date hereof, to deliver at the Chambers of the Right honourable the Lord Chief Justice *Lee*, in *Serjeant's Inn*, an Account of the Principal and Interest which you now claim to be due to you, on the Mortgage of the Office or Place of Marshal of the King's *Marshalsea*, together with such Sums of Money as you have, from time to time, received, for the Sale or Alienation of such Places or Offices as have been filled up by you, as Mortgagees of the said Office; to the Intent, that if you shall consent and agree (upon Payment of what shall appear to be justly due to you for the same) to deliver up the Grant, heretofore made by the Crown, of the Office or Place of Marshal to *William Lenthal* Esquire, deceased, and his Heirs, for ever (which said Grant is assigned over, in Trust, for your Use) Application may be made to his Majesty to pay off the said Mortgage; or, in case of your Refusal, to Parliament, to enforce so reasonable a Proposal. I am,

       Gentlemen,
         Your humble Servant.

(B) In Appendix N°. 3.

King's Bench Prison	Dr.			*Per Contra*	Cr.		
An Account of	*l.*	*s.*	*d.*	Nett Money received	*l.*	*s.*	*d.*
Money due to *Thomas*				for the Fees and			
Martin Esquire, and				Profits of the Office			
others, Assignees				of Marshal of the			
of the late Earl of				*King's Bench* Prison,			
Radnor, from the				from *Hilary* Term			
King's Bench Prison.				1727, to *Easter* Term			
Hil. Term} By a Receipt				1748 inclusive, the			
1st Geo. 2d.} then				Sum of			
made, by the Master							
of the *King's Bench*							
Office, there appeared due to the said							
Thomas Martin, and							
others, the Sum of	21, 361	16	6		10, 149	14	4
To Interest for the							
same, to *Hilary* Term							
1748, being Twenty-one Years,							

APPENDIX, N°. 4.

A Table of Fees to be taken by the Marshal of the *King's Bench* Prison, in the County of *Surry*, for any Prisoner or Prisoners committed, or coming into Goal, or Chambers Rent there, or Discharge from thence on any Civil Action.

Settled and established on the 17th Day of *December* 1730.

		l.	*s.*	*d.*
1stly.	To the Marshal, for every Prisoner committed on any Civil Action,	0	4	8
2dly.	To the Turnkey on the Master Side,	0	1	6
3dly.	To the Marshal, on the Discharge of every such Prisoner,	0	7	4
4thly.	To the Deputy Marshal, on the Discharge of One or more Action, Executions, or other Charges, and no further Fee, though there be ever so many Actions,	0	4	0
5thly.	To the Clerk of the Papers, for the first Action upon the Discharge,	0	3	0
6thly.	To the Clerk of the Papers, for every Action, Execution, or other Charge, to be paid on the Discharge,	0	0	4
7thly.	To the Deputy Marshal, upon the Commitment of any Prisoner, in Court, or at Judges Chambers, in any Civil Action, if carried to the *King's Bench* Prison,	0	1	0
8thly.	To the Clerk of the Papers, for the same,	0	1	0
9thly.	To the said Deputy Marshal, for a Surrender, in Discharge of Bail, be there never so many Actions,	0	1	0
10thly.	To the Clerk of the Papers, for each Action upon such Surrender,	0	0	6
11thly.	To each of the 4 Tipstaffs, 2*s.* 6*d* for each Prisoner, committed by the Court, and carried to the *King's Bench* Prison, in the whole	0	10	0
12thly.	To the Tipstaff that carries any Prisoner, committed at a Judge's Chambers, to the said Prison,	0	6	8
13thly.	To the Marshal, for the Use of Chamber, Bed, Bedding, and Sheets, for each Prisoner, if provided by the Gaoler at the Prisoner's Request, for the First Night, the Common Side of said Prison,	0	0	6
14thly.	For the like Use, for every Night the Prisoner shall remain in Custody, after the First	0	0	1
15thly.	And if Two lie in a Bed, 1*d.* each	0	0	2
16thly.	For the like Use, for every Prisoner that goes on the Master Side, the First Night,	0	0	6
17thly.	For the like, every Night after the First,	0	0	3
18thly.	And if Two lie in a Bed, 2*d.* each,	0	0	4

No other Fee for the Use of Chamber, Bed, Bedding, or Sheets, upon the Commitment or Discharge of any Prisoner on any Civil Action.

APPENDIX Nº. 5.

Office of the Marshal	Dr.			Contra	Cr.		
	l.	s.	d.		l.	s.	d.
To sundry Expences in 1747.	831	12	2	By various Fees in 1747.	885	18	3
To Dº. in 1748.	831	12	2	By Dº. in 1748.	752	3	1
To Dº. in 1749.	781	12	0	By Dº. in 1749.	702	1	7
To Dº. in 1750 to 51.	774	2	0	By Dº. in 1750 to 51.	752	3	6
	3,218	18	4		3,092	6	5

To Law Charges, &c. for Four Years.   *John Ashton*, Marshal.

The Naked Truth (1755)

The *Naked Truth* appeared anonymously on or about August 27, 1755. It was advertised that day in the *Public Advertiser*.[1] It must have been completed during that month, for it cites an article that had appeared in that paper on July 30, 1755. The second edition, which appeared soon after September 6, 1755,[2] incorporated a number of corrections and additions, including a second dedication and an appendix concerning General Braddock's defeat at Great Meadows on July 9, 1755.

The evidence that Oglethorpe wrote *The Naked Truth* seems persuasive. Apparently no other author has ever been suggested; and a copy of the first edition in the British Library bears the signature, or ascription "Oglethorpe."[3] It appears in a hand similar to that in two letters that Oglethorpe wrote to his friend Marshal Keith in late 1755 and the spring of 1756.[4] The circumstances of publication reinforce the attribution. In the second edition, *The Naked Truth* is designated number 1 of a new periodical, like the short-lived *Sailor's Advocate*; and the author promised, "I . . . shall, from Time to Time, publish such Things as I shall think fit for your service" (pp. vii–viii). On October 3, 1755, the *Public Advertiser* announced, "Soon will be published, Naked Truth, No. 2" (p. 4). The "third edition" (perhaps a new impression, but more likely merely a new issue) was advertised there a few days later, on October 6. However, although the first three "editions" were widely advertised, the fourth and fifth were not advertised at all, and number 2 never appeared. Such a pattern fits in with the activities of Oglethorpe at the time. In the summer and early fall of 1755 he had ample time for writing, as he had lately been deprived of virtually all his former activities. In September, however, he petitioned the king for the reactivation and command of his disbanded Georgia regiment; and when in October he found that his *bête noire*, the Duke of Cumberland, had passed him over for any command at all, he had no leisure for writing. He was preparing to leave England as soon as he could, for he feared that in his resentment he might become involved in a duel with one of Cumberland's hangers-on.[5]

The internal evidence seems to confirm the ascription. The views seem

Oglethorpe's, and the classical parallels follow his frequent practice. He had used the mathematics of finance before, notably in *A New and Accurate Account*, and he was to do so later, in his Corsican letters. The author's praise of Admiral Edward Vernon (1684–1757) and General Thomas Wentworth (1693–1747) is especially suggestive. Vernon was a longtime friend of Oglethorpe, and he may have suggested the title by his attack on the Ministry in *A Specimen of Naked Truth from a British Sailor* (1746). Wentworth had presided at Oglethorpe's second court-martial. Oglethorpe's Irish heritage, through his mother, and his American experiences may have led him to address the pamphlet to "THE PEOPLE OF *Great Britain, Ireland*, and *America*." When the author cites the ability of the Spanish in 1718 to supply the invading army of De Lede on Sicily in spite of the British fleet offshore, he may well have been remembering his own brief service in Italy and Sicily at the outset of that campaign.[6] And his futile effort to capture St. Augustine is conjured up when the author laments how the Spaniards "could withdraw into inaccessible Places, and leave you to lose your Troops and Fleets."

In *The Naked Truth* Oglethorpe developed with considerable detail his contention that war with France would afflict all except some moneylenders and a few fortunate officers. Not only would the families of the soldiers and sailors suffer greatly, but the increased taxes and interest would entail hardships upon the poor, the middle class, and the country gentry. Like William Pitt,[7] Oglethorpe developed the adverse effects that war would have upon Britain's economy, which was already suffering from an unfavorable balance of trade. With its different tax system, Oglethorpe reasoned, France could finance a war with much greater ease and prospects of success. Like Pitt again, Oglethorpe was also concerned for the devastating effect of war upon England's sinking fund.

The Naked Truth was of course neither the first nor the last opposition to a declaration of war against France and against subsidizing foreign nations such as Prussia and Russia for the protection of Hanover—whither King George II had retired for his usual summer vacation. In the *Gentleman's Magazine* and the newspapers for the past year, many among the merchant group, especially, had opposed a war with France, and particularly an expedition into the Ohio country. However, as both Oglethorpe and Pitt may have realized, they were attempting to oppose a military policy that had become virtually inevitable; for when the news reached England of Colonel George Washington's defeat at Fort Necessity, on July 4, 1754, the Duke of Cumberland rapidly consolidated his influence to assure a military, rather than a diplomatic solution to the Anglo-French disputes.[8] Indeed so powerful was Cumberland at the time that Oglethorpe's anonymity in *The Naked Truth* may have had a special cause. He usually withheld his name, but here even the publisher adopted a pseudonym, "A. Price."[9] The unusual ironic style of the pamphlet seems appropriate for a thwarted general who perhaps realized that he was opposing Cumberland in a hopeless cause.

Since there were only two actual editions, I have based my text upon the first, but have incorporated the additions, corrections, and substantive changes that Oglethorpe made in his second edition, specifying these in the notes. *The Naked Truth*, incidentally, is apparently the only pamphlet of Oglethorpe to be translated.[10] A French version by Edmé Jacques Genet appeared in "London" (Paris?) in 1755 as *La Vérité Révelée*.

THE NAKED TRUTH.

——Ridentem dicere Verum

Quis Vetat——

[Printer's ornament.]

LONDON:

Printed for A. PRICE, in *Fleet-Street*.

M.DCC.LV.

[Price Six Pence.]

TO THE
PEOPLE
OF
Great Britain, Ireland, and America.

THO' not one in one Thousand of you will read, or even hear of this Dedication, yet you have the most right to the following Pages. The Matter they treat of may affect you and your Children for many Generations.

They are writ to give you what Light my Experience furnishes, before you form your Judgment on a Matter entirely in your own Powers; that is, to chuse whether you will be silent, or will cry aloud.

This is a Thing entirely dependent on yourselves, every free-born *English* Man, and Woman too, has a Right to cry and hollow as loud as they please.

The Voice of the People is the Voice of God,[11] was the Doctrine of the *Whigs* in King *Charles* the Second's Reign, and I have not heard it denied yet publickly. Certainly every reasonable Man must allow, that Governments were formed and submitted to for the Good of the People; *Salus Populi suprema Lex esto.*[12]

The People have, in different Countries, parted with more or less of their natural Freedom, to obtain the Benefits that arise from the Protection and Convenience that the Conjunction of Numbers give; Numbers cannot live together without Order, which must be maintained by Individuals submitting their Differences to the Judgment of others.

Wars cannot be carried on without submitting to the Orders of the Commander; nor Money raised for paying Armies and Fleets, without submitting to Taxes. All these Submissions are so far departing from natural Liberty. Those Nations who have parted with fewest of their natural Rights, or, in other Terms, have preserved most Privileges, are the happiest; nay, they are the most powerful, in Proportion to the Extent of their Dominions; as the People of *Europe*, and of them the Republicks and limited Monarchies, are much more powerful, in Proportion to their Extent of Land, than the absolute Governments of *Asia*.

How weak are the *Turks, Persians* and *Moguls*, who rule over such immense Regions, where the People have no kind of Privileges. The *Venetian* Republick hath resisted the whole Strength of the *Turkish* Empire, and maintained itself against them for many Ages. The *Switzs* are the freest People in *Europe*, and their Country, though small and barren, has, without mercenary Armies, maintained their independent Sovereignty against the great and aspiring Houses of *Austria* and *Bourbon*, and are respected by all *Europe*.

Holland grew populous by Liberty, and if their Extent of Country was to be compared with *France* or *Spain*, their Wealth and Power surpasses all Comparison. Indeed they have of late declined; but that hath been proportionably to the Privileges of the People's being lessened by the Encroachments of the Oligarchy, or Rulers, who would have ruined them, and sold them to *France*, had they not been rescued by the Spirit of the People, who, rising, chose a Stadtholder.

Freedom of the People is therefore the Preservation of the Power and Wealth of States. Amongst other Privileges the Freedom of Writing and Speaking is of the highest Consequence, as the using that Liberty may support or destroy a Nation.

The Voice of the People always was regarded with high Reverence by wise Princes, especially by those of this Nation. It is of serious Consequence, that the People of this Realm should be well instructed. I join with Mr. TRENCHARD, where he says, "The People are never mistaken, but when they are bribed or deceived."[13] Now, to prevent *you, the People*, from being deceived, and thereby misled into a general Clamour, is the End of these Papers. All I wish is, that you would hear, read, and be well informed, before you enter into a general Cry; and that you will believe me to be, with the highest Veneration, and sincerest Affection,

Your devoted, humble Servant.

Second DEDICATION *to the* PEOPLE.

THE Reception you gave to the first Impression of this Pamphlet, obliges me, in Gratitude, to give it you corrected, with Additions. On the *Naked Truth*'s appearing, the Clamour ceased. This proved it was not the Voice of the People, but a Cry work'd up by Art, which is as different from the Voice of the People, as the Yelping of Curs, on the throwing a Bone amongst them, is from the Roaring of the Lion, which maketh the Forest tremble.[14] This is the Cry of the People, who roar not but on high Occasions, when they feel real Grievances; for Millions must feel before they will join in one Voice. Then the Roar is dreadful, and not to be withstood. The Lion roared when the Parliament and People felt the Oppression of the Army, under the Command of *Lambert, Harrison, &c.* He roared so loud, that it frighted them and their Army into Holes and Corners.[15] He roared again when King *James* pinched the People in their Liberties and Religion, and he roared so loud, that he frighted King, Queen and Priests out of the Realm.

The Lion might roar if he was really hurt, if the Christian Protestant Religion and Liberty of Conscience were subverting.

Or if the Multitude was pressed by Taxes and Wants, so as not to be able to subsist.

Or if they saw a Mercenary Military Power grow so fast as to threaten Destruction to the Civil Magistrate and Constitution.

Or if they saw a Ministry betraying the King and People to *France*.

Or if, under the specious Name of Subsidies, they were betraying his Majesty, and making the Kingdom tributary to a powerful foreign Potentate, and putting the Power of the Seas into their Hands.

Or if they should so break through the Parliamentary Faith, which hath appropriated the Funds to paying the Principal and Interest of the Publick Debt, and by applying appropriated Money to Subsidies should neglect paying the National Creditors.

These or such like National Grievances might raise the Voice of the People; but it will not be raised by those Deceivers who would use it as a Means to enrich themselves, by engaging the People in a ruinous and expensive War.

It was to prevent you, the People, from being deceived, that I ventured to print. I find you were not deceived, but that those who strove to deceive you called the Noise they made your Voice. As you have already favoured me, I hope the Continuance, and shall, from Time to Time, publish such Things as I shall think for your Service, and am, with the highest Veneration and sincerest Affection,

Your most Obliged
and Devoted
Humble Servant.

NAKED TRUTH.

———Ridentem dicere Verum
Quis Vetat——— [16]

NAKED TRUTH is always disagreeable to weak Minds. As they compose the Bulk of Mankind, she is most hateful to the Multitude. To tell the Truth to the People, is almost as dangerous as to tell it to a Tyrant.

Phocian and *Socrates* were poisoned by the People of *Athens* for telling them *Naked Truth*.[17] The virtuous *Lacedemonians* hated Disguise, and loved Simplicity and Nakedness so much, that their Laws obliged the Virgins to dance almost naked:[18] Yet even these *Spartans* stoned *Lycurgus*, and beat out one of his Eyes, for telling them *Naked Truth*.[19] If this was the Consequence in better Ages, you, Reader, must think me mad, who, in the Dregs of Time, venture to publish *Naked Truth* to *Britain*.

To love one's Country, and to be virtuous in a bad Age, hath often been called Madness. *Nat. Lee*, the Poet, say'd, "To differ from the People was the Definition of Madness; and therefore that himself and the few Wits were locked up in *Bethlehem*, by the infinitely more numerous Blockheads at large." [20]

Democritus the Philosopher was the first who discovered to the *Greeks*, that the Earth was a Globe, by the Shadow it cast in an Eclipse on the Moon. The Magistrates of his City sent, in pure Love and Sincerity of Heart, to *Hippocrates* the Physician, to come and cure the Philosopher *Democritus* of Madness. When he came, they told to *Hippocrates* the fatal Symptoms, that he said the World was round, and that our Feet pointed at the Feet of other Men on the other Side of the Earth; therefore either they or we must stand on our Heads. But they urged, to prove him still more lunatick, that he despised Money, and refused publick Employments. *Hippocrates* shook his Head, got out of Town in a Hurry, and sent a Horse-load of Hellebore to the the Magistrates, but none to *Democritus*.[21]

Solon and *Brutus*, I mean the first, was called mad, and desired to be thought so.[22] The hireling Wits that flattered Tyrants gave the same or worse Appellations to the second *Brutus*. But *Cowley* says of him,

> *The Heroick Exaltations of the Good*
> *Are so far from understood,*
> *We count them Vice. Alas! our Sight's so ill,*

> *That Things which swiftest move seem to stand still.*
> *We look not upon Virtue in her Height,*
> *On her supreme Idea, brave and bright,*
> *In the original Light;*
> > *But as her Beams reflected pass*
> > *Thro' our own Nature, or ill Custom's Glass:*
> *And 'tis no Wonder so,*
> > *If with dejected Eye*
> > *In standing Pools we seek the Sky,*
> *That Stars so high above may seem to us below.*[23]

Let the World think what they please, if the *Printer will venture Printing*, I'll furnish Copy, and will tell my Country *Naked Truth*, tho' it may be against the present enthusiastick Ardor, that bears down all before it.

I know it is as dangerous to write against popular Prejudices as against Tyrants; and yet it is cruel to flatter the People, nay it is worse, it is being in some Measure *Felo de se:* For if we let the frantick Zeal, and false Magnanimity of the People proceed,[24] and do not undeceive them, we must bear our Share in the publick Taxes, and perhaps universal Ruin that it may draw on.

Perhaps it may be less harsh, and therefore have more Effect, to speak of the past, than at once to rush on, in stripping naked the present Folly. Oil makes a Razor cut, and Example may, like Oil, smooth whilst it sets the Edge. Example is the Tutor of the Wise, as Experience is to Fools: We have both Example and woful Experience in our own Days, of giving Way to popular Clamour and national Prejudice. Let us call back a few Years, and see with what Ardor the Merchants cried out for a *Spanish* War; a few Ships were plundered; a Captain lost his Ears,[25] publick Clamour was raised, no Satisfaction would go down; even Men of Sense supported the Clamour, because it supported the Party: They were not ashamed to hear, nay to repeat, *We can crush* Spain, *let loose your Navy; let loose your People to just Revenge*; you will humble *Spain* in a Year; you will take all her Ships, nay her *America*. Even wise Men were not ashamed to say, they could starve the vast Continent of *Spain*, by prohibiting our People from furnishing Provisions, and trading with them. Nothing was so ridiculous that did not go down; the Price of our Corn lowered for want of that Market, and it hath never rise since,[26] because the *Spaniards* gave Encouragement to their own Tillage, and fell into a Trade, by which the *Hamburgers* and *Dutch* supplied them from *Poland* and *Barbary* with Wheat, *France* with Fish from *Newfoundland*, and the Vallies of their own Mountains with double the

Number of Cattle they used to do. This last was occasioned by the Encouragements which your Prohibition of selling *Irish* Beef to them forced them to give. The Laziness and Oppression of the Government had discouraged Agriculture; but you awaked them; they encouraged it; and you, by prohibiting a Trade to give them a present Distress, gave it a new Turn, and have lost it for ever.[27]

Our sanguine Hopes of Conquest were as much baulked as our starving them into Submission; we sent a noble Fleet, covered the Seas with our Ships, and the Islands with our Soldiers, but what Return! We buried twenty thousand Men without a Battle, without the Sword of a Foe; there was hardly a Man killed, except a few Hundreds at St. *Lazarus*. Did we take one Province, or one Town, except *Porto-Bello?* Did we keep even that or any one spot? This cannot be laid to the Charge of the Officers or Men; the Admiral was as brave a Man, and as good an Officer, as *England* ever bred; he was distinguished in Queen *Anne*'s Wars, an Age of Heroes. To the Merit of a brave and experienced Officer, he added the uncorruptable Integrity of *Cato*, and the Plainness and Roughness of his Manners were, perhaps, Virtues too high for an Age of Fribbles. The Officers of the Land Forces were as valuable as the Age has produced, and Lord *Cathcart* had distinguished himself also in Queen *Anne*'s Wars; General *Wentworth* was a Man of excellent Sense, Temper, and Courage,[28] and shewed it afterwards on several Occasions; General *Guise* was a brave and exact Officer,[29] the Sailors and Soldiers were good; Whence then came the Disappointment? From the War's being improper, and drove on by popular Prejudices. By believing those popular Clamours, or not daring to oppose them, the Government was forced to carry on the War in Sun-burnt Climates, where the Enemy could withdraw himself into inaccessible Places, and leave you to lose your Troops and Fleets, by opposing to you the Sun and Air only.

Some Prizes you took at Sea of great Value, but did not the Expence out of the Publick Stock load the Poor with Taxes? And did there come as much back to the Captains and Captors as the Publick spent? If there did, this was but giving the People's Money to Officers and Sailors; but it was worse, a Squadron cost one Million perhaps fitting out;[30] the Prizes taken might be two hundred thousand Pounds; the Taxed lost a Million, the Captors got two hundred thousand Pounds, the Publick loses eight hundred thousand Pounds.

We sent a Squadron to conquer *Peru*, one Ship of it got round the World, and took a glorious Prize; but that was owing to the Perseverance of the Commander;[31] for out of five, only one could perform the Voyage. Were we to write in the Stile of the Antients, he perhaps was preserved by the Genius of *England*, to renew her antient Discipline, and gain those Victories at Sea that obtained a Peace. When after many unsuccessful Battles at Land, *Bergen* and *Maestritch* taken, and no Place remaining able to prevent the entire Conquest of *Holland*, our Successes at Sea saved *Europe* from Chains, by forcing *France* to give up her Conquests. We said, that *England* did not get a Foot of Ground.——But what then, Did *England* get by that *Spanish* War, to which it was pushed by Clamour? *Why it got* TWO WARS, *that, and the* French, *which followed it;* for had we not engaged in the *Spanish* War, and thereby forced *Spain* into the Arms of *France*, the latter would not have ventured to attack the House of *Austria*, or to have made a dependant *Bavarian* Emperor. *Spain* would have been jealous of *France*, and would have assisted us and the House of *Austria*, had she not, by our Rashness, been forced to seek Defence from *France* against our Fleets.

We also got more by those two Wars; we got rid of a wise Statesman, and a prudent experienced Ministry. Besides getting rid of this pacifick Ministry, *England* got a Number of PATRIOT ORATORS,[32] *and they got Places.*

> *Aut si non aliam venturi fata Neroni,*
> *Invenire viam scelera ipsa Nefasque,*
> *Hac Mercede placent*——[33]   LUC.

We got the spending of eighty Millions; the Nation got forty Millions in Debt; and Contractors, Stockjobbers, Jews and Brokers got Plumbs; Emperors Kings; and Electors got Subsidies; and at last *England* got a Peace.

These Things we did get, and most of them stick by us; and we had like to have got the Pope, the Pretender, the Devil and all; but these, thank Heaven, we did not get; but no Thanks to the clamorous hot-headed Multitude, that drove wiser Heads into those Measures, which brought us to fight with inferior Numbers, *Pro Aris & Focis;*[34] every serious Man must shudder to think what Dangers Providence delivered us from; how often his Majesty and the Royal Family were exposed, how often the Nation was on the Edge of Destruction, and rescued by a Scene of Wonders! And, indeed it was all wonderful, that *England*, assisted by no Ally but whom she paid, could hold out a War; yet are there Numbers, that want to embark us in a new War.

To be sure it is the Interest of the Disaffected, if there are any such, to engage us in a War; they have no other Chance for their desperate Cause; besides, out of Revenge for the Treatment the *French* gave to their Master,[35] they would naturally do all the Mischief they can, and that is nothing but Growling, so doubt not the Disaffected will all growl for a War; and yet in this, as in all other their Hopes, they will be disappointed; for *France* will never assist them; she has disobliged their Master too much ever to forgive or trust him.

The Stock-jobbers, Usurers and Jews, certainly will cry out for the Honour of *England*, for they wish us grinning Honour,[36] that the Interest of Money may rise; but they too may be disappointed; for if a War should grow too heavy, how shall Interest be paid, and the Principal they have in the present Funds will fall in Proportion to the rising of Interest; so they will lose more on the Principal of their tied-up Money, than they can get by the rise of Interest on their floating Cash.

Ladies will be glad of a War; their Lovers may get Commissions, and so they may get rid of old ones, and have new; they may be glad of higher Interest, but they will be mistaken; for they will lose by the selling of their Capital; suppose the Government should be by Clamour drove into a War, and should be obliged to borrow at above 3 *per Cent.* whatever they borrow at above, so much lower must the Capital of the present Funds fall; thus, if a Lady has a 1000 *l.* in the 3 *per Cents*, and the Government should borrow at 3½ (which it is hoped they may not be forced to do) that Instant the 3 *per Cents* fall proportionably, and she cannot sell out at a Price so as to put out her Money in the new Funds; instead of her 1000 *l.* she may perhaps not be offered 900 *l.* Pounds for her Stock; but if the Government should be still harder pushed (which God forbid) and be forced to borrow at 4 *per Cent.* her Stock of 1000 *l.* in the 3 *per Cents* will be worth but 750 *l.* so she will have a worse Capital, and gain nothing by the rising of the Interest of Money.[37]

The Officers must cry out for War, lest they should be believed Men that feared Action. Yet *Hannibal*, and, before him, *Phocian*, very pretty Fellows, as Capt. *Bluff* says, in those Days, when they found their Nation overmatched, advised Peace; but Capt. *Bluff* says, *Hannibal* would be nothing at all in our Days.[38] As for the Sons of War and Glory, perhaps a War with *France* at this Juncture, single-handed, may not be for their Glory nor Advantage. By the present Scheme of the Orators there is to be no War on the Continent; that is to say, there is to be a War and no War. But this is the Orators War, as the last was the Merchants War, therefore the Orators can best tell how it is to be carried on; if then they know their own Child, which it is a wise Father that does, this War is not to be a Land War, and Soldiers are not Seamen; so Soldiers can have no Share in the War, unless they be amphibious Soldiers; your amphibious irrational Animals are Otters and Beavers; and your amphibious rational Animals are Marines; therefore no Land Soldier can wish for a War in this Circumstance, but who wishes to be a Marine; now no Dragoon wishes to be a Marine;[39] therefore no Dragoon can wish for a War. This Syllogism is to shew my Logick.

As for Sailors and Marines, they are in the right to talk for a War, that they may eat. Prizes are rare good Things. But why Parsons cry out for War, who are to pay more Taxes, and consequently eat worse, is worth discussing; they who are Men of Peace, and as Protestants are not for superstitious Fasting, why should they cry for War? It surely is not that People admire what they know least; Is it that they do so because their Patrons do so; and that the Way to Preferment is, *Jurare in Verbo Majestri?*[40] Or is it, that they love to read News and hear of bloody Battles? Surely it is not the Interest of the Church, nor of the spiritual Members of it, to have War. War not only lessens their Income, by encreasing the Land-Tax and other Taxes, but lessens Surplice Fees, Dues of Weddings, Christenings, and Burials; for the Thousands that fell in *Flanders* and the *West-Indies* saved their Burial Fees.

But seriously, Clergymen of all Denominations, whether Church or Dissenters, should stem these strange Clamours of the People for War. They have Learning, and from all History know, that rash Wars, undertaken against stronger Nations, have been the Ruin of the Freedom of States, as unavoidable defensive Wars have been their Honour and Preservation; that the Clamours of the People should never be employed to spur on Princes; they are always apt enough for War, from the Hopes of Power and Glory. The Cry of the People should be for Peace, particularly if the Strength of the Enemy is vastly superior. The best of Books says, if a King comes with 20,000 against one who has 10,000, he sendeth to make Peace, whilst yet in the Way.[41]

It is hurting a Prince or Ministry greatly to urge them by popular Clamour to War. A magnanimous Prince hearing such Clamours is unwilling to stem them, lest his Glory should suffer as sloathful, which Reproach a generous Prince abhors more than Death; and a wise Minister must give Way to the joint cry of the People and urged-on Courage of the Prince, tho' he knows the Danger, and would rather give the Advice of *Phoebus* to the daring Youth;

Parce puer stimulis & fortius utere loris.[42]

Orators have a Right by Prescription to clamour for War. *Demosthenes* did so, and by the Torrent of his Eloquence drove the *Thebans* and *Athenians* quite mad, so that those two Cities declared War against *Alexander the Great; Thebes* was taken, sacked, burnt, and the Inhabitants kill'd or sold for Slaves; and *Athens* lost her Liberty:[43] The great *Cicero* helped to ruin his Country by such Behaviour; he encreased the popular Cry, when *Pompey* was in *Greece*, and husbanding with the utmost Care the Army committed to his Charge, for in that Army he knew the whole Safety of *Rome* lay; he, like *Fabius*, wisely declined fighting with *Caesar*, but the general Cry was for Fighting; *Pompey* despised Common Fame, and stood firm to his Judgment and the Welfare of *Rome*; but when *Cicero* joined the popular Cry *Pompey* yielded, and marched to the fatal *Pharsalia*.

The Nobles, it is said, join the Cry: They can have no sinister Motive: But they are more tender of Honour, therefore are sensible of the least Touch. But *Plebeians* of humbler Minds should strive to temper their heroick Heat; it is the *Plebeians* must give and pay most of the Taxes. *Plectuntur Achivi*,[44] War makes great Armies, and many Provisions for the younger Branches of great Families; and notwithstanding the Marriage Act, there are not quite Heiresses enough for all the younger Brothers of noble Families, some are left Food for Powder.[45]

The Merchant, Manufacturer, Ship-builder, and infinite Numbers employed in fitting out Shipping, may cry for War. Great is the *Diana* of the *Ephesians*,[46] say the Shrine-makers. Perhaps they would be less violent, would they but consider what a desperate Reckoning was paid for their short Harvest at the Beginning of the last War; and how miserably Trade suffer'd in the End, for the quick Demand the first fitting out of great Fleets occasioned.

The News-writers certainly must be for War; next to political Sedition and private Scandal, it is the best Mart for their Wares; but they will not be so much advantaged as they expect; for if more Papers are vended, new ones will be set up.

By its appearing to so many Bodies, to such Multitudes of People,[47] that a War is for their private Interest, they join in a common Cry, and a War becomes a popular Clamour; yet almost every one will be hurt by the very Thing they cry out for; but this they do not know,[48] for want of giving themselves Time to consider.

In mixed Governments, where the Oligarchy or Rulers have the executive Power, but limited by the People in their general Meetings, it happens often, that the Rulers are for War, and privately stir up Clamours for that

Purpose, because they have the Disposal of the Monies and Preferments which are increased by War. Thus the Roman Senate push'd the People to War, till they wasted the Strength of the *Plebeians*; so that they destroyed all Equality, bought the Lands which the Weight of the Services in War forced them to sell, and oppress'd them to the highest Degree; so that the Conquests of *Rome* increased the Misery of the *Plebeians* to such an Excess, that they tried the *Gracci* and *Marius*,[49] and at last made themselves Slaves to *Caesar*, that since they could not be free from the Senators, they might at least make their senatorial Tyrants equally Slaves with themselves.

In mixt Monarchies, the Crown often made use of the Ardor of the Brave, and the Necessities of the unquiet Part of the People, to raise a Clamour for War, which encreases the Power of the Crown. As all Taxes and Offices are in the Disposition of the executive Part of the Government, the Kings in the *Gothick* Constitutions cannot raise Taxes, but when raised, they increase his Power amongst other Things, by the Number of Officers in the Collection and Distribution in his Nomination;[50] so that frequent Wars add so much Power to the Crown, as must in the End make it absolute. This *Henry* VIIth was so well acquainted with, that he pretended Wars with *France*, to make his Advantage of the good-natur'd Courage of the People of *England*; they granted Subsidies, he raised Troops, and then gave up the very disputed Points for Peace. But his End was obtained, the Nobility were made Dependant by expensive Preparations for Campains, the People were tamed by Taxes, and his Power encreased by the Number of Tax-gatherers, and by the Sums saved, and not expended. This Policy of Wars, true or false, have been made use of in *France*, *Spain*, and all the *Gothick* or *Germanick* Kingdoms, to raise the Crown, and depress the People, till this Policy has drove Liberty out of most Parts of *Europe*. In *Turky* a Clamour for War is not the Engine of the State,[51] but of the one Part of the Court or Ministry against the other. Thus Cara Mustifa, or Black Mustifa, got the Ulama or Law to join the Janissaries or Army, and the Levants or Naval-Soldiers all in one Cry for War,[52] whereby he got the Command of the greatest Army, and thereby the most Wealth that a Grand Vizier could acquire. At first he was hated by the Mufti and Captain Bashaw; but the Artifice was this, by which he gained his Point; at the first the Sultan disliked a War, and the Mufti, or Head of the Law, was utterly against it, so was the Testedar, or Treasurer; but Mustifa (without appearing himself in it)[53] engaged the Captain Bashaw, or Lord High Admiral, who was tied by Affinity to the Mufti, to come into the Clamour for a War. He was made to believe it should be carried on by Sea only, and so debase the Vizier, and aggrandize his naval Power. The Mufti came in for the Sake of Affinity, the War began. The Vizier turn'd it all by Land, attacked the *Germans*, and besieged *Vienna*; the Mufti and the Captain Bashaw, highly nettled, turns the Cry against Cara Mustifa,[54] who lost the Battle of *Vienna*, and then his Head.

Dionysius rais'd by his Artifice a Clamour for a War;[55] and said, that the Senators were pacifick, and gave up the Honour of the City. The *Syracusans*, hurried into it, named him General against the *Carthaginians*; he soon made a Peace with them, and became Tyrant of *Syracuse*. *Agathocles* followed the same Steps, with the same Success,[56] and, like the other, began by abusing the Senators and praising the Army. This was so known a Trick in *Greece*, that it gave Rise to the Fable where the Wolf gravely advises the Shepherd to turn out the pacifick fawning Dogs of the Senate, and to give the keeping of the Sheep to the warlike Wolves.[57]

It is surprising, that there ever should be a popular Cry for a War, when there is not a Man in *England* but must lose by it, except some few Officers, Paymasters, and Contractors, by Sea and Land.

The labouring People, who are the Numbers and Support of every Realm, are the first and most pinched by War; the strongest and ablest are pressed into the Sea, or persuaded into the Land Service; and the old Parents, Wives and young Children, dependant on their Labours, left a Charge to Parishes, and if not relieved must starve. The Seamen press'd, the Merchant Ships now lye loaded by the Walls,[58] unless they by Favour can get a Protection; and the Power of granting such Favour augments the Power of the Crown, more than our Ancestors would have thought convenient when they disputed the Ship-money.[59] All Ships cannot have Protections; for if all had, no Men would be left to be press'd, therefore great Numbers must lye by the Walls,[60] whilst the Markets they were design'd for are supplied by neutral Nations; and thus the Channel of Trade is turn'd, and the Merchant hurt, whose Wares rot on Board, which should answer his Bill of Exchange, and enable him to pay his Tradesmen; the Tradesmen and Manufacturer are hurt, by the Merchants being disabled from buying and paying, and the whole Trade of the Kingdom grows dull and heavy. The Poorest suffer first, and by Continuance the Rich grow poor.

But the greatest Sufferers by War are the Country Gentlemen of Estates, and the Owners or Proprietors of the Stocks and Funds.

The Country Gentleman, besides paying an increas'd Land-tax from two to four Shillings in the Pound, must pay more for all foreign Commodities, for Tea, Sugar, Wine, Silks, Hollands, &c. rises proportionably to the Risk of Navigation, and *English* Commodities sell worse, for Corn, Cloth, &c. must be sold cheaper to the exporting Merchants, to enable them,[61] in a foreign neutral Port, to sell at equal Prices with the neutral Ship that pays no Insurance; therefore the *English* Commodity must be sold so cheap, as to enable them to sell at an equal Price with the Foreigner, and this must fall on the prime Cost paid to the *English* Grower or Manufacturer. The Country Gentleman cannot get by preferring his Sons in the Army, it is great Lords, or Members of Parliament, may perhaps do so; he can scarce get an Ensign's Commission without buying; that is to say, he must give three or four hundred Pounds for an Ensign's Commission, which brings in about fifty Pounds a Year; and the Son must pay about fifteen or twenty Pounds for Regimentals, besides Equipage, and must live at an Expence far above his Pay; therefore he pays for the Liberty of keeping his Son in the Service. It is urged there is Advancement; there is so, but all Advancements require higher Expences, proportionable to the Pay; so that no Officer can lay up that lives handsomely, and Equipages and other Accidents forces most (tho' prudent Men) into Debt. A Son in the Army is more Expence to his Father, than if he kept him in his own House, and much more than if he bred him to the Law, Physick, Divinity, or Merchandize; and yet the Benefit Tickets in those Professions are better, and the Way to them easier and less expensive. The Lord Chancellors, Archbishops, Doctors, and Merchants, as *Radcliffe, Sloane, Heathcote, Delmy, Crasteen,* &c.[62] left greater Estates than any General, except the Duke of *Marlborough,* ever did; and he made not his by his Pay, so much as by his Wife's and his own Frugality; and by having the Secret, turn'd his Money in the Funds; for he must win who sees the Bottom of the Cards.

As the Country Gentleman and landed Men must lose by War, so must the Proprietors of the Funds and Stocks; for the Money they have is tied down at 3 *per Cent.* and if they sell, they must do it at such a Discount, as to lose more upon the Principal, than they get by advancing upon a new Loan; and should they sell out at Discount, and lend at a high Interest; on a Peace they will be paid off or reduced. Suppose a Man should sell at 90, to lend on new Loans at 4 *per Cent.* to the Government, as soon as a Peace comes he will be reduc'd to 3 *per Cent.* then the 110 *l.* which he sold out to lend 100, will bring in but 3 *per Cent.* so he will have lost 10 *per Cent.* by the Transaction.

It is said by some, that the Sinking Fund is engaged to be applied to pay the publick Debts now in being. If that should be punctually applied, and one Million yearly, or whatever it were, paid to the old Creditors, the Government might borrow easier of new Men; nay, the very Money paid off of the old Debt would be lent on the new. As soon as the Government borrows at 4 *per Cent.* the present Proprietors have lost the fourth Part of their Principal for every present Use. Are they to pay a Daughter's Fortune, or Bill of Exchange? Instead of selling 1000 *l.* in the 3 *per Cents* to do it, they must sell above 1300, if Stock is fallen to 75, which is the Proportion between 3 and 4 *per Cent.* But if the Father hath agreed to pay 1000*l.* Fortune, and has only 1000 *l.* Stock in 3 *per Cents*, he can give but 750 *l.* which may perhaps break the Match.

Having mentioned only how far this Clamour for War may affect People in their private Interest (but this can have little Influence in this disinterested Patriot Age) therefore it is necessary I should shew how it will affect the Publick. If it were not for the publick Advantage, and the Honour of the Nation, not a Jew nor Broker would clamour for War. If not moved by their tender Sense of the Glory of the Nation, What Contractor would cry *Down with the* French? It is to be sure a pure disinterested Patriot Spirit, that makes them wish to furnish the Publick for nothing. Therefore let us consider, if this Clamour is for the Good or Honour of the Nation, and if so, we ought to join in the Clamour; but if it is ruinous to the Nation, then surely we are not obliged to join in a destructive Cry.

France in the last War kept 450,000 Men by Land and Sea; 20,000 of which were at Sea, and those may be reckoned to cost three Times as much as Landsmen; so that would make in the whole the Expence of 490,000 Men. *England* kept about 100,000 Men, of which about 45,000 at Sea, which esteemed as three to one, makes 190,000 Men; this indeed makes them above double our Number.

The *Romans* looked on Superiority of Numbers with Respect, so as to make it proverbial, that *Hercules* was not a Match for two;[63] but that is not conclusive to *Britain*, every London *Apprentice is stronger than* Hercules, and therefore every *Englishman* can beat three *Frenchmen;*[64] *so that's settled; Britain* alone is above a Match for them, as to their Strength in Men.

With respect to Revenue, *France* in Peace raises about 300 Millions of Livres, which is not 15 Millions Sterling; in War she raises 18 or 19 Millions Sterling. *England* raises by the Malt Tax 750,000 *l.* and Land Tax in Peace, at 2 *s.* 1,000,000; in War at 4 *s.* makes 2 Millions; as for the other Taxes, they are appropriated either to the Civil List, or to pay the Interest of 80 Millions Debt, and the Surplus to sink the Capital of the Debt; the Surplus is called the *Sinking Fund.* Some think this *Sinking Fund may in a War be applied to the yearly Charges of the War;* but it is not probable the Parliament will *alter the Appropriation;* for it was on the Strength of that Appropriation, that the publick Creditors submitted to a Reduction, that thereby the Capital might be secure, tho' the Interest was lessened. Now as the 3 *per Cent.* and 3 one-half *per Cent.* are considerably under Par, I suppose the Sinking Fund will be inviolably applied to pay off the old Debts, and then the present Creditors will have the Benefit of lending their Money out at high Interest, if the Government should be forced to give a high Interest, which I hope they will not.

I say, if the Government give a higher Interest than 3 *per Cent.* they will certainly apply the Sinking Fund to pay the old Debt as appropriated; because it is Justice to the old Creditors, and *England* has always acted with Justice and Punctuality to their Creditors, which is what has maintain'd their Credit; and the Parliament will certainly not do any Thing to damp Credit, when there is most Use for it; therefore I am persuaded they will be punctual in applying the Sinking Fund to pay the present Debt.

I said, I thought the Government would not be forced, I hoped, to give above 3 *per Cent.* I think so, because all those zealous Patriots that clamour for War, I suppose, will lend at 3 *per Cent.* out of their Zeal; and this is the more necessary, because all above the Land and Malt must be borrowed, or new Taxes must be laid. Now new Taxes may either be on Things not taxed before, or by augmenting those already taxed. As for Things not taxed, few are to be found, unless such as oppress the Subject, and impoverish him so, that he will not be able to spend in some other Branch already taxed what he now doth; so it will stop some other Stream, as much as it augments this new Branch of Revenue.

With respect to augmenting the present Duties or Excises, that would hardly answer; for by Experience it is found, the higher Duties are, the less they bring in; several Experiments have been made, and by lowering Duties, the Revenue hath been augmented. The War must probably be carried on by borrowing as many Millions a Year as is wanted, and giving an Interest. Therefore it is most necessary to keep up Credit, that the Lenders may be willing to accept a low Interest; and nothing can contribute more *to keep up Credit,*[65] *than to apply the Sinking Fund inviolably to paying off the Debt.*

There is the more Reason to cherish Credit, since one great Source of Borrowing is stopped, I mean Lotteries. *They used to be Resources that never fail'd;* but unfortunately the last was made (by taking 10 *per Cent.*) a little too disadvantageous, and it is probable new Lotteries will not fill.

With respect therefore to Money; we are to begin a War with 80 Millions Debt, and 2,750,000 *l.* Sterling for Expences of the Year, with a Power of going further into Debt, against a Nation that raises about 15 Millions Sterling for the Year, and who cannot go into Debt, for no Body will trust them.

In short, we have more Ships, they have more Horse and Foot; and as for Money, we have already spoke fully.

> But antient *Pistol* says,
> "What is Money? Dust;
> *Fit only to enthral the mounting Soul,*
> *And knock down Courage to black* Erebus." [66]

What signifies the Money, if they have more Money we can beat them; we will go and take their Money, it will increase our Strength; so that is settled. *It appears plainly by a War, we shall regain all the Virtues of* Cato, *we shall acquire Poverty, which is the Nurse and Mother of all Virtue; we shall augment our Courage and Skill in War by Practice; our Patience I doubt not will be exerted also; and as for Chastity, that Virtue will certainly abound; for the Increase of Taxes, and Decline of Trade, will lessen Letchery, and* Sine cerere & Baccho frigit Venus.[67] *As we shall abound with all Virtues, we shall be secure to carry on the War single-handed at Sea successfully. There is but this Accident against us. If they find themselves weaker at Sea, they may perhaps be Poltroons enough to stay in their Ports, and we can't sail up to* Paris *without some new Inventions; but sure such a Thing may be obtained from some of our Projections. The Broad-wheel Philosopher doubtless can do such a Trifle as carry a Fleet over Land.*[68] *But if this should fail, and yet, if they will not come out of their Ports they can't hurt us. Perhaps they may join the* Spaniards, *and help them to attack* Port Mahone, *or* Gibralter; *for a Fleet of Men of War, some say, cannot in calm Weather hinder Troops landing on Islands in the* Mediterranean, *which was, they pretend to say, proved in* Sicily *in* 1718, *when Lord* Torrington *was not able to hinder Succours getting to the* Marquis de Lede's *Army. They may perhaps try another Way to hurt us, and march into* Westphalia. *Why, if they should do so, we have nothing to do but to* subsidise *all* Germany,[69] *the King of* Prussia *amongst the rest, if we can get him; besides* Russia, Sardinia, *and even* Turkey, *must not be forgot, least the Sultan should give a Diversion to* Russia *or* Hungary. *We are a rich People, this will be but a Trifle, at the worst it will be but borrowing* 80 *Millions more at* 5 *per Cent; and after a Peace, reducing all Debts to* 1½, *and then the same Fund that pays the Interest of* 80 *Millions at* 3 *per Cent. will pay that of* 160 *at* 1½.

All this is great; if therefore the *French* should not be content to carry on the War by Sea only, and should make it general through *Europe*, we must *subsidise*;[70] the Difficulty will be how to pay them; if we must send Specie from hence, the remitting those vast Sums must drain the Cash; and if the Money that circulates, 80 Millions of Paper, is lessened beyond a certain Degree, it will risk a Stagnation.

The Antient *Pistol* has shewn we can have Paper enough, which, whilst it is current, is Money; therefore we must strive to keep it so, and not by sending out the Specie make a Stagnation.

The Subsidies to *Prussia* and *Russia*, and the Empress Queen, must be balanced by Cash, since the Balance of Trade to those Countries is already against us; and whatsoever greater Demand they shall have on us, must be paid by sending Gold or Silver, since they do not want more of our Merchandize than they already have; for if they did, there would not be a Balance against us. The Subsidy must be equal to the Number of Troops with which they act against *France*; for if the War should be begun on our own Account, and not, for their own Cause, they will expect we should pay the Expence; and indeed there are none of them able to act against *France* at their own Expence. The King of *Prussia* can maintain his Troops in his own Country, and this with great Difficulty and Oeconomy; but it will cost double to act in the Field with the same Number of Troops, as it does to keep them in Time of Peace; therefore if he takes the Field with 100,000 Men, it cannot be reckoned less than a Million a Year. He was engaged last War on the *French* Side, but when he found it convenient he quitted them, and joined them again when he thought it for his Advantage. How can we then be certain of any Engagement from that Quarter. One is hardly sure of one's Bargain, where the Auction is still open to the best Bidder.

Another small Difficulty in all Engagements with him is, whether they may not disoblige the Court of *Vienna*; and if ever *Vienna* and *France* should agree, what then would be the Case; could we and *Prussia*, and all the Protestants in *Germany*, stem such a Tide. This is a Measure *Rome* hath long laboured, and proposed many Expedients to bring about.

If *Russia* acts with 30,000 Men, we know what the Charge of that, and the *Vienna* Subsidies were last War; we know that we were forced to raise 6,000,000 over and above Land and Malt, *&c.* and encrease the Debt more than that Sum in one Year: Suppose we should be oblig'd to go on at that Rate with a new War, How many Years can we hold it? And what Acquisitions in *America* can be equal to it? Could we not purchase *Quebec,* and all the *French* Northern Colonies for a less Sum? And is it probable, that we shall be able to keep them, if we should be successful?

Since I wrote the above, I find the last Question answered by the most magnanimous *Hurlothrumbo.* He writ it, I suppose, aware of the Objection at *White's,*[71] *viz.* that a War at Sea with *France* could be no Bett; since we have a great deal to lose, and *France* nothing.

Now by the equitable Laws of Gaming, when Judgment is asked, if a Man cannot win he cannot lose, so it is no Bett. If we beat the French *Fleet, ours cannot sail up to* Paris; *but if they beat ours* Ware Cat; *therefore it is plain it is no Bett. Now* Hurlothrumbo, *with great Sagacity, proves that the* French *do not throw a Levant,*[72] *but that we may get as well as lose, therefore it is a Bett. To support this, the heroick* Hurlothrumbo *leads on our Armies to victory, more rapid than those of* Caesar *in* Pontus. *He beats the* French *out of* North America; *then he shews how by his Victory in driving the* French *out of* Canada, *and the Continent of* America, *we shall get Millions enough to pay the national Debt. There are, says he, more* Indians *a hundred Times about* Canada *and* Mississippi, *than about* Hudson's Bay. *But the Company gets* 20 *Pound a Year by every* Indian *that trades with them. Now with great Moderation he only supposes the new acquired* Indians *will be worth but half as much,* 10 *Pound yearly each; so you need only take the Profit of the* Hudson Bay *Company, and multiply by* 50, *and the Produce will be the Millions promised.*

Quebeck, Cape-Breton,[73] *and all the* French *Places in* North America, *subdued,* Canada *being a cold Country, where the Lakes and Rivers, five Times as wide as the* Thames, *are frozen in one Night, and the Snows continue all the Winter Months without one Thaw.* Hurlothrumbo, *in Tenderness to his victorious Army, marches them from these frozen Climates, and like a Deluge pours them down Southwards, to the burning Sands of* Florida. *He wafts them over the Gulf Stream to* Cuba,[74] *conquers that Island, and* Hispaniola *and* Porto Rico.

These Conquests atchieved, the Advantages of the War appear; besides the Millions arising from the Northern Indians, *we shall not only have full Satisfaction for the Grievances from the* Spaniards, *but may oblige those proud* Spaniards *to pay us the Indulto they now allow to the King of* Spain, *for bringing home the Treasure.*

You see here, Reader, a Proof that supports the Clamour for a War; you see here what surprising Advantages will attend a War. Perhaps you may honour me with supposing, this flows from my luxuriant Fancy. But I would not be so unjust, as to rob the magnanimous *Hurlothrumbo* of his due Praise.—This Proposal is in sober Sadness printed in the *Publick Advertiser* of *Wednesday, July* 30, 1755.[75]

It is to be hoped, that those who cry loudest for War, do it out of Zeal for his Majesty, the Protestant Succession, and the Publick Good; if so, let them shew it by paying the proper Respect to his Majesty, waiting our Sovereign's Will; and when he has declared it, co-operating with it; and till then not joining in any Cry, merely to perplex those at the Helm.

A Ship was bound from Newfoundland *for* London, *with a great Number of Passengers on board, most good Sailors, returning from fishing, coming by the* Goodwins *for the River, It was hazy Weather, and blew a Storm; the Passengers run up and make a prodigious Noise and Clamour, all out of a good Zeal and anxious Eagerness to save the Ship; the Noise was so great, as it almost stunned the Pilot. When up runs the Captain, D—— your Zeal, Gentlemen,—Do you know what you do, by disturbing the Pilot in such Weather.—Such as he wants he will call for—As for the rest, take my Chest of Liquors, go down, be drunk and be d——d; but don't musse the Pilot, when one false Stroke at the Helm may send us all to the Bottom.*

POSTSCRIPT.

Whilst I was writing this I find Insurance rises, and is already got to 20 *per Cent.* on homeward bound *West India* Ships. Three *per Cents* are fallen to near 92. Wheat is about six Pounds a Load, and Woolen Goods and all *English* Manufactures lay dead on Hand; all foreign Goods, and Materials for Manufactures rise. These are the Effects of the Rumour of War. Privateers are fitting out in all the Ports of *France* and *England*. If they are permitted to act Trade will lose its Channel, and the industrious Trader indeed may buy and pay, but the Privateer will be the Customer, purchase with Powder and Bullet, undersell him that pays in Money, and spend the Produce in Wine and Women. It is said the *Dutch* have abandoned the barrier Towns, which looks as if they would maintain a Neutrality, and Profit of Trading without Insurance.

FINIS.

APPENDIX

IT is with great Grief that I find the Conjectures in the first Edition of this have been but too fatally fulfilled. It was Clamour that precipitated Major General *Braddock* to his Ruin. The Projectors engaged the Press on their Side, then called the Noise they had paid for the Voice of the People.

Is not this a direct Copy of Mr. *Wentworth*'s Expedition,[76] spoken of before? Have not those who by their Clamour pushed this Gentleman on to a desperate impracticable March much to answer for? The idle Words they threw about may be Sport to them, but might not the Shades of those who now lie unburied in the Woods on the *Ohio* say, Though it was Sport to you, it was Death to us? Let a News-writer, or Coffee-house Talker, only think that the Bodies of some Hundreds of his Countrymen, perhaps some of his Acquaintance, are now torn by Wolves, or eaten up by Bears, in the Wilds of *America*, because his Cry, in common with others, occasioned the sending them thither. But the Projectors, who have begg'd Millions of Acres in *America*, now lay the Blame on the brave Gentleman who was killed in striving to make their Project succeed. Nay, they are not ashamed to cry out, that his Courage was a Fault; that he should have staid when he knew the Woods were lined with Men. Can Creatures capable of reasoning thus, have any Remains of Modesty. It is insulting the Common Sense of their Hearers. Why these very Projectors, and the *North American* News-writers hired by them, insisted on the Government's sending Troops from *Europe*, to dislodge the *French* from their Posts on the *Ohio*. For this very Purpose Major General *Braddock* was sent, with two Regiments, from *Europe;* it was his Duty to obey those Orders which the Projectors and the *American* Representations had obtained.

What did Major General *Braddock* do? He obey'd his Orders, with much Labour and Care marched through the greatest Part of the Wood, surmounted infinite Difficulties, and, finding a Piece of open Ground at the Meadows, intrenches there, and makes a Place of Arms to support his Communication; he advances the *Indians* into the Woods, to scower them as far as the first *French* Post. On the 4th of *July* his *Indians* are repulsed, their Chief taken and kindly treated by the *French*. Major General *Braddock*, to retrieve this, marches forward, with 1200 Men; and on the 9th his Advance-Guard is attacked and disordered; he supports them, strives to recover the Day, but receives his Death's Wound in the Attempt, and his

Party was totally routed. This is all the certain Account we yet have, and enough to prove, that the Misfortune was owing to Clamour. It was that which occasioned the *American* Force, which all together was but equal to one great Attempt, to be divided into three different Bodies, and thereby the Loss on the *Ohio*. It was not so extraordinary that they should be defeated where they were, as it was that they got so far, and that they should not have sooner been catched on their long March and routed; and, considering how many Difficulties they had to pass, after they were defeated, it is more surprising, that any should escape, than that many should be kill'd and taken.

Two Squadrons, under excellent Admirals and Commanders, sail, one to hinder the *French* from supporting their Attempts in *America*, but it can only intercept two *French* Men of War; the rest got safe, with their Troops, to the Place of Destination; we lose one Man of War in *Hallifax*, and the Squadron is sickly, by Infection from the Fever, occasioned by the Confinement of the press'd Men. The other Squadron knows that part of the *French* Fleet is in *Cales*, takes all Measures to engage them in their Return to *Brest*; but the *French* Squadron sails, takes an *English* Man of War, the *Blandford*, and carries her into *Brest*; the Squadrons have taken several Prizes; But is not paying Squadrons to make Prizes of Merchantmen breaking Windows with Guineas? Thus ended the Campaign, occasioned by Clamour, which proves, that Kingdoms cannot be blocked up by Fleets.

I shall conclude by warning my Readers of an Attempt to raise a popular Clamour. The *Dutch* Papers have, some Time since, thrown out Paragraphs, to try how we should relish a *Muscovite* Assistance; in one they say, we are to have a *Muscovite* Squadron to guard our Channel when our Fleets are sent to *America*; in another they say, we are to give to the *Russians* 60,000 *l.* yearly, and 500,000 *l.* when they shall march 75,000 Men for our Assistance. This is so extraordinary a Proposal, that I suppose it can only exist in a *Dutchman* or *Russian*'s Head; no *Englishman*, surely, could wish to see our Natives wasted in *American* Expeditions, and the Safety of the Nation trusted to the Fleet of an Empire who have already subdued half the World, and to be obliged to pay them 500,000 *l.* yearly, a Sum this Nation cannot pay in Specie out of the Realm: Would it not be a Temptation to them privately to encourage *France* to make a War, that they might be required to march? And if Masters of a Squadron in our Seas, Would they not be able to levy it on us if we did not pay? Was not such a kind of Treaty with the *Saxons* the Ruin of the *Britons?* The Proposal is so improbable, that I should not have mentioned it, had I not found it often repeated with a kind of Approbation in those News-Papers, from whence the former *American* Cry which hath proved so fatal began. I mention this that the Reader may be warned, and not join in a Cry for *Russian* Subsidies, before the Matter is considered by our Superiors.

FINIS.

Some Account of the Cherokees (1762)

Oglethorpe's brief "Some Account of the Cherokees" appeared on July 29, 1762, in the *London Chronicle* and the *Gazeteer and London Daily Advertiser*. It was there attributed to the general.[1] Ettinger seems to have been the first biographer to mention it.[2] It was probably elicited by the publicity that attended the visit of three Cherokee chiefs to England in the summer of 1762, and it probably responded to some of the censure of their conduct during their visit, especially their drinking and wenching.[3] I reprint from the *London Chronicle*.

Some account of the Cherokees, as given by Lieutenant General Oglethorpe.

ON the back of Georgia and Carolina are three considerable nations, called the Cherokees, Chickasaws, Creeks, or Uschesees.[4] The Cherokees inhabit among the mountains, from whence the river Savanna descends. These Indians are not the most warlike, nor of the larger stature;[5] but are more accustomed to labour and live upon corn than to procure their sustenance by hunting. They have about 5000 warriors or hunters;[6] for the Indian nations are divided into two kinds of men: Those who they call warriors, or hunters, are like the ancient gentlemen in Europe, whose single profession was arms and chace.

These Indians look upon the end of life to be living happily. For this purpose their whole customs are calculated to prevent avarice, which they say embitters life; and nothing is a severer reflection among them, than to say that a man loves his own. To prevent the rise and propagation of such a vice, they, upon the death of any Indian, burn all that belongs to the deceased,[7] that there may be no temptation for the parent to hoard up a superfluity of arms and domestic conveniencies, their chief treasures, for his children. They strengthen this custom by a superstition, that it is agreeable to the souls of the deceased to burn all they leave, and that afflictions follow them who use any of their goods. They cultivate no more land than is necessary for their plentiful subsistence and hospitality to strangers. They use neither horses nor ploughs in agriculture; but instead of ploughing or digging, hoe their fields by common labour. The rest of the year they spend in hunting; and when they are injured by any other nation, as supposing one of their own nation to be killed, they send to demand satisfaction; but if this is refused, they make reprisals upon the first they can take of the nation that committed the injury. Thus their wars begin, which are very frequent, and carried on with great rage, there not being any people in the world braver, or more dextrous in the use of their arms and manner of fighting among woods and mountains, none more patient of labour, or swifter on foot.

Shipping Problems in South Carolina (1762)

This hitherto untitled letter appeared on December 8, 1762, in *Lloyd's Evening Post, or British Chronicle*. It was first attributed to Oglethorpe by Ettinger (*Oglethorpe*, 287). He was probably correct. The signature "Britannicus et Americanus" designates an author who felt himself both a Briton and an American; and the writer dated his letter from Soho, which was Oglethorpe's residence at that time. Moreover the author shows the same mercantilist concerns that Oglethorpe had voiced as early as *The Sailors Advocate* in 1728: the need to develop shipping for the export of colonial raw materials. Oglethorpe's correspondent may have been Lieutenant Governor William Bull, Jr., the son of his deceased friend.

The text is that of *Lloyd's Evening Post*, with two obvious typographical errors silently corrected.

To the EDITOR of LLOYD's EVENING POST.

SIR,

TAKING up the Daily Advertiser of yesterday, at St. James's Coffee House, I was not a little surprized to see the Exportation of the Province of South Carolina so very trifling to what it might, and ought to be, when compared with its annual exportation between the months of December and September. I had scarce got home to my house in Soho, before I received the following letter from a person of the first rank in that province, which, for the publick good, I could not help sending you; this letter was brought me from that province, by the fleet just arrived here.

"THE prospect of great crops still continues as great as when I wrote you last; the hurricane season being now over, we have nothing to prevent its being the richest crop ever known of rice, since the first settlement of the colony. But I am sorry to inform you, we have suffered much already for want of vessels to *convey* it to the European markets; I mean the crops of the last year, which did not exceed seventy thousand barrels of five hundred neat weight, of which number many thousands still lye on our hands. What to do with our present great crops I know not, for should we want ships to take it away, it must perish with us, or be given to the hogs, it being principally rice, which is a perishable commodity in these hot climates. Some few vessels have been here and took in rice for London, and for Cowes, and the markets, at the extravagant freight of eight pounds ten shillings per ton, and by that means it was sold for less than four shillings sterling per hundred weight; nor do I know whether it will turn out to the advantage of the shippers, unless it should bear a proportionable price in Europe, to make amends for the great freight paid here. But the loss falls very heavy on the Planters of the province; for it being so excessively cheap, they cannot clear the expenses yearly incurred by planting, by which means the Merchants here must lye out of their money perhaps double the time they should, consequently must suffer for want *of making* remittances home to the Carolina Merchants of London, who must also be sensible of the great inconvenience attending the want of shipping here, which, in fact, is the very reason they have not the value of their goods, shipped here every year, returned in the commodities of the province annually; for it is well known, if the Planters could vend their produce, they would lay out double the money with the Merchants they do at present, and could always pay them the full price of their goods. I am concerned for the good of the province, and have set the matter so clear to you, that you may know the true state of it; for I am greatly concerned to see any place, where I am so much concerned in public matters, suffer, especially in the station you know I am in, and whose greatest happiness would be to see the province flourish. The crop, it is said, and with the greatest foundation, cannot be less than 150,000 barrels, of 500 weight neat each barrel."

So real and warm a zeal, as my friend here expresses himself, will most certainly excite every lover of his country's interest, and all encouragers of trade and commerce, the bulwark of this kingdom and nation, to remedy the inconvenience and misfortunes attending the want of shipping, and proper vending the produce. Let the rice be shipped to different parts of Germany, and let a number of vessels be sent over, which would lower freight, by which means the province there would reap a competent benefit, returns made properly to the Merchants here, ships have a reasonable freight, and the markets of Great Britain and Germany have it reasonable. The shipping, this bulky commodity would employ constantly, would find employment for great numbers of our sailors and seamen, that now must be discharged from the Royal Navy. This would also be a means of its being sent higher up the Rhine, than it has ever yet been; and the quantity encreasing yearly, and had on reasonable terms, would also invite the Merchants to ship it where it has never yet been sent, to the remoter parts of the European continent. The Province, grown richer by this means, would send yearly larger quantities to Europe, which must all pay a duty in England; which duty, we are very sensible, is far from being inconsiderable to the national advantage, as the duty is high, and no one who deals in that commodity can be insensible of it. But, whilst vessels are wanting to take off the crops, it must be dear throughout England, Holland, Amsterdam, Rotterdam, and other parts, whilst it lies useless to every one in its own clime.

It is also to be much lamented, that we are greater encouragers of the Indigo made in the dominions of France and Spain, than that made in our own dominions; though it is well known, by the trial of some of the best Dyers in England, that the Indigo, of the growth and produce of our colonies of Carolina and Georgia, is equal in goodness to the best French and Spanish; but prejudice, and want of judgment, have given the preference to French and Spanish, to the great hurt of our own interest, in discouraging the colonies. It is to be hoped, the encouragement of hemp will not be as that of the indigo has been. They are now making, in the two above-mentioned colonies, hemp which is equal to the best Russia hemp, as we have already seen by some small quantity sent over this and the last year. This is also a bulky commodity, which would encourage shipping; and, instead of sending our money to foreign countries, we should send it to our own colonies, where we should get it again in return for British commodities.

Soho, Dec. 5,   BRITANNICUS ET
1762.   AMERICANUS.

Three Letters on Corsica (1768)

In May of 1768, in the *Public Advertiser*, Oglethorpe published three letters on Corsica. That same year James Boswell reprinted them in his *British Essays in Favour of the Brave Corsicans*, identifying them, in his own copy, as Oglethorpe's.[1]

To most Englishmen in 1768, Corsica was a romantic island where the virtues of the simple life of Nature held sway—and especially the love of liberty. It suddenly became an object of national concern because of James Boswell. From October 12 to November 20, 1765, Boswell made apparently the first visit of the century by an Englishman to the mountainous interior. There he came to know and admire Pascal Paoli and to appreciate the independent spirit of the Corsicans, who wished to free themselves from both Genoa and France. Boswell hoped to persuade, or force, the British Ministry to disclaim a proclamation of 1763 that condemned the Corsicans as rebels and threatened with the charge of treason any Briton who gave them assistance. Utilizing the newspapers to arouse initial interest in Corsica, he published, early in 1768, his *Account of Corsica, The Journal of a Tour to that Island; and Memoirs of Pascal Paoli*. Boswell's book made the island an object of national concern, and Paoli a hero.

It also brought Boswell and Corsica to the attention of James Oglethorpe. As soon as he learned that the author was in London, Oglethorpe, in Boswell's words, "did me the honour to call on me, and approaching me with a frank courteous air, said, 'My name, Sir, is Oglethorpe, and I wish to be acquainted with you.'"[2] In late April and May Boswell continued to call, apparently to discuss with Oglethorpe the letters that the general was writing for the *Public Advertiser*.[3] For a while Oglethorpe became for Boswell almost a surrogate father. Their collaboration led to the most satisfying aspect of Oglethorpe's later life: his friendship, through Boswell, with the most eminent and interesting literary men of London, such as Goldsmith and Johnson.[4] It was perhaps Boswell's encouragement also that led to Oglethorpe's subsequent series of letters to the press: the Adams letters, the Faber letters, those supporting Lord North, and perhaps others yet unidentified.

In his three letters on Corsica Oglethorpe attempted to demonstrate the invalidity of British isolation of Corsica in the face of French oppression, and he concentrated upon the three issues that Joseph Foladare has named the most effective arguments for British intervention: "the commercial advantages of trade with Corsica, the threat to the balance of power in Europe resulting from French occupation of Corsica, and the consequent danger to all British commerce in the Mediterranean."[5]

Oglethorpe's praise of his first letter in his second, submitted under a different pseudonym, was merely indulging in the conventional practice of "puffing," in which he had already engaged in the preface to *A New and Accurate Account*.

I reprint the Corsican letters as they appear in the *Public Advertiser*, with Boswell's introductory paragraph.

To the Printer of the Public Advertiser.

SIR,

As Corsica is now become an Object of serious Concern to this Nation, it is surely a Subject which should employ a Part of the Attention of your Political Correspondents, and well deserves a distinguished Place in every one of the public Papers of this great, free Country. I send you a Letter from Bristol, which you will see is the Production of no ordinary Writer. It contains strong Facts and solid Reasonings, with such Inferences as I apprehend ought somewhat to alarm such among us as look a little farther than the transient Riots of Home Faction. While we are occupied with intestine Cabals, France is steadily pursuing her enlarged Schemes of Tyranny. I should have made Copies of the enclosed for several of our News-papers; but I hope such of them as are animated with the Spirit of Liberty, will not scruple to transcribe from the Public Advertiser any masterly Essay of such a Tendency as this.

I am, SIR,
A Constant Reader.[6]

SIR. *Bristol, April* 1768.

THE Paragraph in some of the News, that it is reported the French will send an Army to support the Genoese in subduing the Corsicans, hath struck the Trading Part of this City with Terror. We already feel the Loss of Trade by the French Encroachments since the Peace. If under Pretence of helping the Genoese, they should render themselves Masters of Corsica, we must be then totally cut out of the Mediterranean Trade: That Island commands the Coast of Italy and Straits of Bonifaccio, and with the Ports of Sicily, now in the Hands of the Family Contract,[7] totally locks up the Passage to Turkey, and the East of Sicily. The Corsicans are excellent Corsairs; from them the very Name is derived: They would furnish Sailors, which the French Navy want in Time of War, and in Time of Peace. Corsica would give a great Vent to many of their Commodities, and their little Vessels be of great Use in conveying the French Manufactures to the Coast of Barbary, Italy, and the Levant. The Corsicans have Timber, and other Materials cheap, and therefore cheap Freight. The Inconvenience of letting that Island fall to the French is great; but it may be said, how can we hinder them from helping their Allies the Genoese? We answer, that by the Treaty of Peace the French are not to augment their Dominions,[8] and by taking this Island they do so.

But the Frenchified Pensioner will say, they do not intend to take it, but only reduce the Rebel-Subjects of the Genoese to due Subjection to their Sovereign, the State of Genoa.—This is mere quibbling; Genoa itself is in Subjection to France. Do not the Kings of France, even from antient Times, claim Genoa? Did not Genoa in the late War take a Garrison from them? Let even the Frenchified Pensioner himself lay his Hand on his Heart, and ask himself the Question, if he thinks, on a new War's happening, the Genoese would not again favour the Family Contract? He must own, he can't deny that they would. Nay, indeed, they dare not refuse a French Garrison; but so far from refusing, they would beg one, as they did in the former War. It is therefore highly necessary to interfere in Time; but your Bourbonite Pensioner will cry aloud, that it is criminal to support Rebels. In Answer I say, I have not proposed to support Rebels, but only to hinder the French from augmenting their too formidable Monarchy with the Island of Corsica, which would in it's Consequences enable France to drive our Squadrons out of the Mediterranean Seas.

But if I did propose the succouring the valiant Corsicans, I can justify that Proposition. No Englishman can deny that Sovereigns, as well as their Subjects, are bound by the Laws.

On that Maxim Queen Elizabeth acted when she assisted the Flemings and the Hollanders; and on the same the Kings and Parliaments of England acted when they, by continual Support for near a Century, at last enabled them to constitute the free State of the United Provinces;[9] which State helped us to support the Balance of Europe, and maintain our own Liberties from French Slavery.

Did not Queen Elizabeth aid the City of La Rochele, and the Princes against the King of France?[10]

Did not Gustavus of Sweden help the People of Dantzick against the then King of Poland? and Dantzick is under the Polish Monarchy, but hath Privileges. Gustavus, on the Application of the Dantzickers, succoured them.[11]

Did not our late King, and the House of Brandenburg, interfere in protecting the People of Thorn against their Sovereign the King, and Republic of Poland?[12]

Did not the House of Austria support Saint ta Remo against these very Genoese, when they broke in upon their Privileges?[13]

The French cannot deny, that it is the Usage of every Sovereign Power in Europe to interfere in Support of the Privileges of their neighbouring People. It is according to the Law of Nature and Nations. If a neighbouring Prince turns a limited into a despotic Government, it affects all his Neighbours; for a limited Monarch cannot, by his Ambition, do so much Mischief to his Neighbours as when rendered despotic. The Privileges, and Power of his People, will hinder his entering into offensive Wars; but despotic Tyrants can use the whole Force of their People, to the Destruction of their Neighbours.

With what Face can the French object to our assisting the Corsicans against the Genoese, who have broke through all their Privileges, and all the Laws of Humanity; when the French Kings assisted the Catallans against Philip and the People of Messina; and the People of Naples against their undoubted Sovereigns the Kings of Spain? The French also assisted the Duke of Braganza to become King of Portugal. And have they not lately interfered and assisted the Magistrates (whose Term was expired) against the People of Geneva, who are the Sovereigns?[14]

I am, SIR,
Your humble Servant,
An ENGLISH MERCHANT.

To the Printer of the Public Advertiser.

SIR,

I SAW a letter from Bristol in your Paper of the 3d inst. which, with great Propriety and Spirit, demonstrates the Damage England would sustain from Corsica's falling into the Hands, or under the Influence of France. That Letter has only showed the Damage to England; but this is far from being the greatest Evil which must follow such an Acquisition to France; it would justly alarm Mankind, for it must affect the Independency of every Sovereign in Europe, and facilitate the universal Monarchy which the House of Bourbon has so long pursued.

Your Bristol Correspondent hath demonstrated, that the Acquisition of Corsica will make France Mistress of the Mediterranean; now from thence follows that France, being safe on that Side, will be able to double her Efforts against Germany and Holland.

The Diversions caused by our Fleets aiding in the Attacks on Thoulon, have more than once distracted the Arms of France, and made abortive her ambitious Projects; but the Acquisition of Corsica will for ever make her safe in that most tender Part.

The Strength for Defence of the Coasts of Provence and Languedoc, and the Squadron at Thoulon, is always computed in the State of France at 60,000 Men; but after this Event 7,000 would be more than sufficient for that Service; so they might have 53,000 Men more to assist in destroying Germany.

Europe felt too fatally in the late War the cruel Impressions the French Forces made in the Empire; and had 53,000 Men been added to their Army, the Consequence would probably have been very dreadful.

Not only Germany, but Holland would soon feel the Effect attending the Encrease of French Power; for if the Mediterranean were theirs, the Dutch must hold their Trade to Turkey, Italy, and the Levant, at the precarious Will of a French Minister, and not only their Foreign Trade, but their Liberty and Independency would be in the greatest Danger.

Should France once feel that she hath an absolute Superiority in Germany (which we have above shown, Success in this Measure will give her) she would then no Doubt display her Moderation.

Denmark also, whose Commerce by her Monarch's Attention to it is greatly encreased, will be affected in Point of her Trade; so will Sweden, Hamborough much more. Venice will be rendered entirely dependent on the French, when they have a decided Superiority in the Mediterranean, and have all to fear from the Interest their antient Rivals, the Genoese, will have with the French Ministry. As for the King of Sardinia, he will be most immediately affected; Fleets in the Ports of Provence and Corsica entirely cut off all Communication from Villa Franca and Nice, his only Ports, and renders the Assistance of English Squadrons most dangerous and precarious; so that not only Sardinia must be lost on the first Efforts of a War, but Piedmont will be open on the Side of Genoa, as Savoy is on the Side of France, and the Benefit of the Barrier, which the Alps makes, will be useless. From Corsica or France every Wind will carry Forces to Lerichy, or the Riviera de Genoa; and Armies can from thence march to Turin without passing the Alps.

France makes use of every Acquisition to encrease her Fleets and Armies. When the Father of Corruption was Minister, and slept over the Helm of State, Britain perceived not that France had acquired Loraine.[15]

When Patriots complained of Sir Robert for suffering it, his venal Tribe cried, "Lord, what a Trifle is that! It has no Sea-port, no Trade; what signifies Loraine?" But France put it under such Regulations as that it furnishes and supports Recruits of 30,000 Men, that is to say, it adds 30,000 Men to her Armies.—If she should acquire Corsica, we may easily conceive what Advantages she would gain by considering what Strength that Island now has. The Free Corsicans are about 200,000 Souls, of which 40,000 are able to bear Arms, and are enrolled; besides which, in the Territories under the Genoese there are 25,000 Souls, about 5,000 fit to bear Arms, besides their regular Troops.—[16] You see by this what a Number of fighting Men this Island would add to France, and as they are Islanders, and mostly employed in fishing, and other Sea-Services, they would contribute to the augmenting their Number of Sailors; an Article they must aspire to, and want greatly.

MONITOR.

To the Printer of the Public Advertiser.

SIR, *Bristol, May 5, 1768.*
IN my last I gave the Alarm on the Danger we are in from the French getting Corsica; I tolled the Bell that stronger Hands might come in and ring a Peal; and I find I was not mistaken by an Introduction, wrote with great Energy and Judgement, which was prefixed in your's. I knew no other Way of Access to the Great but by your Paper. They read it, and I hope these Letters in your's will give them Notice, their Wisdom will then cause them to enquire, and on finding the Evil, they will procure the Remedy.

Many of the most successful Measures taken by Government have arisen from Hints given in the Public Papers; and I hope you may be as successful in preserving Corsica, as Mr. Trenchard and the Craftsman were in saving Gibraltar after Lord Carteret had sent the famous Letter, giving Hopes of delivering it up to the Spaniards.[17] That was a glorious Rescue of a most important Place; but that Place, and Minorca too, will be useless if Corsica should be under French Influence.

I endeavoured to shew in my last how injurious and dangerous such an Acquisition, made by France, would be to his Majesty the King of Great-Britain, his Power and Dignity.

I shall in this shew more at large what great Advantages may arise from cultivating the Trade to Corsica.

The chief Objection is, that the Corsicans are Outlaws and Rebels; the Genoese call them so; but Men must not always be believed in their own Cause. — Let us hear the Corsicans. They say, and swear too, that they are no Rebels nor Outlaws, but a free People; and that the Genoese are Tyrants that have robbed, murdered, and assassinated many of their Nation, and would be Usurpers if they would let them.

A trading Nation doth not, nor cannot enter into the Character of those they trade with. Mr. Wilkes was an Outlaw; but have the Taverns refused to draw Wine for him? or a Shoemaker or Draper to sell him Shoes or Cloth for his ready Money?[18] The Pope is a very sad Fellow, and we burn him along with the Devil once a Year,[19] yet we trade to Civita-Vecchia. Tunis and Algiers are Pirate States, yet we keep Consuls, and trade with those Pirates and Infidels. The King of Prussia was put under the Ban by the late Emperor, that is, was declared a Rebel and an Outlaw; yet that was so far from hindering our trading with him, that the Nation gave him 600,000 l. yearly to make up for the unjust Treatment he received from French Influence.

Meer Jaffier was a Rebel to the great Mogul, the tyrannical Usurper of India. Jaffier was a Traitor to the Tyrant in whose Service he was, and whom he forsook in Fight, and yet Clive was made a Lord for helping this double Rebel Jaffier.[20]

For my Part, I find no Scruple in trading to the free Corsicans; they have dealt very honourably with my Factors at Leghorn, and paid in Goods when Money was scarce, for they chiefly trade by Barter.

If French Troops should be in the Island, there is an End of our Trade, and the French will acquire the many Hundred Thousands of Pounds a Year, which we might acquire if that Trade was open.

Now these free Corsicans invite us to trade with them. The Island produces excellent Wine, famous even in the Roman Times. There are various Sorts; some is extremely luscious and strong. They have also Oil, Bees-Wax, and several other Articles, very beneficial. They give good Prices for Hard-Ware and Cloathing of all Kinds, Turnery, and almost every Commodity, as they have no Manufactures; and so much the better for the Vent of our Goods. They make nothing but a Kind of coarse Rugs, with which their Poor are cloathed, and some fine Guns and Gun-powder.

They have about 200,000 Inhabitants, who, if they only consume Two Pounds Value one with the other of our Manufactures, it would make a

Vent of 400,000l. a Year; no small Object at a Time when all our Manufactures lie on our Hands for Want of Markets, and the poor Manufacturers starve, or run away for Want of Employment.

I myself know a good deal of Corsica; my Agents at Leghorn are still better acquainted with it;[21] nor is that Island unknown to the learned World, as there is a modern Account of it, highly approved by them.

I do not doubt, Sir, but by your Means the governing Part of this Kingdom will be acquainted with the Interest of the Commercial Part, and that they will procure for us a free and open Trade to Corsica, and thereby acquire the Blessings of many Thousands, as well as the highest Reputation.

I am, SIR,
Your humble Servant,
AN ENGLISH MERCHANT.

The Adams Letters (1773–1774)

The four Adams letters appeared in the *Morning Chronicle* on November 10 and 25, 1773, December 22, 1773, and January 25, 1774.[1] The first of the four was attributed to Oglethorpe by Phinizy Spalding, quoting Boswell's response after he received a copy in a letter from the general: "I am clear that I recognise the *heart* of General Oglethorpe."[2] Apparently Oglethorpe did not send the three subsequent Adams letters to Boswell, perhaps because he assumed that the Scot could easily find the principal English newspapers in Edinburgh. Boswell's ascription does not guarantee that the letters were actually written by the general. Nevertheless they seem to be Oglethorpe's. To ensure the perpetuation of the small farms offered by the Georgia Trustees, he had insisted that each should be inherited by the oldest male heir. In 1773, moreover, the topic of luxury and consequent depopulation seems to have been one of his favorite topics. This was apparently the principal topic discussed when Oglethorpe entertained Boswell, Dr. Johnson, and Goldsmith on April 13, 1773, and again on April 27, 1773. On that occasion Oglethorpe "harangued on the mischiefs of enclosing, by depopulating."[3]

As for the signature, it should evidently be read as "Adam's"—a descendant and emulator of Adam: "When Adam delved and Eve span / Who was then the gentleman?" On December 24, 1773, a derivative letter appeared in the *Morning Chronicle* from "A Son of Adam."

The Adams letters concern a problem that had plagued England since the middle of the century—the enclosure of common land by private acts of Parliament for the benefit of wealthy and influential landowners. Whether enclosure was economically necessary, as many contemporary politicians then asserted and as most economists today allege,[4] was not Oglethorpe's issue. In his last letter he admitted that enclosure if properly managed would benefit the nation. But he was concerned that enclosure as it was then practiced, unrestricted, led only too often to the destitution of those whom enclosure dispossessed. Here Oglethorpe placed himself with such a humanitarian as Oliver Goldsmith, whose *Deserted Village* he praises. Whether Oglethorpe's letters had any effect in Parliament is uncertain, but parliamentary restrictions upon enclosure began during the year in which the last letter appeared.

My text is that of the *Morning Chronicle*.

For the MORNING CHRONICLE.

To the KING.

LETTER I.

SIRE,

MUCH has been said, and many letters have appeared, on the subject I intend to pursue in the following course of my address to your Majesty. Truly sensible that you mean to be *a father to your people*, to remove every obstacle to *their* happiness, I have chosen rather to apply to you than to the ear of an inattentive or intrusted Minister. I would wish to turn your attention to the plain tale of a plain man. I would hope, that if, in the course of explaining my meaning, I make use of terms your Majesty may think *harsh*, that you will impute it to the warmth of my zeal for my country and not from any disrespect to a King I sincerely honour.

Your Majesty, as a man of letters,[5] has no doubt read Dr. Goldsmith's amiable poem of the "Deserted Village."[6] On the cause of that desertion I mean to address you. I mean to endeavour, to shew that the basis of that poem is *truth*, and to point out the particular means which have been the cause of that general emigration from the country, and the cause of the capital being filled with objects of distress and nuisance. When I have done that, I will point out the means of restoring agriculture, and of *re peopling the now deserted country*. I hope to carry conviction with me, as I will advance nothing but facts; and then you, who wish to be *the best of Kings*, will listen to my advice, and remove what now threatens to destroy your country, and fill your capital with wretches (through misery) ripe for every mischief. Formerly, a man, with a wife, and perhaps seven or eight healthy children, occupied a small cottage on an extensive common, where by right he could feed a few sheep, rear a few calves and poultry; and his wife *keep the market*, and reasonably sell the produce of his labour; his children (useful members of society) assisted the neighbouring farmers; and content and happiness crowned their labours. In this situation the man of power and interest finds him, and perhaps dispersed over the common twenty more families, who all equally contribute to render labour and provisions reasonable. From a mistaken notion that the *inclosing* this common will operated for the public good, he applies for the *inclosure*, obtains it, and beggars every family on the spot. The parents, unable any longer to obtain a subsistence, either perish miserably, or betake them to a parish workhouse. The children, if boys, seek for refuge in London, and either are enticed to America, or become a public nuisance in the streets; and after insulting magistracy by every desperate act, are made terrible examples of the justice of that law they violate. The daughters, an easy prey to vice, infest our streets, and, by way of revenge, communicate disease on, perhaps, the authors of their misfortune. The markets, deprived of those who used to bring them a constant supply, become thin; the *single farm*, raised on the ruins of twenty, has a master whose fortune enables him to feed the market as he pleases; *he will have his price, or he will not sell at all;* he knows he engrosses every commodity, and that necessity must yield to his demand. Not so, when the honest smaller dealers, anxious to support their families in the necessaries (not the luxuries) of life, endeavoured to undersel each other, that they might obtain a reasonable profit, and hasten home to their expecting families. *The Gentleman Farmer* wants not this; his price is fixed; and as he knows the necessity, encreases his demand; his fortune will enable him to run the risque of loss, and his family are not in want.

To what can all this be owing, but the great number of inclosures? The poor farmer has no vote in the House, else they would not have passed so tamely. Every sessions produces miseries, and your Majesty (*misguided*) puts the cruel fiat.[7] How much better must it be (and here let me apply to your interest) to have, within the space of 300 acres, thirty loyal, healthy subjects, than one single family, consisting at most of seven or eight, and to have your country markets supplied by people who *must sell*, than by those who *will sell only at their own price?* The rage of inclosing, too much encouraged, is the foundation of these evils. By these wretches, made desperate by distress, you are insulted in public, and their friends and relations curse you in private; your poor are starving, your markets empty; and your verging the miserable alternative of being *very poor*, or *very rich*, either aristocracy or despotism must be the consequence. From the first, good Lord deliver you! and from the last deliver the nation! For remember this, if you put all power into the hands of your *Barons*, what has happened in *former* reigns may happen *now*.[8] Endeavour to preserve the middling sort of people in their independency, as the strongest support of your crown, and enrage them no further by giving your consent to inclosures; the fallacy of which shall be the subject of my future letters to expose, and from facts to prove, that every assertion I make is founded in *truth*.

I am, Sire,
Your Majesty's
Most faithful subject,
ADAMS.

For the MORNING CHRONICLE.
LETTER II.
To the KING.

SIRE,

THAT those who solicit for enclosures are wrong, I promised in my last to endeavour to shew, that I would try to convince them, that they had not acted for their own interest, and that every line I in future wrote, should be founded in fact. I mean to keep my word, hoping that the royal ear, ever open to redress real grievances, will not be shut to so plain a tale as I shall endeavour to lay down.

I some time ago saw a letter in this paper signed *Hants*, complaining that the farmers could not go to church, without being upbraided by the parson, as the cause of the dearness of corn, by not bringing it to market. I cannot help thinking the honest parson wrong; he mistook the real cause. How can the farmer be supposed to grow the same quantity of corn he did in former years, when his farm is let to him on the condition of laying a certain portion of it down in grass? he is debarred the use of the plough, and how is he then to be able to supply the market with corn? Some years ago, before the rage of inclosing took place, the corn produced in the distant counties bore such an average to the price in London, as made it worth the farmer's while to send it up to the London market, thereby amply supplying the capital. Importation was not then necessary, but now, when almost every farm in the distant counties is injured by the *enclosures*, when not a third part of the corn is raised, it throws the London market into the hands of a set of men who make the basest use of it; no longer curbed by the corn being sent from the inland counties, they are left at liberty to make every advantage of importation, and raise the market at their pleasure. The farms in these counties have been, and are so disadvantageously let, that few if any can succeed. They raise but very little corn, and what they now do raise, becomes not worth their while to send to the London market, indeed scarcely supplies the want of the country round them. As a proof of which, it sells even at their own country market for two shillings per bushel, or nearly that sum upon an average, *more* than it will fetch at London. The printed prices of corn published in the Daily Papers, will sufficiently prove this.

Another misfortune which has arisen from these inclosures is, that even the number of cattle that used to be raised on these commons are much decreased. Let any man say, who used to travel the country, whether, instead of seeing 4 or 5000 sheep, and a number of other cattle, on these commons and fields before inclosed, he sees now more than perhaps as many hundreds, and those obliged to be sent to he market, (and by that means fall into the hands of the engrossers) to make up their rents, for rent the landlord must and will have. Our fields now, instead of being covered with the necessaries of life, are *encumbered* with a useless breed of horses, bred either to support our own luxuries, or to be sold to our enemies to use against ourselves. Corn,[9] the natural produce of our soil is neglected; cattle, the necessaries of life, our farmers are disencouraged from breeding, and the enclosures are filled with nothing but horses, which tho' they bring profit to individuals, can never be of any real benefit to the nation at large. How then can our great men be so wilfully blind to the natural good of their country? Would they but encourage the raising corn, and breeding cattle, with the same avidity they do that of horses, how much more profitable (and I will prove it really so) would it be to them? Plenty might once more be seen in the country, and our now "deserted villages," be once more peopled. Suppose only the profit of raising the necessaries of life, and that of horses equal, yet let them consider how many more hands are employed in the one than in the other, and let them reflect how many families they may sustain by raising the one, when to raise the other a servant or two is only necessary. We have many well meaning men among the great, who want only to be convinced; some already are, and may their example have the wished effect!

Some little time since, I had a conversation with a gentleman, from whose discourse I gathered, that he had some connection with the Duke of Marlborough;[10] he seemed to intimate that his Grace had seen his error, and was determined to let his estates in smaller farms, and encourage by every means the use of the plough, and the breed of cattle. If his Grace does so, a few years will convince him of the truth of my assertions. He will see plenty once more smile on his estates; they will be peopled, and that not with wretches worn out with misery, ready to raise commotions at every turn, and offend those laws that prevent them from a maintenance, but with a set of honest, industrious men, and their families, contentedly raising the necessaries of life, and happy in themselves. Should this method be adopted by those in power, the number of useful subjects would be increased; husbandry encouraged, and the capital not be so pestered with country vagabonds; in the country every member of the family is useful, but send that family to London, and they become pests to society: it is therefore your Majesty's interest, as the Father of your People, to keep them there, and to have a number of subjects contentedly pursuing their own business, rather than have a number of desperate wretches, insulting you in public, and in private plotting every mischief.

I am, SIRE,
Your Majesty's most faithful subject,
ADAMS.

For the MORNING CHRONICLE.

To the KING.

LETTER III.

SIRE,

DETERMINED at every leisure hour to pursue a subject that, in my poor opinion, must redound to the happiness and ease of your people, as well as to the honour of yourself; your plain subject pursues, as he promised, his plain tale. In my last I think I proved that the breeding horses, instead of cattle, were prejudicial to this kingdom: would it not then be certainly better to stop the exportation of them, at least till there was in this kingdom a proper and sufficient stock of store cattle raised? Our enemies would not then be able to fight us on any future war with our own horses, and the kingdom you govern would not be, as now, starving for want of food; we have had the blessing of the Heaven's mild winters and plentiful summers, yet we complain of want of provisions: where can this want arise? I endeavour to point it out; read then, I humbly beseech your Majesty, these letters with attention; they may shew the means of obtaining plenty, peace, and happiness, and I am sure you wish them to be obtained.

The gentry have been at a great expence in inclosing; they might make them useful, but as they now manage, they only help to starve us, and throw both country and capital into confusion: they should lessen their farms, and plough up at least two parts in three of the old usually ploughed land, instead of laying it down for grass. It always must be admitted, that three inclosed acres will produce as much corn as four acres in a common field, and what with the old land being ploughed up as well as the former, the useless, barren, common land, producing corn, clover, or other fodder;

they might make three acres produce as much as six before inclosed; they might still feed as many useful cattle as might be sufficient for the consumption of the kingdom, or even more. The farmer will then have a sufficient stock to supply the market, and be better able to pay his rent; he will have it in his power to employ more hands; the labourer need not then seek a miserable shelter in a workhouse, or, what is worse, in London; dairying would revive, and notwithstanding the seeming encreased expence for labour, the profits would more than equal it, and happiness and content would return again to the door of the cottager. But this can never be done unless the farms are lessened; two hundred pounds per annum ought to be the largest; if smaller, it would still be the better.

And here let me intreat your Majesty to consider the petty deputy tyrant of a county, the original landlord, for the sake of letting one farm for more than he could do when divided into twenty, consents to the suffering one man to rent the whole; this man has but one family, and the other nineteen must remove from the spot, because they become needless on it; how nearly approaching to aristocracy is this, and where will be your power and authority supported, if you thus negligently depopulate your country, and create, by suffering inclosures, a set of absolute tyrants, who deprive you by every inclosure of a number of useful subjects? The Duke of Marlborough, I am informed (to his credit) is so sensible of this, that he is determined to lessen his farms; nay surely the example of that worthy man, Sir George Savile, in Ireland,[11] would be a sufficient lesson, his tenants there are numerous and well supplied with all the necessaries of life; they have not joined the rioters, but are happy and contented; can this arise from any other than a conviction that his method is right? his farms are small, the culture of the country is considered, and plenty and peace are the consequence.

The Dutch who formerly only occasionally supplied our markets, now become every year necessary to us; 'tis a melancholy truth that, happen but a scarce season, and without importation, we starve; will they not take advantage of our indolence, and from factors become the masters of our markets? Those counties which formerly had large numbers of ricks,[12] which on an unfavourable season they would have thrashed out, and supplied the markets, now have few or none; and what must be the consequence of a real scarcity, your own good sense can too easily foresee: discourage then the breed of horses, stop inclosing (unless under certain limitations) and you may restore your subjects to their homes, and your nation to plenty; the contrary you have experienced in part, and may your wisdom and love for the people, prevent the dreadful alternative of perishing by famine, or violating the laws.

I am, Sire,
Your most faithful subject,
ADAMS.

For the MORNING CHRONICLE.
To the KING.
LETTER IV.

SIRE,
THAT your Majesty's wisdom may prevent your people from the dreadful alternative of perishing by famine, or for violating the laws, is my most sincere wish; to prevent it my endeavour; in which attempt I still persevere, and continue a series of letters, which I hope will, one time or other, meet your Royal attention; and that the King who wishes to be the Father of his people, will one day listen to the advice of a faithful subject.

That inclosing would be of service to the public, *if properly managed*, there is no doubt; it would employ more poor people, especially if plowed, and be worth more in proportion than before inclosed; but not if managed as now, when the breed of horses destroy that provender, which ought to be preserved for the more useful part of the creation. Was the land inclosed to be parcelled into small farms, and a certain portion of the farm tied down by the lease to be plowed, we must have a larger quantity of corn at market, the lesser farmer would breed more sheep, more oxen, more calves, and more poultry than the larger farmer, and, of consequence, the larger number of them being brought to market, would lessen the price.

Our men of property deceive themselves; anxious only to squeeze from their tenants a certain yearly sum, that they may figure in the greater splendor at the Pantheon, Ranelagh, and the more infa— s C— 's.[13] They neglect the proper management of their estates, and delegate their power to a steward, who, as I said before, is the Deputy Tyrant of a county, he must furnish his master with a yearly sum, and if he can squeeze more, it is his own. Honesty and industry has no chance here; the farms of 500, 600, or 1000l. a year, are taken by men whose payment is certain, because their property enables them to keep up the markets and sell at their own price. The landlord here is well paid; but the poor have the price of provisions set above their reach: they may complain, but their refuge is a parish workhouse. Now, were but the farms reduced to 100l. 150l. or even 200l. a year, and one half of it plowed, it would enable the small farmer to pay his rent as well as the larger, and I will maintain it, that one small farm, the smaller farm, would bring, in the course of a year, more useful, necessary provisions to market, than one of a 1000l. a year It would not answer for a small farmer to breed more horses than what might be necessary for his own use; or if he did, it would only be of that sort which are really useful, not a set of creatures bred and kept for the use of luxury only, who eat the bread of idleness, and consume that provinder which would suffice to maintain those animals, whose flesh the poor of our days seldom get the taste of. His wife (not the luxurious pride of the village, whose Sunday dress creates the envy of the poor) would not be above the management of the dairy; she would sell her own produce, keep the market herself, and in consequence sell cheaper than when she delegates the honor of selling, to a servant. Her family, instead of seeking a supply of clothes from London, would be contented with what they met with at a country town. Pride and ostentation would set far from her door, and while she sold by retail her wholesome provisions, she would in her bargains feel for the distresses of the poor. Not so the unfeeling larger farmer, who contracts by wholesale with the London dealers; he feels for no distress, his fortune prevents him from being sensible of misery, and he considers not how many families he starves, if he returns but the gain into his own pocket.

From what I have now said, let your Majesty judge, if I do not set the misery of the poor in a fair light? If inclosing ought to be suffered, unless tied down to parcel the inclosure out into small farms? If the breed of horses ought to be encouraged, and whether the breed of the more useful cattle ought to be neglected? Your Majesty's wisdom will tell you the contrary*. I have endeavoured to point out the means of prevention; may it succeed: if not, I have done my duty, as your Majesty's sincere well wisher.

And I am, Sire,
Your Majesty's most faithful subject,
ADAMS.

Jan. 21, 1774.

---

*Your Majesty will please to observe, that on the trial of the late unfortunate Cox,[14] a person appeared as an evidence there, who acknowledged himself an agent from the King of France, to procure horses for remounting the French cavalry.

The Faber Letters (1778)

Oglethorpe's Faber letters were first ascribed to Oglethorpe by Phinizy Spalding.[1] At least two Faber letters, copies of which the general sent to Boswell, were published in *Bingley's Journal*, apparently on April 7 and 14, 1778, and others may have followed.[2] They embody many of the same charges that Oglethorpe made in his letter to Boswell on March 21, 1778, where he also accused the members of Parliament, the "Westminster Boys," of rapine and bribery.[3]

As with "Adams," the "Faber" signature was probably intended as generic, recalling the Latin *faber*—"workman" or "artisan." The subscription "An old Antigallican" points towards France exclusively, although the Bourbons occupied the Spanish throne as well as the French and were united by the Family Compact. The term "antigallican" had been used by various writers since midcentury and by a London club since about 1755; and the Oglethorpe booksale catalog (item 498) shows *Letters relating to the Antigallican Privateer* (1758). Oglethorpe may have by "old" suggested a longtime conviction, or he may have merely recognized his own age—eighty-one.

Oglethorpe may have sent his letters to a paper with a limited circulation because Bingley had elicited his sympathy. Because the editor had continued John Wilkes's antiministerial *North Briton*, he had been imprisoned for two years, without trial, in the King's Bench Prison, with which Oglethorpe was of course quite familiar. Indeed Bingley had published his newspaper from the prison.

The Faber letters develop the apparently simplistic premise that England's divisions all stemmed from plots of the Bourbons. Oglethorpe could not indict the French people, although he had fought against them under Frederick the Great.[4] His closest family ties were in France and that part of Savoy which was soon to become part of France—with his sister Eleanor's family (Mézières), his sister Louisa Mary's (Bassompierre), and his sister Francis Charlotte's (Bellegarde); and it was to a French nephew that he was to will his estate.

Doubtless Oglethorpe overstated his case. George III apparently believed that he could maintain a peaceful coexistence with France; and many members of Parliament clung to the ideal of an *entente cordiale*. But Oglethorpe's suspicions of French espionage and English venality were not the fancies of an elderly paranoid. He had grown up in a family devoted to undercover activity on behalf of the Old Pretender, and he doubtless occasionally served as their youthful courier. Under the notorious transvestite the Chevalier d'Eon and the famous dramatist Beaumarchais,[5] the French secret service had recently become remarkably active and proficient in England.

The charge of bribery is more complex. It was in the interest and purpose of the French to keep out of power their chief adversary, William Pitt, while they prepared for what seemed to them an inevitable conflict. Pitt's supporters were in a small minority; and of those who opposed him, few were overly scrupulous about accepting Gallic gifts, apparently ignoring the old proverb *Timeo Danaos et dona ferentis*. The legal definition of bribery at the time was restricted to characterize venal judges; and a form of bribery was apparently a way of life for the administration and Parliament.[6] Members of Parliament usually obtained their seats through the bribery of voters—in gifts and entertainment—and they expected to be compensated. Those who opposed administrative and parliamentary bribery were few and far between. When Edmund Burke exposed the unscrupulous Warren Hastings for his wholesale peculations in India, few in the House of Lords even bothered to vote, and those who did, acquitted him.

The Cat let out of the Bag.
To the ANTIGALLICANS.
NUMBER I.
(*To be continued.*)

T*HE mine*, at which the French have long laboured, is sprung. But I must excuse myself for charging the French nation, who are a gay and agreeable people, with the crimes of their oppressors, the *Bourbonites:*[7] it is these who are the instruments of that tyranny, which has for *ages* oppressed France, and tore Europe to pieces by cruel wars.

The whole attention of the *Bourbonites*, ever since they bought the *peace*, has been by artifice to get what they could not obtain by arms.

Delenda Carthago was the maxim of the *Romans*,[8] and pursued, in spite of defeats, for ages, till they extirpated the *Carthaginian* race and *language*.

Destroy England has been the maxim of the tyrants over the Frenchmen, from the *Philips* and *Charles's*, of *Valois*, to the *Lewis's*, of the *Bourbon race*. This they have uniformly pursued; and always baffled in arms, by treachery and intrigues, have regained what they lost by open war.

The same influence by which they obtained the last *peace* of Paris,[9] they exerted to gain an ascendant in our Councils. They bribed all our under clerks that would submit to be corrupted; they flattered and deceived the great; they spread the enchantment of pleasure, the net by which they caught the youth; and plaid off the passions of the aged statesman against each other. They sent legions of friseurs and dancers amongst the women; and pimps, taylors, and cooks, dispersed themselves into all the rich families; and by this means the Bourbonite ministers maintain spies, and make us pay them.

The first use the Bourbonites made of their influence, was driving out their much-dreaded Mr. Pitt. They hired all the scriblers they could get, to set the people of England against our most useful ministers, and the King's truest friends. They infatuated the then new Ministry, and made them disoblige the King of *Prussia*, the *House of Brunswick*,[10] and all the *Protestant German Princes*, who zealously assisted us in the war. They made a cat's foot of Grenville,[11] and he cut off and refused to pay the forage, &c. furnished by those princes to our troops in the utmost necessity. They also put the mad idea of a great financier in his head, suggested the stamp act, stirred up the avarice of his heart against the Americans, which leven of avarice remaining in the offices, has brought on our present distress. They turned their arts against all who had been dangerous to them in the war. They by intrigues made a revolution in *Russia*, and took away the life of Peter the IIId. for having assisted our allies.

The army which had done such wonders in America, was an object they thought it their interest to destroy; their under-hand arts prevailed on Ministry to send them to *East Florida*, and somber unhealthy climates, where the most part perished.[12]

By the same arts they set the Ministry on tireing out, or opposing every great man, who had or could be useful to us; even the universally admired and beloved Granby, Conway, and Hawke,[13] the conquerors at Minden and sea, were tired out of employment.

They set on their hireling Grub-street scriblers to defame *Clive;* they set Burgoyne to spout at him in the House of Commons.[14] The glorious contrast! These got Lord George, of *Minden*,[15] to be Director of the War in America; and the pompous orator, Burgoyne, to be General of the army from *Canada*, and now he gives balls at Boston.[16]

George, well-known to Prince Ferdinand, of Brunswick; and Burgoyne, that had abused and attacked Clive in Parliament—Clive, who with not 400 English, and a few Indians, had scattered an army of 60,000 men, brought millions of money to the nation, and revenged the tortures of the Black-Hole, on the black tyrant Soubah.[17] Burgoyne has shook the senate; and now a prisoner, he gives balls at Boston.

Brethren

You see by this, that the Bourbonites, whom you so nobly opposed, and have often disappointed in their designs of ruining us, have again brought us to the edge of destruction. By you the nation was roused, and you assisted Mr. Pitt's efforts. France's projects were overturned, and Europe, America, and India, were saved from their claws. Let us again rouze the nation, and assist in persuading *Chatham* to take the pilotage, and steer the realm into a port of safety; and let us strain every nerve to support our country.

I am,
Your humble servant,
R. FABER,
An old Antigallican.

FOR BINGLEY'S JOURNAL.

NUMBER II.

To the ANTIGALLICANS.

The Cat let out of the Bag.

Brethren,

THE *Bourbonite hirelings* are in the highest agitation, and terrified at the glorious spirit of reconciliation, which shews itself on the hopes of *Chatham*'s advice being followed with perseverance. They dread the rage of united Britons; and to prevent it, they spout all their venom. They disguise themselves under every shape; some as advocates for liberty, some as zealous friends to the King, some as Dissenters; but all drive the main point, which is blowing up divisions, and hindering measures being determined and pursued.

In one of the morning papers* there was an excellent letter, which shewed the writer perfectly acquainted with the secret measures of the Bourbonites, and their dark artifices, and well he may, for he shews himself one. He speaks of the steps taken after the infamous *peace*, "to this purpose, their mercenary writers and runners, of whom legions were every where employed, gave out, that we were ruined by our successes, disgraced by triumphs, and beggared by the greatness of our acquisitions. They villainously propagated that the war was ruinous, destructive, and bloody."[18] All this to degrade our victories, and the great Minister who conducted us to them. It is true, the war was destructive, ruinous, and bloody, but it was so to the Bourbonites, whose ambition and eternal usurpations made it necessary.

The above-quoted excellent paper flowed from the direction of the Bourbonites; for with all these bold truths against Ministry, he drives at the main point of our enemies, the dividing us; he throws on the Scots and Tories the measures which the Bourbonites directed; by this he blows up rage between Britons. Nothing shews more the deep arts of the Bourbonites in disguise than this instance, where their hireling wears the mask of a patriot.

*In the Gazetteer, March 30, signed *"A Plain Dealer."*

With respect to the Scots, they furnish numbers of the most valuable men, and the nation in general valiant and hardy. The landed gentlemen of England, and the country people through the kingdom, and in London too, were mostly Tories whilst the spirit of parties lasted; but the nonsense of parties ended when *Mr. Pitt* received the direction of the *State*, under George the Second. The reviving those odious distinctions are the fruits not of Scots or Tories, but of Bourbon influence. The same who were corrupted to make the peace, were obliged to follow the directions of the Bourbonites, in whose hands their lives were, since they could at any time prove the money they had bribed them with. From that time the Bourbon influence has been as strong in England as in France. It is that influence there made the gang here follow such measures as have divided America from us, has urged a distinction between Whig and Tory, between cyder and malt counties, churchman and Presbyterian, England and Scotland, England and Ireland; every man who helps to enflame differences, is doing the business of Bourbon, and must be esteemed a Bourbonite hireling, or a fool who does their scavengers work, without finding the gold.

Another laboured point of the Bourbonites, is to frighten us, and make us believe we have no strength. Their strongest argument is, you did not shew your strength; the reason is, their influence blinded us. This appears strongly in one instance. The militia, by the present mode of raising it, is not poor thirty thousand men. The strength of England was tried and known when Ministers had sense, and knew how to use the strength of the nation.

Chamberlayne's exact account is an abstract from the records and returns now in the Tower, and shews our ancestors knew how to make use of the strength of England. It is worth while to look seriously at the act for the militia, the 12th of Charles the IId. And at

Angliæ Notitia.

By EDWARD CHAMBERLAYNE.

The Eighth Edition.

Printed in the Savoy, 1674. Part II. p. 160.

"*There is the standing militia by land.*"

These are commonly called the train-bands of every county, whereof the number is so great, that in only five of the bigger counties of England there are to be found well provided 40,000 able, lusty men, ready to assist the King upon all occasions, so that in all times of peace the King hath 140,000 men enrolled, and wholly and solely at his disposing, for the defence of his kingdom of England.

P. 161. In 1588, upon expectation of the Spanish Armada, stiled Invincible, there went forth from the Queen's Commissions to muster in all parts of England, all men that were of perfect sense and limb, from the age of sixteen to sixty, except noblemen, clergymen, University students, lawyers, officers, and such as had any public charges, leaving only in every parish so many husbandmen as were sufficient to till the ground.

In all these musters there were then numbered three millions; but of those fit for war, about six hundred thousand.

In another muster of Queen Elizabeth, there were found in all England fit for war, of common soldiers, about 400,000, and of those armed, and trained 185,000, besides horse near 40,000; and that the nobility and gentry were then able to bring into the field, of their servants and followers 20,000 men, horse and foot, choice men, and excellent horses, and in all fit for war, and ready upon all occasions 642,000, leaving sufficient to till the ground and to furnish trades, besides nobility, gentry, &c.[19]

The numbers of the men in the realm, I fear, are lessened by the acts of oppression, made by the Bourbonite hirelings at Westminster; but you see there are men enough; there are also ships, arms, and provisions enough, not only to defend Britain and Ireland, but even to penetrate into the heart of France.

The wisdom to create unanimity and obedience, and to use that obedience towards preserving the King, and the liberties and properties of the people, and the constitution in church and state, is only wanting.

The scripture says, "A poor wise man saved the city."[20] We know Lord Chatham is not rich, because he would not plunder. As for his wisdom, let his actions answer, and the opinion of the nation.

His Majesty's goodness, we may hope, will be prevailed on by the prayers of the nation, to use the wisdom and experience of this Peer, whom Providence has still preserved, able to assist in this perplexing situation.

I am, Brethren,[21]

Three Letters Supporting Lord North (1782)

glethorpe's three letters supporting the Ministry of Frederick, Lord North (1732–92), appeared in the *Public Advertiser* on March 14, 19, and 22, 1782. They appear to be his last publications and are unusual in bearing his signature. Ettinger was the first biographer to mention them.[1]

Although many Americans associate the name of Lord North with oppressive measures taken against the Colonies, in 1782 North certainly wanted reconciliation with America, but was placed in an impossible position by King George III, who refused North's pleas for peace and rejected his offers to resign. The opposition, led by Fox, was just as confused. At the end of February 1782 it passed a motion against continuing the war with America, but refused to state a position regarding peace terms.[2]

Oglethorpe's suggestions concerning taxation, in his third letter, reflect the principles and measures already stated by North on March 11, 1782;[3] but the precise manner of differentiation is Oglethorpe's own. His exception of the playhouse from the new taxation had been anticipated in the debates by Charles Howard, Earl of Surrey and later eleventh Duke of Norfolk.[4] Oglethorpe's support of North was of course futile for a minister whose resignation was inevitable. It came on March 20—the day after Oglethorpe's second letter appeared.

My text follows that in the *Public Advertiser*.

To the Printer of the Public Advertiser.

MINISTERS *keep their* PLACES.

SIR,

IF the Independent Country Gentlemen were to *speak out* their honest Sentiments, it would defeat the Purposes of designing Men, who like the Quack Doctor, talk a great deal of a Disorder without proposing a Remedy, and without having, like him, any Thing more in View than the Gratification of their own Purposes, at the Expence of our National Credulity.

I was led to this serious Refection, Mr. Woodfall, by the honest Exertions of Sir John Delaval,[5] who, after asserting his Independency on every Set of Ministers and Men, and that he spoke from Conviction and Principle, declared in Favour of Administration for the great Reasons which should regulate the Conduct of every upright Representative of the People, namely, because "the Men in Opposition to Government had no Plan; and that as they complained of public Evils without offering a Remedy, they acted at Random," which convinced Sir John, as it should convince every candid Man that we cannot have a better Ministry than the present, and that they ought in Reason to keep their Places until a better Set of Men produce themselves to succeed them.

Mr. Woodfall, I honour the worthy Baronet for his sterling Sense and sound Policy, which conveys to my Mind stronger Reasons against the Declamation of the Minority, and in Favour of Lord North's Administration, than all the long Speeches made for and against Ministers.

The Minority say "our Struggle with numerous and powerful Enemies is great." Admitted. — They add, that "the unequal Contest rendering the Event precarious, our Situation is dangerous and alarming." Admitted also. — But while we admit the National Struggle, and are sensible of the Danger, what is the *Conclusion?* The Minority can certainly take no Merit in telling us what we know. We cannot be blind to what we all see, nor ignorant of what we all feel, as the inevitable Consequence of contending with numerous, though unprovoked, Enemies!

Then where is the great Merit of the Minority? Where is the Wisdom and Virtue of which they boasted so much with the good-natured, credulous, and deluded Public?

In the Name of Common-sense let me ask the honest Gentlemen in Opposition and their Partizans in what their Merit consists? They say we are in Danger, and yet do not offer a Remedy. Not a single Thing,

Mr. Woodfall, have these State Physicians prescribed to save the Body Politic in the Hour of Danger and approaching Dissolution! Indeed in the Stile of the Mountebank, they *modestly* advise us to discard all the Faculty,[6] as ignorant, unprincipled Men, and to trust our Lives and Fortunes intirely to them, of whose Wisdom we have but slight Proofs, and of whose Virtue we have strong Suspicions.

But, to be serious, Mr. Printer, how long is the Nation to be amused and abused by these Men of *Words?* Let me tell them, in the Language of Sir John Delaval, that they have no Plan of Operations for the Public Service, and therefore the present Set of Ministers ought to be supported, until others can be found, with more Wisdom and Virtue, to fill their Places; which, in my Conscience, I do not believe will easily be found.

OGLETHORPE.

For the Public Advertiser.

On a CHANGE *of* MINISTERS.

To Lord NORTH.

MY LORD,

ALTHOUGH *Opposition* thought themselves sure of turning *out* the present Set of Ministers, and putting other Men *in*, who are better calculated to promote the Purposes of the Leaders of the *Minority;* yet the Letters of "One in the Secret" have,[7] I believe, convinced the Public in general, that they are quite mistaken and disappointed, and, by consequence, that *Administration* will stand their Ground, and persevere, with the best Intention, to promote a *Reconciliation* with America, that his Majesty's Forces may be more effectually employed against foreign Enemies, until a good Cause and the Assistance of Providence shall reduce our Foes to Reason, and to such a Peace as shall be consistent with the Dignity of his Majesty's Crown, and the Security and Happiness of his Subjects.

My Lord, this Intelligence is very important to the Nation, and I will contribute my Share of Justice to "One in the Secret," by acknowledging that the Reasons he has assigned against the Minority, and in favour of your Lordship's Administration, have convinced me, as, I dare say, they have every candid Man, that the sudden Attempt of the Minority (though well meant by a few worthy Members) was, in general, a *Party Trick* to surprize Ministers, and to take the *Posts of Honour* by Storm, in which they were so secret, so active, and had advanced so far, that they would not give Ministers Time to *capitulate*, insisting on their surrendering at the *Discretion* of Enemies who discovered, by the violence of their Conduct, that they had little Discretion in them.

My Lord, as the Attack of the Minority was precipitate, so their Expectations were sanguine; and as they have totally failed in the *former*, so they are intirely disappointed in the *latter*.

My Lord, you have been more than a *Dozen Years* at the Helm, and if you are not a *Dozen more* it will be your own Choice. I am sure you are too well fixed in the *Saddle* to be shaken off, by any Man, or Set of Men, in the Kingdom. I know, my Lord, that notwithstanding your acknowledged Talents, we want the *Abilities* of some Men in Opposition, but we do not want their *Principles*. It may be said of the Minority as that brave Tar, Admiral Boscawen, said of the Scotch, "They make excellent *Soles*, but damned bad *Upper Leathers.*"

My Lord, as Ministers have weathered the Storm with which they were threatened by the Minority, and as the Fortune of War seems again in our Favour, I congratulate your Lordship on the Prospect of Success, and on the Appearance that the Wisdom and Virtue of your Administration will disappoint domestic Foes and foreign Enemies, and (as "One in the Secret" has prophecied) with the Blessings of Heaven upon a good Cause, that Lord North will still render this Nation happy, great and flourishing.

OGLETHORPE.

For the Public Advertiser.

On TAXATION.

To Lord NORTH.

My Lord,

THE Method of raising *Taxes*, when they are inevitable, discovers the Ability and Principle of the Financier. Taxes being an unavoidable Contribution of People, to the necessary Support of the State, they are only oppressive and odious in Proportion as they are injudiciously laid. When they are laid upon the proper Objects that can and ought to contribute to the Burthens of Government, and the industrious Part of the Community are excused, as much as the Nature of Things will admit, then the Minister becomes *popular*, because the Tax (being unavoidable) is laid on the proper Objects of Taxation.

Your Lordship is the most popular Financier we have had for many Years, because you have paid due Attention to the Objects of Taxation for the Purpose of Revenue; and by charging them where they can be best borne, you have excused, as much as possible, those which were not so able to bear them. Hence it is evident that your Lordship discovers a great Knowledge of the Art of Finance, and a great Regard to the Interest of a trading Nation, by making as light as possible the Burthens of the industrious Part of the Community.

The People feel and acknowledge the good Effects of this sound Policy, and your Lordship is, by Consequence, a very popular Minister in regard to Finance, which is the greatest Object of a commercial Nation, that is greatly in Debt. I wish, my Lord, with all my Heart, that you were as fortunate in every other Circumstance of your Administration. But, to be all Perfection, is more than the People can, in Reason, expect, or your Lordship aspire to. It may be the noble Ambition of a great Mind, but it is beyond the Acquisitions of human Accomplishments.

To confine myself to the single Business of FINANCE, as Money will be much wanted, permit me, my Lord, to prepare the Way to a Supply which will produce much Good to the Government, without Inconvenience to the Subject.

The Art of Taxation consist in Taxes being *productive* for Government, and *proportioned* to the Ability of the People, who will bear the Burthens of their Country, when they arise from Necessity, and are laid with *Judgment*.

A Tax upon LUXURY is sound Policy in the first Instance, by raising a large Supply of Money when it is much wanted; and in the Second, by excusing other Objects, which are more useful to Society, but less profitable.

Were all Public houses to take out an annual Licence at Three Guineas, Coffee-houses at Four, Taverns at Five, and *Places of Dissipation and public Entertainment and Amusement** (the Playhouses excepted) more in Proportion,[8] it would raise a considerable annual Sum for the Use of the Nation, upon the most constitutional and rational Principle. I will venture

---

*Written before the Taxes were known.

to prophecy that the Tax would not lessen the *Frequency* of the People, nor, by Consequence, the Number of such Houses.

My Lord, these and similar Objects, which are greatly indulged and much benefited by a very mild Government, should be made to contribute very handsomely to the Support of that State to which they are indebted for every Indulgence and Blessing they enjoy, which is allowed to be very great.

OGLETHORPE.

Appendix 1:
Spurious Attributions

From time to time a number of works have been inaccurately attributed to Oglethorpe or so listed under his name that they seem to be cataloged as his:

A Brief Account of the Establishment of the Colony of Georgia, under Gen. James Oglethorpe, February 1, 1733 (Washington, 1835) is listed under Oglethorpe in both the *Catalogue Générale des Livres Imprimés de la Bibliothèque Nationale: Auteurs*, 231 vols. (Paris, 1924–81), 126:741; and in *The National Union Catalog: Pre-1956 Imprints*, 754 vols. (London, 1968–81), 427:678. In 1924 Leonard Mackall showed that this publication, which was several times reprinted, was Peter Force's compilation of several articles that had appeared in the *Charles Town South Carolina Gazette*. See Mackall's "The Source of Force's Tract, 'A Brief Account of the Establishment of the Colony of Georgia,'" in *American Historical Review*, 30 (1924–25):304–8.

A Full Reply to Lieut. Codogan's Spanish Hireling and Lieut. Mackay's Letter (London, 1743) is listed under Oglethorpe in *The National Union Catalog*, 427:678, and is attributed to Oglethorpe in *Bibliotheca Americana*, ed. Joseph Sabin, Wilberforce Eames, and R. W. G. Vail, 29 vols. (New York, 1868–1936), 13:538–39; and in Mackall's *Catalogue of the Wymberley Jones De Renne Georgia Library*, 3 vols. (Wormsloe, 1931), 1:111. In 1954 John Tate Lanning showed that the work, actually hostile to Oglethorpe, was written by James Killpatrick (later Kirkpatrick), of Charleston and London. See Lanning's Introduction, p. xvi, to *The St. Augustine Expedition of 1740, reprinted from The Colonial Records of South Carolina* (Columbia, 1954).

"*The History of the Rise, Progress, and Present State of the Colony GEORGIA; with the Attempts made upon it by the Spaniards, and their total Defeat. Interspersed with Original Papers*" appeared in John Campbell's augmented edition of John Harriss's *Navigantium atque Itinerantium Bibliotheca, or a Complete Collection of Voyages and Travels*. This enlarged edition was first issued in 120 numbers, for subscribers. The proposal was printed in *The General Advertiser* for March 15, 1744; and the first number appeared in or about April 1744. The Georgia history, which comprises numbers 91–93, probably appeared in late 1746, when, Campbell tells us, he was working on that section. The second impression, in volume 2, appeared in 1748.

When Boswell read the account, he commented, "It appeared to be the General's own."[1] Boswell's conjecture has some justification. Oglethorpe evidently furnished Campbell with or guided him to published materials, apparently provided some unpublished documents (like the treaties with the Indians and the congratulatory letters from colonial governors), and responded to Campbell's queries. But Campbell would doubtless have credited the account to the general if he had written it. There is little new narrative. Even Oglethorpe's repulse of the Spanish invasion of Georgia is given as it appears in Lieutenant Sutherland's account.[2] The account is based primarily upon printed sources and is arranged to follow the narrative as it appears in Benjamin Martyn's *An Account, Showing the Progress* (1741). Royal Agent for the Georgia Colony from 1765 until his death in 1775, Campbell probably paid the general full credit in his closing remarks:

> One thing more I must observe before I conclude this Section, which is, that if there be any thing in it, or indeed in any of those relating to the *British* Plantations, which ought, in a particular Manner, to claim the Attention of the Public; it is, in a great Measure, due to the Lights afforded by the Honourable *James Oglethorpe*, Esq; from whom, if the Author has caught any of that generous Spirit, which inclines a Man to bind all his Thoughts, and turn all his Labours to the Service of his Country, it is but just that he should acknowledge it; and this he is the more ready to do, because if there be any Merit in his Performance, capable of making it known to, and esteemed by, Posterity; he would willingly consecrate it as a Mark of Esteem and Gratitude, for the many Informations he has received, and the right Turn that has been given to his Inquiries, by that knowing and worthy Person, who is equally happy in rendering the greatest personal Services himself to the Community, and by infusing the like Disposition in others, both by his Example and Conversation.[3]

An Impartial Account of the late Expedition against St. Augustine (London, 1742) was listed under Oglethorpe in *The National Union Catalog*, 427:678, and *The British Library General Catalogue of Printed Books to 1975*, 360 vols. (London, 1979–87), 240:456. It was attributed to Oglethorpe in Sabin's *Bibliotheca Americana*, 13:539. In 1954 Lanning showed that this work also was written by Killpatrick. See Lanning's Introduction, xiv–xv, xxiv–xxv.

"Niederlassung in New-Georgien, und desen Beschreibung," in *Allgemenine Historie zu Wasser und Lande*, 21 vols. (Leipzig, 1747–74), 16:631–40, is listed under Oglethorpe in *The National Union Catalog*, 427:678. The account seems to date from about 1739 and is a German translation from *Histoire Générale des Voyages*, 15 vols. (Paris, 1746–59), compiled by the Abbé Antoine François Prévost, called Prévost d'Exiles, author of *Manon Lescaut*. It is not a translation from any work of Oglethorpe.

Neuste und Richtigste Nachricht von der Landschaft Georgia in dem Engländischen Amerika (Göttingen, 1746) is listed in *The National Union Catalog*, 427:678, as a German translation by Johann Matthias Krämer from Oglethorpe's *New and Accurate Account* and was attributed to Oglethorpe in Sabin's *Bibliotheca Americana*, 13:539. It is not a translation of Oglethorpe's tract.

Appendix 2: Probable Attributions

Although Oglethorpe's preference for anonymity or pseudonymity was conventional for an English gentleman, it has made it impossible to identify many of the letters that he must have written to the newspapers during the course of his life. Only in his final series of letters, in 1782, did he use his own name. Fortunately Amos Aschbach Ettinger and Phinizy Spalding have identified several as his, and I have added others. I have, however, resisted the temptation to add Oglethorpe items on the grounds of his favorite subjects and his style. In working with the corpus of Daniel Defoe, I have seen how the temptation for attributing anonymous works to him has misled bibliographers from the eighteenth century to the present. One should especially be suspicious of letters signed "O." or even "J.O." Many different writers possessed and employed these initials; and John Oakman, in particular, published a good deal of verse above his initials. Similarly, one must be suspicious of placing too much importance upon the residence from which the letter is dated. Most writers to the newspapers did not give their residence, and Oglethorpe apparently did not ordinarily designate his, though he did so in a letter to the press in 1762. But most of the letters dated from Grosvenor Square or Grosvenor Street could not be Oglethorpe's. I do, however, reprint a letter signed "Omega" as probably the work of Oglethorpe. Of "A Refutation of Calumnies" Oglethorpe was certainly one of the authors, perhaps the principal one.

A Refutation of Calumnies (1742)

On November 29, 1742, the *New-York Weekly Journal* published the sworn testimony of General Oglethorpe and several of his officers refuting some of the South Carolinian charges that in the St. Augustine campaign of 1740 the general had been negligent and incompetent not only in commanding the Carolina regiment, but in his direction of the entire campaign.[1] Dated September in a manuscript copy sent to the Trustees, the refutation was sent to the *New-York Weekly Journal* with added attestations dated November 4. The primacy of Oglethorpe's signature here does not prove his authorship: he was listed first as the commander, and it was George Cadogan who later responded most fully to the Carolinian accusations, in his *Spanish Hireling Detected* (London, 1743).[2] But Oglethorpe suffered more than anyone else from South Carolinian aspersions, and after the Spanish threat had dissipated, he had time to respond.

The South Carolinian version of the expedition, which unfortunately is the only account easily available, had in May been published in James Killpatrick's anonymous *Impartial Account of the late Expedition against St. Augustine under General Oglethorpe*.[3] Almost a year earlier, on July 3, 1741, after hearing the report of a joint investigative committee, both houses of the South Carolina Assembly had voted their confidence in Vander Dussen, blamed Oglethorpe, and ordered their full version of the report to be published.[4] But publication had been delayed, and many South Carolinians were refusing to serve again under Colonel Alexander Vander Dussen,[5] this time for the relief of Frederica. Perhaps to restore confidence in him, on July 12, 1742, the *South Carolina Gazette* published the Assembly's commendations.

Although the following testimony clears Oglethorpe only from some of the charges made concerning the retreat of the South Carolinian troops from St. Augustine, it suggests that the vilification that he then received from South Carolina for all aspects and phases of his generalship—and the deprecation that he still receives from some historians—was and remains inadequately informed.

My text is that of the *New-York Weekly Journal*.

A REFUTATION OF CALUMNIES 339

THERE being inserted in the *Carolina Gazette* from *July* the 5th to *July* the 12th 1742, in that Part thereof which is there called the Honourable *John Fenwick*, Esq; his Speech to Col. *Vander Dussen*, many extraordinary things, and one particularly which we cannot help taking Notice of, *viz.*

> "*And when Commodore* Pearse *had also set Sail, and left you* (viz. Vander Dussen) *alone upon that Island* (viz. Anastasia) *with the Force only of this Province, for your having brought off notwithstanding (under the Blessing of God) with such good Conduct, all the Artillery which the General had declared* impossible *to be done, and preserved the same, together with all your Men, Craft, &c. at that deplorable Juncture, when in all human Probability, the whole would have fallen into the Enemy's Hands, and happily compleated your Retreat without any Loss.*"

WE think ourselves obliged in Justice, not only to Capt. *Pearse* and the Officers and Seamen of that Squadron, but to His Majesty's Service, and to the World, which may be deceived by the above Assertion, to declare, That the same is not Fact, and that Mr. *Vander Dussen* and the *Carolina* Regiment were not left upon *Anastasia* alone. That they did not alone bring off the Artillery, and that they did not compleat the Retreat, but on the contrary, that General *Oglethorpe* with a Part of his Regiment, in which was Major *Heron*, Capts. *Desbrisay & Dunbar*, Lieutenant *James Mackay*, Ensigns *Tolson, Mackay, Sutherland, Cathcart, Stewart & Wemess*, and Quartermaster *Wansell*, formed the Rear in the Retreat upon the Main, for that he with that part of his Regiment, the *Indians, Rangers & Highlanders* stayed on the Main within half Cannon Shot of the Gates of *Augustine*, to restrain any Sallies from the Town till the Artillery, excepting one Piece of Cannon which was left behind burst, and all the Men and Stores were embarked from *Anastasia*, and till he saw all the Craft with them on Board, sailed out of the Harbour, and the Men of War also sailed.

AND we do also declare that the only Battery which did engage the half Gallies the Day of the Retreat, was managed by Mr. *Mace*, and Men paid by General *Oglethorpe*, and guarded by a Detachment of his Regiment, and that, under the Command of Ensigns *Mace* and *Hogan*, and that the said Battery did force one of the Gallies aground.

THERE was upon *Anastasia* besides Mr. *Vander Dussen*'s Regiment, some of the General's Regiment which stayed to the very last with the Artillery, and a large Party of Sailors also were left by Capt. *Pearse*, and the Captains of the Men of War on *Anastasia* to the last, and helped to bring off the Cannon, and were paid by General *Oglethorpe*'s order for every Gun they brought off. And Mr. *Vander Dussen* was so far from compleating any Retreat, that a Party of General *Oglethorpe*'s Regiment commanded by Mr. *Hogan*, marched in the Rear of the *Carolina* Regiment, and after that Regiment had marched off, the General in the Rear of his own Regiment secured the Retreat.

> *James Oglethorpe,*
> *Alexander Heron. Lieut. Col. & Maj. of General*
>   *Oglethorpe's Regiment,*
> *George Dunbar, Captain,*
> *James Mackay Capt. Lieutenant,*
> *Primrose Maxwell, Lieut. & second Aid de Camp,*
> *George Cadogan Lieutenant,*
> *Thomas Eyre, Ensign & Sub Engineer,*
> *Probart Howarth, Ensign,*
> *Samuel Mackay, second Ensign,*
> *Solomon Chamberlain second Ensign,*
> *William Robinson Adjutant,*[6]
>
> The above is an exact Copy from the Original. Test
> *Francis Moore,*

WHEREAS the Names of Lieutenants *Maxwell & Cadogan* are sign'd to the foregoing Paragraph in which they do not appear to have been Present in the Retreat, they think it necessary to add the following Explanation.

AT the first Raising of the *Carolina* Regiment, the General to assist that Province in disciplining their Men, dispenced with the Duty of us, who were then second Ensigns in his Regiment, and we were accordingly appointed Officers in that Service, *viz.* Mr. *Maxwell,* Capt. Lieutenant, and Mr. *Cadogan,* Lieutenant. That upon the first Promotions we were both appointed Captains. As this obviates an Objection which might be made by some who dare to Print what they cannot Sign,[7] it also enables us to add the following Particulars, which could not occur to other Persons.

AFTER the Orders were given for a Retreat, Capt. *Dunbar* by the General's Order came from the Camp on the Main to *Anastasia* in the General's Cutter, and assisted in embarking the *Carolina* Regiment, and after the whole were gone off, Capt. *Dunbar* returned to *Point Quartelle,* and stayed there till Col. *Vander Dussen,* and the greatest Part of his Regiment was landed, and then went and reported to the General that Col. *Vander Dussen,* was landed safe at *Point Quartelle,* which is seperated from *Augustine* by an Arm of the Sea, which together with a Party of the General's Regiment which marched in our Rear, was a great happiness to us, for the *Carolina* Regiment marched in such Disorder that the van, which the Col. generally led, was seldom less than four Miles from the Rear. And at the first Night's halting Col. *Vander Dussen,* lay in the Front and Mr. *Maxwell* in the Rear, at the distance of two Miles, and that the Regiment never joyn'd till they came to St. *John's* where the Col. arrived several Hours before the whole came up.

THAT a Day or two after the *Carolina* Regiment came to St. *John's,* Mr. *Max-*

well Rode back from thence twelve Miles towards St. *Augustine*, where he met the General and his Regiment in their march to St. *John*'s.

> *Primrose Maxwell,*
> *George Cadogan,*

The above is an exact Copy from the Original.

> *Francis Moore*

This Day appeared before us, Mr. *Francis Moore*, and declared upon Oath, That the Annexed Paper was exactly and truly Copied by him from the Originals which remains in his Hands. GIVEN under our Hands and the Seal of this Town of *Frederica* this 4*th* of *November*, 1742.

> *Thomas Hawkins,*
> *Thomas Marriott,*

Praise for John Howard (1777)

The letter praising the philanthropist John Howard (1726?–90) for his *State of the Prisons in England and Wales* appeared in the *General Evening Post* for June 14, 1777, signed "OMEGA." "OMEGA" was probably James Oglethorpe. The long *O* would fit Oglethorpe, and the paragraph length is consistent with that of the general's late letters to the press. The prefatory reassurance that the author is not here "puffing" his own work suggests a writer who had resorted to the practice, as Oglethorpe had done in his appeal for benefactors and in his *New and Accurate Account* in 1732 and in his second Corsican letter in 1768. Moreover, of all Englishmen, Oglethorpe would have been the first to praise his worthy successor in the humanitarian work of prison reform that he had himself initiated almost half a century earlier. It was apparently the first praise of the book, which had been advertised in the *Morning Post* on May 16, 1777, as published "This Day." Perhaps Oglethorpe's attention was drawn to the advertisement because he was at the same time advertising a new edition of his *Sailors Advocate*.

The letter does not attempt to review the book, as did the reviewers in the *Monthly Review* for July 1777 (57:8–14) and the *Gentleman's Magazine* for September and December (47:444–47, 596–97). Instead, recognizing the need for public expression of outrage in order to pressure Parliament to enact legislation that he had long ago suggested and that Howard now clearly showed the need of, Oglethorpe remined the public that the prisons were still a national disgrace.

My text follows that of the *General Evening Post*.

To the Editor of the GENERAL EVENING POST.

SIR,

A Recommendatory letter, designed to engage the attention of the public to a new performance, comes always with a suspicious aspect. This piece of author-craft has been so often practised, that the world is sufficiently aware of it; and when the stile and sentiment of a fresh publication are thus trumpeted into notice, the reader is as much disgusted as if he had caught the self-applauding author in the fact.

I should be sorry to injure a work of such distinguished merit as Mr. *Howard's State of Prisons*, by an ill judged commendation of it, and therefore think it needful to premise that I never in my life saw that gentleman, or am in the least acquainted with him. If I write to recommend his book, it is for the sake of the subject, and to assist, as far as by such means it can be assisted, the cause of those unhappy persons, whose crimes do not call more loudly for the vengeance of the law, than their miseries for the compassion of the public.

We are directed by a principle of natural equity to suppose every man innocent, however accused, till he is legally proved to be guilty. What a multitude of contradictions to this principle are to be found in our English prisons? where not only criminals capitally indicted, but even offenders in a less heinous degree, while yet unsentenced, suffer hardships through neglect, such as no authority could inflict upon them. The law says to a felon when it condems him, You shall return to the place from whence you came, and there wait for your execution: but it does not add, There you shall be stifled with filth, there you shall pine with hunger, be devoured by vermin, and infected with disease, till you become a more insufferable nuisance to society than all your crimes have made you. The case of debtors is still more deplorable, who in many prisons, though not considered as criminals, fare but little better.

But it is no part of my business to declaim upon the subject. Mr. Howard's book will convince his reader, beyond the power of all declamations, that these allegations are true: and I wish that his comparison of English with foreign management in this instance, may excite a spirit of emulation in those who have it in their power to redress the evil he points out; an evil that, if universally known, would shock the humanity of every nation under heaven.

I shall only add, that if Mr. Howard has spared neither expence, nor time, nor health, in pursuit of his inquiries upon this subject through half the goals in Europe, it may be reasonably hoped and expected that his narrative will not be entirely neglected; but that the benevolent part of mankind amongst us will give it due attention, and be willing to avail themselves, without danger or inconvenience, of the information he has acquired at the hazard of his life,

I am, Sir, &c.
OMEGA.

Notes

Preface

1. It is ironic that this piece, which Oglethorpe told Boswell had been published, was apparently never printed. It seems certain that "Lord Egmont [John Percival, the second earl of Egmont] was sent to him and got [the] instruction" (Boswell Papers, Yale University Library, M208:1). Apparently Oglethorpe believed that it had been "published in pamph[let] to settle Island of St. Johns'"— i.e., printed with Egmont's proposal to settle Prince Edward Island. Oglethorpe's legal document is mentioned in a postscript to the table of contents of the rare extended version, printed about 1765, of *To the King's most Excellent Majesty, the Memorial of John Earl of Egmont;* but it is not printed there. Of this memorial, several copies of the brief, early edition have survived; but I have been able to locate only one copy of the later, enlarged edition—in the Public Archives of Nova Scotia. The historian of eighteenth-century Prince Edward Island, Professor John Michael Bumsted, of St. John's College, Winnipeg, agrees that the instruction was evidently never printed. I am indebted to Nicolas de Jong, Provincial Archivist of Prince Edward Island, who informed me of the copy in the Nova Scotia Archives, and to Wendy Duff and Philip L. Hartling, Librarian and Microfilm Archivist there, who kindly provided me with a microfilm. To Professor Bumsted, author of *Land, Settlement, and Politics on Eighteenth-Century Prince Edward Island* (Kingston, 1987), I am indebted for his note of April 4, 1991.

Quisquis amissam

1. James Boswell, *Boswell: The Ominous Years*, ed. Charles Ryskamp and Frederick A. Pottle (New York, 1963), 97.
2. Levin Theodore Reichel, *The Early History of the Church of the United Brethren* (Nazareth, Pa., 1888), 65.
3. Boswell, *Boswell: The Applause of the Jury, 1782–1785*, ed. Irma S. Lustig and Frederick A. Pottle (New York, 1981), 129.
4. As general models for Oglethorpe's poem, Professor Harris suggests the apotheosis of Daphnis (Julius Caesar) in Virgil's *Eclogue* 5; and he points out the following Horatian echoes. In line 2 "pius frustrà" seems to evoke Horace's *Odes* 1.24.11–12: "tu frustra pius heu non ita creditum / poscis Quintilium deos." More

generally the first stanza evokes *Odes* 2.20.21ff. In line 10 "Fama *Quam* pennâ" seems to echo *Odes* 2.2.7-8: "illum aget pinna metuente solvi / Fama superstes." By 1714 Oglethorpe may have owned several editions of Virgil (items 26, 39, 606, 792, 1009, and 2189), and two of Horace's *Opera* (566 and 1528). See *A Catalogue of the Entire and Valuable Library of General Oglethorpe, Lately Deceased* (London, 1788). Since this booksale catalog embodies also the smaller library of the Reverend Mr. Samuel Pollen and since I have discovered no way of separating his books there from Oglethorpe's, my assigning any book from the *Catalogue* to the general represents a probability rather than a certainty.

A Duel Explained

1. Mr. Sharpe may have been a son of the Bishop of London's friend John Sharp, Archbishop of York — perhaps Thomas Sharp (1693-1753), the father of Granville Sharp, friend of Oglethorpe half a century later.
2. It was reprinted in *Applebee's Original Weekly Journal* for March 31, 1722, and in Amos Aschbach Ettinger, *James Edward Oglethorpe: Imperial Idealist* (Oxford, 1936), 82-83.

The Sailors Advocate

1. Prince Hoare, *Memoirs of Granville Sharp, Esq., composed from his own Manuscripts* (London, 1820), 489, 160.
2. Hoare, *Memoirs*, 2d ed. (London, 1828), 2:238n.
3. Sir Edward Knatchbull, *The Parliamentary Diary of Sir Edward Knatchbull*, ed. A. N. Newman, Camden Society, third series, vol. 94 (London, 1963), 75.
4. Daniel A. Baugh, ed., *British Naval Administration in the Age of Walpole* (Princeton, 1965), 149-50; Knatchbull, *Diary*, 78.
5. See J. Robert Hutchinson, *The Press-Gang Afloat and Ashore* (London, 1913); Baugh, *British Naval Administration*, 147-240; Baugh, ed., *Naval Administration, 1715-1750*, Navy Records Society, vol. 120 (London, 1977), 89-190; and Christopher Lloyd, *The British Seaman, 1200-1860: A Social Survey* (Rutherford, N.J., 1970), 112-72.
6. Hutchinson, *Press-Gang*, 1-17; Lloyd, *British Seaman*, 16-17, 82-86, 150-72; Baugh, *British Naval Administration*, 224-25, 233.
7. Lloyd, *British Seaman*, 173-80.
8. Baugh, *British Naval Administration*, 227.
9. To these proposals, Leslie F. Church devoted most of his attention in his analysis of *The Sailor's Advocate*, in *James Edward Oglethorpe: A Study of Philanthropy in England and Georgia* (London, 1932), 25-29.

10. A single sheet folio, the Orelbar pamphlet is tentatively dated 1720—before the author entered Parliament.

11. Aaron Lambe's single sheet folio *A Proposal for the Encouragement of Seamen; by Reviving a Register* (London, 1727); and Thomas Robe's *Ways and Means Whereby His Majesty may Man his Navy* (London, 1726).

12. Great Britain, Parliament, *The Journals of the House of Commons* (London, n.d.), 21:22, hereinafter cited as *JHC*.

13. *JHC*, 21:52.

14. Also in February there appeared views similar to Oglethorpe's in *Some Considerations on the Reasonableness and Necessity of Encreasing and Encouraging the Seamen*, attributed to Daniel Defoe, and *The Encouragement and Increase of Seamen Consider'd*, which was perhaps elicited by Oglethorpe.

15. Agnes Mary Clerke, "Samuel Molyneux," *Dictionary of National Biography*, hereinafter designated *DNB*; Baugh, ed., *Naval Administration, 1715–1750*, 98–106. Baugh (p. 91) tentatively identified Thomas Corbett as the author.

16. Baugh, ed., *Naval Administration, 1715–1750*, 102.

17. For example, see Lloyd, *British Seamen*, 154. Oglethorpe's pamphlet, Lloyd attributed tentatively to Thomas Robe (p. 181).

18. *JHC*, 21:74.

19. 1 George II, stat. 2, cap. 14, sect. 15: Great Britain. *The Statutes at Large*, ed. Danby Pickering, 46 vols. (Cambridge, 1762–1807), 15:481, hereinafter cited as Pickering's *Statutes*.

20. *JHC*, 21:79.

21. *JHC*, 21:135.

22. 1 George II, stat. 2, cap. 14, sects. 12–13: Pickering's *Statutes*, 15:480–81.

23. *JHC*, 21:147.

24. *JHC*, 21:168.

25. Baugh, ed., *Naval Administration, 1715–1750*, 161.

26. One piece of evidence seems to point to the Goldsmith copy as representing the corrected state: the 1777 reprint follows it rather than the Kress. But all the rest of the evidence points to the Kress. It corrects a misstatement given in the Goldsmith; and page 18, where the correction occurs, embodies only twenty-nine lines in the Kress copy, an abnormally short page in a pamphlet where the norm is thirty or thirty-one lines and where there are sometimes thirty-two. Moreover page 6 is incorrectly paginated in the Goldsmith copy, the *i* is missing from the *if* on the same page, and periods are missing on pages 18 and 20. All these errors are corrected in the Kress state. Apparently Oglethorpe used a copy of the uncorrected state for the 1777 edition, forgetting that on one page he had corrected the text. Copies of the uncorrected state are found also in the New York Public Library, the Huntington Library, and the Library of the University of Chicago. The University of Indiana Library has a copy of the rare corrected state.

27. Milton's phrase occurs in *Paradise Lost*, 4.393–934. *The Library of Oglethorpe* shows editions of 1669, 1688, and 1719 (items 419, 1459, and 1071).

28. In the debates in the House of Commons, Sir Charles Wager, a Lord of the Admiralty, maintained that the care of seamen could not be improved. See Knatchbull, *Diary*, 78.

29. Oglethorpe quotes Sir Edward Coke, *Le Quart Part des Reportes* (London, 1610), sig. [B6].

30. Oglethorpe compares Sir Robert Walpole with Julius Caesar, who, according to Cato, in Joseph Addison's *Cato* 4.4.109, lost all sense of shame after his victory at Pharsalia. Oglethorpe later quoted from the play in a conversation with Dr. Johnson and Boswell on April 14, 1778. See Boswell, *Boswell in Extremes, 1776–1778*, ed. Charles McC. Weis and Frederick A. Pottle (New York, 1970), 278.

31. Oglethorpe, not Granville Sharp.

32. *The Library of Oglethorpe* lists (item 266) a copy of Sir John Fortescue's *On the Laws of England*, trans. Robert Mulcaster (London, 1599), but there Fortescue merely glances at the Admiralty Court, in ch. 32, fol. 73, verso. Perhaps Oglethorpe remembered John Selden's extensive note concerning the Admiralty Court in his edition of Fortescue—*De Laudibus Legum Angliae* (London, 1616), Notes, 31–37. On December 24, 1776, Oglethorpe sent "a very old edition of Fortescue" to Granville Sharp. See Hoare, *Memoirs*, 1st ed., 163.

33. Oglethorpe quotes from sections 5 and 6, evidently from Pickering's *Statutes*, 15:468, 469, italicizing Pickering's roman in sec. 6.

34. Apparently attracted by the black letter type that was still occasionally used in England, especially for printing statutes, either Oglethorpe designated them for that purpose in his first appendix or the compositor decided to use them there. They also appear for emphasis in the central essay and the final letter. For black letter, which never appears in Oglethorpe's other publications, I have substituted italic, pointing out in the notes the rare appearances of italic in the three sections where black letter is substituted for the same purpose.

35. The national stock, secured through the Bank of England and a few other companies, as a source of revenue.

36. Samuel Daniel, *The Collection of the History of England*, 4th ed. (London, 1650), 121. *The Library of Oglethorpe* lists this edition, item 932.

37. The Magna Charta, cap. 29. Italicizing *Magna Charta*, Oglethorpe presumably quoted from his copy of the Barthelet edition of 1531–32 or from his copy of Great Britain. *The Statutes at Large*, ed. Joseph Keble (London, 1676), 4, hereinafter cited as Keble's *Statutes*. See *The Library of Oglethorpe*, items 1267 and 941.

38. 16 Charles I, cap. 5 was concerned with the recruitment of sailors.

39. The Petition of Right, of May 27–28, 1628, maintained that no freeman ought to be committed to or be detained in prison, or otherwise restrained, without cause.

40. Oglethorpe's unorthodox reference cites Keble's *Statutes*, 795, section 43, not 48.

41. This phrase is italicized.

42. The "Ostend ships" were apparently the *Prince Eugene* and the *Stahremberg*, commissioned by "the authorities at Ostend" for use against the Spaniards in the Pacific. See Sir William Laird Clowes, *The Royal Navy: A History*, 7 vols. (London, 1897–1903; rpt., New York: AMS Press, 1966), 3:316–17.

43. The first edition reads "dreadful morality."

44. A year later, on the floor of the House of Commons, Oglethorpe put the loss at "near 4000"; and in response Sir Charls Wager "said he had a list of every man dead on that expedition, which amounted in all to but 1900 men." John Percival, first Earl of Egmont, *Diary of Viscount Percival*, ed. R. A. Roberts, Historical Manuscripts Commission, 3 vols. (London, 1920–23), 3:346–47. In his *Naval Administration*, 327, Baugh put the figure above three thousand.

45. It was apparently this Baltic expedition in which Admiral Wager admitted the loss of "above 500." See Percival, *Diary*, 3:347.

46. In 1725 Lord Chancellor Sir Thomas Parker, first Earl of Macclesfield, was found guilty of defalcation of funds in his custody.

47. This entire sentence is italicized.

48. *Viz.* is italicized.

49. The earlier state reads, "the purser is the first creditor, and if he runs away, no other is paid." Originally Oglethorpe apparently did not realize, or perhaps forgot, that the buyer of the sailor's prospective wages frequently managed to collect the wages of even those who had deserted.

50. The phrase is italicized.

51. The first edition reads "*The Duth method.*"

52. The black letter here apparently reproduced that in Oglethorpe's copy of Keble's *Statutes*, 316–17, 345; 7 Henry VII, cap. 1, par. 1; and 3 Henry VIII, cap. 5, par. 4.

53. Italics appear in this title and all subsequent titles of the appendix except in Number IV.

54. The word *pressing* appears in black letter. The writer of this section may have been John Barnard, a member of the parliamentary committee. Although he had become an Anglican, Barnard had once been a Quaker.

55. In the 1777 edition "Shoe-beacon" became "Sohoc-beacon." In 1542 this warning signal was called the "horse-shoe beacon." It is now Maplin Light. The man of war was the *Flamborough*. Its captain, John Hildesley, had a bad reputation within the Navy. On April 23, 1717, a complaint was lodged in the Admiralty against him for drawing his sword and making a disturbance among the workmen at the Navy Yard, also for "cursing and swearing and abusing the Officers, and that he would kick the Builder over the wharf." (Baugh, ed., *Naval Administration, 1715–1750*, 46, 48; see also 49, 140–41.) In March of 1721, Hildesley attempted to help

restore Governor Robert Johnson to power in South Carolina. With five ships, he sailed into the harbor of Charleston and, as commander of the militia for Berkeley County, furnished eighty sailors as militiamen for Johnson's abortive attempt. In August 1923 L. G. Carr Laughton printed a letter from the Lords of the Admiralty giving the official account of the incident narrated in *The Sailor's Advocate* (*Mariner's Mirror*, 9:240–42); and in 1931 "W.S." added notes excerpted from the evidence taken at the hearings of the case (*Mariner's Mirror*, 17:397–98). This evidence seems to confirm the accuracy of the account published by Oglethorpe.

56. The apprentices were William Risham and George Whalebone.

57. In this paragraph *Sailors Hardships* is italized; and in the following, *Letter* and *Service*.

58. In this paragraph are italicized *forgery*, *Sheriffs*, and *Crown*.

59. Recorded as having deserted.

60. *Indulgences* is italicized.

61. The phrase is italicized.

A Preliminary Report on the Fleet Prison

1. Knatchbull, *Diary*, 88–89. Charles Selwyn (1689–1749) later defended the new colony of Georgia in the House of Commons. Knatchbull's assertion that Sir William had stabbed Bambridge's underling is correct. The press uniformly reported only that Sir William had stabbed Bambridge himself, and so Oglethorpe stated in his appendix to his report on the Marshalsea Prison. In his own defense, however, Bambridge asserted that Sir William had attacked his assistant also, in a separate incident (*Mr. Bambridge's Case* [London, 1729?], 2).

A Report from the Committee . . . Relating to the Fleet Prison

1. *JHC*, 20:303.

2. *JHC*, 21:264.

3. See Baine, "The Prison Death of Robert Castell and Its Effect on the Founding of Georgia," *Georgia Historical Quarterly* 73 (1989): 67–78.

4. *JHC*, 21:237.

5. Moses Pitt, *The Cry of the Oppressed* (London, 1691), 84–86.

6. A "Newgate solicitor," Thomas Bambridge, along with Thomas Corbett, acquired the freehold of the Fleet Prison from John Huggins and was sworn warden of the prison on November 16, 1728. After the investigation, Bambridge was accused of the murder of Robert Castell; and when he was acquitted, he was tried again on the appeal of the widow, who was doubtless subvented by Oglethorpe. Again acquitted, he was then tried for felony on the charges of his prisoner Elizabeth Berkeley. Though found not guilty of these indictments, Bambridge was by

the unanimous vote of the House of Commons deprived of his freehold of the Fleet and disabled forever from again holding the office of warden there. Despite his legal protests and his self-exculpation in *Mr. Bambridge's Case*, he was never able to regain his post. After apparently resuming his legal practice, he died in his chambers in London on July 11, 1741. Reportedly he cut his own throat. He is pictured by Hogarth in both the sketch and the final painting of Oglethorpe's committee visiting the Fleet.

7. *The Historical Register . . . for the Year 1729*, 128n.

8. On March 10 the *Daily Post* announced a visit planned for that day.

9. Sidney James Webb, Baron Passfield, and Beatrice Potter Webb, *English Prisons Under Local Conditions* (London, 1922; rpt., Archon, 1963), 28.

10. *JHC*, 21:283, 310, 374; Great Britain, Parliament, *Journals of the House of Lords* (London, n.d.), 23:438; Pickering's *Statutes*, 16:88 (2 George II, cap. 32).

11. James Boswell, notes toward a biography of Oglethorpe, Boswell Papers, M208:1, Yale University Library; *The Register of Admissions to Gray's Inn, 1521–1889*, ed. Joseph Foster (London, 1889), 369.

12. *JHC*, 21:387n. The Fleet report also appeared in *Journals of the House of Lords*, 23:404–34; and it was reprinted in 1729 in Dublin. The body of the report was included in Abel Boyer's *Political State of Great Britain* in the number for April of 1929 (37:359–77). All three major reports were reprinted, with the exception of Appendix B in the Marshalsea report and minor compressions elsewhere, by William Cobbett in his *Parliamentary History of England*, 36 vols. (London, 1806–20), 8:706–53, 803–26.

13. Particularly oppressive during the reigns of James I and Charles I, the Court of the Star Chamber was abolished in 1641.

14. This act, 16 Charles I, cap. 10, was entitled "An Act for the regulating of the privy council, and for taking away the court commonly called the star-chamber." See Pickering's *Statutes*, 7:338–42.

15. Oglethorpe focuses upon the specific charge to investigate the use of charity monies. See 22–23 Charles II, cap. 20, sec. 11: Pickering's *Statutes*, 8:372.

16. The Magna Charta.

17. This was Richard Tyrell of Asshton, in Essex. At his death, in 1566, his executors acted until his eldest son, Edward, attained his majority.

18. After the Great Fire of 1666 destroyed the prison, the prisoners were temporarily housed in Caron House, in South Lambeth. Sir Jeremy's grant came in September 1667, and he evidently sold the grant before he died in 1677.

19. During these years the Fleet was successively held by Edmund Pierce, Thomas Dickenson, Thomas Bromhall, Escrick Howard, and Richard Manlove, who was deprived of his office for abuses, extortion, and escapes.

20. Although Colonel Baldwyn Leighton was granted wardenship in 1690, William Weedon Ford continually contested his right to the prison.

21. Leighton was still living in 1703, but Huggins's patent was dated July 22,

1713. Perhaps this patent confirmed an earlier one. Henry Hyde, second Earl of Clarendon, sold his patent to Thomas Bambridge and Dougal Cuthbert in August of 1728. During his wardenship Huggins exercised his office by deputy, preferring to live at his leisure in St. Martin in the Fields, where he was a vestryman, or at his estate in Headly Park, Hampshire, where from time to time he entertained members of Parliament. A man of genteel pretensions, he acquired the books of Sir Isaac Newton and had his library painted by Sir James Thornhill, whom he had evidently helped to become Royal Historical Painter. He was later charged with the death of Edward Arne, who died while Thomas Guybon was acting as deputy. Huggins was acquitted. In Hogarth's painting of the committee examining the Fleet, tradition names Huggins as the shadowy figure at the extreme left (easily visible in S. Bull's engraving a century later), his back turned upon the proceedings—so depicted by Hogarth "out of consideration for his friend's feelings." See R. B. Beckett, "Hogarth's Early Paintings: III 1728/9: The Gaols Enquiry," *Burlington Magazine* 90 (1948): 225. Huggins died in 1745.

22. For a detailed look at the case of Thomas Periom, Periam, or Perrin, see the following report on the Marshalsea Prison.

23. Vains, who ran a coffee-house, subsequently testified at Bambridge's second trial for the murder of Castell.

24. Bishop, who had paid two hundred pounds for his position as tipstaff, had been at the Fleet at least as early as 1723/24, when he attacked Major Wilson. Bishop was a prisoner himself, at least from June 25, 1728.

25. After Reed's first escape, in 1724 or 1725, Bambridge claimed that he paid five hundred pounds to Reed's creditors and thereafter put the prisoner in chains. In 1726 Reed escaped again.

26. A man who neglected his business and allegedly left his wife and family to starve, Edward Arne earlier appeared as the improvident upholsterer of Addison and Steele's *Tatlers* 155, 160, 178, and 232. He became thereby the prototype of the improvident newsmonger, frequently an upholsterer, as in Arthur Murphy's *The Upholsterer, or What News?* (1758). Since 1786, when John Nichols combined the two in his edition of *The Tatler*, he has often been confused with his first cousin Thomas Arne, father of the composer of "Rule, Britannia." Perhaps at one time Edward and Thomas Arne shared "The Two Crowns and Cushion," for both lived in King's Street and were "upholders," members of a small guild that then numbered about 144 and that combined upholstery with the sale of second-hand wares. In 1725 Edward was the "servant" of the guild, then located at Exeter Change, and was arrested for debts to some of the other members. By this time he was reduced to the clothes he was wearing, his seal, his gold-headed cane, and his gold watch. Ostracized by his fellow prisoners for his eccentricities, he was eventually confined in a dungeon over an open sewer, where he had neither heat, proper food, nor proper care. He soon died. In the trial for his murder, Warden John Huggins

managed to shift the blame to his agent John Barnes, who had fled, and to the deceased deputy, Thomas Guybon.

27. After Bambridge was removed from office, Cuthbert took charge about March 22, 1729.

28. See Oglethorpe's appendix A.

29. Captain John Macphreadris, described by John Mackay as a "Gentleman worth 100000 Pounds" (Mackay, *A True State of the Proceedings of the Prisoners in the Fleet-Prison*, 37), was confined, along with eighty or a hundred other prisoners, for tearing down partitions in the prison (*Mr. Bambridge's Case*, 1–2). Bambridge claimed that he was then merely visiting the prison and was not employed there.

30. Richard Corbett, tipstaff and keeper of a sponging house adjacent to the Fleet, was taken into custody on April 2, 1729, to stand trial for the murder of Castell.

31. Lieutenant Jenkin Leyson, or Lyson, was committed to the Fleet by Lord Chief Justice Eyre on January 18, 1728.

32. An officer of the superior courts at Westminster.

33. Thomas Hogg was transferred to the Fleet from the King's Bench Prison on December 10, 1726, and again committed to the Fleet, by Chief Justice Eyre, on May 3, 1727.

34. Thomas Guybon, or Gybbon, came to the Fleet in 1724 and served for a while as Huggins's deputy.

35. "An act for the relief of insolvent debtors," 6 George I, cap. 22: Pickering's *Statutes*, 14:291. Charles Fitch, or Fytche, was Clerk of the Enquiries under Guybon.

36. In a letter to the editor on November 24, 1988, Mr. D. Crook, of the Search Department of the Public Record Office wrote, "Only three of the five Committment Books he [Oglethorpe] mentions have survived. PRIS 1/2 is the one which begins, as he says, on 26 March 1708, and it ends on 4 November 1713. PRIS 1/4 is the one beginning on 6 May 1728, its last entry being made on 13 June 1729. The only other for that period, PRIS 1/3, runs from 9 February 1725 to 6 May 1728. The gap between 1713 and 1725 was presumably filled by the two volumes now wanting. . . . None of the other items he mentioned seems to have survived, and there are no other records of the Fleet Prison before 1729 except two earlier Committment Books, for James II—William and Mary, and for 1699–1700. . . ." I am grateful to Mr. Crook and the Public Record Office for microfilm copies of the three extant books, which have been a major source of my information concerning the prisoners.

37. David Boyce, or Boyes, was in the Fleet by 1725 and complained to Chief Justice Eyre of being overcharged. Bambridge maintained that Boyce, Booth, and Kilbury all escaped before he had custody of the prison.

38. William Kilbury, or Kilberry, was confined to the Fleet by order of Lord

Chief Justice Gilbert on July 20, 1726. He testified at Bambridge's second trial for the murder of Castell.

39. William Booth was committed to the Fleet by Justice Pangellys on December 7, 1726.

40. William Talure, Tayleur, or Taylor was committed to the Fleet by Justice C. J. Tracey on May 7, 1726, and was transferred back to the Fleet from the King's Bench Prison on October 28, 1727. Bambridge claimed (*Bambridge's Case*, 1) that Barnes, King, and Talure were never in his custody.

41. James Barnes became a prisoner in the Fleet during Hilary Term, 1724. He soon became a runner and watchman for Guybon, with liberty of the gate. He escaped when the order for his arrest arrived.

42. Pickering's *Statutes*, 8:371: 2–3 Charles II, cap. 20, sec. 9.

43. This toy ship apparently found its way into the possession of Lord Chief Justice Sir Robert Eyre, according to the testimony recorded by Luke Kenn, in "Minutes of the Proceedings of the Committee appointed to Enquire into the State of the Goals of this Kingdom, touching a Charge against Sir Robert Eyre," p. 8. See Rodney M. Baine, "The Oglethorpe Prison Committee and Lord Chief Justice Robert Eyre," *Journal of Legal History* 10 (1989): 343–51.

44. Sir Edward Herbert (1648?–1698), titular Earl of Portland, became Chief Justice of the Common Pleas in 1687.

45. Jacob Mendez Solas, or Jacob Mendez, a Portuguese Jew turned Christian and baptized, was apparently a jeweler. He testified at Bambridge's trial for felony and later contributed five guineas to the the Georgia Trustees via Dr. William Berriman, rector of St. Andrew Undershaft. Solas is probably the kneeling figure in Hogarth's portrait of the Fleet committee. Bambridge maintained that Solas was put in irons before he had any concern in the Fleet Prison.

46. In his *Case* Bambridge responded that Sinclair, or Sinkler, insulted, "collar'd, struck, and kick'd him" until he was rescued by the watch (p. 2). Sinclair testified at the appeal for the murder of Castell.

47. John Everett, turnkey and taphouse keeper at the Fleet, was executed at Tyburn for highway robbery on February 20, 1730/31, before he could give evidence concerning Chief Justice Eyre. When the first rope broke, he was strung up again. An alleged autobiography was published and circulated for the occasion.

48. Peter King, first Baron King, of Ockham (1669–1734), was Lord Chief Justice of the Common Pleas from 1724 until 1725.

49. My long dash substitutes for space left blank for the insertion of Guybon's first name, Thomas. In *JHC*, 21:280, an asterisk was substituted for the space.

50. John Holder was an old offender. A debtor in the Fleet as early as March of 1702, he escaped during that month. He was accused in the House of Commons of sending to Cadiz two ships, the galley *Cloudsley* and the frigate *Holder*, heavily insured for forty thousand pounds, and of having Mate Robert Acres transfer the

cargo of the *Cloudsley* to the *Holder* and then burn the galley. One of the officers confessed to the committe of the House (*JHC*, 13:796, 826–28). Warden Ford was ordered prosecuted because of Holder's escape.

51. Major George Wilson, or Willson, a merchant of Leeds, was in the Fleet by 1723 (Mackay, *True State*, 21) and was later confined there on June 13, 1726. Bambridge confined him in the strong room for alleged drunkenness and insults. John Pigot, or Piggot, was committed to the Fleet by Lord Chief Justice Robert Tracey on May 19, 1726. Bambridge said that Pigot was discharged from prison.

52. William Pindar was an underling and probably a prisoner in the Fleet by 1724, when he attacked Major Wilson. He was certainly committed to the Fleet on November 20, 1728. Thomas King, an accomplice of Bambridge, was committed to the Fleet on November 22, 1726. Apparently none of the four were ever charged for their alleged offenses.

A Report from the Committee . . . Relating to the Marshalsea Prison

1. *JHC*, 18:131; 20:86.
2. *JHC*, 20:360.
3. *Daily Journal*, March 29, 1729, p. 1.
4. For an analysis of this court and its problems, see William Buckley, *The Jurisdiction and Practice of the Marshalsea and Palace Courts* (London, 1827).
5. *London Evening Post*, March 19, 1730, p. 2.
6. Sir Philip Meadows the younger (d. 1757) was made Knight Marshal of the King's Household on July 2, 1700.
7. Contrary to the recommendations of Oglethorpe's committee and of the House of Commons, Darby was never charged with a crime. Even before Acton became his deputy, Acton seems to have run the prison as head turnkey, for Darby seems to have been rarely at the prison after 1725. Of the parish of St. George the Martyr, Acton served for four years as a butcher with a Mr. Haysey before becoming turnkey at the Marshalsea.
8. 22–23 Charles II, cap. 20, sec. 10: Pickering's *Statutes*, 8:372.
9. Punishing a prisoner if he refuses, or is unable, to pay garnish—the fee demanded of a new prisoner.
10. 12 George I, cap. 29: Pickering's *Statutes*, 15:331–33.
11. Sir Thomas Gresham (1519?–1579), the founder of Gresham College, left ten pounds a year for debtors in each of six London prisons.
12. Sir John Bennett (d. 1724) should be distinguished from John Bennett, Esq., an M.P. who served as Master of Chancery from 1717 until his death in 1739.
13. Clerk of the Papers for five years, Grace remembered the Marshalsea before Acton arrived there. He testified at Acton's trial for the murder of Thomas Bliss.

14. 11 George I, cap. 21: Pickering's *Statutes*, 15:231.

15. Sir John Darnall the younger (1672–1735) usually cooperated fully with the keeper of the prison under his jurisdiction. He testified for Acton at his trial for the murder of Thomas Bliss and defended Bambridge in his trial for the murder of Castell.

16. Lionel Cranfield Sackville, first Duke of Dorset (1688–1765) served as Lord Steward of the Household from 1725 to 1730 and again later.

17. John Campbell, second Duke of Argyll (1678–1743), a relative of Oglethorpe, was Lord Steward of the Household from 1718 to 1725.

18. 11 George I, cap. 21: Pickering's *Statutes*, 15:231.

19. For details concerning Thomas Bliss, see Acton's trial for his murder, in *A Complete Collection of State Trials*, ed. T. B. Howell, 33 vols. (London, 1809–26), 17:461–510.

20. Since John Darby was himself only deputy warden of the prison, terminology for Acton's role as his deputy was awkward. Acton was sometimes called chief turnkey, but he was certainly "farmer," or deputy leaser of the prison.

21. See the report on the Fleet, n. 26.

22. See ibid., n. 25.

23. For Bishop, see ibid., n. 24.

24. On May 25, 1728, the *London Evening Post* reported, p. 2, "Last Monday a charitably disposed Lady came to the Marshalsea Prison in Southwark, and discharg'd thirty poor Debtors for Sums not exceeding 50 Shillings each, besides the Fees of the Prison."

25. For Pindar, see the Fleet report, n. 52.

26. See also the preliminary report on the Fleet. In Oglethorpe's reports Bambridge is always the aggressor; but in Bambridge's version of this incident, after Sir William stabbed one of the keepers "three several times," the next morning he stabbed Bambridge himself "with a Shoemaker's Paring-Knife, provided on purpose, without any other Reason or Apology, for so doing, than *Damn you take that to your Heart*" (*Case*, 2). On March 3, 1729, a grand jury at the Old Baily indicted Bambridge for an assault on Sir William "with an Intent to murther him," but at the same time indicted Sir William for an assault on Bambridge (*Daily Post*, March 4, 1729, p. 1). Apparently neither case was brought to trial. It is probably Sir William who appears before the committee as the slight figure in the foreground in Hogarth's sketch of the committee investigating the Fleet Prison.

A Preliminary Report on the King's Bench Prison

1. John Mackay, Senior, was not an agent of the committee, but the attorney for the prisoners. In 1729 he dedicated to the committee his *True State of the Proceedings of the Prisoners in the Fleet-Prison*.

A Report from the Committee . . . Relating to the King's Bench Prison

1. Knatchbull, *Diary*, 100.
2. Percival, *Diary*, 1:46.
3. Ibid., 1:49.
4. *JHC*, 21:444.
5. See Baine, "The Oglethorpe Prison Committee," 343–51.
6. Oglethorpe cites the Calendar of Postmortem Inquisitions, 11 Henry VI, No. 43. The office of Marshal of the King's Bench Prison was ancillary to the office of Marshal, or Earl Marshal of England from at least as early as 1246, when Roger le Bigod, fourth Earl of Norfolk, was created Earl Marshal, with the ancillary posts of Marshal of the King's Bench Prison and Marshal of the Exchequer. Until 1572, when Thomas Howard II, fourth Duke of Norfolk, was executed, these offices were bestowed upon the earls and later the duke of Norfolk, though the offices were temporarily separated when the Norfolk line failed or the heir was under age—i.e., following the death of Thomas de Brotherton, Earl of Norfolk (1300–1338), and during the minority of John Mowbray, fourth Duke of Norfolk (1444–76). During these intervals and after 1572 the offices reverted to the Crown and were separately appointed.
7. See Great Britain, Parliament, *Rotuli Parliamentorum*, 6 vols. (London, 1767–77), 3:343–44.
8. Sir John Cutler (1608?–1693) was a parsimonius but civic-minded financier. He lent Lenthall more than twenty thousand pounds and left his daughter, Lady Radnor, above sixty thousand pounds, including his equity in the King's Bench Prison.
9. Nor did Oglethorpe discover the circumstances of the Lenthall title in 1752, when he again reported on the King's Bench Prison. In the subsequent report of 1753, however, Sir William Calvert managed to clarify Lenthall's title. On May 15, 1616, King James I had granted the marshalship of the King's Bench to Sir William Smith, "his Heirs and Assigns, to be exercised by him or themselves, or sufficient Deputy or Deputies, for ever" (*JHC*, 26:680). Thus the Crown and Parliament were virtually powerless to reform the prison because of the terms of James's careless grant and Parliament's subsequent legislation of 1708, confirming Lenthall's title. On May 16, 1631, Sir John Rous acquired the office, and on May 13, 1669, William Lenthall acquired it from Rous. However Sir John Lenthall (not to be confused with his nephew Sir John Lenthall, Speaker of the House of Commons) was acting marshal from at least as early as February 27, 1633, and continued to act, by deputy, until he died. He had evidently purchased the reversion of the marshalship some decades before he actually acquired it, for Sir John Rous admitted that he held it in trust for John Lenthall and his heirs (*JHC*, 26:680–81). After Lenthall's death in 1668, his grandson William Lenthall became marshal and successfully resisted legal and parliamentary efforts to remove him. After William died, childless,

in 1702, efforts to establish responsibility in the management of the King's Bench Prison were for decades thwarted by the legislation that Oglethorpe cites.

10. 8–9 William III, cap. 27: Pickering's *Statutes*, 10:89–98.

11. As Cutler's executor, Boulter assigned the mortgage of the King's Bench to Radnor by deed poll on January 17, 1700.

12. Charles Bodville (Robartes), Earl of Radnor (1660–1723), was the heir of Robert Robartes, styled Viscount Bodmin.

13. Although Joseph Studley owned only a twentieth part in the King's Bench, he seems to have managed financial affairs for the others as well.

14. As appears later, Richard Mullens became deputy warden in January of 1724.

15. Sir John Pratt (1657–1725) was made puisne judge in 1714 and served as Lord Chief Justice of the King's Bench court from 1718 until his death. Sir John Fortescue Aland (1670–1746) was a justice of the court from 1701 until he retired in 1726. Sir Robert Raymond, later Baron Raymond (1673–1733), was in 1720 attorney general, then in 1724 puisne judge of the King's Bench, and in 1725, Lord Chief Justice. In his rulings and summaries he helped to clarify the distinction between murder and manslaughter, especially in the trials of Bambridge for the murder of Castell.

16. James Reynolds (1686–1739) was puisne judge from 1725 until 1730. The painter Sir Joshua Reynolds was his nephew.

17. Sir John Holt (1642–1710) was Lord Chief Justice of the King's Bench from 1689 until 1710. Praised as *Verus* in *Tatler* 14, he was apparently independent and conscientious.

18. This may have been the murder described in *The Miseries of Goals, and the Cruelty of Goalers* (London, 1729), 15–16.

19. The interesting legal fiction developed here seems to have been ignored by the London newspapers.

20. See the account of the charity monies for the King's Bench Prison in *The Miseries of Goals*, 25–27.

21. 2 George II, cap. 20: Pickering's *Statutes*, 16:44–45.

22. See 8–9 William III, cap. 27, secs. 19, 22: Pickering's *Statutes*, 10:97–98.

23. The surviving books of the King's Bench Prison are now in the Public Record Office. To the list of marshals given by Oglethorpe can be added the names of Joseph Coling, in 1678; a Mr. Glover, removed from his office in 1686; a Mr. Farrington; a Mr. Church; and a Mr. Ford, all in 1698. Gimbert is "Gunibert" in the 1752 report.

24. Sir John Gonson attained some popularity in his addresses, from the bench, to the grand juries of Westminster. These addresses were frequently printed in the newspapers and were often reprinted as pamphlets. Sir John became a Georgia Trustee on March 13, 1733.

An Appeal for the Georgia Colony

1. The appeal was excerpted and summarized in the *London Magazine* for August 1732 (1:197-98). The editor of the *London Journal*, Francis Osborne, attained perhaps his greatest fame by being "beaten" by Dr. Johnson, for rudeness.

2. Benjamin Martyn, the new secretary for the Georgia Trustees, might conceivably have written the appeal: he had already used Oglethorpe's manuscript of *Some Account* for his own *Some Account of the Designs of the Trustees*, which he read to the Trustees on August 3, less than a week after Oglethorpe's appeal appeared; and he later embodied other passages from Oglethorpe's manuscript in his *Reasons for Establishing the Colony of Georgia* (1733). All his known writings on behalf of the colony, however, were first read, approved, and published by the Trustees. The general's were not. It seems quite unlikely that Martyn would have been so officious as to obtrude upon Oglethorpe's special province as newspaper publicist. Internal evidence enforces the ascription to Oglethorpe: like Oglethorpe's separate Georgia tracts, this appeal opens with classical models; and just as in the Preface of *A New and Accurate Account* the author pretends to have only recently come upon *Select Tracts*, so here the author pretends to be unfamiliar with the exact intentions of the Georgia Trustees. Such ruses were the stock in trade of the "puffer." Finally, the rare quotation of Eccelsiastes 9:15 reappears in Oglethorpe's second "Faber" letter.

3. Publius Cornelius Scipio, *Africanus Major*.

4. Terence, *Heautontimorumenos* 1.77, with "nil" altered to "nihil." Later, in *The Naked Truth*, Oglethorpe quoted from Terence's *Eunuchus*. The Library of Oglethorpe lists the 1706 Dacier edition of Terence (item 988) and the Echard edition of 1718 (item 1059).

5. He will not increase his fees by writing needless prescriptions.

6. Hippocrates, the Greek physician idealized in the Middle Ages and the Renaissance, was doubtless intended to suggest Sir Hans Sloane (1660-1753). President of the Royal Society, Sir Hans never refused a needy patient and gave his salary to charity and his fortune and his collections to the nation. His friend Oglethorpe served as a trustee for his donation to the British Museum. Sir Hans contributed to the Georgia colony and in 1734 treated Tomochichi's dying companion.

7. Decius (Publius Decius Mus the elder or the younger?) could be intended for Colonel Charles Selwyn (1688-1751), one of the most active members of the prison committee and a Georgia Trustee; but was more likely meant for Colonel George Carpenter (c. 1695-1749), who was soon to be elected President of the Trustees.

8. Massala (Marcus Massala, *Niger?*) was surely Lord Chief Justice Sir Robert Raymond, whose probity Oglethorpe praised in his prison reports.

9. Cornelius (Publius Cornelius Scipio, *Africanus Major?*) may have been Oglethorpe's cousin John Campbell, second Duke of Argyll.

10. The well-to-do Captain Thraso appears in Terence's *Eunuchus*.

11. Alphus, a name unfamiliar to readers of the classics, was doubtless intended for Sir Gilbert Heathcote, Mayor of London and Governor of the Bank of England, who had been pilloried as a miser by Alexander Pope in three of his poems. One of the richest commoners, with large estates, Sir Gilbert spoke in Parliament for the Georgia colony and used his influence in the bank on its behalf. His nephew George Gilbert Heathcote was an active member of the prison committee and served as treasurer of the Georgia Trustees.

12. *An Account of the Sufferings of the Persecuted Protestants in the Archbishoprick of Saltzburg*. Translated from the German, probably by the Reverend Frederich Michael Ziegenhagen's secretary, the book was apparently in the press in May of 1732.

13. The Society for Promoting Christian Knowledge (SPCK).

14. Ecclesiastes 9:15: "Now there was found in it a poor wise man, and he by his wisdom delivered the city."

15. A favorite phrase of Oglethorpe. See his *Some Account of the Design of the Trustees for establishing Colonys in America*, ed. Baine and Phinizy Spalding (Athens, 1990), 11; and his letter to Bishop George Berkeley of May 1731, in Benjamin Rand, ed., *Berkeley and Percival: The Correspondence of George Berkeley and Sir John Percival* (Cambridge, 1914), 276–77.

16. For material here Oglethorpe drew on his *Some Account*, 11.

17. These two sentences come from *Some Account*, 11–12. In the following sentence I have substituted angled brackets for Oglethorpe's retangular ones.

18. On April 18, 1732, Richard Smith, a bookbinder, and his wife Briget hanged themselves after killing their two-year-old child. Smith left letters explaining these deaths, and these letters were published not only in the London newspapers, but separately, as *An Exact Copy of Some Genuine Letters Wrote by the late Unhappy Mr. Smith* (London, 1732).

19. Writers on civil law.

20. This long sentence, with the exception of the opening phrase, appears in *Some Account*, 42.

21. Compare ibid., 48.

22. Compare ibid., 45.

23. Compare ibid., 45–56.

24. Compare ibid., 15.

Select Tracts Relating to Colonies

1. By Verner W. Crane, "The Promotional Literature of Georgia," *Bibliographical Essays: A Tribute to Wilberforce Eames* (Cambridge, Mass., 1924), 290–91; and by Leonard Mackall, ed., *Catalogue of the Wymberley Jones De Renne Georgia Library*, 3 vols. (Wormsloe, Ga., 1931), 3:1336c.

2. Thomas Coram to Henry Newman, November 20, 1732, Rawlinson MS D.839, fol. 130, Bodleian Library, Oxford University, from a photostat kindly furnished by the Bodleian. For a fuller account of Oglethorpe's editorship, see Baine, "James Oglethorpe and the Early Promotional Literature for Georgia," *William and Mary Quarterly*, 3d series, 45 (January 1988):104–5.

3. John Nichols, *Literary Anecdotes of the Eighteenth Century*, 9 vols. (London, 1812–15; rpt., New York: AMS, 1966), 2:17.

4. *The Library of Oglethorpe*, items 292, 562, 1111, and 1864.

5. Although eighteenth-century English translations identified the author as Jan de Witt, he furnished at most only a few chapters, and not that on colonies. See Herbert H. Rowen, *John de Witt, Grand Pensionary of Holland, 1625–1672* (Princeton, 1978), 391–98.

6. See especially Fayrer Hall, *The Importance of the British Plantations in America* (London, 1731); the enlarged, third edition of Joshua Gee's *The Trade and Navigation of Great-Britain Considered* (London, 1731); the newspapers; and *Gentleman's Magazine* and *London Magazine*.

7. A favorite adventurer and author for Oglethorpe, Raleigh was twice quoted in *Some Account*. Oglethorpe apparently owned several editions of Raleigh's *History of the World* (*The Library of Oglethorpe*, items 503, 717, 1160, 2113, and 2350); and on his first voyage to Georgia he apparently carried with him Raleigh's *Discoverie of . . . the Empyre of Guiana* (London, 1596). According to the *South Carolina Gazette* for March 24, 1732/33, "Mr. *Oglethorpe* has with him, Sir *Walter Raleigh*'s written Journal, and by the Latitude of the Place, the Marks and Tradition of the *Indians*, it's [Savannah is] the very Place where he [Raleigh] first went a-shore and talk'd with the *Indians*."

8. Arthur Wodenoth, *A Short Collection of the Most Remarkable Passages from the Originall to the Dissolution of the Virginia Company* (London, 1651), 2, paraphrased by Oglethorpe rather than quoted. Oglethorpe cited Wodenoth again in his *New and Accurate Account*.

9. According to Michael Kiernan, "The essay appears to have been written . . . c. 1619–22." See Sir Francis Bacon, *The Essayes or Counsels, Civil and Morall*, ed. Kiernan (Cambridge, Mass., 1985), 239. The essay was first printed in the edition of 1625. In his capacity as solicitor-general, Bacon may have helped to write the second charter of the Virginia Company.

10. Niccolo di Bernardo dei Machiavelli.

11. William Penn, *Some Account of the Province of Pennsilvania*, published by Benjamin Clark shortly after Penn's patent was granted, on March 4, 1681, with no price listed. Charles M. Andrews also said that it was printed in 1680 and "never sold," but he may have based his statement on Oglethorpe. See *The Colonial Period of American History*, 4 vols. (New York, 1934–38), 4:337 and n. 3.

12. I have been unable to identify the source of this quotation; the writer may have been Thomas Penn, with whom Oglethorpe was corresponding at this period.

13. Sir Josiah Child, *A New Discourse concerning Trade* (London, 1692), reprinted from one of Oglethorpe's copies, apparently of the 1698 edition. (*The Library of Oglethorpe*, items 791 and 1111. Item 1111 is undated.)

14. Convicts were among the first Virginia settlers. See Bacon, *Essayes*, ed. Kiernan, 92–95.

15. The Virginia Company then comprised more than a thousand patentees and about a hundred counselors.

16. Kiernan implies (*Essayes*, 239) that Bacon may have seen the manuscript (c. 1610) of William Strachey's *True Repotory* (London, 1625), which criticizes the site selected for the colony.

17. The italics and capitals are Oglethorpe's added emphasis. Bacon surely completed his essay before the Indians massacred 347 white settlers on March 22, 1622.

18. The most celebrated of the dozen or so Indians brought over in 1616 was Powhatan's daughter Pocahontas.

19. Niccolo Machiavelli, *Works* (London, 1680), 22–24, the first paragraph of book 2, with the final words "they were wont" altered to "of the Ancients."

20. Genoa was pillaged and burned by the Saracens in 936.

21. Machiavelli, *Works*, 201, parts of the first two paragraphs, with Oglethorpe's own chapter heading. Oglethorpe's three long dashes indicate the omissions, successively, of a sentence, part of a sentence, and five sentences.

22. Machiavelli, *Works*, 213, again with Oglethorpe's chapter heading. Machiavelli's own heading was "*How the strength of all principalities is to be computed.*" In the first sentence Oglethorpe changed "free" to "safe." Oglethorpe's long dash indicates the omission of part of a sentence.

23. Machiavelli, *Works*, 268–69. Titus Livius was the Roman historian Livy. Oglethorpe reprinted parts of three paragraphs, omitting the first four lines, then skipping the final two sentences of the first paragraph, and finally skipping sixteen lines, indicating omissions by long dashes.

24. Ragusa.

25. Selim I (1467/70–1520).

26. Dinocrates actually designed Alexandria. The anecdote apparently comes from Vitruvius Pollio, *De Architectura*, Preface, 2–3. Although *The Library of Oglethorpe* shows no copy of Vitruvius, the general knew and apparently quoted from Robert Castell's manuscript translation. See Oglethorpe, *Some Account*, xxiv.

27. Machiavelli, *Works*, 281, part of the long opening paragraph.

28. Scipio Africanus Major (236–184/3 B.C.), reputedly incorruptible; Gaius Julius Caesar (100–44 B.C.); Agesilaus II (444–360 B.C.), patriot king of Sparta; Timolean (d. 334 B.C.), opponent of tyranny and protagonist of Benjamin Martyn's 1730 tragedy; Dion (c. 408–354 B.C.), liberator of Syracuse; Nabis (d. 192 B.C.), Spartan tyrant; Phalaris (c. 570/65–554/49 B.C.), tyrant of Acragas and originator of the brazen bull; Dionysius I (430–367 B.C.), tyrant of Syracuse.

29. Lucius Sergius Catalina (c. 108–62 B.C.), the conspirator.

30. Machiavelli, *Works*, 283. Oglethorpe opens in the middle of a sentence and does not finish the paragraph. Machiavelli's "Commonwealth," in the first line, Oglethorpe changed to "virtuous City."

31. Numa Pompilius (715–673 B.C.), reputedly the author of many Roman institutions.

32. Machiavelli, *Works*, 293–94, using Oglethorpe's own chapter heading and opening in the middle of a paragraph.

33. Pelopidas (c. 410–364 B.C.) and Epaminondas (d. 362 B.C.) rescued Thebes from the Spartans in 379 B.C.

34. Tullus Hostilius (c. 673–642 B.C.), legendary third king of Rome.

35. *Aeneid*, 6.813–14. Machiavelli's change of Virgil's "Residesque" to "Desidesque" Oglethorpe kept, but stopped just short of the translation: "No soft unactive people *Tullus* knows / But trains up all promiscuously to blows."

36. Machiavelli, *Works*, 341. The long dashes indicate the omissions, successively, of a phrase, a sentence, parts of two sentences, most of a long sentence, and part of a sentence.

37. In 396 B.C. the Romans besieged and captured Vei, an Etruscan city about ten miles north of Rome.

38. Machiavelli, *Works*, 342, combining two paragraphs. The chapter heading is Machiavelli's.

39. Livy, *Annales*, 5.24.

40. Machiavelli, *Works*, 357, part of the first paragraph, with the omission of four sentences.

41. [Pieter de la Court], *The True Interest and Political Maxims of the Republick of Holland* (London, 1702), 139–46, 153–54. Oglethorpe used De la Court's chapter title, adding the inaccurate ascription to De Witt and the words "A Treatise proving."

42. Not only the Dutch colonies of Cochin, Negapatam, and Ceylon, but the numerous colonies in the East Indies. Just as contemporary references to the East and West Indies often designated the mainland, so vice versa. The subsequent italics are Oglethorpe's.

43. Oglethorpe's compositor erroneously substituted "heard" for "hard."

44. At this point Oglethorpe skipped seven pages without indicating an omission. He also stopped short of the final sentence.

45. Trading groups, rather than colonies in the modern sense. Lyfland was the Dutch name for Livonia.

46. The first half of William Penn's *Some Account*, 1–4, beginning with the second paragraph and omitting Penn's second word there, "then."

47. Caleb was one of the Jewish spies sent into Canaan. Lycurgus, the third prominent Greek of that name (c. 390–325/4 B.C.), was responsible for many naval reforms. The legendary Theseus reputedly united all Attica into one state. Romulus was one of the legendary founders of Rome.

48. Child, *New Discourse* (1698 ed.), 178–94.

49. Here Oglethorpe skipped points six through eleven, Child, *New Discourse*, 179–80.

50. Oglethorpe did not finish Child's sentence (*New Discourse*, 181), but modified the structure in order to complete the sense.

51. Especially the Puritans and the Anabaptists.

52. Cromwell's victory on September 3, 1651.

53. John Graunt, *Natural and Political . . . Observations upon the Bills of Mortality*, 3d ed. (London, 1665), 76, 100–101.

54. Oglethorpe quoted and paraphrased this passage in his *Some Account*, 44.

55. Just before the word "Utensils" Oglethorpe omitted "the *Negroes* and," and after "him" he omitted "it being customary in most of our *Islands* in *America*, upon every Plantation, to employ eight or ten Blacks for one white Servant" (190).

56. Graunt, *Observations*, 88.

57. Since "*Falselet*" was surely the compositor's misreading of Child's *Taffelet*, rather than Oglethorpe's mistake, I have restored Child's original (*New Discourse*, 193) here.

A New and Accurate Account of the Provinces of South-Carolina and Georgia

1. Crane, "Promotional Literature," 289.
2. Nichols, *Literary Anecdotes*, 2:17.
3. See Oglethorpe, *Some Account*, Introduction, xxi–xxvi.
4. See Baine, "Oglethorpe and Promotional Literature," 105–6.
5. Klaus E. Knorr, *British Colonial Theories, 1570–1850* (Toronto, 1944), 77, n. 63.
6. David S. Shields, *Oracles of Empire: Poetry, Politics, and Commerce in British America, 1690–1750* (Chicago, 1990), 58; Knorr, *British Colonial Theories*, 131.
7. John Archdale, *A New Description of that Fertile and Pleasant Province of Carolina* (London, 1707).
8. Milton R. Ready, "The Georgia Concept: An Eighteenth-Century Experiment in Colonization," *Georgia Historical Quarterly* 55 (1971):162, 171, n. 23; Webb Garrison, *Oglethorpe's Folly: The Birth of Georgia* (Lakemont, Ga., 1982), 44, 229, n. 8.
9. Purry had already developed his conviction in his *Memorial Presented to his Grace the Duke of Newcastle* (London, 1724).
10. The bibliographical collation follows: half title, verso blank; title, verso blank; text, 1–76: *²A²a², B–E⁸, F². The preliminaries were obviously printed as part of sheet F. I have not reproduced the half title: "A / New and Accurate Account / OF THE / PROVINCES / OF / *SOUTH-CAROLINA* / AND / *GEORGIA*."

11. *Collections of the Georgia Historical Society*, 21 vols. to date (Savannah, 1840–), 1:42–78; Trevor Reese, ed., *The Most Delightful Country of the Universe: Promotional Literature of the Colony of Georgia, 1717–1734* (Savannah, 1972), 114–56, xvi.

12. It was purchased in 1903 from Henry Stevens, Son, and Styles. This firm acquired it in 1893, from a source it can not now identify. Thomas P. Macdonnel to the editor, August 31, 1989.

13. Mackall, ed., *Catalogue*, 1:32. The judgment may have actually been that of G. W. Cole.

14. Archdale, *Description* (1707 ed.).

15. Thomas Nairne, *A Letter from South Carolina* (London, 1710); 2d ed., 1718; 3d ed., 1732.

16. Nairne, *Letter*, 1st ed., 17–23, 33–34, 35–39.

17. Doubtless a common jest, but Oglethorpe may have had in mind Thomas Shadwell's comedy *The Humorists*, where in act one the quack French doctor Pullim cures Crazy in this way.

18. Archdale wrote that "17 Ships, this Year, came laden from *Carolina*" (*Description*, 11); and Nairne wrote of "two and twenty Sail of *English* Ships" (*Letter*, 1st ed., 57). In his *Description Abregée de l'Etat présent de la Caroline Meridionale*, 2d ed. (Neuchatel, 1732), 11, Jean Pierre Purry stated that there were "up to about 200 Ships annually."

19. "Drawn up at Charles-Town, in September, 1731," Purry's tract was partially translated for the *Gentleman's Magazine* for August, September, and October 1732 (2:894–96, 969–70, 1007–18). This translation was reprinted by B. R. Carroll, ed., *Historical Collections of South Carolina*, 2 vols. (New York, 1836), 2:124–40. Purry apparently brought not 600 Swiss, but about 150, though his colonists totaled some 700 within three years. See Robert L. Meriwether, *The Expansion of South Carolina, 1729–1765* (Kingsport, Tenn., 1940), 35; and Arlin C. Migliazzo, "A Tarnished Legacy Revisited: Jean Pierre Purry and the Settlement of the Southern Frontier, 1718–1736," *South Carolina Historical Magazine* 92 (1992): 232–52.

20. Samuel Butler, *Hudibras*, part 2, canto 1 (London, 1674), p. 251: item 510 in *The Library of Oglethorpe*.

21. Archdale was chosen in 1698 as M.P. for Chipping Wycombe, Buckinghamshire.

22. Oglethorpe is indulging in the conventional eighteenth-century practice of "puffing," praising one's other publications. See, post, his denial of the practice in his praise of John Howard.

23. Benjamin Martyn's *Some Account of the Designs of the Trustees* (London, 1732) appeared both separately and in the newspapers, as in the *Country Journal, or the Craftsman* for August 12, 1732. Actually Martyn produced merely a pastiche of the Georgia Charter and Oglethorpe's *Some Account*.

24. In 1609, through a group of guilds, the City of London began "the Plantation in Ulster," an organization that in 1612–13 became "the Irish Society."

Oglethorpe was especially interested in this plantation because his grandfather Richard Wall had been "transplanted" to Connaught in 1656 and because his mother claimed kinship with the Argyll family through her grandfather Maurice Roche, of Killcoman, Tipperary.

25. "The Society of the Governors and Assistants, London, of the New Plantation in Ulster."

26. In his *Some Account*, 14, Oglethorpe placed the southern boundary of Carolina at 29 degrees longitude, in accordance with the grant of 1665. Moreover, in his later dealings with the Spaniards concerning the Georgia border he apparently insisted on a boundary far south of the Altamaha. See Antonio de Arrendondo, *Historical Proof of Spain's Title to Georgia*, ed. Herbert E. Bolton (Berkeley, 1925), 72–74, 191–92, 298–99.

27. In the map appended to Martyn's *Some Account*, St. Augustine is shown "far south of its actual site." See Louis de Vorsey, Jr., "Oglethorpe and the Earliest Maps of Georgia," *Oglethorpe in Perspective: Georgia's Founder After Two Hundred Years*, ed. Phinizy Spalding and Harvey H. Jackson (Tuscaloosa, 1989), 33.

28. The Pacific Ocean.

29. Pope Alexander VI's concessions of May 4, 1493.

30. The material in this paragraph and the next seems to be paraphrased from John Oldmixon, *The British Empire in America*, 2 vols. (London, 1708), 1:325–29.

31. So Archdale, *Description*, 5; but Oldmixon (1:325) correctly dismissed this inaccurate claim for Cabot.

32. The French King.

33. In the De Renne copy, Oglethorpe deleted "from Invaders."

34. Anthony Ashley Cooper, first Earl of Shaftesbury, "The Fundamental Constitutions for the Government of Carolina," dated July 21, 1669, in the Public Record Office, is in Locke's hand, but Locke was secretary to the proprietors; he seems, however, to have assisted in framing the document. See Maurice Cranston, *John Locke* (London, 1957), 119–20; and John C. Attig, comp., *The Works of John Locke: A Comprehensive Bibliography* (Westport, Conn., 1985), 5–6.

35. In the De Renne copy, Oglethorpe moved "only" from in front of "be."

36. From Edmund Waller, "The Battle of the Summer-Islands." For the changes here in the De Renne copy, see my introductory comments.

37. Thomas Burnet, *The Sacred Theory of the Earth*, ed. Basil Willey (Carbondale, 1965), 149–63.

38. "Some say he bid his Angels turne ascanse / The Poles of the Earth twice ten degrees and more / From the Suns Axle" (John Milton, *Paradise Lost*, 10.668–70).

39. In the De Renne copy Oglethorpe pluralized "Vicissitude."

40. Samuel Purchase, *Purchase his Pilgrimage* (London, 1613), 645, bk. 8, ch. 7 (item 944 in *The Library of Oglethorpe*).

41. According to legend, his beloved son Eos (Aurora) so changed him, out of pity.

42. "Old age withered Tithonus slowly." Horace, *Odes* 2.16.30.

43. In the De Renne copy, Oglethorpe restored the arabic numbers that the compositor had spelled out. Oglethorpe had done the same thing in proofreading *The Sailors Advocate*.

44. See Oldmixon, *British Empire*, 1:161–62.

45. Archdale, *Description*, 8. See also Oldmixon, *British Empire*, 1:344–45.

46. Oglethorpe may have combined Captain John Smith's various estimates of the Virginia Indians interspersed through his *Map of Virginia* (Oxford, 1612), 29–33, and his *Generall Historie* (London, 1624). For an interesting analysis of Indian populations, see Peter H. Wood, "The Changing Population of the Colonial South: An Overview by Race and Region," in *Powhatan's Mantle: Indians in the Colonial Southeast*, ed. Wood et al. (Lincoln, Nebr., 1989), 35–103.

47. Horace, *Ars Poetica*, 206: "That was, when listeners could still be counted."

48. In 1616 Powhatan so instructed Uttamaccomack. See Oldmixon, *British Empire*, 1:285.

49. For the various visits, see Carolyn Thomas Foreman, *Indians Abroad, 1493–1938* (Norman, Okla., 1943).

50. In De Renne, Oglethorpe excised the "somewhat" before "tawny" and added "or olive-Coloured."

51. The fact that in De Renne Oglethorpe had to correct the blunder "Fourpence" to "Four Shillings" here suggests, along with other evidence, that in his absence in 1732, no one read proof except the printer.

52. In the De Renne copy, Oglethorpe changed the comma here to a period, but neglected to capitalize the *t* of "they."

53. This De Renne correction replaces the original "at least, easy Education." Brackets enclose my conjectural readings.

54. Oglethorpe replaced the period after "Suretyship" by a semicolon and added "[in thin]king."

55. In De Renne, Oglethorpe altered "here" to "there."

56. Sir William Petty, *Political Arithmetic* (London, 1690); Sir William Temple, *Observations upon the United Provinces of the Netherlands* (London, 1673).

57. Among the principal advancements to trade Temple lists "The Severity of Justice," with "Workehouses, or Hospitals, as they [beggars] are able or unable to labour" (Temple, *Observations*, 200–201). Most "Rasp-houses" were houses of correction where prisoners were put to rasping wood.

58. Oglethorpe is whimsically exaggerating Temple's remark in his sixth chapter that "the true original and ground of Trade" was "the great multitude of people crowded into small compass of Land" (*Observations*, 187).

59. Oglethorpe is actually quoting Thomas Sheridan, *The Intelligencer*, no. 6.

He was misled because the second, collected edition (London, 1730), advertised the essays as *"By the Author of a* TALE *of a* TUB" — Swift. Although Swift started the journal and contributed to it, Sheridan wrote this sixth number. See the AMS reprint of *The Intelligencer* (New York, 1967), 61–63; and *The Prose Works of Jonathan Swift*, ed. Herbert Davis and Harold Williams, 16 vols. (Oxford, 1939–74), 12:xv.

60. In the De Renne copy, Oglethorpe moved the "and" after "Pounds" to follow "Removal."

61. Here Oglethorpe inserted "of" after "Encouragement" and changed "of Propagation" to "by Propagation."

62. The natural analogy was still timely because of the increased popularity of the controversial *Fable of the Bees, or Private Vices, Public Benefits*, by Bernard Mandeville (London, 1714). Part 2 appeared in 1728; and his final works, in 1732.

63. In De Renne, Oglethorpe deleted "Martyrs and" before "Confessors." Evidently almost twenty thousand Saltzburgers emigrated to East Prussia.

64. Here Oglethorpe corrected his blunder giving credit to the Society for the Propagation of the Gospel in Foreign Parts (SPG), another blunder which suggests that no one read proof except the printer. He also adjusted "have" to "h[as]" and "themselves" to "itse[lf]."

65. In De Renne, Oglethorpe inserted the "about" and supplied the "1" missing in the "10" of "¹⁄10."

66. Bartolome de las Casas, probably from the retelling in Purchas, *Pilgrimage*, 449 (bk. 5, ch. 16).

67. Corrected in De Renne from "2 *Brit. Emp.* Fol.I. p.162."

68. Oglethorpe refers to the acts against the inalienable return of lands and buildings held by the Catholic Church: 26 Henry VIII, cap. 28; 31 Henry VIII, cap. 13, 35; 35 Henry VIII, cap. 14; 37 Henry VIII, cap. 20; and 1 Edward VI, cap. 14: Pickering's *Statutes*, 4:403–10, 455–68; 5:207, 236, 267–86.

69. In the De Renne copy, Oglethorpe deleted the "but" after "Life."

70. Here Oglethorpe clarified by inserting ", South Carolina,."

71. Here he changed "sent" to "send."

72. Here Oglethorpe deleted the repetitive "a Year" and inserted "wh[at]" after "compute."

73. William Houston.

74. In De Renne, Oglethorpe penciled "might" to replace "may."

75. "Sh[illings]" here corrects the deleted "Pence."

76. "More" is Oglethorpe's clarification in the De Renne copy.

77. "An act for granting liberty to carry rice from . . . Carolina . . . directly to any part, of Europe" is 3 George II, cap. 28: Pickering's *Statutes*, 16:182–86.

78. "Homew[ard]" is Oglethorpe's insertion in De Renne.

79. John Selden, *Of the Dominion, or, Ownership of the Sea* (London, 1652). *The Library of Oglethorpe* shows two editions, or copies, items 893 and 1423. Josiah

Burchett, *A Complete History of the most Remarkable Transactions at Sea* (London, 1720). In De Renne, Oglethorpe corrected the misspelling "Martime."

80. Sir Edward Coke, "Ad Lectorem," *Le Quart Part des Reportes* (London, 1610), sig. [B6], recto. In the De Renne copy, Oglethorpe corrected several mistakes, probably the compositor's: he corrected "*ominantium*" to "*dominantium*," "*ego*" to "*ago*," and the period after "*includuntur*" to a comma. He did not, however, correct the blunder *eum* to *eam*, or supply the omitted "*rerum.*"

81. Paul de Rapin-Thoyras, *The History of England*, trans. N. Tindal, 28 vols. (London, 1726–47), 1:391–92. This edition is item 1737 in *The Library of Oglethorpe*.

82. Arthur Wodenoth, *A Short Collection*, 4–16.

83. "Vers 1731 il avait 100 à 106 métiers battants qui produisaient annuellement 30.000 à 40.000 aunes d'étoffes." Albert Demangeon, *La Picardie* (Paris, 1905), 265. Percival told Sloper, on February 16, 1730, that "the manufacture [of wool] at Abbeville was set up the very year ours [the Irish] was ruined, and that by the Irish weavers who were obliged to leave their country for want of business." Percival, *Diary*, 1:48.

84. Percival commented that "the Irish will certainly furnish France with wool by running it thither though a hundred ships were employed to prevent it" (*Diary*, 1:48). See F. G. James, "Irish Smuggling in the Eighteenth Century," *Irish Historical Studies*, 12:299–317.

85. In 1704 Captain Thomas Coram, later a Georgia Trustee, was instrumental in obtaining a bounty on tar imported from the colonies.

86. Although Oglethorpe was himself too busy in Georgia to follow up this puff, he provided Benjamin Martyn with materials for his *Reasons for Establishing the Colony of Georgia* (London, 1733).

A Description of the Indians in Georgia

1. This account, variously titled, was several times reprinted, at first virtually entire, in the *Gentleman's Magazine* for August 1733 (3:413–15) and the *London Magazine* for the same month (2:399–400), then, considerably cut, in Thomas Salmon's *Modern History: Or the Present State of all Nations*, 3d ed., 3 vols. folio (London, 1739), 3:602, and in *A New Voyage to Georgia. By a Young Gentleman* (London, 1735), 57–60. In 1841 this truncated version was reprinted in *Collections of the Georgia Historical Society*, 2:61–64. The account was not included in Peter Force's 1837 reprint of *A New Voyage*.

2. On August 1, 1733, Percival recorded in his *Journal*, "A long letter from Mr. Oglethorp was read, giving a character of the Indians with whom he has made a Treaty," and on the same day he noted in his *Diary*, "A long letter from Mr. Oglethorp received yesterday was read, giving . . . a character at large of the Indians

with whom he has made a treaty." John Percival, *The Journal of the Earl of Egmont*, ed. Robert G. McPherson (Athens, 1962), 31; and Percival, *Diary*, 1:398.

3. On the contrary, according to Charles Hudson, "The Creeks placed a high value on having several wives or concubines, though only the wealthier men could afford it." See his *The Southeastern Indians* (Knoxville, 1976), 199.

4. Evidently when they visited the white settlers, the Yuchis, who lived upriver from Savannah, helped themselves, in approved Indian fashion, to whatever fruits and vegetables they needed.

5. During the Yamacraw's visit to England in 1734, William Verelst painted Tomochichi with his eagle feathers and his buffalo robe.

An Account of Carolina and Georgia

1. Thomas Salmon, *Modern History*, 3 vols. (London: Bettesworth and Hitch, 1739), 3:770–73. This edition was announced in the *Daily Advertiser* on April 9, 1739. Salmon later reprinted various sections from Oglethorpe's "Account" in his *New Geographical and Historical Grammar* (London, 1749) and his *Modern Gazeteer: Or a Short View of the Several Nations of the World* (London, 1746).

2. Thaddeus Mason Harris, *Biographical Memoirs of James Oglethorpe* (Boston, 1841), 312–22. The only "fourth" edition of Salmon's *Modern History* consists of late issues of the octavo edition sold by J. Crokatt and others. I am greatly indebted to Alexander E. Lucas, Reference Librarian at the Newberry Library, for locating and furnishing me with a copy of Oglethorpe's "Account." Henry Bruce excerpted sections from Harris's reprint for his *Life of General Oglethorpe* (New York, 1890), 80–92; but he further confused the provenance of Oglethorpe's "Account" by giving the impression that he took it from an imaginary fourth, folio edition of *Modern History*, which he dated about 1752.

3. Salmon, *Modern History*, Bettesworth's edition, 3:770.

4. For the suggestion about Gascoigne, on whose ship Oglethorpe returned to England in 1734, I am indebted to my colleague Louis De Vorsey, Professor Emeritus of Geography.

5. Captain John Smith so used the word "swamps," at least as early as 1624.

6. "Sir" John Hill called the magnolia "the laurel-leaved Tulip-tree." Later the native Georgian poet Thomas Holley Chivers called it "the wild emerald cucumber-tree" ("Rosalie Lee").

7. See my introduction to this "Account."

8. Probably the Indian name for Jekyll Sound. The Spanish name was Gouadaquini, or Gualquini Sound. Captain George Dymond testified before the Georgia Trustees on January 16, 1740, "That Jekyll Sound can contain twelve Men of War in safety, being well Land Lock'd." See *Colonial Records of the State of Georgia*, ed.

Allen D. Candler, Kenneth Coleman, et al., 32 vols. to date (Atlanta and Athens, 1904–), 1:363. Subsequent references cite this work as *CRG*.

9. When Admiral Francis Hosier's blockade of the Spanish galleons at Porto Bello was raised, in 1727, his forces had been decimated by fever. The admiral himself died of its effects.

10. "Sulwan's Island" in Salmon seems to be the compositor's misreading of "Sulivan's Island."

11. "Makes the entry" in Salmon seems, again, a compositor's misreading.

12. The lighthouse was completed about March 30, 1736 (*CRG*, 21:274).

13. The Vernon River runs just northeast of the Ogeechee. The Westbrook River, which was later called Augustine Creek, was, like the tiny village of Westbrook, named after Oglethorpe's estate at Godalming. The village centered about Walter Augustine's saw mill, about ten miles upriver from Savannah. In this sentence and four sentences later, the compositor's "country" may well be misreadings of Oglethorpe's "county."

14. See Samuel Urlsperger, ed., *Detailed Reports on the Salzburger Emigrants Who Settled in America*, trans. and ed. George Fenwick Jones et al., 18 vols. to date (Athens, 1968–), 3:244, 250, 251, and 5:79, 188; and *CRG*, 20:132–33. Although Henry Parker's mill was on Abercorn Creek, both Ebenezer River (Creek) and Abercorn Creek were outlets of the same stream (*Detailed Reports*, 5:143).

15. For Brims, see Walter A. Harris, *Emperor Brim* (Macon, Ga., 1956), and David H. Corkran, *The Creek Frontier, 1540–1783* (Norman, Okla., 1967), 61–80. Oglethorpe apparently just missed meeting Brims, for the *South Carolina Gazette* for June 2, 1733, called "old Breen" "lately dead."

16. Oglethorpe's use of *buffaloe* for *bison* anticipates by half a century the first example in the *NED*, where the same protest of impropriety is registered.

17. Probably the mountain lion, or cougar (felis concolor).

18. The bobolink.

An Account of the Negroe Insurrection in South Carolina

1. Lieutenant Governor William Bull's reports on October 5 to the Duke of Newcastle and to the Board of Trade and Plantations are not so detailed, and the *South Carolina Gazette* for September 15, 1739, contains nothing about the rebellion. Later issues for that month are apparently not extant.

2. Percival, *Diary*, 3:105, 118.

3. Peter H. Wood, *Black Majority: Negroes in Colonial South Carolina from 1670 Through the Stono Rebellion* (New York, 1974), 320.

4. Phinizy Spalding, *Oglethorpe in America* (Chicago, 1977), 74.

5. Oglethorpe to Verelst, October 9, 1739, Great Britain, Public Record Office,

Colonial Office 5/640:392r, hereinafter cited as CO. Brackets enclose conjectural readings for words obliterated in the MS.

6. On the following day the account appeared in both the *London Daily Post, and General Advertiser* and the *London Evening Post.* It appeared also in the March issues of the *Gentleman's Magazine* (10:127–29) and (excerpted) the *Scots Magazine* (2:138–39). It was published in *CRG,* 22 (2):232–36, with sidenotes added by the editor.

7. CO 5/640:393r–396r. On folio 391r it was addressed "To Mr. Harman Verelst. These" and marked "recd. 13 March 1939." The account was written fair and quite separate, so that it could be sent to a newspaper. Martyn apparently made several copies for this purpose and retained the original. I have italicized the words that Oglethorpe wrote in large script to indicate italics; and I have substituted angle brackets for his square ones.

8. Oglethorpe's implication that the slaves were encouraged to revolt by the Spanish proclamation is regarded by Wood (*Black Majority,* 314) as likely. Oglethorpe apparently began his parenthesis with "then at embargo of," but deleted the last two words.

9. In November of 1738 nineteen slaves of Captain Caleb Davis and fifty others escaped to St. Augustine.

10. Evidently Lieutenant Raymond Demeré. Paul Demeré did not attain this rank until December 1740.

11. Captain James McPherson commanded the Rangers.

12. Joseph Anthony Mazzique, a Spanish physician, and William Shannon, an Irish Catholic who had enlisted in Oglethorpe's regiment. In the previous sentence in the text I have changed Oglethorpe's rectangular brackets to angle ones.

13. Don Pedro Lamberto, with whom Oglethorpe occasionally corresponded.

14. After "Stonehow" (Stono) Oglethorpe wrote "—— miles from Charles Town," but unable to ascertain the distance, deleted the phrase.

15. Alexander Hext, colonel in the militia and a member of the Assembly and the Council, was unmarried. The overseer's wife perished.

16. A member of the Assembly, Royal Spry had a plantation near Pon Pon Bridge; Thomas Sacheverelle's son was in the Assembly.

17. Before "Shot," Oglethorpe wrote "after," apparently intending "afterwards," but then deleted the word.

18. Lieutenant Governor William Bull's reports to Oglethorpe doubtless furnished him with most of the facts he needed for his account. Bull was of course not only warning Georgia, but reporting to his superior officer: since 1737 Oglethorpe had been in command of the armed forces of South Carolina as well as Georgia.

A Thanksgiving for Victory

1. Bolzius translated it to read to his flock and sent it to Germany, where Samuel Urlsperger published it in his *Neunte Continuation der Ausführlichen Nachrichten von den Salzburgischen Emigranten* (Halle, 1743), 1261–63. See the discussion there, p. 1264, and in George F. Jones's *Detailed Reports*, 9:183. The German translation, Thaddeus Mason Harris Englished for his *Oglethorpe*, 387–89.
2. It may have appeared around October 1 in a now-missing issue of the *Virginia Gazette*. The Reverend Mr. George Whitefield included almost the entire proclamation in a letter that he wrote, on January 9, 1742, to a "Mr. T." in Scotland, and that was later published in his *Works*, 6 vols. (London, 1771–72), 2:7–8.
3. Although Oglethorpe exaggerated the Spanish forces and casualties, he doubtless based them upon what he considered reliable reports.
4. See, in Appendix 2, "A Refutation of Calumnies."

The King's Bench Prison Revisited

1. See my "Oglethorpe and the Moravians—After Georgia," *Atlanta History* 35 (1991): 25–31.
2. Not John Howard, Oglethorpe's successor in prison reform, but the Reverend Mr. Leonard Howard, chaplain to the Prince of Wales and "poet laureate" of the King's Bench, in which he was frequently imprisoned because of his improvidence.
3. Ashton (d. 1768) was marshal of the King's Bench Prison from 1749 to 1766. It seems strange that Oglethorpe did not interview Theodore, "King" of Corsica, who was in prison in the King's Bench for debt from 1749 to 1755. For an interesting fictional account of Theodore and his club at the prison, see Tobias George Smollett, *The Adventures of Ferdinand Count Fathom* (1753), chs. 39–42.
4. In his more specific report, Sir William Calvert detailed that "by Indenture, dated the 4th of *February* 1684, the said *William Lenthall*, for securing the Sum of 10,000*l.* and Interest, at 5*l.* 10*s. per Centum per Annum*, mortgaged the Manor of *Latchford* and *Great Haseley*, in the County of *Oxon*, and the Profits of the said Office, to Sir *John Cutler*'s Trustees, therein named; and *Lenthall* covenanted, that he and his Heirs should stand seised of the inheritance and Fee-simple of the said Office, subject to the Payment of the said 10,000*l.* and Interest" (*JHC*, 26:681).
5. By "original Grant or Patent" Oglethorpe apparently meant the patent awarded Sir William Smith in 1617, in which James I resigned to Sir William and his heirs and assigns subsequent control of the King's Bench Prison. Oglethorpe thus left it to Calvert to clear up the title.
6. Sir William Lee (1686–1754), appointed Lord Chief Justice of the King's Bench in 1737, had been one of Bambridge's prosecutors in 1729.

7. Philip Yorke, first Earl of Hardwicke (1690–1764), followed Sir Robert Raymond and preceded Sir William Lee as Lord Chief Justice of the King's Bench.

The Naked Truth

1. On the following day it was advertised in the *Whitehall Evening Post*, p. 2, and the *London Evening Post*.
2. It was advertised on that day in the *Whitehall Evening Post* as forthcoming.
3. British Library shelfmark 102.d.3 (1).
4. Printed in part in the *Reports of the Historical Manuscripts Commission*, vol. 9, appendix, part 2 (London, 1884), these two letters are now in the Scottish Record Office, which supplied microfilm copies, with the kind permission of the owner, James Alexander Elphinstone, Baron Elphinstone.
5. Boswell Papers M208:1, Yale University Library.
6. See Rodney M. Baine and Mary E. Williams, "Oglethorpe's Early Military Campaigns," *Yale University Library Gazette* 60 (October 1985): 75.
7. Owen Aubrey Sherrard, *Lord Chatham: A War Minister in the Making* (London, 1952), 294–95.
8. Ernest Marsh Lloyd, "William Augustus, Duke of Cumberland," *DNB*; Lee McCardell, *Ill-Starred General: Braddock of the Coldstream Guards* (Pittsburgh, 1958), 123, 130; Francis Jennings, *Empire of Fortune* (New York, 1988), 115; Reed Browning, *The Duke of Newcastle* (New Haven, 1975), 217–19.
9. Henry R. Plomer, *A Dictionary of Printers and Booksellers, 1726–1775* (London, 1977), 203; *Monthly Review* for September 1755, 238.
10. For translations of works inaccurately attributed to Oglethorpe, see Appendix 1.
11. "Vox populi, vox Dei." Alcuin to Charlemagne. Alexander Pope Englished it in *The First Epistle of the Second Book of Horace*, lines 89–90.
12. "The wellbeing of the people should be the supreme law." Cicero, *De Legibus* 3.3.8. This quotation opens John Trenchard's *Cato's Letters*, No. 11, for January 7, 1721. See *Cato's Letters*, 3d ed., 4 vols. (London, 1733; rpt., New York, 1969), 1:66.
13. The first edition ends the quotation with "they are deceived or bribed." Oglethorpe follows the sense of *Cato's Letters*, No. 22, for March 25, 1721.
14. Apparently not a quotation and surely not a biblical one. The British lion is of course a national symbol.
15. Major General John Lambert opposed Monk's advance into England in 1659–60 and was subsequently sent to the Tower and then to Guernsey. Thomas Harrison, for a while second in command to Cromwell, helped to expel the Long Parliament and was ultimately executed.
16. Horace, *Satires* 1.1.24, with Horace's "quid" altered to "Quis." Here and

on the title page the first edition of *The Naked Truth* reads "discere," which appears in Horace's *Satires* two lines later.

17. Like Socrates, condemned to drink hemlock (in 399 B.C.), Phocion was condemned in 319 B.C. for advising peace with Macedonia.

18. Edition 1 reads "loved Truth, Simplicity, and Nakedness, so that. . . ."

19. According to Plutarch, Lycurgus, in the process of instituting his reforms of luxury, was pelted with stones at the instigation of the wealthy and had one eye clubbed out.

20. The sense of the quotation appears in William Wycherly's "To Nath. Lee, in Bethlem," in *Miscellany Poems* (1704). Especially suggestive is line 17 there: "For telling Naked Truths, like Mad-Men, stripp'd." "Bethlem" is more familiar to us as "Bedlam."

21. The story may derive from a similar one told by "Democritus Junior" in Robert Burton's *Anatomy of Melancholy* (1621). See the edition of Thomas C. Faulkner et al., 2 vols. (Oxford, 1989), 1:33–37. In the second edition Oglethorpe substituted "Magistrates" for "Citizens."

22. Lucius Junius Brutus may have assumed stupidity to escape vengeance. Like Shakespeare's Hamlet, Solon at one stage of his life apparently pretended insanity. In the third sentence of this paragraph Oglethorpe added "of him" in the second edition.

23. Abraham Cowley, "Brutus," stanza 2, from *Pindarique Odes*, with the first four lines omitted. Edition 1 omits "In standing pools" and substitutes "should" for "may" in the last line. Since Oglethorpe's booksale catalog lists two copies of Cowley's *Works* in the edition of 1669 and one in that of 1684 (*The Library of Oglethorpe*, items 249, 1442, and 1141), Oglethorpe at first evidently quoted from memory or made a hasty and inaccurate transcription.

24. Edition 1 reads "People go on. . . ."

25. Master mariner Robert Jenkins.

26. Edition 1 reads "we lowered the price of Corn . . . and it hath never rise, because. . . ."

27. Edition 2 substitutes the final "it" for "a great deal."

28. Oglethorpe refers to the 1742 campaign of Admiral Edward Vernon and Major General Thomas Wentworth (1693–1747) to land at Porto Bello and march across to the town of Panama; but the venture achieved virtually nothing.

29. The clause concerning General John Guise, who commanded the Sixth Regiment of Foot at Cartagena, was added in the second edition. General Charles Cathcart, eighth Baron Cathcart (1686–1740), commanded the forces sent to attack the Spaniards at Cartagena.

30. In edition 1, "and perhaps" follows.

31. The commander was Admiral George Anson.

32. Oglethorpe's use of "Patriot" here is that set in the same year by Dr. Johnson in his *Dictionary* for "patriotism" — "the last refuge of a scoundrel."

33. "Yet if the fates could find no other way / For Nero's coming . . . / For this boon supreme / Welcome, ye gods, be wickedness and crime." Marcus Annaeus Lucanus, *The Pharsalia of Lucan* 1.33–38, trans. Edward Ridley (London, 1896), 4. Oglethorpe substituted "*Aut*" for "Quod, "*ipsa* "for "ista," and "*venturi*" for "venturo." Schrevelio's edition of Lucan (Amsterdam, 1658) is item 630 in *The Library of Oglethorpe*.

34. "For our homes and our religion," a favorite phrase that appears, for example, in Cicero's *De Natura Deorum* 3.40, and in Sallust's *De Conjuratione Catalinae* 59.5.

35. After supporting the Old Pretender, James Francis Edward Stuart, for several decades, France finally made him feel unwelcome.

36. Oglethorpe evokes Falstaff's characterization of "grinning Honour" in *Henry IV, Part I*, 5.3.59.

37. In edition 2 the numbers that were spelled out in edition 1 are given in arabic figures; "and so" following "Commissions" is deleted; and "Stock on" is changed to "Stock of."

38. In William Congreve's *The Old Batchelor*, 2.1.180ff., Captain Bluff says, "*Hannibal* was a very pretty Fellow in those Days, it must be granted—But Alas Sir! were he alive now, he would be nothing." *The Complete Plays of William Congreve*, ed. Herbert Davis (Chicago, 1967), 52. *The Library of Oglethorpe* lists the 1733 edition of Congreve's *Works* (item 332).

39. Dragoons then fought either on horseback or afoot.

40. "To no one master do I swear fealty."—Horace, *Epistles* 1.14, a favorite quotation that appears in Pope's *First Epistle of the First Book of Horace Imitated*, 24; in Tobias Smollett's *Roderick Random*, ch. 17; and serves as the motto for Samuel Johnson's *Rambler*.

41. Luke 14:31, paraphrased. Edition 1 spells out the numbers.

42. "Spare the lash, my boy, and more strongly use the reins."—Frank Justus Miller. The advice of Phaeton in Ovid's *Metamorphoses* 2.127. Edition 1 reads "*Parce Puer stimulus / Sed major utite Lora*."

43. Oglethorpe added considerably here: the first edition reads, ". . . for War. So did *Demosthenes*. And the great *Cicero*. . . ."

44. "Quicquid delirant reges, plectuntur Achivi." Horace, *Epistles* 1.2.14, used as a motto by Richard Steele for his *Spectator* 180, and his *Englishman* 23.

45. The Marriage Act of 1755 was designed to prevent runaway marriages of wealthy young women to seducers of a lower class; but many younger sons of the nobility and gentry were forced into the military service to become in Falstaff's phrase, "Food for Powder." *Henry IV, Part I*, 4.2.65–66.

46. Acts 19:34.

47. The "to" in this phrase was inserted in edition 2, probably for clarity.

48. Edition 2 deletes "and" before "yet" and inserts "this."

49. Gaius Marius was tried for bribery in 115 B.C., but was acquitted. Tiberius

Sempronius Gracchus II was prosecuted for resisting a tribune but was released. A mob stoned his brother Gaius Sempronius Gracchus.

50. Edition 1 reads "in the Collection" rather than "for the Collection."

51. In edition 1 "Engine" is "Ensign," doubtless a compositor's misreading.

52. Edition 1 reads, "Thus Pare Mustifa, or Black Mustifa, got the Whenca...." Oglethorpe apparently possessed (item 2355 in *The Library of Oglethorpe*) Richard Knolles's *The Turkish History*, 6th ed., 3 vols. (London, 1687–1700), with acounts of the campaign against Vienna by both Sir Roger Manley (2:288–308) and Sir Paul Ricaut (3:92–134).

53. Edition 1 reads "Captain Bashaws" and "Festadur" and lacks the parenthetical material that follows.

54. Edition 1 reads "Pare mustifa."

55. Dionysius I, tyrant of Syracuse (c. 430–367 B.C.).

56. Agathocles secured his election in troubled Syracuse as general and keeper of the peace, then used his soldiers to gain control of the city.

57. Not a fable from Aesop, La Fontaine, or John Gay, but perhaps Oglethorpe's adaptation of the ironic proverb "Set the wolf to keep the sheep."

58. Edition 2 pluralizes "The Seaman" and "Ship."

59. Charles I's levies of ship-money helped to precipitate the Civil War and were declared illegal in 1641. John Hampden was a prominent protestor against the levies.

60. Edition 2 substitutes "therefore" for "so."

61. Edition 2 pluralizes "Merchant" and "him."

62. John Radcliffe, physician (1650–1714), left his fortune for charitable purposes. For Sir Hans Sloane and Sir Gilbert Heathcote, see notes for "An Appeal to Benefactors." Sir Peter Delme (d. 1728) was governor of the Bank of England and mayor of London. His son Peter was a member of Parliament from 1734 to 1754; and his daughter was sought by Percival as a wife for his son. Abraham Crasteyn, a Hamburg merchant, died in 1754 worth four hundred thousand pounds.

63. Although this proverb goes back to Plato's *Phaedo* 38.89, Oglethorpe may have remembered it from Erasmus, *Adagia*, where it appears on p. 115 of his 1629 Frankfort edition (*The Library of Oglethorpe*, item 702). For assistance here I am indebted to my colleague Richard La Fleur, Head of the Classics Department, and to August Krickel, of Columbia, South Carolina.

64. "One *Englishman* cou'd beat three *Frenchmen*." Addison's Sir Roger de Coverley, in the *Spectator* 383 (*The Spectator*, ed. Donald F. Bond, 5 vols. [Oxford, 1965], 3:437).

65. Edition 1 reads "heap up," probably a compositor's misreading.

66. Not a quotation from Shakespeare, but perhaps from a minor play in which Theophilus Cibber enacted his favorite role of Pistol, perhaps from his *Humorists*, never printed, but enacted the previous year at Drury Lane – in 1754. In the preceding paragraph, "for" replaces the "or" of the first edition.

67. "Deprived of food and wine, Love is lifeless." Terence, *Eunuchus* 4.5.6, with "Baccho" substituted for "Libero." *The Library of Oglethorpe* shows both the 1706 edition (item 988) and the 1718, by Echard (item 1059). Edition 2 replaces "Luxury" with "Letchery."

68. Late in 1754 an act was passed requiring all carriages and wagons "of burden" to have wheels at least nine inches broad. This legislation followed extensive debate in the press, as in the *Public Advertiser*, where Oglethorpe may have read the discussions of July 26 and October 12.

69. George Byng, Viscount Torrington (1663–1733), commanded the Mediterranean fleet in 1718–20 and destroyed one Spanish fleet off Cape Passaro in 1718. Edition 1 reads "subsidy all Germany."

70. Edition 1 reads "Subsidy."

71. Oglethorpe compares the writer "T.C." with the protagonist of the burlesque *Hurlothrumbo* (1729), by Samuel Johnson of Cheshire. White's Coffee House was then a popular Tory club where large bets were sometimes laid upon mere trifles. In 1755 it removed to its present location in St. James's Street.

72. To make a wager intending to abscond rather than pay up.

73. Edition 1 reads "Cape-Briton."

74. Edition 1 reads, "He wastes them."

75. Oglethorpe's is not an unfair paraphrase of "T.C.," "The Benefits that will accrue to this Nation by driving the French out of all the Continent of America."

76. Wentworth's expedition against Porto Bello and Panama.

Some Account of the Cherokees

1. "Some Account of the Cherokees" appeared also in *Lloyd's Evening Post, and the British Chronicle* for July 30, 1762, which added to the title "*who often conversed with their Chiefs while he was Governor of* Georgia; *which is the only authentic Account that has even been given of that Nation.*" It was reprinted in the anonymous *An Enquiry into the Origin of the Cherokees* (Oxford, 1762), 20–21. Although an incautious reader of John Phillip Read's *A Law of Blood* (New York, 1970) might assume that Oglethorpe wrote the rest of this pamphlet, Read only seems to attribute it to him, and there is every reason not to do so. See Read, *A Law*, 4 and 279, n. 9; 84 and 305, n. 84; 154 and 309, n. 9. Oglethorpe's account led Philip Thicknesse, as "A PLEBEIAN," to contribute an account of Tomochichi to the *Public Adveriser* for August 14, 1762. For Thicknesse's Georgia journalism, see Baine, "Philip Thicknesse's Reminiscences of Early Georgia," *Georgia Historical Quarterly* 76 (winter 1990): 672–98.

2. Ettinger, *Oglethorpe*, 287, n. 2.

3. See Foreman, *Indians Abroad*, 65–81; and Henry Timberlake, *Memoirs, 1756–1765*, ed. Samuel Cole Williams (Marietta, Ga., 1948).

4. The "Uscheeses," or Yuchis, were members of the Creek Confederacy, but only loosely affiliated. They had their own language.

5. William Bartram, on the other hand, described the Cherokees as "the largest race of men I ever saw." See his "Observations on the Creek and Cherokee Indians" (1789) in *Transactions of the American Ethnological Society* 3 (1853): 28.

6. Oglethorpe did not take into account the ravages inflicted by war and smallpox since his departure. Reports of 1755 place the figure at " 'above three Thousand Men' " or at only 2,590. See Peter H. Wood, in *Powhatan's Mantle*, 63.

7. Southeastern Indians certainly interred personal possessions with the corpse of the deceased. See Hudson, *Southeastern Indians*, 334–35. Their principal motive, however, was to enable the dead to use their possessions in the afterlife.

Three Letters on Corsica

1. The letters appeared on May 2, 19, and 27, 1768. The first appeared also in the *London Magazine* for May 1768 (37:253–55); and the second, in the *London Chronicle* for May 21, 1768, and in the *Gazette* for June 3, 1768. In James Boswell's *British Essays in Favour of the Brave Corsicans* (London, 1768), they constitute the opening series of essays, pp. 3–26. For authorship, see Frederick A. Pottle, *James Boswell: The Earlier Years, 1740–1769* (New York, 1966), 395, 553. For a discussion, see Richard C. Cole, "James Oglethorpe as Revolutionary Propagandist: The Case of Corsica, 1768," the *Georgia Historical Quarterly* 74 (1990): 463–74.

2. James Boswell, *The Life of Samuel Johnson*, ed. G. B. Hill and L. F. Powell, 6 vols. (Oxford, 1934–64), 2:350, n. 2.

3. Pottle, *James Boswell*, 381, 549; Boswell, *Boswell in Search of a Wife, 1766–1769*, ed. Frank Brady and F. A. Pottle (New York, 1956), 163, 166, 167; Cole, "Oglethorpe," 74:465.

4. See Ettinger, *Oglethorpe*, 291–328; and Mary Elizabeth Williams, "Oglethorpe's Literary Friendships," University of Georgia dissertation, 1980.

5. Joseph Foladare, *Boswell's Paoli*, in *Transactions of the Connecticut Academy of Arts and Sciences*, 48:65.

6. This introductory paragraph by Boswell he reprinted as Essay I of his *British Essays*.

7. The Family Compact, or contract, of 1761 had closely united the Bourbon courts of France, Spain, Parma, and the Two Sicilies (Sicily and Naples).

8. The Peace of Aix-le-Chapelle, in 1748.

9. Queen Elizbth dispatched an army to the assistance of the United Provinces in 1585. The Triple Alliance was signed in 1668.

10. In 1572 Elizabeth privately assisted the Protestants besieged in the seaport city of La Rochelle. *The Library of Oglethorpe* shows, item 64, Pierre Mervault's *Journal des Choses plus memorable qui sont passés au dernier Siege de la Rochelle* (Rouen, 1671).

11. Like George III himself, Oglethorpe apparently viewed Gustavus Adolphus as a Protestant champion of Danzig (Gdansk) against the Catholic king of Poland.

12. In 1724 in the "blood-bath of Thorn" (Toron, on the Vistula), ten Protestant citizens were executed with the complicity of the Polish king, Augustus II.

13. The independent coastal city of Sanremo was in 1729 protected by the Austrians when the Genoese threatened its autonomy.

14. Many of these French interventions Oglethorpe saw as selfish, unlike the other, altruistic interventions. In 1640 the French assisted the Catalonians against Philip IV of Spain and in the following year helped to sow dissension in Naples and Sicily, where Oglethorpe himself must have witnessed the Sicilian preference of the Spanish to the Savoyards or the Austrians. In 1640 also, in a revolt against Spain, John II of Braganza became John IV of Portugal, with at least the early recognition of France. In his *Lettres écrites de la Montaigne* (1764) Rousseau condemned the Petit Counseil of Geneva for repressing liberties at the suggestion of Voltaire and the French Minister, Choiseul.

15. In 1736, while Robert Walpole was Prime Minister, France acquired Lorraine under the Third Treaty of Vienna.

16. Oglethorpe took his figures from Boswell's *Account of Corsica* (London, 1768), 253. *The Library of Oglethorpe* shows a copy, item 1723.

17. Apparently Oglethorpe here refers to the unconditional promise that George I made to Spain in June 1721, while Carteret was Secretary of State. Actually a defender of the British claim to Gibraltar, Carteret knew that the promise would be meaningless. See Archibald Ballantyne, *Lord Carteret: A Political Biography* (London, 1887), 73–74, 77; and W. Baring Pemberton, *Carteret: The Brilliant Failure of the Eighteenth Century* (London, 1936), 70 and 338, nn. 37, 38. John Trenchard's first *Cato* letter, of November 5, 1720, emphasized the importance of Gibraltar to England and reassured that "*Secretary Grimaldo*" had promised to keep it. See *Cato's Letters*, 1:5. Trenchard reasserted England's determination in letters of June 30, 1722 (3:148–49), and June 6, 1723 (4:226). The *Craftsman* 35, of April 10, 1727, dwelt upon the importance of Gibraltar.

18. Denied his seat in Parliament and then outlawed, on November 1, 1764, "that Devil Wilkes" became the idol of London.

19. Guy Fawkes Night, November 5.

20. Clive used Mir Jaffir to replace the Nawab of Bengal: Suraj-ud-Daulah.

21. Sir John Dick, British consul at Leghorn, corresponded with Boswell and contributed an essay to his *British Essays*.

The Adams Letters

1. The first three were excerpted in the *General Evening Post* on November 13, 1773, and December 4 and 23, 1773. The first was excerpted in the *St. James Chronicle* on November 11, 1773.

2. Phinizy Spalding, "James Oglethorpe and the American Revolution," *Journal of Imperial and Commonwealth History* 3 (1975): 406, n. 15, quoting Boswell to Oglethorpe, December 3, 1773 (James Boswell MS L995, Yale University Library).

3. Boswell, *The Private Papers of James Boswell from Malahide Castle*, ed. Geoffrey Scott, 18 vols. (Mount Vernon, N.Y., 1928-34), 6:123.

4. See W. F. Tate, *The Enclosure Movement* (New York, 1967), 84-85. Contemporary defenders of enclosure included John Arbuthnot, in his *Inquiry into the Connection between the present Price of Provisions and the Size of Farms* (1773) and the anonymous author of *Advantages and Disadvantages of Inclosing Waste Lands* (1772). Opposed were Stephen Addington, in his *Inquiry into the Reasons for and against Inclosing Open-Fields* (1767, 1772), and John Lewis, in *Uniting and Monopolizing Farms, Plainly Proved disadvantageous to the Land-Owners and highly prejudicial to the Public* (1767, 1772), from the latter of which Oglethorpe may well have drawn.

5. Not an author but a collector and encourager of the arts, George III possessed "a noble collection of books," according to Boswell and Johnson—a library to which Dr. Johnson often resorted and where the king at least once interviewed him on literary subjects and suggested his writing the lives of the poets.

6. Oliver Goldsmith's *Deserted Village* had appeared in 1770.

7. Private acts of enclosure were passed at every meeting of Parliament and were routinely approved by the king.

8. The Magna Carta, as Oglethorpe realized, marked a success not for the common man, but for the aristocracy.

9. By "corn" Oglethorpe of course denotes grain; in England, specifically, wheat.

10. Oglethorpe suggests that George Spencer, fourth Duke of Marlborough (1739-1817), had experienced a change of heart. As Lord of the Manor of Westcote, he had in 1765 enclosed the commons in the tything of Westcote, in the parish of Waldesden, Buckinghamshire. See *JHC*, 30:56.

11. An M.P. for Yorkshire, Sir George Savile (1726-84) voted for the repeal of the Stamp Act, supported religious liberty, was concerned about criminal justice, and opposed press gangs. His Irish estates lay mainly in County Fermanagh. Although Sir George enclosed the commons adjoining his English estate, he apparently protected his less affluent neighbors in doing so. See John Lawrence Le Breton Hammond and Barbara Hammond, *The Village Labourer, 1760-1832: A Study in the Government of England Before the Reform Bill*, new ed. (London, 1920), 30-31.

12. I have substituted "counties," the reading of the *General Evening Post*, for the *Morning Chronicle*'s "countries," evidently the compositor's misreading.

13. The Pantheon and Ranelegh were well-known pleasure gardens. Theresa Cornelys (1723–97), an actress-singer, had purchased Carlisle House in Soho Square in 1760 and was thus for Oglethorpe a most obnoxious neighbor as a manager of assemblies, balls, and concerts. Although she was indicted in 1771 for keeping a "disorderly house," i.e., a house of prostitution, and became bankrupt in 1772, she apparently remained active, to Oglethorpe's annoyance.

14. William Cox was executed for robbery on October 27, 1773, at Tyburn. Two different criminal biographies appeared that year. One reached five editions and an abridgment.

The Faber Letters

1. Spalding, "James Oglethorpe," 13:406–7.

2. The heading "FOR BINGLEY'S JOURNAL" can be detected from the remaing feet of the cropped letters in the second number that Oglethorpe sent to Boswell. I have followed the dates noted on the Yale copies by Mr. or Mrs. Frederick A. Pottle. According to a letter of December 3, 1992, from Mr. Vincent Giroud, curator of the Beinecke Rare Book and Manuscript Library, the Pottles left no indication of their source for these dates. I have been unable to locate any file of *Bingley's Journal* that includes these late issues.

3. Boswell Papers, Yale Library, C2119.

4. See "Oglethorpe's Missing Years," by Rodney M. Baine and Mary E. Williams, *Georgia Historical Quarterly* 69:193–210.

5. Charles Geneviève Louis Auguste André Timothée d'Eon de Beaumont (1728–1810); Pierre Augustin Caron de Beaumarchais (1732–99), author of *The Barber of Seville* and *The Marriage of Figaro*.

6. In his *Political Disquisitions, or an Enquiry into Public Errors, Defects, and Abuses*, 3 vols. (London, 1774–75), James Burgh found bribery to be the normal practice of English kings, and in book 5, devoted to parliamentary corruption, he again found bribery "*our* disease" (1:267). See also Sir Louis Namier, *The Structure of British Politics at the Accession of George III*, 2d ed. (London, 1957); and John T. Noonan, Jr., *Bribes* (New York, 1984), 417ff.

7. The first Bourbon, Henry IV, ascended the French throne in 1589.

8. Cato the Censor (234–149 B.C.) regularly ended his speeches to the Roman Senate with the warning that Carthage must be destroyed.

9. The Peace of Paris (1763) between Great Britain and France.

10. Not the House of Brunswick (Braunschweig)-Lünenburg, of which George III was elector, but that of Brunswick-Wolfenbüttel, headed by Duke

Charles (1735–80) and his brother Duke Ferdinand (1721–92), who commanded the Anglo-German Army of Observation after the Duke of Cumberland departed.

11. George Grenville (1712–70), First Lord of the Treasury from 1762 to 1765.

12. Although some writers described the coasts of East Florida as pestilential, Oglethorpe probably confused the Floridas. In Mobile, in West Florida, in 1765 sickness wiped out the Twenty-first Regiment, and subsequent summers brought wholesale death to the garrison. See Bernard Romans, *A Concise Natural History of East and West-Florida* (New York, 1776), 10–13, 238; Charles Loch Mowat, *East Florida as a British Province, 1763–1784* (Berkeley, 1943), 51; and Peter J. Hamilton, *Colonial Mobile*, rev. ed. (Mobile, 1952), 264–74. The reading "somber" is conjectural.

13. John Manners, Marquis of Granby (1721–70), retired from the army in 1770; Field Marshal Henry Seymour Conway (1721–95) resigned all military command in 1772; and Admiral Edward Hawke, Baron Hawke (1705–1781), retired in 1771.

14. Robert Clive, Baron Clive (1725–74), had been subjected to a parliamentary inquiry in 1772–73.

15. George Sackville, Lord Germaine, had been dismissed from the service after he failed to attack at Minden.

16. After surrendering at Saratoga, John Burgoyne (1722–92) gave at least one ball while he was imprisoned by the Americans at Cambridge.

17. Suraj-ud-Dowlah.

18. "A Plain Dealer," "*Scotch* FRAUD *and English* FOLLY *displayed,*" *Gazeteer and New Daily Advertiser*, March 30, 1778, pp. 1–2. Oglethorpe's quotations are not precise, but are substantially reliable.

19. Oglethorpe follows Chamberlayne faithfully, taking the liberty only of substituting arabic numbers, using the fifth edition of Part II (1764). *The Library of Oglethorpe* shows a copy (item 1933) of an undated edition, presumably this one, a continuation of the eighth edition of Part I.

20. Ecclesiastes 9:15. Oglethorpe had already employed this rare quotation in his appeal for the Georgia colony in 1732.

21. The signature has been torn off in the copy that Oglethorpe sent to Boswell.

Three Letters Supporting Lord North

1. For a discussion of the North letters, see Spalding, "James Oglethorpe," 403–4; and Ettinger, *Oglethorpe*, 316–17.

2. See Alan Valentine, *Lord North* (Norman, Okla., 1967), 2:303–4.

3. See Cobbett's *Parliamentary History*, 22, cols. 1150–62. During March the *Public Advertiser* printed extensive reports from the debates.

4. The earl regarded the theaters as "places not only of rational amusement, but of great instruction and improvement." Cobbett, *History*, 22, col. 1166.

5. According to the *Public Advertiser* of March 9, 1782, Sir John Delaval (1728–1808) "declared himself an independent Country Gentleman, and that he never in his Life received or solicited any Favour from the Administration that had supported them. He could see no Plan which was framed by the Opposition, and he wished them to name any Set of Men who were to carry on the Business of the Country."

6. All the licensed physicians.

7. Letters from "One in the Secret," appearing in the *Public Advertiser* for March 11, 13, and 15, 1782, predicted a "Reconciliation with America (not an abject and disgraceful Offer of Peace on such Terms as they shall think fit to prescribe)" and published "Important Considerations on 'the Proposals for an Accommodation with the Revolted Colonies' as laid before his Majesty."

8. There were various proposals, one for a fixed fee of five shillings; another for a fee from ten to fifty shillings according to the size of the establishment.

Appendix 1: Spurious Attributions

1. *Boswell in Extremes*, 306–7.
2. Patrick Sutherland, *An Account of the late Invasion of Georgia* (London, 1742).
3. John Harriss, *Navigantium atque Itinerantium Bibliotheca*, enlarged ed., ed. John Campbell, 2 vols. (London, 1748), 2:347.

Appendix 2: Probable Attributions

A Refutation of Calumnies

1. In the Egmont Papers, 14206:258–61, in the Hargrett Rare Book and Manuscript Library at the University of Georgia, there is a MS copy entitled "A Certificate relating to Mr. Fenwickes Speech to Colonel Vander Dussen Sept. 1742."

2. *The Spanish Hireling Detected: Being a Refutation of the Several Calumnies and Falshoods in a late Pamphlet Entitul'd "An Impartial Account of the late Expedition against Saint Augustine under General Oglethorpe* (London, 1743). Unfortunately George Cadogan's defense has never been reprinted.

3. James Killpatrick's biased report was reissued in a facsimile edition, with an introduction and notes by Aileen Moore Topping (Gainesville, 1978). Killpatrick responded to Cadogan in *A Full Reply to Lieut. Cadogan's "Spanish Hireling," &c. and Lieut Mackay's Letter, Concerning the Action at Moosa* (London, 1743).

4. This brief report supplemented the full one made during 1741–42 and published as *The Report of Both Houses of Assembly of the Province of South-Carolina,*

Appointed to enquire into the Causes of the Disapointment of Success, in the late Expedition against St. Augustine, Under the Command of General Oglethorpe (Charles Town, 1742). The fuller report was reprinted in London in 1743, and again, in large part, in the nineteenth century, in *Collections of the South Carolina Historical Society*, 4:1–177. In the middle of the present century it has been twice edited and reissued, by J. H. Easterby in *Journal of the Commons House of Assembly, May 18, 1741–July 10, 1742* (Columbia, 1953), 78–247; and by John Tate Lanning in his *St. Augustine Expedition of 1740* (Columbia, 1954). The Carolinan position has been frequently voiced.

5. Colonel Alexander Vander Dussen may have been a member of the Van der Dussen family of Delft or Dordrecht, in the Netherlands. He arrived in South Carolina in 1731, perhaps from Curaçao, with some military experience, and he rapidly became prominent in political and military circles. Mentally disordered, he was removed from the Council in 1756. He seems to have treated ruthlessly not only his slaves, but according to Lieutenant Patrick Sutherland, even his own family. See Walter B. Edgar, ed., *Biographical Directory of the South Carolina House of Representatives*, 4 vols. (Columbia, 1977), 2:685–86; and Robert Wright, *A Memoir of General James Oglethorpe* (London, 1867), 347–48.

6. Alexander Heron arrived in Georgia in 1738, from Bermuda, and became a major in 1740 and lieutenant colonel in 1744. (For military commissions, see W. R. Williams, compiler, "British-American Officers, 1720 to 1763," in *South Carolina Historical and Genealogical Magazine* 33 [July, 1932]: 183–96). After the Georgia regiment was disbanded in 1749, he was assigned to South Carolina. George Dunbar, master of the *Prince of Wales*, recruited and brought over Scots servants as well as Oglethorpe's Indian delegation. Given a grant of five hundred acres at Josephstown and subsequently land at Darien, he served as emissary to the Indians in 1741 and to the British government, for military assistance, in 1743. Given command of the fourteen-gun captured sloop *Walker*, he became captain lieutenant in 1740 and captain in 1741. James Mackay of Scoury, brother of Hugh, arrived in 1733, became ensign in 1740 and captain in 1742. Samuel Mackay became ensign in 1742. Primrose Maxwell became a lieutenant in 1740 and an adjutant in 1741. George Cadogan became lieutenant in 1741 and captain lieutenant in 1747. At Oglethorpe's order, he commanded the general's own company when it removed to Augusta in 1748. Agent to the Cherokees and author of the hitherto anonymous "Ranger's Report of Travels with General Oglethorpe, 1739–1742," Thomas Eyre became ensign in 1740. Probart Howarth became ensign in 1741, lieutenant in 1744, and ultimately colonel in South Carolina, commanding Fort Johnson. Ensign in 1742/43, Solomon Chamberlain died in 1746. William Robinson was probably the Highlander, aged twenty-one, who arrived in 1741.

7. Surely a reference to the anonymous *Impartial Account*.

Index

Abbeville (Picardy), 238, 369 (n. 83)
Abercorn (Georgia village), 249
Acton, William, 355 (n. 7); prosecution of, recommended, 84; trials of, 84, 125, 356 (nn. 15, 19); becomes deputy warden of the Marshalsea, 89, 101, 356 (n. 20); misappropriates charity monies, 94–95; tortures prisoners, 98–100; examined by the committee, 100; its recommendations, 100–101, 117; parliamentary action against, 117
Adam and Eve, 311
Adams. *See* Oglethorpe, James Edward, as "Adams"
Addison, Joseph: *Cato*, 15, 348 (n. 30); *Spectator*, 287, 377 (n. 64); *Tatler*, 352 (n. 26)
Admiralty, British, 7–10, 14–17; office of the, 7, 23, 33; Court of the, 14, 16; its use of impressment, 14–26 passim, 42–43; officers of the, 24–25
Ægypt. *See* Egypt
Æquator. *See* Equator
Agathocles (tyrant of Syracuse), 285, 377 (n. 56)
Agesilaus II (king of Sparta), 179
Aix-le-Chapelle, Peace of, 305, 379 (n. 8)
Alaminas, Antonio de, 245
Aland, Sir John Fortescue, first Baron Fortesque of Credan, 135, 147, 358 (n. 15)
Alatamaha, 212, 248, 249
Alborough, 245

Alexander III (Alexander the Great, king of Macedonia), 178, 283
Alexander VI (pope), 209, 366 (n. 29)
Algiers, 309
Allen (murdered in the King's Bench), 120, 136, 358 (n. 18)
Allen, John, 141
Allen, Joseph, 136, 138, 154–55
Allgemeine Historie zu Wasser und Lande, 336
Alphus. *See* Heathcote, Sir Gilbert
Alps, 307
America (British North America), 192, 196, 198, 248, 291; waste lands in, 164; imports Portuguese products, 165; increase in its population, 226; scene of Gen. Braddock's defeat, 293–94; as refuge of the dispossessed, 313; and Stamp Act, 323; taxation of, 323–24; Burgoyne defeated in, 324; saved by Pitt, 324. *See also* Barbadoes; Georgia; Jamaica; New England; New York; North Carolina; Pensilvania; South Carolina; Virginia
America, French, 210, 238–39, 291, 293. *See also* Canada
America, Spanish, 196–97, 226, 278. *See also* Florida; Mexico; Peru
America, United States of: War of Independence, 202; Stamp Act, 323; British reconciliation with, 328, 330
Amsterdam, 300
Anastasia Island, 339–40

387

Andaluzia, 193, 197
Angola, 253
Anne (queen of Great Britain and Ireland), 3–4, 279
Anne, 200
Anson, Adm. George, 279, 375 (n. 31)
Antediluvians, 215
Antigallican, Old. *See* Oglethorpe, James Edward, as "Old Antigallican"
Antigallicans, 321, 323, 325
Apalachean (*or* Apalatian) Mountains, 209, 213, 246
Apellache (*or* Appellachee) Bay (or Gulf) of, 246, 248
Arabia, 234
Aragon, 197
Arbitrary Punishments and Cruel Tortures, The, 84
Archdale, John, 365 (n. 21); *A New Description of Carolina*, 202, 206–17 passim; as governor of South Carolina, 207
Argyll, John Campbell, second duke of, 96, 356 (n. 17); as "Cornelius," 161, 359 (n. 9)
Armada (Spanish), 236
Arne, Edward, 56, 107, 352 (n. 26)
Arnold, Benjamin, 150
Ashton, John, 260, 262–63, 269, 373 (n. 3)
Asia-Minor, 212
Athens, 164, 277, 283
Athos (mountain), 178
Atlantic (*or* Atlantick) Ocean, 209, 216, 247, 248
Augustine. *See* St. Augustine (*or* St. Augustino)
Augustus II (king of Poland), 305, 380 (n. 12)
Austria, House of, 275, 280, 305. *See also* Vienna, Court of
Austrian Succession, war of the, 280

Backhouse, Thomas, 156–57
Bacon, Sir Francis: "Essay on Plantations," 168, 170, 172–74, 361 (n. 9), 362 (nn. 14–17)
Bahama (*or* Bahamas), 247
Ballard, George, 96
Bambridge, Thomas, 108, 120, 122, 126; as warden of the Fleet, 44–47, 52, 55, 57; and cruelties to Rich, 44–47, 110–12; imprisoned by the House of Commons, 47, 81; resolutions of the committee concerning, 50, 72; resolutions of the House concerning, 50, 79–81, 350–51 (n. 6); disabled from serving as warden, 50, 123, 350–51 (n. 6); runs sponging-houses, 58; and cruelties to Mackpheadris, 58, 66–68; and cruelties to Hogg, 59; allows escapes, 62; neglects records, 62; charges excessive fees, 62–65; and cruelties to Castell, 63–64; accepts presents, 64; and cruelties to Solas, 66, 354 (n. 45); greed of, 66–68, 71–72; malice of, 68–70; and cruelties to Sinclair, 68–70, 354 (n. 46); denies admittance to solicitors and refuses the king's writs, 70; examined by the committee, 70; mistreats Holder, 71–72; income of, 77; shackles Reed, 107–8, 352 (n. 25); abuses discharges, 109; wounded, 111; tried for murder and felony, 350 (n. 6), 351 (n. 15), 356 (nn. 15, 26), 358 (n. 15), 373 (n. 6); *Mr. Bambridge's Case*, 351 (n. 6), 354 (n. 40), 356 (n. 26)
Barbadoes, 189, 192, 194, 197, 198
Barbary, 212, 213, 234, 278, 304
Barnard, John, 349 (n. 54)
Barnes, James, 62, 354 (n. 41); seizes Hogg, 59; conceals fee tables, 64; pulls down Mackpheadris's hut, 67; seizes Sinclair, 69; to be prosecuted,

80, 81; seizes Arne, 107; assaults Rich, 110–11
Bartram, William, 379 (n. 5)
Bassompierre, Louisa Mary, marquise de, 321
Bathurst, Robert, 253
Baugh, Daniel A., 10
Bavaria, 280
Bayley, James, 78
Beaumarchais, Pierre Augustin Caron de, 322, 382 (n. 5)
Bellegarde, Frances Charlotte, marquise de, 321
Bellegarde, François-Eugène Robert, comte de, 321
Bennet, Sir John, 93, 96, 355 (n. 12)
Bergen, 280
Berkeley, Elizabeth, 350 (n. 6)
Berkeley, George (bishop of Cloyne), 360 (n. 15)
Bermudas, 215
Bethlehem Hospital (London), 277
Bettesworth and Hitch (publishers), 245, 370 (n. 1)
Bible, 163, 282, 283, 383 (n. 20)
Bibliotheca Americana, 335, 336
Bigod, Roger, fourth earl of Norfolk, 357 (n. 6)
Bingley, William, 321
Bingley's Journal, 321, 382 (n. 2)
Bishop, Richard: assists Huggins in financial manipulations, 56; assists in escapes, 108; sells share in King's Bench, 142, 146; buys share there, 150
Bishop, William, 260
Black Hole (of Calcutta), 324
Blackwell (legal agent), 261, 262
Blandford, 294
Bliss, Thomas, 84, 99, 356 (nn. 15, 19)
Bloody Marsh (battle of), 256–58, 336

Bluff, Captain (character in Congreve's *Old Bachelor*), 281
Blunt, Samuel, 116, 117
Blythman, Jasper, 141–44
Bodvile, Charles, second earl of Radnor. *See* Radnor, Charles Bodville Robartes
Bonifaccio, Straits of, 304
Booth, William, 62, 354 (n. 39)
Boscawen, Adm. Edward, 331
Boston, 324
Boston Evening-Post, 256
Boswell, James: entertains Oglethorpe, 3; befriends Oglethorpe, 302; *British Essays*, 302; reprints Oglethorpe's Corsican letters, 302; visits and champions Corsica, 302; *An Account of Corsica*, 302, 309; as "A Constant Reader," 304, 379 (n. 6); attributes "Adams" letters to Oglethorpe, 311; visits and corresponds with Oglethorpe, 311, 321, 348 (n. 30), 381 (n. 2); receives copies of "Faber" letters, 321; attributes Campbell's "History" to Oglethorpe, 335; reports Oglethorpe's "Instruction," 345 (n. 1)
Boulter, Edmund, 132, 261, 358 (n. 11)
Bourbon, House of, 275, 306, 321, 323, 326
Bourbonites, 323–27
Bowman (a proprietor of the King's Bench), 142
Boxmen, the running (London guild), 77
Boyce, David, 62, 353 (n. 37)
Boyer, Abel, 11
Braddock, Gen. Edward, 270, 293–94
Brafield, Thomas, 124
Braganza, Duke of. *See* John IV (king of Portugal)
Bramston, Thomas, 252

Brandenburgh, 188; House of, 305. See also Frederick II (king of Prussia)
Bray Associates, 200
Brest, 294
Brief Account of the Establishment of the Colony of Georgia, A, 335
Briggs, William, 152
Brigstock (legal agent), 261
Brim (Creek chief), 250, 371 (n. 15)
Bristol, 15, 198
British Commonwealth, 202
British Library, 204, 270
British Library Catalog, 336
Britons, 294, 325
Brittanicus et Americanus. See Oglethorpe, James Edward, as "Brittanicus et Americanus"
Broad-wheel Philosopher (newspaper writer), 289
Bromfield, Capt. John, 84
Brotherton, Thomas de, earl of Norfolk, 357 (n. 6)
Broughton, William, 152, 153
Bruce, Henry, 370 (n. 2)
Brunswick (Brunswick-Wolfenbüttel), House of, 323, 382–83 (n. 10)
Brutus, Lucius Junius, 277, 375 (n. 22)
Brutus, Marcus Junius, 277
Bull, Lieut. Gov. William, 253–55, 371 (n. 1); 372 (n. 18)
Bull, William, Jr., 298
Bullock (home owner near Stono), 254
Bumsted, John Michael, 345 (n. 1)
Burchet, Josiah: *Naval History*, 234
Burgh, James, 382 (n. 6)
Burgoyne, Gen. John, 324, 383 (n. 16)
Burke, Edmund, 322
Burnet, Thomas: *The Sacred Theory of the Earth*, 215
Burrell, Peter, 6
Butler, Samuel: *Hudibras*, 207
Bygrave (clerk of the papers at the fleet), 78

Byng, Adm. George, Viscount Torrington, 289, 378 (n. 69)

Cabot, Sebastian, 210, 246
Cadogan, Lieut. George, 385 (n. 6); *The Spanish Hireling Detected*, 338, 384 (nn. 2, 3); attached to the South Carolina regiment, 340–41
Caesar, Gaius Julius, 179, 250, 284, 291
Caesars, the, 179
Cain, 210
Caleb, 188, 363 (n. 47)
Cales (Calais), 294
Calvert, Sir William, 259, 357 (n. 9), 373 (nn. 4, 5)
Campbell, John: "History of Georgia," 335–36
Canada, 239, 246, 291, 324
Cape Breton, 291
Cape Fear, 248
Cape Fenesterre, 233
Cape of Good Hope, 27
Capper, Richard, 142
Cara Mustifa, 284, 377 (n. 52)
Carolina: proprietors of, 211, 218; divisions of, 212, 246, 248. See also Georgia; North Carolina; South Carolina
Carpenter, George, 161, 359 (n. 7)
Carter (benefactor to the Fleet), 77
Carter, Lawrence, 125
Carteret, Sir George, 308, 380 (n. 17)
Carthage, 285; its colonies, 185; its strugge with Rome, 215, 323, 382 (n. 8)
Castell, Robert: death of, 49; mistreatment by Bambridge, 63–64; Bambridge tried for murder of, 350 (n. 6), 356 (n. 15); translation of Vitruvius Pollio by, 362 (n. 26)
Cataline (Lucius Sergius Catalina), 179, 362 (n. 29)
Catallans, 306, 380 (n. 14)

Catalogue Générale de la Bibliothèque Nationale, 335
Catalogue of the Wymberley Jones DeRenne Georgia Library, 335
Cathcart, Gen. Charles, eighth Baron Cathcart, 279, 375 (n. 29)
Catholic Church. *See* Rome (the Roman Catholic Church)
Cato "Censorius," Marcus Porcius, 215, 279, 289 (n. 8)
Catooche River, 248
Caucasus, Mount, 234
Cecil, Robert, 31
Chamberlain, Ensign Solomon, 340, 385 (n. 6)
Chamberlayne, Edward: *Angliae Notitia*, 326–27
Chapman, John, 260
Charities, 48; abused at the Fleet, 76–77, 97; abused at the Marshalsea, 84, 93–95, 97, 108–9, 117; abused at the King's Bench, 137–40, 156–58
Charles I (king of Great Britain and Ireland), 377 (n. 59)
Charles II (king of Great Britain and Ireland), 195, 210, 211, 246
Charles Town (*or* Charlestown): shipping at, 206; inhabitants of, 212, 216; plague at, 216; value of land near, 228; harbor of, 248; blacks hanged at, 253; Spanish emissaries at, 253
Cherokees, 243, 296–97, 379 (n. 5); mountains of the, 246
Chickasaws, 297
Child, Sir Josiah, 201; "A Discourse concerning Plantations," 168, 171–72, 192–99, 363–64 (nn. 48–57)
China, 212
Chremes (dramatic character), 160
Cibber, Theophilus, 377 (n. 66)
Cicero, Marcus Tullius, 283
Cities: building of, 176–80

Civita Vecchia, 309
Clarendon, Henry Hyde, second earl of, 56, 211n, 352 (n. 21)
Clarendon River, 248
Clark, Samuel, 155, 157
Clive, Robert, Baron Clive, 309, 324, 380 (n. 20), 383 (n. 14)
Coffin-land (island off South Carolina), 248
Coke (warden of the King's Bench), 152
Coke, Sir Edward, 16n, 203–4, 234–35
Colerain, 208
Coligny, Admiral Gaspard de, 209–10
Collections of the Georgia Historical Society, 202
Colonies, 166–99; Athenian, 164; Roman, 164, 174–76, 181–82, 185, 188, 229; feared by Parliament, 167; benefits of, 167, 170, 174–76, 182–83, 185, 188–99, 218–29, 224–25, 229, 239–40; prove not to depopulate England, 171–72, 189, 192–99; proper colonists for, 172, 176, 219–22, 228; proper produce of, 172–73; government of, 173, 176; locale for, 174, 175–76, 178; militia in, 180; Dutch, 183–88, 197; Portuguese, 185; Greek, 185, 188; Spanish, 185, 197, 239; British, in America, 192; British, in Ulster, 207–8; French, 238–39. *See also* America (British North America); America, French; America, Spanish; Barbadoes; Georgia; Jamaica; New England; New York; North Carolina; Pensilvania; South Carolina; Ulster; Virginia
Committee appointed to Enquire into the State of the Goals of this Kingdom, the: appointed, 44; visits Fleet, 44–45, 50, 54, 66, 108, 352 (n. 21), 354 (n. 45); reports on Fleet,

Committee (*continued*)
46, 56, 107, 108; resolutions of, on Fleet, 50, 72, 79–81, 117; questions witnesses, 70; reports on the Marshalsea, 83, 88; visits Marshalsea, 88, 90–91, 99; feeds starving prisoners at Marshalsea, 92–93; busy with parliamentary duties, 99; resolutions on the Marshalsea, 100–101, 117; reports George Gray, 119–21; resolutions on Gray, 121; supports Gambier petition, 122, 123; enlarged and continued, 125; uncertainty of continuation of, 125; investigates Eyre, 126; visits King's Bench, 126, 136; reports on the King's Bench, 130, 131; recommends prohibiting presents to supervising officials, 140; resolutions of, on the King's Bench, 140, 158

Common Pleas, Court of. *See* Court of Common Pleas

Congreve, William: *The Old Bachelor*, 281, 376 (n. 38)

Constant Reader, A. *See* Boswell, James, as "A Constant Reader"

Constitution (English), 8, 14, 31

Conway, Henry Semour, 324, 383 (n. 13)

Cook, Moses, 116, 152, 153

Coram, Thomas: sends Newman *Select Tracts*, 167, 200; produces tar in America, 238, 369 (n. 85)

Corbett, Richard: keeps sponging-house, 56, 58, 63, 110; refuses prisoners their rights, 58; records no discharges, 59; appointed tipstaff, 60; mistreats Rich, 110–11; invests in Fleet, 350 (n. 6); tried for murder of Castell, 353 (n. 30)

Cornelius. *See* Argyll, John Campbell, second duke of

Cornelys, Theresa, 319, 382 (n. 13)

Cornwall, Velters, 82

Corsica: importance of independence of, to Great Britain, 303–9

Cotton (clerk of the papers), 59, 78

Court, Pieter de la, 168, 361 (n. 5); *The True Interest of Holland*, 183–88, 363 (n. 41–47)

Court of Common Pleas, 49, 50, 70, 73, 76, 110; regulates fees at Fleet, 64–65; rules for Rich's removal from Fleet, 111–12

Court of Record of the King's Palace of Westminster, 84, 89

Court of the Exchequer, 76

Court of the King's Bench, 126, 131, 137, 140, 158, 264; accepts presents, 135–36, 147–48; fines Woodham, 154–55

Court of the Star Chamber, 49, 54, 55

Cowes, 299

Cowley, Abraham, 277–78, 375 (n. 23)

Cox, William, 320n, 382 (n. 14)

Craftsman, 207, 308

Crane, Verner, 200, 203

Crane, William, 84

Crasteen (Crasteyn), Abraham, 286, 377 (n. 62)

Crawford, David, 152

Creeks, 250, 297, 379 (n. 4)

Crull (investor in King's Bench), 142

Cuba, 247, 291

Cumberland, William Augustus, duke of, 270, 271–72

Cumberland Sound, 257

Cuthbert, Dugal, 57, 123, 351–52 (n. 21), 353 (n. 27)

Cutler, Sir John: conveys the Lenthall title to Radnor, 131–32, 141, 259, 261–62, 357 (n. 8)

Daily Advertiser, 203, 299

Daily Journal, 5, 6, 9
Daniel, Samuel, 19n
Dantzick, 305
Darby, John, 356 (n. 20); prosecution of, recommended, 84; illegally leases prison, 88, 101; extortions of, 89–90; fails to post fees, 90; seizes prisoners' seal, 93; lists voluntary prisoners, 96–97; permits crowding, 99–100; censured, 101, 117; never charged with a crime, 355 (n. 7)
Darien (Georgia town), 249
Darnall, Sir John, 94, 96, 356 (n. 15)
Davenant, Charles, 201
Davis, Capt. Caleb, 253, 372 (n. 9)
Dawson (benefactor to the Fleet), 77
Decius. *See* Carpenter, George; Selwyn, Charles, as "Decius"
Dee River, 235
Defoe, Daniel, 337, 347 (n. 14)
Delaval, Sir John, 329–30, 384 (n. 5)
Delmy (Delme), Sir Peter, 286, 377 (n. 62)
Demeré, Lt. Raymond, 253, 372 (n. 10)
Democritus (of Abdera), 277
Demosthenes, 283
Denham, Thomas, 120
Denmark, 188, 234, 307
Denton, Alexander, 73, 76
Deptford, 33
Desbrisay, Capt. Albert, 339
Diana, 283
Dick, Sir John, 310, 380 (n. 21)
Dinocrates, 178, 362 (n. 26)
Dion, 179, 362 (n. 28)
Dionysius I (tyrant of Syracuse), 179, 285, 362 (n. 28)
Dorset, Lionel Cranfield Sackville, first duke of, 95, 96, 356 (n. 16)
Drummond, John, 7
Dublin, 222n, 235n
Dudley, John, 78, 112–13

Dumay, Thomas, 56
Dunbar, Capt. George, 339–40, 385 (n. 6)
Dussen, Col. Alexander Vander, 338–40, 385 (n. 5)
Dymond, Capt. George, 370 (n. 8)

Earle, Giles, 7, 8, 81
East Florida, 324, 383 (n. 12)
East India, 27, 199
East-India Company (Dutch), 185–87, 237
East Indies (Dutch), 187, 197, 213, 214, 237
Ebenezer (Georgia village), 249, 253, 256
Ebenezer River (Georgia), 248, 249
Edgar (king of the English), 234–36
Egypt, 178, 212, 213, 234
Elizabeth I (queen of Great Britain and Ireland), 83; favors colonies, 170; increases size of her navy, 235–36; intervenes in foreign civil wars, 305, 379 (nn. 9, 10); militia of, 327
Elliott, Robert, 120–21
Emigration. *See* Colonies
Enclosure, 311–20, 381 (n. 7)
England, 188, 222, 279–80, 300, 326; liberty in, 22; not depopulated by colonies, 171–72, 197–98; soldiers of, 180, 194; colonies strengthen, 184–85, 189; population of, 193, 195–97; ecclesiastical laws of, 194–95; Jewish immigration to, 197; conquest of Ireland by, 207; birds and fruit of, 214; Indian visits to, 217, 218, 296; emigration policy of, 221–22; generosity of, 227; militia of, 326–27. *See also* Great Britain
English Merchant, An. *See* Oglethorpe, James Edward, as "An English Merchant"

Enquiry into the Causes of our Naval Miscarriages, 9, 11
Eon de Beaumont, Charles, 322, 382 (n. 5)
Epaminondas, 180, 363 (n. 33)
Ephesus, 283
Equator, 234
Escapes (of debtors): from the Fleet, 56, 62, 108, 113–16; warrants for, 61, 153; from the King's Bench, 126, 131–35, 138, 144–46, 149–51; committee recommendations for, 140; no one liable at King's Bench for, 143, 146, 149
Eton, 3, 8
Ettinger, Amos Aschbach, 296, 298, 328, 337
Everett, John, 70, 80, 81, 111, 354 (n. 47)
Eyre, Sir Robert: favors Bambridge, 50; sets fees, 73, 76; investigated by the committee, 126, 127, 354 (nn. 43, 47)
Eyre, Ensign Thomas, 340, 385 (n. 6)

Faber. *See* Oglethorpe, James Edward, as "Faber"
Fabius, 283
Family Compact (*or* Contract), 304, 305, 321, 379 (n. 8)
Fees: at the Fleet Prison, 50, 55, 57, 59, 62–66, 72–75, 112–23; at the Marshalsea, 89–90, 101–2; reduced at the Fleet by Gambier, 124; at the King's Bench, 138, 263, 267–68
Fenwick, John, 339
Ferdinand, Duke of Brunswick, 324, 382–83 (n. 10)
Fesse (kingdom of), 199
Fitz-Simmonds, Robert, 109
Flanders, 188, 197, 282, 305
Fleet Prison: shackling at, 44–45, 54, 55, 66–68; described, 44–45, 57–58, 70–71; history of, 49–50, 54–57; management of, 50; tortures at, 50, 56, 66–67; living conditions at, 50, 57–58, 62–63; mistreatment at, 56, 66–70, 107–8, 110–12; watchmen at, 58; records of, 60–62; strong room at, 66, 67, 69, 70–71, 107; dungeons used at, 66, 70; profits from, 77–79; misuse of soldiers at, 109; improvements at, 124; rents reduced at, 124. *See also* Charities; Escapes (of debtors); Fees; Prisons; Rules; Sponging-houses
Fleet River, 49
Flemings, 305
Flint, Mrs. Dorothy, 3
Flint River, 248
Florida, 291; geography of, 209, 248; French, then Spaniards colonize, 209–10; Spaniards mistreat Indians in, 210; English right in, 211; Indian longevity in, 215; Gulf Stream of, 247; Spaniards shelter Carolina slaves in, 253; fever in, 324, 383 (n. 12); English invade, 338–41. *See also* East Florida
Florida, Gulph of, 209
Foladare, Joseph, 303
Fonseka (Yamacraw warrior), 243–44
Force, Peter, 335
Fort Argyle (Georgia), 249
Fortescue, Sir John (d. 1476?): *De Laudibus Legum Angliae*, 16, 348 (n. 32)
Fortesque, Sir John (d. 1746). *See* Aland, Sir John Fortesque
Fort Necessity, 271
Fort William (Georgia), 257
Fox, Charles James, 328
France, 188, 275, 290; English invasion of, 180; population of, 193, 239–40; English soldiers in, 194;

civil wars in, 209–10; struggle of with Spaniards in Carolina of, 209–10; silk production in, 232; danger of war with, 270–95; gives up conquests, 280; ousts the Pretender, 280–81; sham war against, 284; stronger than England, 287–90; indigo of, 300; threat in Corsica of, 302–10; Oglethorpe family ties in, 321; deceives and bribes the English, 321–27. *See also* America, French; Bourbon, House of; Colonies, French; Navies, foreign, French; Trade, foreign, French
Franklin, Benjamin, 256
Franks, Dr., (dean of Bedford), 79
Frederica, 249, 256–58
Frederick II (Frederick the Great, king of Prussia), 225, 289, 290, 309, 321, 323
Frenchified Pensioner. *See* Pitt, William
Full Reply to Lieut. Cadogan's Spanish Hireling, A, 335
Funds, the: depend on trade, 19; in a war with France, 271, 276, 281, 286–88
Fytche (tipstaff at the Fleet), 60, 353 (n. 35)

Gambier, James, 122–24, 126
Gaols. *See* Prisons
Gascoigne, Capt. John, 245, 370 (n. 4)
Gazeteer and London Daily Advertiser, 296
Gazetteer, 325n
Gee, Joshua, 201
General Advertiser, 335
General Evening Post, 342, 343
Genet, Edmé Jacques, 272
Geneva, 306
Genoa: revitalizes Pisa, 175, 362 (n. 20); as agent of France in Corsica, 302, 304, 305, 307
Gentlemen's Magazine, 271, 342
George I (king of Great Britain and Ireland), 3–4
George II (king of Great Britain and Ireland), 122, 326; prefers voluntary sailors, 8–9, 14–15, 39; creates Georgia, 220; vacations in Hanover, 271; helps Thorn, 305
George III (king of Great Britain and Ireland), 327; Oglethorpe petitions to revive his Georgia regiment, 270; addressed in "Adams" letters, 311–20; as a "man of letters," 313, 381 (n. 5); believes in an *entente cordiale*, 321–22; opposes peace with America, 328
Georgia: appeal for, 159–66, 227; Trustees' purposes in, 164–65; religious liberty in, 165; silk in, 165, 202, 229–33; wine in, 165, 202, 230; for released debtors, 167; history and value of, 201–2, 209–12, 227; geography of, 209n, 212, 246–47; British title to, 210–11; taken from South Carolina, 212; climate, 212–16, 234; fertile soil in, 213; tar and pitch in, 213, 238; flora and fauna of, 213–14, 251; longevity in, 215–16; Indians in, 215–16, 241–43; proper colonists for, 219–20; colony created, 220; economic attractions of, 223–25; blacks and hardened criminals unwelcome in, 228, 252; cotton, drugs, dyeing stuffs in, 230; future trade of, 230–34, 237; rice in, 233; produce of, 238; magnolia of, 246, 370 (n. 6); geography of, 246–49; towns and villages in, 248–49; fish in, 251; malcontents in, 252; Rangers, 252, 255, 339; Spanish invasion of,

Georgia (*continued*)
256–58; indigo and hemp in, 300–301; regiment at St. Augustine, 338–41

Georgia Trustees: praised, 161–65, 208; their intentions, 166; review their publications, 201, 359 (n. 2); named by George II, 220; assistance given by, 220–21; assistance to, 226; land policy of, 227–28; Oglethorpe corresponds with, 241; oppose black slaves, 252

Germany, 306; city states of, 176; English soldiers in, 194; receives Protestants and Jews, 194, 197; Protestant immigrants from, 225–27; allies of, in Vienna, 285; Great Britain subsidizes, 289, 290; rice market in, 300; power of, 307. *See also* Salzburgers

Gibbs (man killed at Stono), 254

Gibraltar, 234, 289, 308, 380 (n. 17)

Gibson, Jacob and Jacomb (money lenders), 10, 14

Gilbourne, Edward, 93–95, 105

Gimbert, Godfrey, 152

Glanville, William, 81

Glover, Henry, 152

Goals. *See* Prisons

Godfrey (man killed at Stono with son and daughter), 254

Goldsmith, Oliver, 302; visits Oglethorpe, 311; his *Deserted Village*, 311–13, 316

Gonson, Sir John, 154–56, 358 (n. 24)

Goulder, Thomas, 78

Gracchi, the, 284, 376–77 (n. 49)

Graccus, Gaius Sempronius II, 376–77 (n. 49)

Grace, John, 94, 355 (n. 13)

Granada, 193, 197

Granby, John Manners, marquis of, 324, 383 (n. 13)

Graunt, John, 195, 198

Gray, George, 119–21

Great Britain, 233, 253; proper immigrants from, 219–20; increased by foreign immigrants, 225–26; silk consumption in, 230–33; rice markets of, 233, 299–300; trade of, 235–39; and dangers of a French war, 271–95; power of the people of, 275–76; losses of, from the War of Jenkins' Ear, 278–80; losses of, from the war of the Austrian Succession of, 280; divisions of people in, 326; taxation in, 331–33. *See also* America (British North America); Colonies; England; Ireland; Navy, British; Scotland; Trade, British

Great Meadows (battle of), 270, 293–94

Greece, 249, 277, 285. *See also* Colonies, Greek

Greenwich Hospital, 26

Grenada, 197

Grenville, George, 323, 383 (n. 11)

Gresham, Sir Thomas, 93, 355 (n. 11)

Grubham, John, 76

Guiana, 170

Guise, Gen. John, 279, 375 (n. 29)

Gulf Stream (*or* Gulph Stream), 245, 247, 291

Gustavus Adolphus (king of Sweden), 305, 380 (n. 12)

Guthrie (legal official of the King's Bench), 262

Guybon (*or* Gybbon), Thomas, 59, 70, 353 (nn. 26, 34)

Habeas corpus: fees for, 58–59; list of those removed by, 60; misused, 69, 75, 108, 110

Hallifax (Nova Scotia), 294

Hamborough (*or* Hamburg), 278, 307

Hampden, John, 377 (n. 59)
Hampstead (Georgia village), 249
Hannibal, 281
Hanover, 271
Hants (newspaper writer), 315
Hardwicke, Philip Yorke, first earl of, 265
Harleain Miscellany, 11
Harris, Robert R., 3, 345 (n. 4)
Harris, Thadeus Mason, 245
Harrison, Thomas, 276, 374 (n. 15)
Harriss, John: *Navagantium atque Itinerantium*, 335
Haslam, Capt. William, 36–38
Haslemere (Surrey), 5–6
Hastings, Warren, 322
Hawke, Adm. Edward, 324, 383 (n. 13)
Heathcote, Sir Gilbert, 286; as "Alphus," 161–62
Hell in Epitome, 83
Henry VII (king of England), 210, 284
Henry VIII (king of Great Britain and Ireland), 83
Herbert, Sir Edward, 64, 354 (n. 44)
Hercules, 287
Heron, Major Alexander, 339, 340, 385 (n. 6)
Hext, Col. Alexander, 254, 372 (n. 15)
Heybord, Humphrey, 138, 154–55
Highgate (Georgia village), 249
Highlanders: in Georgia, 339
Hildesley, Capt. John, 37–38, 349 (n. 55)
Hill, John, 370 (n. 6)
Hilton-head, 248
Hippocrates (English physician). See Sloane, Sir Hans
Hippocrates (Greek physician), 277
Hispaniola, 291
Hoare, Prince, 7
Hogan (ensign of the Georgia regiment), 339, 340
Hogarth, William: portraits of the Committee by, 50, 351 (n. 6), 352 (n. 21), 354 (n. 45), 356 (n. 26)
Hogg, Thomas, 59, 353 (n. 33)
Holder (son of John Holder), 71
Holder, John, 71–72, 354–55 (n. 50)
Holland, 280, 307; need for and use of colonies by, 183–88; charities in, 184–85; emigration to, 184–85, 194, 196, 197; mismanagement of colonies by, 187; population of, 193; English soldiers in, 194; colonies of, do not depopulate, 197; freedom from Spain of, 197; rasp-houses in, 221; fisheries of, 222; power of liberty in, 275; supplies Spain during war with Britain, 278; abandons barrier towns, 292; newspapers in, 294; rice markets in, 300; helped by Queen Elizabeth I, 305; effects upon, by French control of Corsica, 306; begins to control English produce markets, 318. See also Colonies, Dutch; Navies, foreign, Dutch; Trade, foreign, Dutch
Holt, Sir John, 136, 153, 358 (n. 17)
Hooker, Richard: *Weekly Miscellany*, 241
Horace: *Odes*, 3, 216, 345 (n. 4), 367 (n. 42); *Ars Poetica*, 217; *Satires*, 277, 374–75 (n. 16); *Epistles*, 282, 283, 376 (nn. 40, 44)
Hosier, Adm. Francis, 371 (n. 9)
Houlditch, Richard, 142
House of Commons, 324; considers bill for voluntary recruitment of sailors, 9–10; orders changes in bill, 10; recommends voluntary recruitment, 15; throws out references to impressment, 15, 16; hears Oglethorpe's reports on the Fleet, 44–46, 48, 50, 54, 107, 122, 123; *Journals* of, 45, 51, 119, 122, 259; acts on the Fleet reports, 47, 50, 79–82,

House of Commons (*continued*)
122, 124; petitions to, 49; hears
Oglethorpe's report on the
Marshalsea, 83, 84, 88; acts on the
Marshalsea, 117–18; hears
Oglethorpe's report on the King's
Bench, 119, 120, 259, 260; acts on the
King's Bench, 121, 158; assistance of,
sought for Georgia, 228. *See also*
Committee appointed to Enquire
into the State of the Goals of this
Kingdom, the; Parliament, English
House of Lords, 49, 50, 144, 322
Howard, Charles, earl of Surrey, 328, 384 (n. 4)
Howard, John, 127; *State of the Prisons*, 342–43
Howard, Rev. Leonard, 260, 373 (n. 2)
Howard, Thomas II, fourth duke of Norfolk, 357 (n. 6)
Hudson's Bay, 291
Hudson's Bay Company, 291
Huggins, John, 122, 351–52 (n. 21); tortures prisoners, 50; allows escapes, 56; becomes warden of the Fleet, 56; transfers patent, 56–57, 350 (n. 6); refuses to list some prisoners and to release others, 60–61; reprimanded, 68; uses dungeons and shackles, 71; censured by House of Commons, 72, 79–80; to be prosecuted, 80; imprisoned, 81; refuses aid to Arne, 107; mistreats Reed, 107–8; misuses escapes, 108; conspires with Perrin and others, 108–9, 113–17; brings soldiers to Fleet, 109; surrenders Fleet, 123; acts by deputy, 352 (n. 21); tried for murder of Arne, 352–53 (n. 26)
Hughes, Edward, 81, 82, 126
Hull, 198
Hungary, 289

Hurlothrumbo (newspaper writer), 291, 292
Hutchenson (owner of a warehouse at Stono), 253

Impartial Account of the late Expedition, 336, 338
Impressment: press gangs and, 8, 14, 22–25, 34–35; unjust and illegal, 8, 19–20; backed by the Admiralty, 14–16; complained of by the House, 20; origin of, 20; as harmful to recruits and Navy, 20, 22, 24–27, 35, 42; liberty denied pressed men, 20, 22–24; and press officers, 20, 23–25, 34–35, 36–38; spreads disease, 21; induces desertion and piracy, 21, 24; prejudicial to merchants, 22, 285; expense of, 23; and press warrants, 23; press smacks, 23–24, 33–34; excuse for, 25; avoided by Dutch, French, and Swedes, 27, 39; evils of illustrated, 36–38
India: Dutch, 184, 363 (n. 42); English, 322, 324
Indians (American), 190, 201; proper treatment of, 174; visit England, 203, 217; longevity of, 215; in Georgia, 216; length of year for Virginia, 216; war of, with the Spaniards, 216; numbers of, diminished, 216–17; rum fatal to, 217; described, 217, 218, 242–44, 249–50; mistreated by Spaniards, 226–27; converted to Christianity, 226–27, 242; as in need of conversion in New England and Pennsylvania, 227; as Noble Savages, 241–44, 249–50; morality of, 242; revenge among, 242; government of, 242–43; frankness of, 243; eloquence of, 243, 250; food of, 250; health of, 250; attack escaping slaves, 253; in

Canada, 291; as Braddock's allies, 293; as allies at St. Augustine, 339. *See also* Cherokees; Chickasaws; Creeks; Iroquois; Uchees
Ireland, 222, 318, 326; English colonies in Ulster, 198, 207–8; English conquest of, 207–8, 234; silk trade in, 230–31; wool trade in, 238, 369 (n. 84); beef trade in, 279
Iroquois, 216, 218
Islington, 62
Italy, 213, 271, 307; silk in, 165; population of, 175, 193; Jews in, 197; Spanish dominions in, 236; coast of, 304

Jacobites, 3, 280–81
Jacomb, Robert, 10, 14
Jaffier, Meer, 309, 380 (n. 20)
Jamaica, 189, 195, 197
James I (king of Great Britain and Ireland), 236, 357 (n. 9), 373 (n. 5)
James II (king of Great Britain and Ireland), 276
James Francis Edward Stuart (the Old Pretender, prince of Wales), 3, 280–81, 322, 376 (n. 35)
Jekyll, Sir Joseph, 15, 77
Jekyl Sound, 247, 257, 370 (n. 8)
Jemmy (black leader at Stono), 253
Jenkins, Robert, 278
Jesuits, 253
Jews, 197, 281, 287
John (king of England), 264
John IV (king of Portugal), 306, 380 (n. 14)
Johnson, Gov. Robert, 349–50 (n. 55)
Johnson, Dr. Samuel: friendship with Oglethorpe, 302; visits Oglethorpe, 311; converses with Oglethorpe, 348 (n. 30); beats Osborne, 359 (n. 1); *Dictionary*, 375 (n. 32), visits George III's library, 381 (n. 5)
Johnson, Samuel (of Cheshire), 378 (n. 71)
Jones, John, 140–41
Jordain, Peter, 78
Joseph's Town (Georgia village), 249
Joshua, 188

Kaschmere (*or* Kasimere), 234
Keith, Field Marshal James, 270
Kemp (benefactor of Solas), 66
Kendrick, John, 76
Kenn, Luke, 48
Kennet, Basil, 3
Ketleby (master of the King's Bench Court), 153
Kilberry, William, 62, 353–54 (n. 38)
Killpatrick, James (later Kirkpatrick): *A Full Reply to Lieut. Cadogan's Spanish Hireling*, 335; *An Impartial Account*, 336, 338, 384 (nn. 2–3)
King, Sir Peter, 50, 70, 354 (n. 48)
King, Thomas, 80, 81, 355 (n. 52)
King, William, 142
King's Bench, Court of the. *See* Court of the King's Bench
King's Bench prison: preliminary report on, 119–21; supervision and management of, 126–27, 138–39; Lenthall mortgage of, 131, 132–33, 140–42, 261–66; ownership of, 131, 140; prisoners at, 134; rents excessive at, 134, 138, 149; absence of cruelties at, 136; described, 136–37, 260–61, 264–65; prisoners of, denied legal release, 139; profits of, 143, 151–52, 263, 267, 269; marshals of, listed, 152, 357 (n. 6); repaired with charity money, 156–58; creditors of escaped prisoners from, to be helped, 158;

King's Bench prison (*continued*)
   rents lowered at, 237; expansion and other changes in, recommended, 259, 261, 263, 266; as inadequate and unhealthy, 260–61; and disadvantages of the Lenthall mortgage, 261–62, 265–66; warden Ashton of, commended, 262–63; purchase of Lenthall mortgage recommended for, 266; William Bingley imprisoned at, 321. *See also* Charities; Escapes; Fees; Lenthall, William; Rules
King's Marshalsea, the. *See* King's Bench prison
Kircher, Athanasius, 245
Kirk, Rudolf, 3
Knatchbull, Sir Edward, 44, 125, 350 (n. 1)
Knight, Robert, 142, 150
Knorr, Klaus E., 202
Krämer, Johann Matthias, 336

Lacedemonians, 180, 277
Lambert, Gen. John, 276, 374 (n. 15)
Lamberto, Col. Pedro, 253, 372 (n. 13)
Langmore (legal agent), 261, 266
Languedoc, 307
Lanning, John Tate, 335, 336
La Rochelle, 305
Laval, Antoine François de, 245
Leather-Sellers Company, 77
Lede, marquis de, 271, 289
Lee, Nathaniel, 277, 375 (n. 20)
Lee, Sir William, 262, 265, 266–67, 373 (n. 6)
Leghorn, 309, 310
Leickey, Alexander, 78
Leighton, Baldwyn, 55, 351–52 (nn. 20, 21)
Lemy (killed near Stono, with wife and child), 254

Lenthall, William: title of, to the King's Bench, 131, 133, 138, 140, 144, 259, 262, 266, 267, 357–58 (n. 9), 373 (n. 4); mortgages title to Cutler, 131–32, 141–42, 261; heirs of, 132–33, 144, 145, 261
León, Luis Ponce de, 210, 245
Lerichy, 307
Letter from South Carolina, A. *See* Nairne, Thomas
Letters relating to the Antigallican Privateer, 321
Levant, 233, 304, 307, 393
Leyson, Jenkin, 58, 353 (n. 31)
Lime (Lyme Regis), 198
Lincoln, 198
Lisbon, 238
Little Ogechee River, 248
Liverpool, 198
Livy, 182
Lloyd, John, 260
Lloyd's Evening Post, 298
Loader, Hall, 141
Locke, John, 211, 366 (n. 34)
London, 578; City, 15; impressment in, 23–24; Bridge, 83; Tower of, 83; fire of, 83, 222; vagrants in, 163–64, 195; population of, 191, 194–96, 198; plague of 1664–1665, 192, 198; Irish colony and salmon fisheries of, 207–8; Indians visit, 217–18; labor cheap in, 223–25; port of, 299; merchants of, 299–300; as refuge of the dispossessed, 313, 316; markets of, 315. *See also* British Library; Fleet; King's Bench prison; Marshalsea; Newgate; Pantheon, Prisons; Ranelegh; Soho; Southwark; Westminster; Westminster-Hall; White's Coffee House
London Chronicle, 296
London Daily Post, 252

London-derry, 208
London Evening Post, 167, 200
London Journal, 159, 160
London Society for the Plantation of Ulster, 208
Long, Henry, 262, 263–64
Loraine, 307, 380 (n. 15)
Louis XV (king of France), 210
Louis XVI (king of France), 320n
Lowther, Sir James, 15
Lucan, 280
Lucas, William, 157, 158
Lutwyche, Thomas, 15
Lycurgus (Athenian statesman), 188, 363 (n. 47)
Lycurgus (Spartan law-giver), 277, 375 (n. 19)
Lyddal (owner of a house near King's Bench prison), 261
Lyfland (Livonia), 188, 363 (n. 45)

Mace (ensign in the Georgia regiment), 339
Machen, Richard: as marshal of the King's Bench, 134, 152; not liable for escapes, 143; sued over Poulter's escape, 149; as prisoner at King's Bench, 150; runs away, 151
Machiavelli, Nicolo, 170–71; *The Prince*, 168, 175–76, 362 (nn. 21, 22); *Discourses upon Titus Livius*, 168, 177–83, 362–63 (nn. 23–40); *The History of Florence*, 174–75, 362 (nn. 19, 20)
Mackall, Leonard, 203, 355; *Catalogue*, 335
Mackay, Lieut. James, 339, 340
Mackay, James, of Scoury, 385 (n. 6)
Mackay, John, 120, 356 (n. 1)
Mackay, Ensign Samuel, 339, 340, 385 (n. 6)
Mackpheadris, John, 58, 66–68, 353 (n. 29)

Mackpherson, Capt. James, 253, 372 (n. 11)
Maderas, 165
Maestritch, 279
Magna Charta, 19, 55, 348 (n. 37), 381 (n. 8)
Mandeville, Bernard, 225, 368 (n. 62)
Manlove, Richard, 50
Margate, 40
Marius Gaius, 284, 376 (n. 49)
Marlborough, George Spencer, fourth duke of, 316, 318
Marlborough, John Churchill, first duke of, 286
Marriage Act (of 1755), 283, 376 (n. 45)
Marriott (attorney for Woodham), 155
Marshalsea prison: visited by the committee, 83–84, 88; management of, 84; history of, 84, 88–89; described, 84, 90–92; tortures and cruelties at, 84, 91, 98–99; starvation at, 84, 91–92, 95, 98–99, 100; crowding and jail fever at, 84, 91–92, 99–100; abuse of tap-houses at, 89–90; extortions at, 89–90; garnish money at, 89–90; minor mistreatment of prisoners at, 89–92; housing and rents at, 91, 102–5; offices sold at, 95–96; begging box abused at, 97; pirates housed in, 97–98. *See also* Charities; Fees; Escapes; Prisons; Rules
Martin, John, 133, 142–47
Martin, Thomas, 133, 142–43, 145–50, 267
Martin, William, 142–43, 146–47, 266–67
Martyn, Benjamin: *A New and Accurate Account*, 200–201, 203; *Some Account of the Designs of the Trustees*, 201, 207, 359 (n. 2), 365 (n. 23), 366 (n. 27); *An Account, Showing the Progress*, 336;

Martyn, Benjamin (*continued*)
  Reasons for Establishing the Colony of Georgia, 359 (n. 2), 369 (n. 86)
Mary (queen of Great Britain and Ireland), 83
Mason, Joseph, 156–58
Maund, Thomas, 157
Maxwell, Primrose, 340–41, 385 (n. 6)
Mazzique, Joseph Anthony, 253, 372 (n. 12)
Meadows, Sir Philip, 88, 355 (n. 6)
Mediterranean, 289, 305, 306, 307
Meney, Thomas, 152
Messala. *See* Raymond, Sir Robert, as "Messala"
Messina, 306
Metcalf (brewer of Greenwich), 151
Mexico, 248
Mexico Bay (*or* Gulf of Mexico), 213, 246, 248
Mézière, Eleanor, marquise de, 321
Miles, Jeremiah, 78
Milton, John, 15n; *Paradise Lost*, 215, 348 (n. 27), 366 (n. 38)
Minden, battle of, 324, 382 (n. 15)
Minorca, 308
Mississippi, 291
Mississippi River, 248
Moguls, 274, 309
Molyneux, Samuel, 8–9
Monitor. *See* Oglethorpe, James Edward, as "Monitor"
Monthly Review, 342
Montiano, Gov. Manuel de, 253
Moore, Francis, 341
Moore, William, 157
Moors, 193, 197
Moravians, 3, 259
Morning Chronicle, 311, 312
Morning Post, 342
Morocco, 199
Morris, John, 136, 153

Mosdell, Stephen, 152
Moses, 188
Mowbray, John, fourth duke of Norfolk, 131, 357 (n. 6)
Mowbray, Thomas, first duke of Norfolk, 131
Mullens, Richard, 158; reports Gray, 120–21; becomes deputy marshal of King's Bench, 133, 134–35, 146–47, 152, 358 (n. 14); income of, from King's Bench, 134–35, 151–52; compassionate conduct of, 136, 265; accuses Woodham, 138, 154–55; not liable for escapes, 143, 146; examined by the Committee, 146–52; uses charity money for repairs, 156–58
Muscovy. *See* Russia

Nabis, 179, 362 (n. 28)
Nairne, Thomas: *A Letter from South Carolina*, 206
Naples, 306
Nash (home owner near Stono), 254
National Union Catalog, 335, 336
Natolia, 212
Navies, foreign: Dutch, 8, 20–21, 28–29, 237; French, 8, 27–28, 287, 290, 294, 304, 307; Swedish, 8, 29–30; Spanish, 21, 235–36, 248, 327; Russian, 21, 294; Venetian, 27
Navy, British, 287, 300; pay in, 8–9, 15, 17–18; manning of, 15, 23, 26–27, 31–32, 39–43; financing of, 17–18; promotes and defends trade, 18–19; power of, 18–19, 234–37; hurt by impressment, 20–21; Baltick fleet, 21, 23, 26; guard ships, 21, 33–34; West India squadron, 23, 26; Mediterranean fleet, 23, 271, 305, 307; history of, 234–37; ineffectual against France and Spain, 278–80,

294. *See also* Impressment; Sailors, British
Netherlands. *See* Holland
Neuste und Richtigste Nachricht, 336
Newbury, Walter, 78, 113
New England, 216; population of, 192, 194, 195, 198; Indians in, 227
Newfoundland, 237, 278
Newgate, 60, 107, 110, 111, 126, 261
Newman, Henry, 167
Newton, Robert, 84
New York, 216
New York Weekly Journal, 338
Nice, 307
Nichols, John: *Literary Anecdotes*, 167, 200
"Niederlassung in New Georgien," 336
Nile, 178
Nore, the, 33, 34
Norfolk, Roger Bigod, fourth earl of. *See* Bigod, Roger
North, Frederick, second earl of Guildford, 302, 328–33
North Briton, 321
North Carolina, 212, 246, 248
Norway, 234
Numa Pompilius (second king of Rome), 180, 188, 363 (n. 31)

Oakman, John, 337
Ogechee River, 248, 249
Oglethorpe, Eleanor, marquise de Mézière, 321
Oglethorpe, Eleanor Wall, 3, 271
Oglethorpe, Elizabeth Wright, 7
Oglethorpe, Frances Charlotte, marquise de Bellegarde, 321
Oglethorpe, James Edward: education of, 3; linguistic ability of, 3, 204; laments the death of Queen Anne and celebrates the advent of George I, 3–4; duel of, 5–6; reports on Fleet, 44, 46, 48, 54; chairs committee to report on prisons, 44, 50; serves on debtors committees, 49; chairs committees to disable Bambridge and reform prisons, 50–51, 81; studies law at Gray's Inn, 51; presents Fleet resolves, 79–81; presents Marshalsea report, 83, 84, 88; presents Marshalsea resolves, 117–18; reports George Gray, 119–21; supports Gambier petition, 122; moves for printing trials of wardens, 125; begins prison reform, 127; reports on the King's Bench, 130, 259–60; library of, 167, 202, 203–4, 321, 345–46 (n. 4), 348 (nn. 27, 32, 36, 52), 359 (n. 4), 365 (n. 20), 368–69 (n. 79), 369 (n. 81), 375 (n. 23); 376 (nn. 33, 38), 377 (nn. 52, 63), 378 (n. 67), 379 (n. 10), 380 (n. 16), 383 (n. 19); editorial practices of, 167–68, 383 (n. 19); "puffs" his own publications, 200, 207, 303, 342, 365 (n. 22); buys land in South Carolina, 202; memory of, 204; and the Georgia Indians, 241–44; as member of the Royal Society, 245; records velocity of Gulf Stream, 245; has Georgia coast sounded, 247; demands escaped slaves, 253; defensive actions after Stono, 255; as chairman of King's Bench committee, 259; escapes arrest for debt, 259; letters to Keith, 270, 374 (n. 4); petitions George II for reactivation of Georgia regiment, 270; Irish heritage of, 271; second court-martial of, 271; military experience in Sicily and Florida, 271, 380 (n. 15); as "Brittanicus et Americanus," 298–301; friendships with Boswell, Goldsmith, and

Oglethorpe, James Edward (*continued*)
Dr. Johnson, 302; begins series of letters to the press, 302; as "An English Merchant," 306, 310; as "Monitor," 308; corresponds with Boswell, 311, 321, 381 (n. 2); entertains literary friends, 311; opposes enclosure, 311–12; as "Adams," 311–20; family ties in France, 321; as "Old Antigallican," 321; as "Faber," 321–27; provides John Campbell with biographical materials, 335–36; spurious attributions to, 335–36; as "Omega," 337, 342–43; blamed for defeat in Florida, 338; directs retreat from St. Augustine, 338–41; "instruction" for Lord Egmont by, 345 (n. 1); gift to Sharp by, 348 (n. 32); role of, in trials of Bambridge, 350 (n. 6); fails to establish Lenthall title, 357–58 (n. 9); as trustee for the British Museum, 359 (n. 6); fascinated by Raleigh, 361 (n. 7); commands forces of Georgia and South Carolina, 372 (n. 18)

Oglethorpe, Louisa Mary, marquise de Bassompierre, 321

Oglethorpe, Sutton, 51

Ohio River, 293–94

Oldmixon, John: *British Empire in America*, 202, 204

Omega. *See* Oglethorpe, James Edward, as "Omega"

One in the Secret (newspaper writer), 330, 384 (n. 7)

Onslow, Arthur, 5, 15

Onslow, Richard, 5–6

Orelbar, John, 8

Osborne, Francis, 359 (n. 1)

Ostend ships, 21

Ovid: *Metamorphoses*, 282, 376 (n. 42)

Owen, Thomas, 262, 263–66

Pacific, 246

Page, Francis, 73, 76

Palestine, 193

Palichocolas (South Carolina), 255

Pantheon, 319, 382 (n. 13)

Paoli, Pascal, 302

Papal Donation (of Pope Alexander VI), 209

Paris, 289

Paris, Peace of, 323

Parker (of the Merchant-Taylors Company), 76

Parker, Henry, 371 (n. 14)

Parker, Thomas, first earl of Macclesfield, 349 (n. 46)

Parliament, English, 231, 252, 286, 288, 305, 342; Acts of, 8, 10, 14n, 16–18, 31, 32, 54, 55, 60, 62, 84, 89, 94, 131, 136, 139, 144, 149, 227, 233, 261, 283, 311, 314, 326; George II recommends voluntary enlistment in navy to, 8–9, 14–15; spirit of Constitution in, 14; petitions to, 15, 49, 122–24; provides pay for navy, 17–18; fear of emigration, 167; assistance of, sought for Georgia, 228, 392; resists army, 276; ministry of, opposes Corsican independence, 302; members of, charged with bribery, 321–22, 327; debates taxation, 328. *See also* Committee; House of Commons; House of Lords

Parliament, Irish, 208

Pearse, Commodore Vincent, 339

Pelopidas, 180, 363 (n. 33)

Penn, Thomas, 361 (n. 12)

Penn, William: settles Pennsylvania, 171; *Some Account of Pennsilvania*, 168, 171, 188–92, 361 (n. 11), 363 (nn. 46, 47)

Pennsylvania Gazette, 256

Pensilvania, 171, 227

Percival, John, first earl of Egmont, 9, 369 (n. 2); 377 (n. 62); on committee to disable Bambridge, 81; and Irish wool, 369 (nn. 83, 84)
Percival, John, second earl of Egmont, 125, 345 (n. 1)
Perrin (*or* Perriom), Thomas: his escape, 56, 109–10; his case, 113–17
Persia, 212, 274
Peru, 279
Peter III (czar of Russia), 324
Petition of Right, the, 19, 348 (n. 38)
Petty, Sir William: *Political Arithmetic*, 201, 221
Phalaris, 179, 362 (n. 28)
Pharsalia, battle of, 15, 383
Philadelphia, 171
Philip II (king of Spain), 236
Philip IV (king of Spain), 306, 380 (n. 15)
Philip V (king of Spain), 253
Philip and Mary, 35–38, 349–50 (n. 55), 350 (n. 56)
Philpot (warden of the King's Bench), 152
Phocion, 277, 281, 375 (n. 17)
Phoebus, 282
Picardy, 238, 369 (n. 83)
Piedmont, 231–32, 307
Pietas Universitatis Oxoniensis, 3
Pigot (*or* Pigott), John, 71–72, 355 (n. 51)
Pindar, William, 109; mistreats Sinclair, 69; to be prosecuted, 80, 81; imprisoned, 81, 355 (n. 52); mistreats Rich, 110
Pingelly (Pengelly), Sir Thomas, 15
Pisa, 175
Pistol, Antient (dramatic character), 289–90
Pitt, Moses: *Cry of the Oppressed*, 49–50
Pitt, William, first earl of Chatham: opposes war with France, 271; as "Frenchified Pensioner," 305; opposes French, 322, 325, 327, 331
Plain Dealer, A (newspaper writer), 325n, 383 (n. 18)
Plimouth (England), 198
Po, 229
Pocklington, Henry, 50
Point Quartelle (Florida), 340
Poland, 278, 305
Political State of Great Britain, 11
Pomerania, 188
Pompey, 283
Pons Pons road, 254
Pope, Alexander, 179
Port Mahone, 289
Porto Bello, 248, 279
Porto Rico, 291
Port Royal, 248, 255
Portsmouth, 198
Portugal, 165, 185, 233; Portugueze, 253. *See also* Colonies, Portuguese
Poulter (prisoner in the King's Bench): escapes, 134, 149–50; his case, 143; given liberty of the rules, 150
Poultney (surveyor and builder), 260, 261, 263
Powell, Richard, 120–21
Powhatan, 367 (n. 48)
Powis, Sir Littleton, 135, 147–48
Pratt, Sir John, 358 (n. 15); enlarges rules of King's Bench, 127, 151; accepts presents, 135, 147; lowers Mullens's lease, 148
Presbyterian, 326
Pressing. *See* Impressment
Preston, John: has share in the King's Bench, 133, 142, 150; examined, 145–46; appoints Mullens, 146
Pretender, the. *See* James Francis Edward Stuart
Prévost, Antoine François, 336

Price, Robert, 73, 76
Prince Edward Island, 345 (n. 1)
Prisons, 221–22; begging-box at, 48; prison fever at, 48; starvation at, 48; greedy jailers at, 48–49; living conditions at, 48–49, 342–43; government and management of, 49, 50, 55; acts for relief of debtors at, 61; need for reform, 342–43. *See also* Charities; Escapes; Fees; Fleet, Habeas corpus; King's Bench; Marshalsea; Newgate; Rules; Sponging-houses
Protestants, foreign: in Georgia, 202; murdered by Spaniards in Carolina, 209–10; in Germany, 290. *See also* Salzburgers
Provence, 307
Prussia, 188, 238, 271, 290. *See also* Brandenburgh; Frederick II
Publick Advertiser, 270; "Hurlothrumbo" letter in, 291; Corsican letters in, 302, 303, 306, 308; North letters in, 328
Pugh, Matthew, 93–94, 105
Purchas his Pilgrimage, 215
Puritans, 194
Purry, Jean Pierre, 201; latitudinarian fallacy of, 202; sells land in South Carolina to Oglethorpe, 202; *Description Abregée*, 202, 206, 212–33 passim, 365 (nn. 18, 19); settles in South Carolina, 207; as a source of information, 207; *Memorial*, 364 (n. 9)

Quack Doctor (Pullim, in Shadwell's *Humorists*), 329
Quakers, 195
Quebec, 291

Radcliffe, John, 286, 377 (n. 62)
Radnor, Charles Bodville Robartes, second earl of, 259, 358 (n. 12); acquires King's Bench prison, 132, 153, 261, 358 (n. 11); assigns King's Bench to Studley et al, 132–33, 140–43, 261–62; appoints Morris deputy marshal, 153
Radnor, Lady Elizabeth Cutler, 357 (n. 8)
Raleigh (*or* Rawleigh), Sir Walter: as colonizer, 170, 217; *Discovery of Guiana*, 361 (n. 7); *History of the World*, 361 (n. 7)
Ranelegh, 319, 382 (n. 13)
Rapin (Rapin-Thoyras), Paul de, 235n
Raugia (Ragusa), 177
Raymond, Sir Robert, 358 (n. 15); refuses fees and presents, 126–27; 135, 139, 148; care of the King's Bench by, 137, 138–39, 265; gives furniture to King's Bench, 139, 156; accepts present, 148; as "Messala," 161, 359 (n. 8)
Reed, Oliver: escapes, 56, 352 (n. 25); mistreated by Huggins, 107–8
Reese, Trevor: *The Most Delightful Country*, 167, 202
Religion: liberty of, in Georgia, 165; value of, 179–80
Representation of the several Fetters, Irons and Ingines from the Marshalsea Prison, The, 83
Reynolds, James, 135–36, 148, 358 (n. 16)
Reynolds, Sir Joshua, 358 (n. 16)
Rhine, 212, 229, 300
Rhone, 229
Rich, Sir William, second baronet Rich, 44
Rich, Sir William, fourth baronet Rich, 85; shackled by Bambridge, 44–47, 49, 110–12; writes Committee, 46
Risham, William, 38, 350 (n. 56)

Riviera de Genoa, 307
Roberts, J., 207
Robinson, Benjamin, 113, 114, 117
Robinson, John (bishop of London), 5
Robinson, Adjutant William, 340, 385 (n. 6)
Roche, Maurice, 366 (n. 24)
Rogers, William, 116
Rome (the Roman Catholic Church), 210, 253, 290, 309
Rome (the Roman Empire), 249, 283, 287; philanthropy in, 160; management of wars by, 180–81, 284; conquest of Carthage by, 323, 382 (n. 8). *See also* Colonies, Roman
Romulus, 188, 363 (n. 47)
Rose, Thomas, 254
Rotterdam, 300
Rous, Sir John, 357 (n. 9)
Rousseau, Jean Jacques, 380 (n. 14)
Royal Society, the, 245
Rules, the, 48; at the Fleet, 50, 56, 59–60, 114; at the King's Bench, 127, 137, 140, 158
Russia: British subsidies to, 271, 289–90, 294, 295; hemp in, 300; revolution in, 324. *See also* Navies, foreign, Russian
Russia-Company (English), 238

Sabin, Joseph, 335, 336
Sacheverell, Thomas, 254, 372 (n. 16)
Sackville, George, Lord Germaine, 324, 383 (n. 15)
Sackville, Lionel Cranfield, first duke of Dorset, 95–96, 356 (n. 16)
Sailors, British: pay of, 7, 8, 10, 15, 17–18, 25–26, 33, 39–41, 349 (n. 49); need for reform in treatment of, 7–8; length of voyages of, 8; registration of, 8; promissory tickets given for, 8, 10, 15, 26, 33, 40; families of, 8, 41; voluntary enlistment of, 9, 15–16, 32, 39–43; debts of, 10; become pirates, 21; need for, 21, 41–42, 235; treatment of, 25–26, 32–33, 41; power of attorney of, 33, 40–41; in merchant marine, 42; will be increased by Georgia trade, 201; attitudes of, toward French war, 282; employment needs of, when discharged, 300. *See also* Admiralty, British; Impressment; Navy, British
Sailors, foreign: Dutch, 20–21, 28–29; Venetian, 27; French, 27–28; Swedish, 29–30
St. Augustine (*or* St. Augustino), 209n; South Carolinian attack on, 206, 209–10; encourages slaves to escape, 253; Oglethorpe's attack on, 271; his retreat from, 338–41
St. James's Coffee House (London), 299
St. John's River, 246, 248, 257, 341
St. Lazarus. *See* San Lazaro
St. Paul's Parish (South Carolina), 252
St. Simons Island, 257
Saint ta Remo (San Remo), 305, 380 (n. 14)
Salmon, Thomas, 245, 370 (nn. 1, 2)
Salzburgers (*or* Saltzburghers), 162, 225–27, 253
Sandys, Sir Edwin, 170
San Lazaro (fort above Carthagena), 279
Saracens, 175
Sardenia, 289, 307
Savage (tipstaff at the Fleet), 67
Savannah, county of, 248
Savannah River, 212, 249, 255, 297; fish in, 214; harbor of, 247; navigability of, 248
Savannah, town of, 248–49, 256
Savile, Sir George, 318, 381 (n. 11)
Savoy, 307, 321
Saxons, 294

Scarborough, 198
Scipio Africanus Major, 160, 359 (n. 3), 362 (n. 28)
Scipios, the, 179
Scotch (*or* Scots): as soldiers and sailors, 194–95, 331; language of, 253; as people, 325, 326, 331. *See also* Highlanders
Scotland, 222, 326
Selden, John: *Mare Clausum*, 234; edition of Fortescue, 348 (n. 32)
Selimus (Selim I, sultan of the Ottoman empire), 178
Selwyn, Charles, 45, 350 (n. 1); as "Decius," 161, 359 (n. 7)
Senserf and Son (Dutch financial agents), 115
Seth, 210
Shadwell, Thomas: *The Humorists*, 365 (n. 17)
Shaftesbury, Anthony Ashley Cooper, first earl of, 211, 366 (n. 34)
Shakespeare, William, 283, 376 (n. 45)
Shannon, William, 253, 372 (n. 12)
Sharp (duellist), 5–6
Sharp, Granville, 346 (n. 1); establishes Oglethorpe's editorship of *The Sailors Advocate*, 7; contributes to *The Sailors Advocate*, 11, 18; given book by Oglethorpe, 348 (n. 32)
Sharp, John (archbishop of York), 346 (n. 1)
Sharp, Thomas, 346 (n. 1)
Sheridan, Thomas, 222–23n, 367 (n. 59)
Shields, David S., 202
Shippen, William, 15
Sicily, 236, 271, 289, 304
Siddale, Samuel, 113
Sidon, 185
Sinclair, David, 68–70, 354 (n. 46)
Sinking Fund. *See* Funds
Skydoway (Georgia village), 249
Slann, James, 133, 134, 144

Slaves, 190; as a danger to South Carolina, 228; prohibited in Georgia, 252; insurrection of, at Stono, 252–55; escape of, to Florida, 253
Sleswick, 188
Sloane, Sir Hans, 286; as "Hippocrates," 161, 359 (n. 6)
Smith, Capt. John, 217, 367 (n. 46), 370 (n. 5)
Smith, Richard, 164, 360 (n. 18)
Smith, Sir William, 357 (n. 9), 368 (n. 64), 373 (n. 5)
Soame, William, 261
Society for the Promotion of Christian Knowledge (SPCK), 162, 167, 201, 225–26, 360 (n. 13), 368 (n. 64)
Society for the Propagation of the Gospel in Foreign Parts (SPG), 201, 225–26, 368 (n. 64)
Socrates, 277
Soho (London suburb), 298, 301
Solas, Jacob Mendez, 66, 354 (n. 45)
Solon, 277, 375 (n. 22)
Some Account of the Design of the Trustees (Oglethorpe's), 159, 200, 202; mercantile thinking in, 167, 201; diverse purposes of, 201; not read and approved by the Georgia Trustees, 201; passages from reused later, 360 (nn. 17, 20–24), 362 (n. 26)
Son of Adam, A (newspaper writer), 331
Soubah (Souaj-ud-Dowlad), 324
Southampton, Henry Wriothesley, third earl of, 170
South Carolina: silk in, 165; rice in, 165, 206, 213, 233, 299–300; fee for land in, 200–201; Indians an early threat in, 201, 211; cattle in, 206; paper currency of, 206, 212; slaves in, 206, 212, 228; wine in, 206, 214, 230; colony described, 206–7, 209, 212–13, 246–47; under Archdale, 207; history of, 209–11; English right to,

210–11; proprietors of, 211, 212, 218; religious repression in, 211–12; uninhabited part of, 212; climate of, 212–13, 216, 230; soil of, 213; and tar in, 213; flora and fauna of, 213–14; pitch longevity in, 215–16; Indians in, 216–18, 296–97; land policy of, 218–19; Georgia taken from, 220; slaves a danger to, 228; value of land in, 228; devoid of poverty, 229; cotton and oil in, 230; trade in, 230–32; counties of, 248; slave insurrection in, 252–55; and need for shipping, 299–301; indigo and hemp of, 300–301; regiment at St. Augustine, 339–41
South Carolina Assembly, 256, 338
South Carolina Gazette, 335, 338, 339
South Sea Company, 142, 150
Southward, Francis, 152
Southwark, 83
Spain: colonies of, 185, 197, 306; depopulation of, 192–93, 196–97; loses Holland, 197; Inquisition of, 197, 226–27; extirpates French in South Carolina, 209–10; abandons South Carolina, 210; climate, 213; Christianizes Indians in America, 226; rice markets in, 233; commerce of increased, 235–36; Spanish language, 253; invades Georgia, 256–58, 336; supplies troops in Sicily, 271; in War of Jenkins' Ear, 278–80; indigo of, 300; and Gibraltar, 308. *See also* America, Spanish; Florida; Navies, foreign, Spanish; Trade, foreign, Spanish
Spalding, Phinizy, 252, 309, 321, 337
Spangenberg, August Gottlieb, 3
Sparta, 180, 277
Spectator, 377 (n. 64)
Spencer, George, fourth duke of Marlborough, 316, 318, 381 (n. 10)

Sponging-houses, 50, 138, 151; Corbett's, at the Fleet, 56, 58, 59, 63, 110; charges at, 63
Sprye, Royal, 254, 372 (n. 16)
Stamp Act, 323
Stapleton, Isaac, 260
Star Chamber, Court of the. *See* Court of the Star Chamber
Steele, Richard: *Tatler*, 352 (n. 26)
Steere (surveyor and builder), 260, 261, 263
Stein, Baron (prisoner in the King's Bench), 262
Stephens, Thomas, 252
Stephens, William, 252
Stonehow (Stono, South Carolina): rebellion at, 252–55
Strachey, William: *True Reportory*, 362 (n. 16)
Studley, Joseph: acquires interest in King's Bench, 133, 141–43, 262; examined by committee, 143–44; receives profits of King's Bench, 146, 358 (n. 13); appoints Mullens, 146
Sugar Colonies (French West Indies), 239
Sugar Islands (British West Indies), 228
Sulivan's Island, 248
Surman (a proprietor of the King's Bench prison), 142, 150
Sutherland, Patrick, 336, 339
Sutton, William, 152
Sweden, 194, 307. *See also* Navy, foreign, Swedish
Swift, Jonathan, 222, 367–68 (n. 59)
Switzs, 275
Sydall, Alexander, 78
Syracuse, 285

Taffelet, 199, 364 (n. 57)
Talure, William, 62, 354 (n. 40)
Tangier, 234
Tatler, 352 (n. 26)

Taylor, George, 152
T. C. (newspaper writer), 378 (nn. 71–75)
Teky-Sound. *See* Jekyl Sound
Temple, Sir William: *Observations upon the United Provinces*, 221, 222, 367 (nn. 57, 58)
Terence, 160, 289, 359 (n. 4), 378 (n. 67)
Tew, William, 260
Thames, 24, 29, 40, 229, 291
Thatcher, Edward, 76
Thebes, 180, 283
Theodore ("king" of Corsica), 373 (n. 3)
Theseus, 188, 363 (n. 47)
Thicknesse, Philip, 378 (n. 1)
Thomas de Brotherton, earl of Norfolk, 357 (n. 6)
Thompson, James, 84
Thorn (Toron), 305
Thornhill, Sir James, 352 (n. 21)
Thoulon (Toulon), 307
Thraso, Captain (dramatic character), 161, 360 (n. 10)
Thunderbolt (Georgia village), 249
Thwaites, Christopher, 150
Tiber, 229
Timolean, 179, 362 (n. 28)
Tithonus, 216
Tomochichi (Yamacraw chief), 203, 243–44, 370 (n. 5)
Tories, 325, 326
Trade, British: importance of, 18–19, 230, 235–40, 298–301; pays interest on the Funds, 19; hurt and endangered by impressment, 19–22; needs protection from pirates, 21; importance of colonies for, 165, 189–92, 196–98; importance of Georgia for, 201–2, 230–34; effect of South Carolina paper currency on, 206; increased by European Protestant immigrants, 226; in South Carolina, 229, 298–301; in British North America, 235–38; woolen, 237–38; as hurt by war, 285; importance of Corsica for, 304; as hurt by enclosure, 314–16
Trade, foreign: Italian, 165; Portuguese, 165; Dutch, 183–88, 222, 237, 307; Spanish, 236–37; German, 238; French, 238–39; Danish, 307; of Hamburg, 307; Sardinian, 307; Swedish, 307; Venetian, 307
Trapps, Mary, 91
Trenchard, John, 275, 308; *Cato's Letters*, 275, 374 (nn. 12, 13), 380 (n. 17)
Trenches Island, 248
Truth, 277–78
Tullus Hostilius, 180, 363 (n. 34)
Tunis, 309
Turin, 307
Turkey (*or* Turky), 193, 233, 289, 304, 307; Jews in, 197; large armies in, 199; weakness of, 274–75; militarism in, 284; wars with Austria, 284–85
Tybee Island, 248, 371 (n. 12)
Tyler, Wat, 83
Tyre, 185
Tyrrell, Richard, 55, 351 (n. 17)

Uchees (*or* Uschesees), 242, 247, 370 (n. 4), 379 (n. 4)
Ulster, 198, 207–8, 365–66 (n. 24)
United Provinces, 305. *See also* Holland
United States of America. *See* America, United States of
Upsdale, John, 262
Uttamaccomack (Virginia Indian), 217, 367 (n. 48)

Vains, Joseph, 56
Valois, House of, 323

Vei (*or* Veij), 181, 182
Venice, 175, 275, 307. *See also* Navies, foreign, Venetian
Venus, 289
Verelst, Harman, 252
Verelst, William, 370 (n. 5)
Vernon, Adm. Edward: collaborates in *The Sailors Advocate*, 7, 9; writes *A Specimen of Naked Truth*, 271; in war against Spain, 279, 375 (n. 28)
Vernon River (Georgia), 248, 371 (n. 13)
Vienna: siege of, 285
Vienna, Court of, 290
Villa Franca (Italy), 307
Virgil: *Aeneid*, 180, 363 (n. 35); *Eclogues*, 345–46 (n. 4)
Virginia, 192, 198, 209, 246; Raleigh's colony in, 170; produce of, 173, 189; colonists of, 194; climate of, 213; Indians in, 217; settlement of, 236; Virginia Company, 170, 236n, 362 (n. 15)
Vitrivius Pollio, 362 (n. 26)
Voltaire, 380 (n. 14)

Wager, Sir Charles, 21; favors impressment, 14, 16; defends navy, 348 (n. 28), 349 (nn. 44, 45)
Wakeling, Benjamin, 78
Wales, 222
Wall, Richard, 366 (n. 24)
Wallace (tavern owner), 254
Waller, Edmund: "Battle of the Summer Isles," 203, 204, 215
Walpole, Sir Robert: favors impressment, 9, 15, 348 (n. 30); as the "father of corruption," 307
War: English volunteers in foreign, 194; size of armies in, 198–99; types of weapons in, 199; democratic appeal against war with France, 274–76; evils of war with France, 278–80, 282; benefits of, nugatory, 280–83; militarism as the tool of tyrants, 284–85; hardships of, 285–87; French superiority for, 287–89; ironic advocacy of, 289; subsidies necessary for allies in, 290–91; unrealistic expectations from, 291–92; ill effects from rumors of, 292; disasters attending, 293–95
Washington, George, 271
Watson, William, 157, 158
Wellman, William, 147
Wem (Shropshire), 62
Wentworth, Gen. Thomas, 271, 279, 375 (n. 28); expedition of, 293, 378 (n. 76)
Westbrook (Georgia village), 249, 371 (n. 13)
Westbrook River (Georgia), 248, 371 (n. 13)
Westchester (Chester, England), 198
West-India Company (Dutch), 185–86
West-Indies (Dutch), 187, 197
West Indies (English), 21, 195, 197, 282
West-Indies (Spanish), 192, 196, 197, 282
Westminster, 55, 95, 195, 321, 327
Westminster-Hall, 19, 55, 59, 78, 139
Westphalia, 289
Whalebone, George, 38, 350 (n. 56)
Whichcot, Sir Jeremy, 55, 351 (n. 18)
Whigs, 274, 326
White, John, 36–38
White's Coffee House (London), 291, 378 (n. 71)
Whitwood, Mary, 64
Wildey, John, 133–145 passim
Wilkes, John, 309, 380 (n. 18); *The North Briton*, 321
Wilson, Ann, 150
Wilson, Elizabeth, 150

Wilson, George, 71–72, 352 (n. 24), 355 (nn. 51, 52)
Wilson, William, 134, 150
Winchester, 198
Wingrove, Joseph, 260
Witt, Jan de, 168, 171, 183, 361 (n. 5). *See also* Court, Pieter de la
Wood, Peter H., 252, 372 (n. 8)
Woodfall, Henry Sampson, 329, 330
Woodham, Samuel, 127, 138, 154–56
Worcester (battle of), 195
Wycherly, William, 375 (n. 20)
Wyndham, Edmond, 102

Yamacraws, 370 (n. 5)
Yamassee War, 252
Yarmouth, 198

CPSIA information can be obtained
at www.ICGtesting.com
Printed in the USA
LVHW010858051021
699564LV00002B/272